Here's What You Get on the CD:

T he CD included with the second edition of the *MCSE: Windows 95 Study Guide* contains invaluable programs and information to help you prepare for your MCSE exams. You can access and install the files on the CD through a user-friendly graphical interface by running the CLICKME.EXE file located in the root directory.

System Requirements: 486/100MHz, 16MB RAM, 2x CD-ROM, SoundBlaster-compatible sound card, 640x480, 256-color display, Windows 95/NT 4 or later.

The Sybex CD interface is supported only by Windows 95 and Windows NT. To access the CD contents from Windows 3.x, you must use File Manager.

Custom Exam Review Software

Test your knowledge with custom exam preparation software. Make sure that you know all that you need to know by reviewing all of the questions found in the chapters. Explanations of correct answers are also provided. To install the exam review program, run SETUP.EXE in the EXAM folder. (During installation you may be prompted to allow the program to update system files. The file that is updated is OLEPRO32.DLL. this is a Microsoft DLL and should not cause any problems; however, as a precaution, we recommend that you back up this file prior to installing the test program.)

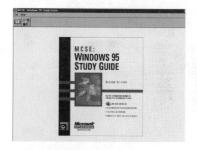

Network Press MCSE Study Guide Sampler

Preview chapters from the best-selling line of MCSE study guides from Sybex. We've also included a copy of the Adobe Acrobat Reader, which you'll need to view the various preview chapters. From the core requirements to the most popular electives, you'll see why Sybex MCSE Study Guides have become the self-study method of choice for tens of thousands seeking MCSE certification.

Microsoft Train_Cert Offline Update and Internet Explorer 4

Look to Microsoft's *Train_Cert Offline* Web site, a quarterly snapshot of Microsoft's Education and Certification Web site, for all of the information you need to plot your course for MCSE certification. You'll need to run *Internet Explorer* 4 to access all of the features of the *Train_Cert Offline* Web site, so we've included a free copy on the CD. To install the *Train_Cert Offline* Web site to your system, run the SETUP file located in the MICROSFT\OFFLINE folder.

Please consult the README file located in the root directory for more detailed information on the CD contents.

MCSE: Windows 95
Study Guide

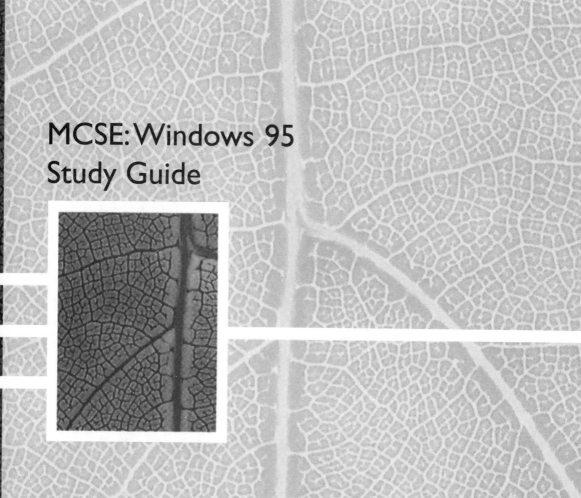

MCSE: Windows® 95
Study Guide
Second Edition

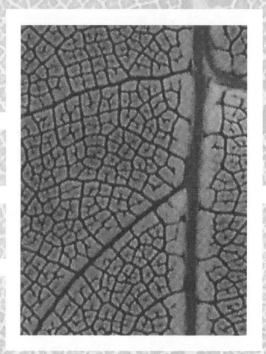

Lance Mortensen
Rick Sawtell
with Duane Benson, Alex Conger,
Blake Ferrin, Max Holloway,
Tracy Johnson, and Mike Spinola

San Francisco • Paris • Düsseldorf • Soest

Associate Publisher: Guy Hart-Davis
Contracts and Licensing Manager: Kristine Plachy
Acquisitions & Developmental Editor: Neil Edde
Editors: Suzanne Goraj and Marilyn Smith
Project Editor: Davina Baum
Technical Editors: Jim Cooper and Bill Ross
Book Designer: Patrick Dintino
Graphic Illustrator: Patrick Dintino
Desktop Publisher: Robin Kibby
Production Coordinator: Rebecca Rider
Indexer: Nancy Guenther
Companion CD: Molly Sharp and John D. Wright
Cover Designer: Archer Design
Cover Illustrator/Photographer: Image Bank

Screen reproductions produced with Collage Complete.

Collage Complete is a trademark of Inner Media Inc.

Library of Congress Card Number: 98-84651
ISBN: 0-7821-2256-6

Manufactured in the United States of America

10 9 8 7 6 5 4 3 2 1

October 9, 1996

Dear SYBEX Inc. Customer:

Microsoft is pleased to inform you SYBEX Inc. is a participant in the Microsoft® Independent Courseware Vendor (ICV) program. Microsoft ICVs design, develop, and market self-paced courseware, books, and other products that support Microsoft software and the Microsoft Certified Professional (MCP) program.

To be accepted into the Microsoft ICV program, an ICV must meet set criteria. In addition, Microsoft reviews and approves each ICV training product before permission is granted to use the Microsoft Certified Professional Approved Study Guide logo on that product. This logo assures the consumer that the product has passed the following Microsoft standards:

- The course contains accurate product information.
- The course includes labs and activities during which the student can apply knowledge and skills learned from the course.
- The course teaches skills that help prepare the student to take corresponding MCP exams.

Microsoft ICVs continually develop and release new MCP Approved Study Guides. To prepare for a particular Microsoft certification exam, a student may choose one or more single, self-paced training courses or a series of training courses.

You will be pleased with the quality and effectiveness of the MCP Approved Study Guides available from SYBEX Inc.

Sincerely,

Holly Heath
ICV/OCV Account Manager
Microsoft Channel Programs, Education & Certification

MICROSOFT INDEPENDENT COURSEWARE VENDOR PROGRAM

This second edition of the book, just like the first edition, is dedicated to you, the reader. We hope that this book will be of value to you, and that you can pass your Windows 95 test and have a fulfilling career in computers.

Acknowledgments

I would like to thank my parents for sacrificing to buy that Atari 800 back in high school. Thanks also go to my many friends, including Stu and Dalice for playing games with me and keeping me sane while I wrote this book. Rick, it has been great to work with you—can't wait until our next book. Thanks to Duane, Alex, and Max for helping out, too.

I'd like to thank Neil, Davina, Marilyn, and Suzanne, along with all the others at Sybex (Rebecca and Robin), for being such a great crew to work with. I realize that this book, and the professional quality of it, wouldn't have been possible without you.

Thanks go to the many people who have sent in comments (almost always positive) and corrections (we really do try to make the book 100% accurate, but sometimes typos, errors, or bad wordings slip in). Rick, Sybex, and I realize that this second edition of the book is a better book because of your involvement and suggestions.

As always, thanks to Luann for being supportive and understanding. I know these books are harder on you than they are on me. Thanks to Bryce, Jessany, and Devin, for being such cute kids, and thanks to Logan, for being born right during final deadlines. I'm glad you kids would rather wrestle with Daddy than do anything else (even watch Disney). Don't grow up too fast.

Lance

I would like to thank Sharron and Dick (my Mom and Dad) for buying me that first computer and being so supportive of my growing enthusiasm for the hi-tech computer industry. Thank you for helping me choose the right college and the right major and for all the support, both financial and emotional. I would also like to say thanks to Lance for bringing me in on this project, and to all the people at Sybex—Neil, Davina, and especially Marilyn and Suzanne—who made sure all of my *T*'s were crossed and my *I*'s dotted.

A special thanks to Melissa (my love and inspiration) for putting up with me during those long nights with deadlines looming. Your support and affection are always a blessing. Finally, a thank you to Kenya (my neurotic cat), who would carry on lengthy discussions about the quantitative nature of the universe while I typed away.

Rick

Contents at a Glance

Table of Contents

Table of Exercises

Introduction

There's an old Army reserve commercial where a person can't get employed because he has no experience, and can't get experience because he can't get employed—a classic "Catch-22" situation. Although certification is best used in conjunction with real-life experience, it can go a long way in making up for lack of experience.

The value of certification is undeniable. Many people get certified just to compete in the job marketplace. For example, if you were an employer and you had two candidates with the same experience, but one was also certified, which one would you hire? The fact is that even though the number of certified professionals has grown tremendously, the demand has grown at least as fast as, if not faster than, the number of certified people.

Whether you are just getting started or are ready to move ahead in the computer industry, the knowledge and skills you have are your most valuable assets. Microsoft, recognizing this, has developed its Microsoft Certified Professional (MCP) program to give you credentials that verify your ability to work with Microsoft products effectively and professionally. The Microsoft Certified Systems Engineer (MCSE) certification is the premier MCP credential, designed for professionals who support Microsoft networks.

Is This Book for You?

If you want to become certified as an MCSE, this book is for you. The MCSE is *the* hot ticket in the field of professional computer networking. Microsoft is putting its weight behind the program, so now is the time to act. This book will start you off on the right foot.

If you want to learn techniques that you can apply in your day-to-day work as a systems engineer or administrator, this book is for you, too. You will learn about the fundamentals of Windows 95 operations, ranging from installation to optimizing and monitoring performance to running on a network. You will also find troubleshooting information for each topic.

MCSE: Windows 95 Study Guide (2nd ed.) provides clear explanations of the fundamental concepts you must grasp both to become certified and to do your job effectively and efficiently. Our intention in writing this book was not merely to help you pass the MCSE tests. We have tried to make the book comprehensive and detailed enough that it will remain a valuable resource for you once you have passed your test and become a certified systems engineering professional.

What Does This Book Cover?

Think of this book as your guide to Microsoft Windows 95. It begins with an overview of the Windows family, and then continues with the following topics:

- Installing Windows 95

- Booting Windows 95

- Windows 95 architecture and memory

- Customizing and configuring Windows 95

- The Windows 95 registry

- Running Windows and MS-DOS applications

- Managing disk resources

- Printing from Windows 95

- Communications features in Windows 95

- Mobile computing

- E-mail and fax transmittal

- Plug-and-Play support

- Configuring the display

- Multimedia features

- Troubleshooting Windows 95

The old Windows 95 exam was numbered 70-63, and was scheduled to be replaced in April 1998 by the new Windows 95 exam, numbered 70-64. The authors have taken the beta version of the 70-64 exam (which, in theory, allowed us to see all of the questions from each of the different forms of the test), and have designed this second edition of the study guide to help prepare you for the new version (70-64) of the test. If you have already passed the 70-63 test, you will not be required to pass the 70-64 test (at least not as of now).

This book (and the test) also heavily emphasizes networking issues, including the following:

- Windows 95 networking components

- Installing and configuring TCP/IP

- Connecting to Windows NT networks

- Connecting to Novell NetWare networks

- Setting up user profiles

- Using system policies

- Remote administration with Windows 95

How Do You Become an MCSE?

Attaining MCSE status is a serious challenge. The exams cover a wide range of topics and require dedicated study and expertise. Many who have achieved other computer industry credentials have had troubles with the MCSE. This is, however, why the MCSE certificate is so valuable. If achieving MCSE status were easy, the market would be quickly flooded by MCSEs, and the certification would become meaningless. Microsoft, keenly aware of this fact, has taken steps to ensure that the certification means its holder is truly knowledgeable and skilled.

To become an MCSE, you must pass four core requirements and two electives. Most people select the following exam combination for the MCSE core requirements for the 4.0 track, which is the most current track:

Client Requirement

70-64: Windows 95

or

70-73: Implementing and Supporting Windows NT Workstation 4.0

Networking Requirement

70-58: Networking Essentials

Windows NT Server 4.0 Requirement

70-67: Implementing and Supporting Windows NT Server 4.0

Windows NT Server 4.0 in the Enterprise Requirement

70-68: Implementing and Supporting Windows NT Server 4.0 in the Enterprise

For the electives, you have about ten choices. The most popular elective is:

70-59: Internetworking with Microsoft TCP/IP on NT 4.0

Other electives are:

70-81: Implementing and Supporting Microsoft Exchange Server 5.5

70-26: SQL Server Administration for 6.5

70-18: SMS Administration for 1.2

70-87: Implementing and Supporting IIS 4.0

For a complete description of all the MCSE options, see the Microsoft Train_Cert Offline Web Site on the CD that comes with this book, or go directly to www.microsoft.com\train_cert.

Where Do You Take the Exams?

You may take the exams at any of more than 800 Authorized Sylvan Testing Centers around the world. For the location of a testing center near you, call (800) 755-EXAM (755-3926). Outside the United States and Canada, contact your local Sylvan Registration Center.

To register for a Microsoft Certified Professional exam:

- Determine the number of the exam you want to take.

- Determine when and where you want to take the test. If you don't know where any testing centers are, you can ask Sylvan when you register.

- Register with the Sylvan Registration Center that is nearest to you. At this point, you will be asked for advance payment for the exam. At this writing, the exams are $100 each. Exams must be taken within one year of payment. You can schedule exams up to six weeks in advance or as late as one working day prior to the date of the exam. You can cancel or reschedule your exam if you contact Sylvan at least two working days prior to the exam. Same-day registration is available in some locations, although this is subject to space availability. Where same-day registration is available, you must register a minimum of two hours before test time.

You can now register for tests on the Internet. The address at the time of this writing is www.slspro.com/msreg/microsof.asp. If that doesn't work, try www.microsoft.com/mcp as a starting point.

When you schedule the exam, you'll be provided with information regarding appointment and cancellation procedures, ID requirements, and the testing center location.

What the Windows 95 Exam Measures

The Windows 95 exam covers concepts and skills required for the support of Windows 95 computers running on a network. It emphasizes the following areas:

- Planning and installation

- Remote administration and system policies

- Printing on both the local computer and on a network

- Network protocols and their configurations

- Being a client and/or server in both the Windows NT and NetWare networking environments

- Troubleshooting

If we could rename the exam to be precisely descriptive it would be "Supporting Windows 95 as a client and as a file and print server on NetWare and Windows NT networks, using System Monitor, Remote Administration, and System Policies as needed." Over half of the questions deal with Windows 95 connected to some sort of network. Chapters 11, 12, 13, 14, 15, and 16 of this book are critical to passing the test.

The exam focuses on fundamental concepts related to Windows 95 operations, as well as how to make Windows 95 function in a networked corporate environment. Careful study of this book, along with hands-on experience with the operating system, will be especially helpful in preparing you for the exam.

Tips for Taking the Windows 95 Exam

Here are some general tips for taking the exams successfully:

- Arrive early at the exam center so you can relax and review your study materials, particularly tables and lists of exam-related information.

- Read the questions carefully. Don't be tempted to jump to an early conclusion. Make sure you know *exactly* what the question is asking.

- Don't leave any unanswered questions. They count against you.

- When answering multiple-choice questions you're not sure about, use a process of elimination to get rid of the obviously incorrect questions first. This will improve your odds if you need to make an educated guess.

- Because the hard questions will take up the most time, save them for last. You can move forward and backward through the exam, unless the question specifically states that you cannot go back. At this time the Windows 95 test allows you to go back and amend previous answers, but that is always subject to change.

- This test has some exhibits (pictures). It can be difficult, if not impossible, to view both the questions and the exhibit simulation on the 14- and 15-inch screens usually found at the testing centers. Call around to each center and see if they have 17-inch monitors available. If they don't, perhaps you can arrange to bring in your own. Failing this, some have found it useful to quickly draw the diagram on the scratch paper provided by the testing center and use the monitor to view just the question.

- One of the keys to correctly answering Microsoft tests is figuring out just what it is that you are being asked. Most test questions are in the form of a story problem—cutting through the fluff and understanding the issue involved is most of the battle. You may want to look at the answer choices and "reverse-engineer" the question.

- Many of the Multiple Rating Items (MRI) questions that ask you "How well does this solution address the problem?" are very intimidating at first, because they are very long. My strategy is to look at the solution and compare it against each desired outcome, keeping track of whether it works or doesn't. The available responses will sometimes consist of a count of the number of items that were successfully accomplished, which is the running total I have kept in my head. Sometimes the question will end with a list of the objectives, and you will be asked to specify if they were fulfilled or not. I found these much easier, as I could look at the solution and see if it fulfilled each individual objective.

■ This is not simply a test of your knowledge of Windows 95; you'll need to know how it is implemented in a network. You will also need to know about Windows NT, NetWare, protocols, and other networking issues in order to pass the test.

How to Use This Book

This book can provide a solid foundation for the serious effort of preparing for the Windows 95 exam. To best benefit from this book, you might want to use the following study method:

1. Study a chapter carefully, making sure you fully understand the information.

2. Complete all hands-on exercises in the chapter, referring back to the chapter so that you understand each step you take.

3. Answer the exercise questions related to that chapter. (You will find the answers to these questions in Appendix A and on the CD.)

4. Note which questions you did not understand, and study those sections of the book again.

5. Study each chapter in the same manner.

6. Before taking the exam, try the practice exams included on the CD that comes with this book. They will give you an idea of what you can expect to see on the real thing. We have added many additional questions to this second edition of the book, in order to help you better prepare for the test.

7. Use resources available on the Internet to help supplement and update your training preparation. The best place to start is the Certification area on Microsoft's Web page, www.microsoft.com/mcp. When you are ready to get more details about a particular test or objective list, the www.microsoft.com/train_cert Web site is another invaluable resource.

If you prefer to use this book in conjunction with classroom or online training, you have many options. Both Microsoft-authorized training and independent training are widely available. See Microsoft's Web sites (www.microsoft.com/mcp and www.microsoft.com/train_cert) for more information.

To learn all the material covered in this book, you will need to study regularly and with discipline. Try to set aside the same time every day to study, and select a comfortable and quiet place in which to do it. If you work hard, you will be surprised at how quickly you learn this material. Good luck.

Exam objectives are subject to change at any time without prior notice and at Microsoft's sole discretion. Please visit Microsoft's Training & Certification Web site (www.microsoft.com/Train_Cert) for the most current exam objectives listing.

What's on the CD?

The CD contains several valuable tools to help you study for your MCSE exams:

- The Microsoft Train_Cert Offline Web Site is a good place to start. It provides an overview of Microsoft's training and certification program and the process of becoming an MCSE.

- The exercise questions and answers from each of the chapters in this book are included in a simple-to-use exam preparation program.

- Sample applications are supplied for some of the hands-on exercises in the chapters.

How to Contact the Authors

We welcome any of your comments, suggestions, and feedback.

You can e-mail Lance Mortensen at:
LMWin95@aol.com

You can e-mail Rick Sawtell at:
Quickening@msn.com

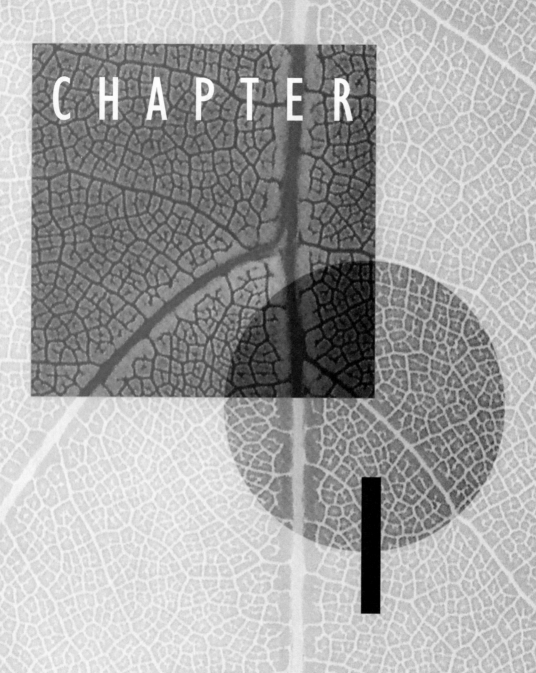

CHAPTER

1

The Windows Family

Understanding the history of the Windows operating system will help you to see where Windows development is going. With this knowledge, you will be able to better support the current products your system uses, as well as plan for the future.

Microsoft has split the Windows family into two distinct sides: the Windows 95/Windows 98 side and the Windows NT side. Microsoft has always excelled at coding software that was before its time. Remember when Windows NT was the butt of all the computer jokes? Now it is a force to be reckoned with, as it slowly takes over both the client and server roles.

Whether or not you use Microsoft Windows as your operating system is no longer the big decision it once was. The real decision is which version of Windows to use: Windows 95 or Windows NT. Both operating systems have their advantages and disadvantages. The key to deciding between them is knowing what those advantages and disadvantages are, and how your company will be affected by them.

The future of Windows 95 is starting to become clearer, although we can't predict all the changes for the next release. Windows 98 seems more of an evolutionary product, rather than the revolutionary product that Windows 95 was. Whatever the future holds, it is always important to remember an ancient Chinese curse: "May you be born in interesting times."

This chapter begins with a brief history lesson, and then explains the differences between Windows 95 and Windows NT. We will then look at how Windows 95 fits into a stand-alone or networking environment. Finally, we will take a glimpse at the future of Windows 95.

The History of Windows 95

The Windows family started in 1985 with the 1.0 16-bit version. In 1987, Windows 2.*x*, or Windows 286, was released. Although it supported Dynamic Data Exchange (DDE) and overlapping windows, it was still mostly used as a glorified menu program. Windows 386 (version 2.10) added pre-emptive multitasking of DOS programs and the concept of virtual machines (see Chapter 4 for details about Windows and virtual machines).

Windows 3.0 was released in 1990. Its enhanced mode took advantage of the 386 protected architecture. Windows 3.0 was the operating system that convinced people to switch from DOS-based programs to native Windows programs, because the new enhanced mode enabled applications to run much better than their DOS counterparts.

Windows 3.1 was released in 1992. The operating system was more stable in this version, which also included multimedia support. In the same year, Windows for Workgroups 3.1, then 3.11, was released. These versions added Microsoft Mail and better networking integration.

By this time, Microsoft knew that an entirely new operating system was required to take advantage of the power of the personal computer and to provide better multitasking and network functionality. Windows NT 3.1 was first released in 1993. Although this looked like earlier versions of Windows (due to the similarity of the interface), Windows NT acted more like a mainframe operating system designed to replace the older DOS-based operating systems. The current version is NT 4.0, which has a Windows 95-type user interface. Windows NT is a fully protected mode (32-bit) operating system, with some compatibility sacrificed for new features.

Work on Windows 95 started in 1992, and it came onto the market in August 1995. Windows 95 incorporates many features of the Windows 3.*x* family, as well as features from the Windows NT family. Windows 95 continues to be the most popular of the Microsoft operating systems for many reasons, such as its ease of use, low hardware requirements compared to Windows NT, and backward compatibility.

Windows 95 is a revolutionary operating system when compared with Windows 3.*x*. Chapter 5 focuses on many of the new features in Windows 95, and other chapters provide more details on how to install, configure, and troubleshoot new Windows 95 components.

Design Philosophies of Windows 95

The programmers of Windows 95 had some definite goals in mind when they created Windows 95, including the following:

- **Compatibility:** Windows 95 was designed to run on existing hardware and to be able to run software better than Windows 3.*x*.

- **Speed:** Windows 95 was designed to be at least as fast as Windows 3.*x*, and considerably faster when given newer software and hardware. New 32-bit, protected-mode caching components are one of the reasons for better performance.

- **Reliability:** Windows 95 was designed to better recover from GPFs (General Protection Faults) and hung (nonresponding) programs.

- **Ease of use:** Windows 95 was designed to be easier to use than Windows 3.*x*. With Plug-and-Play support, less time and effort are required to configure hardware and software.

- **Robust, integrated networking:** Windows 95 was designed with 32-bit, protected-mode network drivers and protocols, making networking faster and more reliable.

Windows 95 is an almost clean break from earlier versions of Windows. Like all major upgrades, there will probably be some hassle and pain involved. However, once you convert to Windows 95, you may actually believe that all of those commercials were closer to the truth than you realized. Although Windows 95 won't cure all of society's ills (it didn't increase my gas mileage, after all), it's still a darn good product.

Windows 95 versus Windows NT Workstation

Many companies struggle with the decision of whether to use Windows 95 or Windows NT Workstation on the desktop. There are two overriding things to consider when looking at the two operating systems:

- Windows 95 stresses compatibility.

- Windows NT Workstation stresses security.

Windows 95 is a mixture of 32- and 16-bit components. It can even use 16-bit device drivers. Windows NT Workstation is a pure 32-bit operating system, and it controls all access to hardware resources. Applications are allowed access to hardware resources only through NT itself. If applications try to directly access hardware, NT will stop them. Windows 95, on the other hand, tries to control access to hardware resources, but if an application needs or wants to access hardware directly, it can. This makes Windows 95 inherently less stable than Windows NT Workstation, but much more compatible with older legacy applications and utilities.

Windows 95 and Windows NT Workstation have many things in common. Both systems have the following features:

- Can run 16-bit applications

- Can run 32-bit applications

- Use preemptive multitasking

- Provide multithreaded support

- Can share files

- Can be a personal Web server

- Have user profiles available

- Can enforce system policies (NT 4.0 and later)

- Replace INI files with the registry

- Can be a client for Microsoft

- Can be a client for NetWare

- Run on Intel-compatible CPUs

However, there are also some big differences between the two programs. Table 1.1 lists the differences between Windows 95 and Windows NT Workstation.

T A B L E 1.1 Differences between Windows 95 and Windows NT Workstation	Item	**Windows 95**	**Windows NT**
	Can use 16-bit drivers	Yes	No
	Supports Plug and Play	Yes	No*
	Can run DOS applications	Yes	Most**
	Can run 16-bit applications in separate address space	No	Yes
	Supports multiple CPUs	No	Yes

	Item	Windows 95	Windows NT
TABLE 1.1 (cont.) Differences between Windows 95 and Windows NT Workstation	Certified for C2 security	No	Yes
	Requires secured logon	No	Yes
	Runs on Alpha, PPC, MIPS	No	Yes***
	Stated minimum RAM	4MB	12MB
	Realistic minimum RAM	16MB	32MB

*NT 5.0 will add Plug-and-Play support.
**DOS applications that attempt direct access to hardware resources are not allowed by NT.
***Until NT 5.0; then only Intel-compatible and DEC Alpha CPUs will be supported.

The question is not, "Which one is better?" You need to ask, "Which one is right for me and my company?" Although Windows NT Workstation is positioned as the premier client platform, Windows 95 has some advanced capabilities, as you will discover in this book.

Integrating Windows 95 into an Environment

There are three general ways of integrating Windows 95 into an environment.

Microsoft ✓ ***Exam Objective***

Develop an appropriate implementation model for specific requirements. Considerations include:

- Choosing a workgroup configuration or logging on to an existing domain

- As a stand-alone computer

- As a member of a workgroup

- As a member of a Windows NT Domain or other type of server-based network

Each of these various ways of integrating Windows 95 will be discussed below.

Stand-Alone Installations

The easiest way to install Windows 95 is as a stand-alone installation. Most home computers are installed this way, as well as many laptop computers.

The major advantage of a stand-alone installation is that it doesn't rely on other computers, which means that any problems you encounter can quickly be determined to come from that one computer.

The major disadvantage is the lack of connectivity. Without a connection to other computers you are dependant on the old "sneaker net," which means you copy data to floppies and run the floppies around with your sneakers. (We had an advanced version called "Frisbee net," where we would take the floppies and throw them back and forth, but it still wasn't very good.)

Workgroup Configurations

Windows 95 can participate in a workgroup, which is a grouping of computers with no central server. Windows 95 can connect to other computers via a network (be a client) and use resources on other computers as if those resources were its own. Windows 95 can also allow other computers to connect to it (act as a server) and can share both folders and printers to clients connected via a network.

The major advantage of a workgroup is that a dedicated, expensive computer is not required—Windows 95 comes with all the software you need to be both a client and a server. Each computer can be configured as a client and/or server in the workgroup.

The major disadvantage of a workgroup model is that because there is no central server, each Windows 95 computer may be set up slightly differently, thus requiring clients to remember many passwords. For example, the password to use the laser printer hooked to the secretary's computer may be *jazz* but the password required to print to the color printer hooked to the salesman's computer may be *sun.*

Workgroups, as well as the sharing of folders and printers, are covered in depth in later chapters.

Workgroup security models are based on passwords (called Share level security), which means that anyone who knows the password can gain access to shared resources. This is inherently insecure, as you can NOT limit access to certain users—you can only hope that users you don't want to have access never learn the password.

Windows NT Domain or Other Server-Based Configurations

Windows 95 has the ability to join an existing Windows NT domain. This allows Windows 95 to still act as a client and/or server, with the added benefit of having a centralized database for users, passwords, and security. Windows 95 comes with software to join a Windows NT domain as well as a NetWare server environment. Other types of server environments can also be supported by adding additional components to Windows 95. Joining a domain will be covered in later chapters.

The major advantage of joining an existing domain is that all security is centrally controlled. In a correctly configured environment, you will have only one user name and password. Your single user name can then be assigned rights to various printers and folders. Windows 95 can still operate as a client, a server, or both in a domain environment.

The major disadvantage is that you will need a dedicated server computer, with Windows NT Server, NetWare, or some other type of high-end server software. Joining and maintaining a domain is also more complex than creating and maintaining a workgroup.

Because the security model of a domain is based upon users and groups (called User level security) you can limit access to people based on their user account, or on group membership. This is the best form of security available for Windows 95. Joining a domain is the preferred option for most businesses.

The Future of Windows 95

More than 70 million copies of Windows 95 have sold so far, and 3 to 5 million more copies are selling each month!

The newest versions of Windows 95 include the B, or OSR2 (including OSR2.5), release, which offers various additional features such as support for larger partitions (covered in Chapter 8) and integration of all of the Windows 95 patches. Most of the features of Windows 95B can be added to earlier versions of Windows 95 by simply visiting the Microsoft Web site (www.microsoft.com) and downloading them. Windows 98 (code name "Memphis") is scheduled to ship mid- to late 1998. Enhancements will include all of those that Windows 95B has, as well as integrated Internet Explorer 4.0 capabilities and features, and support for all the latest hardware technologies, including USB ports and dual monitors.

It's clear that Windows 95 (and Windows 98) will continue to be one of the major operating systems in use for quite some time to come.

Review Questions

1. Your company is upgrading its computers. The choice is between Windows 95 and Windows NT. You want to support user profiles, the registry, and 32-bit applications, but you have many DOS applications that access the video card directly. Which operating system should you choose, and why?

   A. Windows 95

   B. Windows NT

   C. Both A and B would work fine.

   D. Neither A nor B would work.

2. How many CPUs can Windows 95 support?

A. 1

B. 2

C. 4

D. Unlimited

3. Which of the following support Plug and Play? (Select all that apply.)

A. MS-DOS

B. Windows 95

C. Windows NT Workstation

D. Windows NT Server

4. Which of the following support multithreaded, multitasking applications? (Select all that apply.)

A. MS-DOS

B. Windows 95

C. Windows NT Workstation

D. Windows NT Server

5. What is the revised version of Windows 95 called?

A. Windows 96

B. Windows 95-a

C. OSR1

D. OSR2

6. Which network model has no dedicated server?

   A. Stand-alone

   B. Networked

   C. Workgroup

   D. Member of an NT Domain

7. In which model can Windows 95 be both a client and a server? (Select all that apply.)

   A. Stand-alone

   B. Networked

   C. Workgroup

   D. Member of an NT Domain

8. Which model would be appropriate for the home user with one computer?

   A. Stand-alone

   B. Networked

   C. Workgroup

   D. Member of an NT Domain

9. Which model would be most appropriate for a large company?

   A. Stand-alone

   B. Networked

   C. Workgroup

   D. Member of an NT Domain

CHAPTER

2

Planning and Installing Windows 95

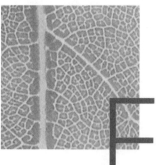

E ven though Windows 95 is a newer operating system with much more functionality than was provided in Windows 3.*x*, installing it is a relatively simple process. The Windows 95 setup is so simple that novice users could run the setup process on their home PC with few (if any) problems. For the systems engineer, Windows 95 provides a wide array of configuration options. Combined with a special startup file, these options can allow for "hands-free" installations of both Windows 95 and additional applications like Microsoft Office.

Although installation of Windows 95 is a simple process, as a systems engineer you know how important planning an installation can be. In this chapter, we will cover the following:

- An overview of the installation process

- A comparison of installation mediums: floppy, CD, or network

- A new installation versus an upgrade of Windows 3.*x*

- System requirements for both hardware and software

- An administrator's "to do" list before beginning installation

- The installation itself

- Uninstalling Windows 95

- Dual-booting issues

- Batch setups: BATCH.EXE, NetSetup, and INFINST.EXE

- Troubleshooting installation problems

Whew! That may seem like a lot of information to cover, but remember, the better your initial installation plan, the fewer maintenance headaches you will need to deal with down the road. You should read the entire chapter before attempting an actual installation of Windows 95 (Exercise 2.1).

Installation Process Overview

The installation process for Windows 95 runs like any Windows 3.*x* installation. You no longer interact with the MS-DOS text-based environment. If you launch the Setup program from the MS-DOS prompt, it will create a minimal installation of Windows 3.*x*. This minimal installation will provide just enough functionality for Setup to continue running in Windows protected mode. This requires about 600KB of conventional memory. Usually, you will run Setup from within the Windows 3.*x* environment by opening File Manager and navigating to the SETUP.EXE program for the Windows 95 installation.

Viewed from the workstation's perspective, the installation process is in two parts: real-mode setup and Windows protected-mode setup.

Real-Mode Setup

Part of the setup process needs to run in real mode. This is done to ensure that the current system metrics will allow for a successful setup. The real-mode portion of the setup process involves the following:

- **File system:** Setup runs ScanDisk to check for problems with the MS-DOS FAT (file allocation table) and will attempt to fix any problems it finds. It would not be wise to install a new operating system to a disk that is not working properly.

- **Windows 3.x:** Setup then attempts to locate a version of Windows 3.x. If one is found, Setup queries the user if it is okay to use this version of Windows for the setup process. If the user does not choose OK, a minimal version of Windows is installed, and the setup process continues from there.

- **System metrics:** Setup now runs system checks to make sure the system can run Windows 95. Things like the CPU, hard disk space, and MS-DOS version are checked.

- **Memory managers:** Setup continues by looking for an Extended Memory Manager like HIMEM.SYS. If it doesn't find a memory manager, it loads one. (Windows 3.x will not run without an Extended Memory Manager.) Setup will also load a disk-caching utility like SMARTDRV if one is not already present.

- **Terminate-and-stay-resident programs (TSRs):** The next step is to unload any TSRs that are known to cause problems with a setup. These are normally loaded in your CONFIG.SYS or AUTOEXEC.BAT file. The Setup program will remark out known problem TSRs. If the program isn't sure, it will leave the TSR there.

Many anti-virus programs will place extra information into the files as they are placed on your system, and will thus render Windows 95 unrunnable.

Protected-Mode Setup

After the real-mode setup procedures, Setup switches to the Windows 3.x protected-mode GUI (graphical user interface) and finishes the setup process. Setup now goes through the hardware-detection process, copies files, modifies boot records, and finally reboots and runs. The details are discussed in the following sections.

Hardware Detection

Setup begins the hardware-detection process by determining if Plug-and-Play components are installed on your PC. The second step of the detection process will use safe methods of detecting hardware. It does this by looking for entries in the AUTOEXEC.BAT and CONFIG.SYS files. Several *.INI files might also be searched. If you specified any hardware items that are not listed in these files, Setup will use an invasive method of detection. This means that the Setup program will start sending messages to particular memory locations (base I/O addresses) and different IRQ channels. These messages could crash the setup process. Do not be alarmed; this is part of the normal setup process. If this occurs, simply power off the computer (do not use Ctrl+Alt+Del), and then restart it. Setup will continue to run properly.

You should power on all peripheral devices (such as scanners, printers, and modems) before the detection process begins. This allows the Setup program to talk with the hardware.

The Setup program keeps a detection log file called DETLOG.TXT, which contains a list of all of the components found in your system. The whole setup process is logged to a file called SETUPLOG.TXT. This file contains everything that happened during the setup process, including any crashes. You can delete these files after the setup process has completed successfully. As an administrator, you may find it useful to keep a backup copy of the DETLOG .TXT file, since it lists the hardware items and their base I/O addresses and IRQ settings.

Microsoft ✓ *Exam* *Objective*

Diagnose and resolve installation failures.

There are three points at which the setup process might stop or stall: before, during, or after hardware detection. Setup will analyze the errors that are recorded in the log files and try to either find a solution or skip the error and continue with the setup process. If Setup fails before the hardware detection phase, it recovers by reading SETUPLOG.TXT to determine where the system stalled, what portions need to be redone, and what portions to skip.

If Setup fails during hardware detection, the DETCRASH.LOG file is created. It contains information about the detection module that was running and the I/O port or memory resources it was accessing when the failure occurred. When the detection process finds this file, it automatically runs in Safe Recovery mode to verify all the devices already detected, and then skips all detection modules up to the failed module. Safe Recovery then skips detection and any attempts to configure the failed module—in effect, skipping the action that caused the failure—and continues the detection process, starting with the next module.

> The DETLOG.TXT and SETUPLOG.TXT files are built by Windows 95 during the setup phase and can be useful for troubleshooting your system.

Once the detecting phase has been completed, Setup will create the Windows 95 system registry and begin loading it with the detected hardware.

Windows 95 Files

Next, the Windows 95 files are decompressed and copied to the appropriate location on your hard disk. This process can take several minutes.

Boot Record Modifications

The boot records are now modified. Files that are modified include your CONFIG.SYS file, which is copied to a new file called CONFIG.DOS. The new CONFIG.SYS file looks similar to the old one, but may have lines remarked out. This means that Windows 95 has replaced a real-mode driver with a protected-mode version that will run when Windows 95 is started. Your AUTOEXEC.BAT file also has similar modifications.

> If none of your applications require real-mode drivers, you can delete both your CONFIG.SYS file and your AUTOEXEC.BAT file. On our PCs, we have removed the CONFIG.SYS file completely. We have kept the AUTOEXEC .BAT file because it loads an anti-virus program and has a PATH statement. The PATH statement is useful if you go to a command prompt from within Windows 95. In the past, you normally had a portion of the PATH statement directed to your DOS directory, thus providing you with access to the DOS commands from anywhere in the system. The DOS commands have been replaced by 32-bit versions, which support long filenames. These are stored in the \Windows\Command directory. You should modify your PATH statement appropriately.

The MSDOS.SYS file is also replaced. The new MSDOS.SYS file is a flat ASCII file rather than a binary system file. The file contains options for delaying the boot process, specifying double-space drivers, and so on. It looks a lot like the old-fashioned *.INI files. The end of the MSDOS.SYS file is filled with *x*'s. These are here for place holders. *Do **not** delete them.* The MSDOS.SYS file must be at least 1024B for backward compatibility with some programs. See Chapter 3 for information about setting options in MSDOS.SYS.

Finally, your IO.SYS file is replaced and loads the new drivers needed to run Windows 95.

After this final phase of the operation, you are now running in Windows 95. After the modification, you will need to run the UNINSTAL.EXE program if you want to return to your old operating system for some reason (uninstalling Windows 95 is discussed later in the chapter).

Reboot and First-Run Procedures

Next, the system is rebooted and run as a Windows 95 operating system. Then the first-run procedures begin. These include tasks like setting up short-cuts in your Programs group, converting old group files into shortcuts, setting the time zone where you live, and so on.

Depending on your hardware configuration, the system might need to be rebooted again to finish the first-run procedures.

Installation Mediums

You can install Windows 95 using several different mediums: floppy disk, CD-ROM, from a network, or as a shared installation.

The floppy disk installation provides all of the functionality you need to run Windows 95. The CD-ROM version has additional tools and utilities that are not shipped with the floppy disks. These tools and utilities are located in the \Admin folder and contain things like a System Policy Editor, batch setup programs, and a host of samples. The CD-ROM is also more convenient, since you do not need to continually swap disks in and out of the drive.

The CD-ROM version of Windows 95 also includes an electronic version of the Windows 95 Resource Kit.

You can also do a setup across the network. This allows you to install an administrative version of Windows 95, which will decompress all files needed for a setup and allow you to configure administrative features that will apply to all Windows 95 installations performed from here. Another way of doing a network installation is to place all of the files located in the \Win95 directory on the CD-ROM onto a network drive. Then all you need to do is log on to the server, go to that shared directory, and run the SETUP.EXE program. This is similar to a stand-alone setup, except that the data is coming from the network share rather than the local PC.

Another option is to create a shared installation of Windows 95, which means that each PC will use the shared version of Windows 95. This has the advantage of being very easy to configure, because you need to make modifications to only one PC. The disadvantages are increased network traffic and a large load on the server. In this type of environment, a minimal number of files will be copied to the local PCs. The local PC will also have its own local swapfile. If you decide to go a step further and use diskless workstations, your server will need to accommodate the swapfiles.

As an administrator, you can create hands-free installations using batch setup files and a network server for distribution. We will look at this technique in more detail at the end of this chapter.

New Installation versus Upgrading

When you install Windows 95 from a Windows 3.1*x* system, the upgrade version will search the current system for several files that indicate that you already have a current version of Windows. If it does not find them, it may ask you to put the Windows 3.*x* Installation Disk 1 into the floppy drive for confirmation.

Rather than upgrading, you can install Windows 95 from a machine that has just been formatted. To do this, you will need a full installation copy of Windows 95, not the upgrade version. As you might expect, the full installation software is a bit more expensive than the upgrade.

During normal Windows 3.*x* usage, you will inevitably install software on your system. Many of these programs will add their own *.DLL files to your Windows directory. When you remove that software, the removal process may not remove those *.DLL files. You may have several megabytes of files in your Windows directory that are never used. A full installation has the advantage of getting rid of all of these unused files. You can accomplish much the same thing by deleting your \Windows directory before doing an installation.

Another advantage of installing to a clean system is that you can set up your system to dual-boot. All you need to do is create bootable floppy disks for each operating system, and then install the operating system. For example, when you want to run Unix, you put your Unix boot disk into the drive, and away you go.

The disadvantage of installing to a clean system is that you must reinstall all of your applications after you have installed Windows 95. When you install Windows 95 over a Windows 3.x system, the Windows 95 setup is smart enough to add your old software to the new platform. This includes your computer name, workgroup name, and icons from the old Program Manager. However, if you specify a directory other than the current Windows directory during a partial upgrade, you may need to reinstall your old applications.

If you have the time, we suggest a full installation onto a recently formatted hard disk. This will get rid of any unused files from old programs and give you the cleanest possible system to start with.

If you already have Windows 3.x and you wish to do a full install, you do not have to buy the full installation version of Windows 95. Format your hard drive and then do an upgrade installation of Windows 95. During the setup process, the upgrade will look for some particular files from Windows 3.x. All you need to do is have your Windows 3.x Installation Disk 1 handy. You can also use the Windows for Workgroups Disk 1 or an OS/2 installation disk.

System Requirements

The Windows 95 operating system has minimum requirements for software and hardware. These minimum requirements, along with the recommended hardware and software, are presented in the following sections.

Hardware Requirements

Here are the minimum and recommended requirements for hardware:

Hardware Requirements	Hardware Recommendations
386DX processor or later	486DX 66MHz or later
4MB RAM (8MB to run Exchange, Internet Explorer 4.0, or Outlook)	16MB RAM for good performance
3.5 high-density floppy or CD-ROM drive	CD-ROM drive (for the Windows 95 CD-ROM version)
50–55MB free hard disk space (the actual system will use 32MB with all options installed, but temporary files used during setup will need the extra room)	More is recommended (at least double the amount of RAM in your system) for swapfile use
VGA card (Windows 95 does not support CGA or EGA)	SVGA card with at least 2MB of VRAM

Other recommended hardware is a pointing device (mouse, TouchPad, or other) and a fax/modem.

Windows 95 Setup requires approximately 470KB of conventional memory.

Software Requirements

For your software, the Windows 95 installation requires Windows 3.*x* for an upgrade installation, or the more expensive Full System copy of Windows 95, and one of the following forms of DOS:

- MS-DOS 3.2 or later

- DR DOS

- Novell DOS

- IBM PC-DOS

- OS/2 configured to dual-boot with MS-DOS

Your best choice is MS-DOS 6.2*x*. Up until MS-DOS 5.0, many OEMs had their own flavors of DOS. We recommend version 5.0 as a minimum, both because it is a standardized version and it is the earliest flavor of MS-DOS that supports dual-booting.

Windows 95 Version B (OSR2) can add support for the FAT32 file system. FAT32 can support 2 terabyte (2000 gigabyte) drives whereas normal MS-DOS FAT supports up to 2GB drives. FAT32 does have the following advantages and disadvantages:

- FAT32 drives can access up to 2TB.

- FAT32 clusters are smaller than MS-DOS FAT, meaning better utilization of disk space.

- Existing disk utilities that do not ship with Windows 95B (OSR2) cannot perform low-level maintenance on the FAT32 drives. This includes compression and defragmenting. The OSR2 disk utilities do work, however.

- FAT32 drives cannot be accessed directly by other operating systems, including Windows 95 version 1. This is only a problem if you are planning on dual-booting your Windows 95 OSR2-FAT32 machine.

Before You Install

The following is an administrator's "to-do" list of things that should be taken care of before you begin a Windows 95 installation.

Although this information is not covered on the Windows 95 certification exam, it will give you a jump start on becoming a solid, practical MCSE and not just a person with a certification.

1. Create an MS-DOS boot disk.

If everything blows up, you'll still have an out. This disk should have a copy of your current CONFIG.SYS file (including any special drivers like the ones for your CD-ROM and network interface card), AUTOEXEC .BAT file, the double-space program (DRVSPACE or DBLSPACE) if used, as well as the ATTRIB, DEFRAG, EDIT, FDISK, FORMAT, SCANDISK, and XCOPY programs.

To create an MS-DOS boot disk, place a new floppy into the drive and format it with the following parameters:

```
Format A: /S
```

This will format the disk and place the system files needed to boot on it. You then need to manually copy over the files specified above. If you already have a floppy disk with the files on it and want to make it an MS-DOS bootable, run the following command:

```
Sys A:
```

This will place the necessary boot files onto the floppy disk.

2. Run ScanDisk on your hard disks.

ScanDisk will look for problems with your file structures and try to fix them. Files live in clusters. The cluster size depends on the number of cylinders and heads configured in the CMOS for your hard disk. The FAT points to the starting cluster of a particular file. If the file spans more than one cluster, the end of the first cluster will have a pointer to the next cluster location where the rest of the file is located. Sometimes a cluster will point to a cluster where the continuation of the file does not reside. This is known as a *lost cluster* and can be detected by ScanDisk. ScanDisk will allow you to delete these lost clusters or to convert them into files that you can look at.

3. Run the Defrag program for full defragmentation—consolidate free space and sort clusters.

Files that are dispersed all over your hard disk are said to be *fragmented*. To consolidate free space (move clusters together so that the drive arm does not need to travel as far) and place files on contiguous clusters, you should run the Defrag program with the /F parameter:

```
Defrag /F
```

This will optimize your hard disk's performance, because the files can be read more quickly.

4. Consider making your disk partitions smaller.

FAT and Windows VFAT look at files with a granularity of a single cluster. On a 1GB hard drive, formatted as a single drive, a single cluster will be approximately 32KB. This means that if you have a 12-byte file, it will take up 64KB of disk space. By making two disk partitions of 500MB each, your 12-byte file will now take up 16KB rather than 32KB.

Microsoft Plus! and Windows 95B (OSR2) include a disk-compression utility called DriveSpace3 that will allow you to compress your hard drive with "no compression." This virtualizes your clusters in such a way that 12 bytes take up only 12 bytes of hard disk space. With this type of compression, you have the added advantage of more disk space, with the low overhead of a mapping table. This is much faster than real compression, which will actually look for patterns in your files and then crunch the files. See Chapter 8 for more information about the Plus! software.

5. Remove any TSRs that you do not need.

If Windows 95 is unsure about a TSR, it will leave it in the CONFIG.SYS or AUTOEXEC.BAT file. These TSRs will take up conventional memory, even if Windows 95 has a protected-mode driver that could be used.

Make sure you leave the networking and CD-ROM TSRs if you are going to use those for your setup process. Disable all anti-virus utilities, screen savers, disk-scan utilities, undelete utilities, UMB managers, disk caching, and menu systems in your CONFIG.SYS and AUTOEXEC.BAT files. Replace third-party memory managers like QEMM and 386MAX with HIMEM.SYS and EMM386.EXE before running Setup. Disable all ROM shadowing, because it can conflict with the proper detection of video cards, disk controllers, and other peripherals. Once you are finished editing these files, you need to reboot the system so that they can be cleared from memory.

6. Disable laptop suspend features.

Many laptops have a suspend feature that kicks in after a predetermined interval of user inactivity. If you are installing to a laptop computer, make sure that you disable this feature.

7. Back up your system.

If you have the available space, making a backup copy of your system is always a good idea. This allows a quick recovery in case of problems during the setup process. If disk space is at a premium, you should back up registry files (*.DAT), initialization files (*.INI), program groups (*.GRP), password files (*.PWL), network configuration files, login scripts, and any user documents used by applications.

8. **Check network software and hardware.**

Make sure that the network software is running correctly before you start Windows 95 setup. Windows 95 uses the settings from the existing network configuration to set up the new configuration. If an unused network card is installed on your machine, remove it.

9. **Design and test your installation scripts.**

You can automate the Windows 95 setup procedures by using batch setup files. See the section "Creating Batch Setup Scripts" later in the chapter for details.

The Windows 95 Installation

There are some optional switches that you can set for the Setup program. To view the different options, run Setup with the /? parameter. The options are different for an MS-DOS setup and a Windows 3.x setup, as summarized in Tables 2.1 and 2.2.

TABLE 2.1	**Switch**	**Description**
MS-DOS Setup Program Switches	/ID	Disable check for hard disk space.
	/IL	Install Logitech series C mouse.
	/IM	Disable memory check.
	/IN	Do not run the network module.
	/IS	Disable ScanDisk from running.
	/T:<path>	Location for temporary setup files. The directory must already exist before Setup begins.
	<batch>	Specify a batch file to run with Setup.
	/?	Help

TABLE 2.2	Switch	Description
Windows 3.*x* Setup Program Switches	/ID	Disable check for hard disk space.
	/IM	Disable memory check.
	/IN	Do not run the network module.
	/IS	Disable system check.
	/T:*<path>*	Location for temporary setup files. The directory must already exist before Setup begins.
	/?	Help

There are three parts of the Windows 95 Setup Wizard, as you can see in the opening screen shown in Figure 2.1:

- The first step gathers system information and will prompt you for additional information.

- The second step decompresses and copies the Windows 95 files to the appropriate directories. It also allows you to create a Windows 95 Startup disk. If you choose to create this disk, the files listed in Table 2.3 will be added to the disk.

- The final step is a reboot of your system and then final configuration, including the migration of old Program Manager groups.

FIGURE 2.1

The opening screen of the Windows 95 Setup Wizard

	FILE	DESCRIPTION
T A B L E 2.3 Windows 95 Startup Disk Files	ATTRIB.EXE	File attributes tool
	CHKDSK.EXE	Mini version of ScanDisk
	COMMAND.COM	Command interpreter
	DELTREE.EXE*	File-delete utility capable of deleting subdirectories as well as their files
	DRVSPACE.BIN	MS DriveSpace compression driver
	EBD.SYS	Flag to identify this as a Windows 95 Startup disk
	EDIT.COM	Editor
	FDISK.EXE	Disk partition utility
	FORMAT.COM	Disk format utility
	IO.SYS	System boot file
	MSDOS.SYS	Boot options
	REGEDIT.EXE	Registry editor
	SCANDISK.EXE	ScanDisk disk utility
	SCANDISK.INI	ScanDisk configuration file
	SYS.COM	System boot file
	UNINSTAL.EXE	Utility to remove Windows 95 and return to previous version (available only if you installed an upgrade to a different directory than your original Windows 3.x location)
	XCOPY.EXE*	Extended file copy utility

*Files you should add as an administrator.

Exercise 2.1 shows the steps for a sample installation. At various points in the installation process, we will talk about different options you might choose and how those options affect the functionality of Windows 95. One of the choices you will encounter at the outset is which type of setup you want. The exercise takes you through a Custom setup, which presents a choice of all the options, including all accessories, as shown in Figure 2.2.

F I G U R E   2.2

Installing options with the Custom setup

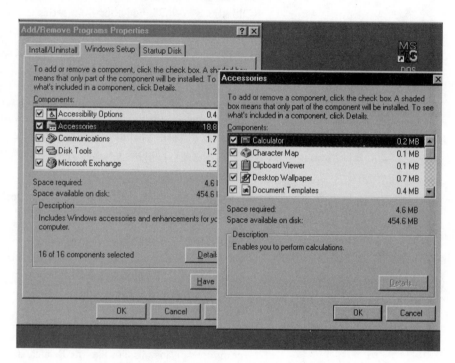

Please install **all** the options. We will be using many of these utilities throughout the rest of this book.

EXERCISE 2.1

Installing Windows 95

1. Start up your computer.

2. If you are setting up from Windows 3.*x*, start Windows and go to the File Manager. Navigate to the installation directory. For the CD-ROM, this is \Win95. For floppy disks, this is the root directory on Disk 1. If you are installing from the MS-DOS prompt, skip to step 3.

3. Run the SETUP.EXE program. You can use the optional switches listed in Table 2.1 (MS-DOS) or Table 2.2 (Windows 3.*x*).

4. The Windows 95 Setup Wizard starts (Figure 2.1). During the first stage—gathering system information—the Setup Wizard asks you if you want it to automatically detect hardware or if you want to install it yourself. Choose the automatic detection option and click on Next.

5. The Setup Wizard will ask you which Setup Options you wish to install. There are four choices:

   ■ **Typical:** This is the system default setup. It is recommended for users with desktop computers. It will automatically perform most of the steps of the installation with little input from you. You just need to confirm the installation directory and indicate whether or not to create a Startup disk.

   ■ **Portable:** This setup is useful for mobile users with portable computers. It installs files like the Briefcase and support for direct cable connections. It also includes options for advanced power management, such as shutting down the hard drive and screen during periods of inactivity.

   ■ **Compact:** This option is for users with a limited amount of hard disk space. It will install the minimum set of files needed to run Windows 95.

   ■ **Custom:** This option allows you to specify exactly which components of Windows 95 you wish to install. You must use this option if you wish to install mail and fax support.

Choose Custom to see all the options.

6. To make specific changes, click on the checkboxes next to the options you wish to install. Click on the Accessories option. You will note that only 4 of 16 accessories have been selected. Click on the Details button. You will see another dialog box (Figure 2.2) with more options from the Accessories section. Select *all* the options and click on OK. Make sure that all options are selected, including any underlying Details options for each selection. When you are finished, click on Next.

7. The next screen asks you to enter your name and company name. Fill in the required information and click on Next. The Setup Wizard may ask you to confirm your choices. Do so by clicking on OK. If you are presented with a license agreement, read it and click on I Agree. You may also be prompted to give a CD Key. This would be located on the jacket of your CD and consists of 10 digits. For OEM versions, the key might be a 20-letter alphanumeric key. When you're finished, click on OK.

8. You have reached the second stage of the process. You are asked if you want to make a Windows 95 Startup disk. Click on the Yes option, and then click on Next. This creates a Windows 95 emergency boot disk. The files listed in Table 2.3 will be added to the disk.

9. Windows 95 copies the files needed to complete the setup process. It copies only the files that are needed based on the options you have chosen in previous steps.

10. The third and final stage is a reboot of the system and final configurations. The reboot will start your system with the new Windows 95 drivers. You will see the Windows 95 logo screen. During this stage, the following occurs:

   ■ The Windows 95 logon screen appears. Your password file list is started at this time.

   ■ Windows 95 gets the hardware configurations from the registry created during the detection phase and initializes Plug-and-Play devices.

- Windows 95 creates and adds the Control Panel, Start menu shortcuts, and Help files. It also sets up default PIFs (Program Information Files) for MS-DOS-based programs. The *.GRP files used by Windows 3.x Program Manager are also converted to shortcuts and placed on the Start menu under Programs. If you installed an upgrade and placed the installation in a directory other than the \Windows directory, you can run GRPCONV (select Start ➢ Run and enter **GRPCONV**) to convert those groups.

- You will be prompted to choose your time zone.

- If you installed Microsoft Exchange, a Setup Wizard for installing MSN, MS Mail, MS at Work Fax, and default TAPI settings appears. You can click on Cancel and do this setup at another time by simply double-clicking on the Inbox icon on your Desktop. (See Chapter 19 for information about Microsoft Exchange.)

- The Printer Wizard runs. You can add printers at any time from within the Printers folder. (See Chapter 13 for information about printing.)

11. You may need to restart your system for all of the final configuration changes to take effect.

Uninstalling Windows 95

Windows 95 can be uninstalled from your computer if, during the setup, you chose to save your previous configuration—that is, you chose to install Windows 95 to a directory other than your \Windows directory.

To uninstall Windows 95, boot your system using the Windows 95 Startup disk and then run the UNINSTAL.EXE program. This process does not just go through your system and delete the Windows 95 installation directory. It actually analyzes your current Windows 95 configuration and files and looks for changes, and then makes adjustments as needed. This analysis process can take several minutes. After the uninstall process has completed, it will leave many of the Windows 95 files on your system. You can go through and delete these files if you choose.

You will probably need to do some minor configuration changes on your old Windows 3.x system to return it to its pre-Windows 95 upgrade condition.

Dual-Booting Issues

Usually, Windows 95 is used to replace an older operating system. However, you can configure Windows 95 to dual-boot with MS-DOS, Windows 3.x, or Windows NT. Dual-booting with OS/2 is not supported using the Windows 95 boot manager. You can, however, dual-boot with other operating systems using other boot managers like IBM's OS/2 Boot Manager.

Dual-booting should be used by advanced users who need access to multiple operating systems. The average user should never need an old version of Windows 3.x or MS-DOS.

You can dual-boot your system by pressing F4 to revert to your old operating system, or by pressing F8 for a configuration menu. You press either of these keys during the boot-up phase. You will see a system graphic at the top of the screen listing your CMOS specifications; shortly thereafter (usually about a second), you will see a line that says:

```
Starting Windows 95
```

When you see that line, hit your function key. This line will stay up for only about two seconds, so you must be quick. To have it stay up longer, you need to modify the BootDelay entry in the MSDOS.SYS file.

To enable dual-booting, you must set the BootMulti parameter to 1 in the MSDOS.SYS file. The entry should read:

```
BootMulti=1
```

See Chapter 3 for information about setting options in the MSDOS.SYS file.

Dual-Booting with Windows 3.x and MS-DOS

To dual-boot with Windows 3.x, you need to be able to dual-boot with your old version of MS-DOS. You must be using MS-DOS 5.0 or later in order to be able to dual-boot.

Since Windows 3.*x* loads on top of MS-DOS, you only need to be able to reload your old version of MS-DOS to run Windows 3.*x*. This can be most easily accomplished by installing Windows 95 into a directory other than your old Windows 3.*x* directory. Setup will preserve your old copy of Windows as well as the AUTOEXEC.BAT and CONFIG.SYS files. These files will be renamed AUTOEXEC.DOS and CONFIG.DOS. When you dual-boot, these files will be swapped with the current Windows 95 versions. The Windows 95 version of the boot files will have a .W40 extension.

You must be using MS-DOS 5.0 or later in order to be able to dual-boot with MS-DOS and/or Windows 3.*x*. Windows 3.*x* and MS-DOS 5.0 through 6.22 do not support long filenames. Be careful if you are modifying Windows 95 files. Avoid using older Windows 3.*x* utilities that are not Windows 95-compatible, like PC Tools and Norton Utilities. Both of these products have newer versions that are Windows 95-compatible.

If you are installing software to run on both your Windows 3.*x* and Windows 95 installations, you should install those files in the Windows 3.*x* directory, and then create shortcuts for them in Windows 95.

Dual-Booting with Windows NT

The easiest method for installing dual-booting with Windows NT is to first install Windows 95 and then install Windows NT to a different directory. Windows NT will automatically configure its boot files.

If you have already installed Windows NT and are planning to install Windows 95 to dual-boot with NT, you need to make a few minor modifications to the Windows NT boot files and then continue with a command-line installation of Windows 95. Exercise 2.2 shows the steps for modifying NT and continuing with a Windows 95 setup.

Windows 95 cannot read Windows NT's NTFS partitions, and Windows NT cannot read a FAT32 partition.

EXERCISE 2.2

Setting Up for Dual-Booting after NT Is Installed

1. Boot up the system to MS-DOS rather than Windows NT. (Press the F4 key during the boot sequence.)

2. Remove the read-only status of the BOOTSECT.DOS and BOOT.INI files. You can do this by using the following MS-DOS commands:

   ```
   attrib -r BOOTSECT.DOS
   attrib -r BOOT.INI
   ```

3. Make a copy of BOOTSECT.DOS for backup, naming it something like BOOTSECT.BKP.

4. Run the Windows 95 Setup program from the command line and specify a directory other than Windows NT.

5. Rename BOOTSECT.DOS to BOOTSECT.W40 and rename BOOTSECT.BKP to BOOTSECT.DOS.

6. Using an editor like Notepad, add the following entries to the BOOT.INI file:

   ```
   [BOOT LOADER]
   TIMEOUT=30
   DEFAULT=C:\WINNT

   [OPERATING SYSTEMS]
   C:\WINNT="Windows NT"
   C:\BOOTSECT.DOS="MS - DOS v6.22" /Win95dos
   C:\BOOTSECT.W40="Windows 95" /Win95
   ```

7. Reboot the computer. The Windows NT dual-boot menu will appear for 30 seconds. If you do not make a choice in that 30 seconds, it will default to Windows NT.

Creating Batch Setup Scripts

The Windows 95 Setup program can use a special file called MSBATCH .INF, which contains setup configuration options. If you then run the Windows 95 Setup program and specify the setup file, the options that you created there will be automatically selected.

By studying the setup options carefully, a savvy administrator can create a setup script that will perform the installation automatically. All you need to do from a client workstation is navigate to the server containing the setup files and run the Setup program with your batch file as a parameter (Setup <batch-name.inf>).

Once you have created the batch file, you can run a utility called INFINST .EXE to add other batch setup scripts to the MSBATCH.INF setup script. This will allow you to add other applications to the setup of Windows 95. Imagine spending a few hours to create a large setup script and then having Windows 95 install "automatically," along with Microsoft Office Professional and any other third-party applications that have an *.INF file.

Creating a Setup Script Using BATCH

BATCH.EXE is a file located on your Windows 95 CD in the \Admin\NetTools\ NetSetup folder. Before using this program, you should read the BATCH .TXT file associated with it, and also go through the Help file inside the BATCH.EXE program.

The Windows 95 Resource Kit, Appendix D, provides a lot of information about creating setup scripts. You should refer to this appendix prior to creating batch setup scripts.

Run the BATCH.EXE program and answer questions to create your batch setup file. Figure 2.3 shows the opening screen. You can set as many or as few parameters as desired. There are options for installing network components, installation options (Typical, Portable, Compact, and Custom), and optional components (available if you choose a Custom installation). When you are finished making your choices, click on Done. A BSETUP.INF file will be created.

FIGURE 2.3

The BATCH.EXE program can help you create your own Windows 95 setup scripts for automated installations.

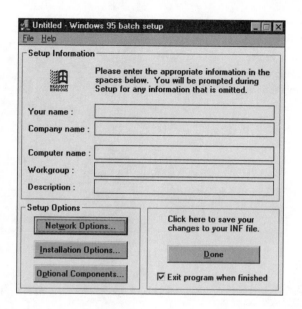

Run the Windows 95 Setup program and include the name with a fully qualified path of the .INF file as an argument, as in:

```
D:\Win95\SETUP C:\Scripts\BSETUP.INF
```

You can also use a UNC name for the path, like:

```
\\NTServer\Win95\Setup \\NTServer\SetupScripts\BSETUP.INF
```

The file will be used by Windows 95 Setup, and later copied to the MSBATCH.INF file.

Some setup messages cannot be automated by the batch setup script. These are described in the Windows 95 Resource Kit, Appendix D.

Creating a Setup Script Using NetSetup

The NetSetup program essentially does the same thing as the BATCH.EXE program does. You can also specify a setup server.

NetSetup is located in the \Admin\NetTools\NetSetup folder on your Windows 95 CD-ROM. Figure 2.4 shows the opening screen of the NetSetup program.

FIGURE 2.4

NetSetup allows you to create an installation server and setup scripts.

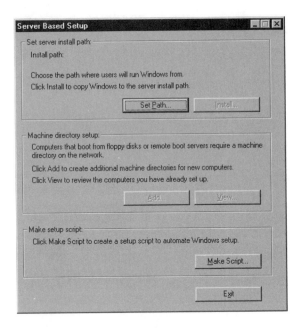

The \Admin folder is not available on the floppy disk version of Windows 95.

When you designate a setup server, you will need to specify the source path as well as where the shared files will be installed, as shown in Figure 2.5. Depending on the choice you make here, the files will be installed in their compressed format, or an administrative type of install will occur in which all files will be decompressed and placed on the server. Follow the steps in Exercise 2.3 to install Windows 95 files onto a source server.

EXERCISE 2.3

Creating an Installation Server Using NetSetup

1. Insert the Windows 95 CD into the drive and navigate to the \Admin\NetTools\NetSetup folder.

2. Run the NetSetup program (Figure 2.4).

3. Click on the Set Path button and specify the name of the shared folder on the distribution server where you want to store the installation files. Click on OK after you have entered the path.

EXERCISE 2.3 (CONTINUED FROM PREVIOUS PAGE)

4. Click on the Install button. NetSetup asks you for the source path (Figure 2.5).
5. Enter the current location of the source installation files (for example, **D:\Win95**).
6. Specify how the users are allowed to install Windows 95:
   - If you select Server, Windows is to run from a server. Most files will be copied to the server in expanded format.
   - If you select Local, Windows is to run from a local machine. Most files are copied to the server in compressed format.
   - If you select User's choice, the user determines how Windows is used (either Server or Local). All files are copied to the server in expanded format.
7. Click on OK to install the files to the server.
8. Once the files have been copied to the server, you can create a setup script based on these settings. To do this, click on the Create Default button.

FIGURE 2.5

Setting the source path for the setup server

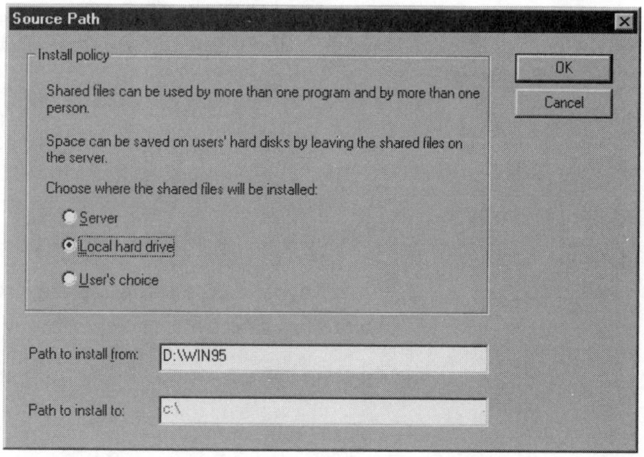

NetSetup uses the System Policy Editor interface to configure setup scripts, as shown in Figure 2.6. Follow the steps in Exercise 2.4 to create a setup script using the NetSetup program.

FIGURE 2.6

NetSetup uses the System
Policy Editor interface.

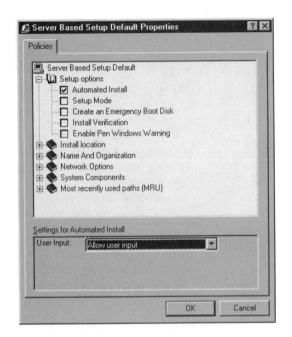

EXERCISE 2.4

Creating a Setup Script Using NetSetup

1. Start the NetSetup program located on the Windows 95 CD in \Admin\NetTools\NetSetup.

2. Click on the Make Script button.

3. In the Server Based Setup Default Properties dialog box (Figure 2.6), make your selections and specify any settings.

4. Click on OK when you are finished.

5. To use your setup script, run Setup with the new script as a parameter, as in:

```
SETUP C:\Scripts\MySetup.INF
```

Modifying Setup Scripts to Include Additional Applications

The INFINST.EXE tool can be used to integrate .INF (and related) files into the NetSetup installation scripts. To use this utility, first run NetSetup and create a network installation of Windows 95 (Exercise 2.3). You can then use the INFINST tool, located on the Windows 95 CD-ROM in the \Admin\NetTools directory, to add external components to the batch script.

The INFINST tool will update the MSBATCH.INF file located in the root installation directory. Components that are integrated as separate applications will have entries added to the [Optional Components] section of the MSBATCH .INF file. Other components will have entries in the appropriate locations.

Refer to Appendix D of the Windows 95 Resource Kit for more information about the INFINST.EXE program.

Troubleshooting a Windows 95 Installation

Troubleshooting the installation process can be a lengthy and cumbersome procedure. This is due to the fact that you may need to continually reboot to try fixes that you have made. In the following sections, we discuss troubleshooting techniques:

- Setup hangs

- Hardware-detection troubleshooting

- Post setup boot problems

- Post setup networking problems

Microsoft ✓ ***Exam Objective***

Diagnose and resolve installation failures.

A good place to start troubleshooting in general is during the boot process. You can press the F8 key when you see the "Starting Windows 95" message to bring up the Startup menu. This menu contains options that allow you to control the boot process. See Chapter 3 for details.

Setup Hangs

You can run into problems during several different aspects of the setup process. These problems could cause the Setup program to hang. Here are some typical problems and suggested solutions:

- Setup hangs while making a Startup disk.

Run Setup without making a Startup disk. After completing Setup, create a new disk using the Add/Remove Programs applet in the Control Panel. You could also remove the line:

```
device=symevnt.386
```

from the [386enh] section of the SYSTEM.INI file and rerun Setup.

- Setup hangs during the "routine check on your system" while running the ScanDisk program.

Try to find out why ScanDisk is hanging by running a virus check first and then running ScanDisk by itself. If this doesn't fix the problem, you can bypass the ScanDisk portion of the setup by specifying the /IS switch, as in:

```
Setup /IS
```

- Setup hangs, but there is still hard disk activity.

Just wait; Setup is still processing.

- Setup hangs during the reboot process.

Look for entries in the SYSTEM.INI file that point to an old swapfile. Comment them out by placing a semicolon as the first character on the line:

```
;This line has been remarked out.
```

- Setup fails to complete.

If this is due to a power failure, power on the machine and let it continue processing. If you get a menu with the options Safe Recovery or Run Full Setup, choose Safe Recovery. Safe Recovery will utilize the crash recovery feature of the Windows 95 Setup program.

Hardware Detection

If Setup fails during the hardware-detection process, you can try to track down the problem by looking at the DETLOG.TXT file. This file is a log of everything done during the detection process.

The detection process uses the DETLOG.TXT file by writing the problems there. The Setup program will append entries to the bottom of the file. Every time the detection process begins a session, it will add [System Detection] to the file. You can peruse the file for those entries and look for problems.

If you are having problems detecting a particular piece of hardware, you should choose a Custom installation and deselect items that might use that piece of hardware. For example, if your modem is not being detected correctly, you should deselect The Microsoft Network (MSN), Exchange, and Fax items. You can also reinstall those pieces of hardware using the driver disks supplied by the vendors.

If you continue to have problems, you can remove those devices from your system and then reinstall them one by one using the Add New Hardware Wizard in the Control Panel (see Chapter 5).

Post Setup Boot Problems

If your system is having difficulty booting after Windows 95 Setup has completed, you can check for the following:

- Remove third-party memory managers like QEMM and revert to the old HIMEM.SYS and EMM386.EXE.

- Try running a Safe mode boot (press F5 after the "Starting Windows 95" message appears). If this works, you have potential problems in the CONFIG.SYS file with TSRs or some other real-mode driver.

- If Safe mode fails, run ScanDisk to make sure that the file system is still intact.

Microsoft ✓ *Exam Objective*   **Diagnose and resolve boot process failures.**

Post Setup Networking Problems

If you are having network problems after Windows 95 setup, try removing all network adapters from the Network Control Panel. Add them back one by one and test their functionality.

If Microsoft Client for NetWare is not working, try using the real-mode Novell clients IPX/ODI and VLM or NETX. If these work, your protected-mode driver needs modification.

Some flavors of real-mode TCP/IP can hang Windows 95 during the boot process. Use the Microsoft TCP/IP client that ships with Windows 95.

See Chapters 9 through 12 for information about Windows 95 networking.

Summary

In this chapter, we covered the installation process from the workstation's point of view. We looked at different installation mediums and their advantages and disadvantages. You can install Windows 95 using floppy disks or CD-ROM, or over a network. (The floppies do not contain administrative files.)

We next discussed the difference between a clean installation and an upgrade from Windows 3.x. If you have the time, a full installation to a recently formatted hard drive is suggested, because this will get rid of any leftover files from old programs and give you the cleanest possible system to start with. If you cannot do this, an upgrade installation is preferable to setting up in a separate directory, because the upgrade will migrate Windows 3.x configurations to Windows 95. The upgrade to a separate directory is required if you wish to dual-boot with MS-DOS and Windows 3.x.

Before getting into the details of installation, we provided an administrator's "to-do" list before installation. As an administrator, you should create emergency boot disks as well as backups of key programs and files before beginning the setup process. You can help the setup process by pre-configuring your boot files. Removing TSRs and third-party memory managers from the CONFIG.SYS and AUTOEXEC.BAT files can save you time down the road. It's also a good idea to run ScanDisk and Defrag before beginning an installation. Another consideration is anti-virus software—make sure it is unloaded or disabled during the setup process.

Then we covered the installation process. Setup has a real-mode and protected-mode portion. The real-mode setup is mainly concerned with checking and configuring the current system to handle Windows 95. The protected-mode portion does the hardware detection, decompression, file copy operations, and reconfiguration of boot files. It also handles the migration of old Windows 3.x groups to Windows 95 Start menu items.

You should choose to make at least one Windows 95 Startup disk when the Windows 95 Startup Wizard gives you this option. This will allow you to boot to a Windows 95 command prompt in the event of an emergency. Adding selected files to this disk can be useful for maintenance and troubleshooting.

Next, we looked at dual-booting issues. Dual-booting is supported for DOS/Windows 3.x and Windows NT. Before dual-booting can occur, the BootMulti=1 entry needs to be set in the MSDOS.SYS file.

You also learned about using setup scripts to create "hands-free" installations. You can create setup scripts using the BATCH.EXE or NetSetup program. If you would like to have other applications, such as Microsoft Office 97, automatically installed as part of the Windows 95 setup, you can use the INFINST.EXE tool to add entries to the MSBATCH.INF file.

We concluded with a section on troubleshooting. We looked at some common setup problems and their possible resolutions.

We want to stress that the better your initial installation and configuration are, the fewer headaches you will deal with down the road. Take the appropriate amount of time to plan and configure your installations.

Review Questions

1. The real-mode portion of the setup process does all of the following except:

    A. Runs ScanDisk

    B. Runs Defrag

    C. Finds a current installation of Windows

    D. Checks the CPU, hard disk space, and MS-DOS version

2. The protected-mode portion of the setup process does all of the following except:

    A. Detects hardware

    B. Modifies boot records

    C. Runs run-once procedures, including migration of Windows 3.*x* program groups

    D. Removes TSR programs from the CONFIG.SYS and AUTOEXEC.BAT files

3. Which of the following can be used to install Windows 95? (Select all that apply.)

    A. Floppy disks

    B. Network server

    C. Shared installation on a network server

    D. CD-ROM

4. To dual-boot with Windows 3.*x*, you must do which of the following? (Select all that apply.)

   A. Run the DUALBOOT.EXE program.

   B. Install Windows 95 to a directory other than the current Windows directory.

   C. Create a bootable floppy disk for Windows 3.*x*.

   D. Set the BootMulti=1 property in the MSDOS.SYS file.

5. What are the minimum hardware requirements for Windows 95? (Select all that apply.)

   A. 386DX processor or later

   B. 12MB of RAM

   C. 50 to 55MB free hard disk space

   D. VGA card

6. What is the minimum version of MS-DOS needed for an installation of Windows 95?

   A. MS-DOS 6.22

   B. MS-DOS 5.0

   C. MS-DOS 4.1

   D. MS-DOS 3.2

7. As an administrator, which of the following should you do before installation of Windows 95? (Select all that apply.)

   A. Uncompress your hard drive.

   B. Run ScanDisk and Defrag.

   C. Remove TSRs from your CONFIG.SYS and AUTOEXEC.BAT files.

   D. Make a backup of user files and boot files.

8. What can the Windows 95 Startup disk be useful for?

    A. Booting to the Windows 95 command prompt for maintenance and troubleshooting

    B. It is necessary to have the Startup disk to run any version of Windows 95.

    C. It is necessary to have the Startup disk to run a dual-boot version of Windows 95.

    D. Creating new disk partitions, because Windows 95 cannot read NTFS partitions

9. To uninstall Windows 95, you need to run the UNINSTAL.EXE file on the Windows 95 Startup disk. What does this program do?

    A. Deletes the current Windows 95 directory and reverts to your old Windows 3.*x* system

    B. Analyzes your current Windows 95 settings and reverts to your old system by making changes to specific files

    C. Loads a new version of Windows 3.*x* on top of Windows 95

    D. You cannot uninstall Windows 95.

10. The Windows 95 boot manager supports dual-booting with which of the following? (Select all that apply.)

    A. Windows NT

    B. Windows 3.*x* with MS DOS 5.0 or later

    C. OS/2

    D. MS-DOS 3.2

11. To enable dual-booting on Windows 95, you must do which of the following?

A. Set `DualBoot=1` in the CONFIG.SYS file.

B. Set `BootMulti=1` in the CONFIG.SYS file.

C. Set `DualBoot=1` in the MSDOS.SYS file.

D. Set `BootMulti=1` in the MSDOS.SYS file.

12. You can create batch setup scripts using which of the following programs? (Select all that apply.)

A. NewBatch.EXE

B. BATCH.EXE

C. NetSetup.EXE

D. INFINST.EXE

13. The NetSetup program has what additional feature that BATCH.EXE does not have?

A. You can install an administrative version of Windows 95 for server-based distribution.

B. You can specify network clients.

C. You can specify custom setup options.

D. You can specify a default Windows setup location.

14. During the setup process, what three files does Windows 95 use?

A. DETLOG.TXT

B. SETUPLOG.TXT

C. BOOTLOG.INI

D. DETCRASH.LOG

15. Which file contains everything that occurred during the Windows 95 setup procedures, including any crashes and reboots?

    A. BOOTLOG.TXT

    B. INSTALL.LOG

    C. SETUPLOG.TXT

    D. DETLOG.TXT

16. Which file contains all of the successfully detected hardware devices and their associated parameters?

    A. BOOTLOG.TXT

    B. INSTALL.LOG

    C. SETUPLOG.TXT

    D. DETLOG.TXT

CHAPTER

3

The Boot Sequence

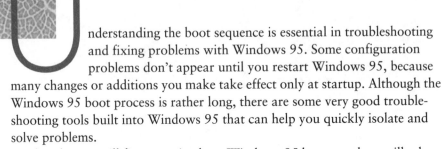

nderstanding the boot sequence is essential in troubleshooting and fixing problems with Windows 95. Some configuration problems don't appear until you restart Windows 95, because many changes or additions you make take effect only at startup. Although the Windows 95 boot process is rather long, there are some very good troubleshooting tools built into Windows 95 that can help you quickly isolate and solve problems.

This chapter will first examine how Windows 95 boots, and we will take a detailed look at each of the steps. We will then examine how the boot process can be configured and controlled. Next, we will see how the emergency boot disk can be helpful for troubleshooting. Finally, we will look at one more way to control how Windows 95 starts up—through WIN.COM command-line switches.

Elements of the Windows 95 Boot Process

The Windows 95 boot process takes place in several discrete steps:

- BIOS bootstrap

- Master boot record and boot sector

- Real-mode boot

- Real-mode configuration

- Protected-mode boot

Each of these steps is described in the following sections.

BIOS Bootstrap

The computer's BIOS handles this step prior to the actual boot. It performs the following tasks:

- Performs the Power On Self Test (POST). The POST detects and tests memory, ports, and basic devices, such as the keyboard, video adapter, and disk drives. Newer versions on some systems even support CD-ROM drives.

- Identifies and configures any Plug-and-Play devices. If the system has a Plug-and-Play BIOS, it will look for and test any Plug-and-Play devices installed.

- Locates a bootable partition on the boot drive. The BIOS has a setting for the order in which you want the system to look for the bootable partition. The default setting on most systems is floppy drive, then hard drive, then CD-ROM (if supported). This sequence can be changed if you want to check the drives in a different order.

- Loads the master boot record (MBR) and the partition table of the bootable drive, and executes the MBR

MBR and Boot Sector

After the MBR finds the bootable partition on the hard disk, it passes control to the boot sector in that partition. The partition contains the boot program and a table of disk properties and characteristics. The root directory is located, and IO.SYS is executed. IO.SYS is basically DOS. In Windows 95, it takes over the functions of both IO.SYS and MSDOS.SYS from previous versions of MS-DOS.

WARNING

Boot viruses affect the boot process at this point, which may cause the loading of both Windows 95 and Windows NT to fail. There is a chance that booting off a clean floppy (your emergency boot disk, discussed later in the chapter) and running the command Fdisk/MBR will restore the master boot record and nondestructively eliminate the boot virus. You may also use a DOS-based anti-virus program.

Real-Mode Boot

Once IO.SYS has been executed, the real-mode boot process begins:

- MSDOS.SYS is checked for boot configuration parameters. MSDOS.SYS does not perform the same function as in previous versions of DOS. In Windows 95, MSDOS.SYS is a text file where you can control certain options of the boot process, as explained later in this chapter.

- "Starting Windows 95" is displayed, and the system waits for a function key to be pressed. The default time Windows waits before continuing is two seconds. This time can be changed by an option in MSDOS.SYS.

- LOGO.SYS is displayed, if it exists. IO.SYS has a copy of the default Windows 95 image if LOGO.SYS cannot be found. The image can be disabled by pressing the Esc key.

- If DBLSPACE.INI is present, DRVSPACE.BIN is loaded.

- SYSTEM.DAT is checked.

- SYSTEM.DAT is loaded if it is present and valid; otherwise, the backup of SYSTEM.DAT (SYSTEM.DA0) is loaded. After a successful boot, whichever file was loaded updates the other.

- If the system detects that double-buffering is necessary, it is loaded.

- Based on detected hardware, a hardware profile is chosen, or the user is prompted to choose one.

- IO.SYS reads CONFIG.SYS, if it exists, and processes its commands.

- IO.SYS reads AUTOEXEC.BAT, if it exists, and processes its commands.

Real-Mode Configuration

CONFIG.SYS and AUTOEXEC.BAT are not necessary with Windows 95, but if they are present, they will be processed by IO.SYS. If CONFIG.SYS does not exist, Windows 95 will automatically load HIMEM.SYS, IFSHLP.SYS, SETVER.EXE, and several environment variables. CONFIG.SYS will override these defaults.

Protected-Mode Boot

The protected-mode boot process proceeds as follows:

- WIN.COM is automatically executed after AUTOEXEC.BAT is run.

- WIN.COM loads VMM32.VXD and any virtual device drivers referenced in the registry and SYSTEM.INI that are not already part of VMM32.VXD.

- The processor is switched into protected mode, and the virtual device drivers are initialized.

- The core Windows Kernel, GDI, and user libraries are loaded along with the Explorer shell and network support (if present).

- Any programs in the Start Up group are executed.

- The last step is to run any programs located in the registry at Hkey_Local_Machine\Software\Microsoft\Windows\CurrentVersion\RunOnce. After an item is successfully run from the RunOnce key, its entry is removed from this key.

Configuring and Controlling the Boot Process

Windows 95 takes care of the boot process for you, and most actions are executed in accordance with their default settings. However, Windows 95 provides some ways for you to control the boot process. The Windows 95 Startup menu offers options for various boot modes. Another way to set boot options is by editing the MSDOS.SYS file. The following sections explain both approaches.

Using the Windows 95 Startup Menu

Microsoft ✓ ***Exam Objective***

Diagnose and resolve boot process failures.

To start previous versions of Windows, you entered the WIN.COM command. If you had problems with Windows, you could boot to a DOS prompt, fix the problem, and restart the system. Even if WIN.COM loaded in AUTOEXEC.BAT, you could bypass it for troubleshooting purposes by remarking it out.

Windows 95 still has WIN.COM but, because Windows loads automatically, you don't need to use it. So what do you do if you need to bypass loading the GUI (graphical user interface)? The easiest way to do this is with the Windows 95 Startup menu. This menu has various options for loading Windows, booting directly to a command prompt, or even loading a previous version of MS-DOS.

You can access the Startup menu by pressing the F8 key after the system POST beep. This is when you see the message:

```
Starting Windows 95
```

When this message appears, you can press F8 (you have two seconds by default. You can change this by editing the BootDelay= parameter in the MSDOS.SYS file discussed later in this chapter).

You can also set an option to have the Startup menu appear each time you boot up the system. The Startup menu will look something like this:

```
Microsoft Windows 95 Startup Menu

    1.   Normal

    2.   Logged (BOOTLOG.TXT)

    3.   Safe mode

    4.   Safe mode without compression

    5.   Safe mode with network support

    6.   Step-by-step confirmation

    7.   Command prompt only

    8.   Safe mode command prompt only

    9.   Previous version of MS-DOS

Enter a choice:    1
```

Your Startup menu will display some or all of these choices, depending on which options are installed on the system, as follows:

■ The Safe mode without compression option will appear only if you have a compressed drive in the system.

■ The Safe mode with network support option will appear only if you have network software installed on the system.

■ The Previous version of MS-DOS option will appear only if you installed Windows 95 over an existing version of DOS.

The first option, Normal, loads Windows in the usual way. The other options are described in the following sections.

Windows 95 also has shortcut keys associated with several Startup menu options. Table 3.1 lists the key combinations you can press after the POST beep.

	Shortcut Key	Startup Menu Equivalent
T A B L E 3.1 Startup Menu Shortcut Keys	F8	Startup menu
	F4	Previous version of MS-DOS
	F5	Safe mode
	Shift+F5	Safe mode command prompt only
	Ctrl+F5	Safe mode without compression
	F6	Safe mode with network support
	Shift+F8	Step-by-step confirmation

The Logged (BOOTLOG.TXT) Option

BOOTLOG.TXT is a text file that can be created by Windows 95 during the boot process. This file records each of the devices and drivers, including all of the protected-mode (virtual) drivers, as the system attempts to load it, and whether the loading was a success or failure. BOOTLOG.TXT is automatically created during the first boot sequence following a successful setup. After that, Windows 95 creates this file when you choose the Logged option from the Startup menu.

You can use the information in the BOOTLOG.TXT file to diagnose driver loading failures, determine whether or not the driver was found, and learn about driver initialization failures. To find load failures in the BOOTLOG.TXT file, you can use an editor like NotePad and search for the keyword "Failed." A typical BOOTLOG.TXT file may look something like the one shown in Figure 3.1.

FIGURE 3.1

A BOOTLOG.TXT file

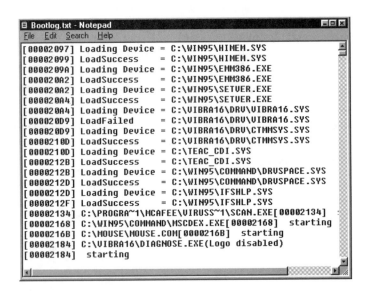

The Safe Mode Option

Safe mode is a way of booting Windows 95 with the minimal set of drivers needed to function. Bypassing the normal loading of hardware and software is useful for troubleshooting. You can use the Device Manager to troubleshoot suspected hardware problems and conflicts (see Chapter 21 for more information about using the Device Manager for troubleshooting). You can also edit INI files, or any other files, that may be causing problems.

Windows 95 will automatically boot to Safe mode if there is a drive failure or conflict.

When you choose to boot in Safe mode from the Windows 95 Startup menu, several things happen:

- You see the message "Windows is bypassing your startup files" in place of "Starting Windows 95."

- Windows does not load the registry, CONFIG.SYS file, or AUTOEXEC .BAT file. Windows also ignores commands in the LOAD= and RUN= lines of WIN.INI.

- The HIMEM.SYS and IFSHLP.SYS files are loaded.

- WIN /d:m (the WIN.COM switch for starting Windows 95 in Safe mode; WIN.COM switches are discussed later in this chapter) is executed.

When you boot Windows 95 in Safe mode, you will see a dialog box reminding you that you are running in Safe mode, as shown in Figure 3.2. Click on OK to continue into Windows. When you reach the Windows Desktop, you are again reminded by the words *Safe mode* appearing in each corner of the screen.

While Windows 95 is in Safe mode, you can remove hardware devices by using the Device Manager, but you cannot add hardware. This can be useful if you think a certain device is causing problems during bootup. Boot to Safe mode, remove the device, and reboot the system. This step can be repeated as many times as necessary to find the hardware causing the problem.

The Safe Mode without Compression Option

This option allows you to boot the system in Safe mode without loading the disk compression driver. You might choose this option if you suspect that a corrupted disk compression driver, or the compressed drive itself, may be causing boot problems. Compressed drives are *not* available when you are in this mode.

FIGURE 3.2

Windows 95 reminds you
that it is running in Safe
mode (notice the
messages in the corners).

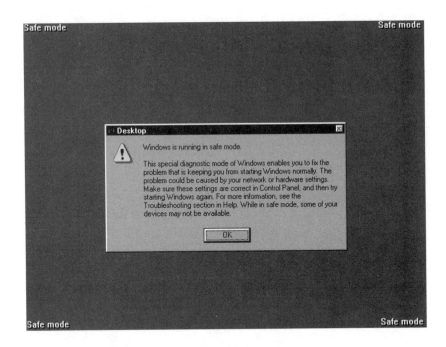

The Safe Mode with Network Support Option

This option boots the system in Safe mode, but does load the real-mode network drivers. You might choose this option when you need to access a network resource to load additional or replacement software or drivers from a network resource.

The Step-by-Step Confirmation Option

This option allows you to see each item loaded in IO.SYS, CONFIG.SYS, and AUTOEXEC.BAT, and to decide whether or not each command is executed. This is a very valuable tool for troubleshooting when you suspect that a command or driver is responsible for boot problems. By stepping through these commands, you can see which items execute properly, and which, if any, are not loading properly. The success or failure of each command will help you determine the command or driver that is not working correctly. As you step through each command, you will see:

```
[Enter=Y, ESC=N]?
```

To run the command or load the driver, press Enter or Y. To bypass the command or driver, press Esc or N.

In Exercise 3.1, we will select the Step-by-step boot option so we can see Windows 95 load the various support files it needs to operate.

EXERCISE 3.1

Starting Windows 95 with Step-by-Step Confirmation

1. Restart Windows 95.

2. When the screen says "Windows 95 loading..." press the F8 key (you have about two seconds).

3. Choose the Step-by-step confirmation option from the Startup menu (it will be number 5 or 6 depending on whether compression is installed).

4. At each prompt, press Enter or Y to run the command. This is the same as doing a normal boot. After Windows 95 has gone through all the steps and booted, you should notice no differences from when you boot normally.

The Command Prompt Only Option

This option boots you to the Windows 95 equivalent of a DOS prompt. The Windows 95 GUI is not loaded, and neither are protected-mode drivers. CONFIG .SYS and AUTOEXEC.BAT, if they are present, are executed.

The Command prompt only option boots quickly and can be useful if you need to edit a file before going into Windows, or for running DOS-based programs. You can also use this option to take advantage of the command-line switches available with WIN.COM, which are discussed later in this chapter. You can go to Windows from the command prompt by typing WIN.

The Safe Mode Command Prompt Only Option

This option is the same as Safe mode except that the GUI is not loaded. CONFIG.SYS and AUTOEXEC.BAT are bypassed, as is the registry and any protected-mode drivers. This option can be useful if you need to get to a command prompt quickly and don't need to have drivers and devices loaded.

Previous Version of MS-DOS

This option will load a previous version of DOS if it is present on the system and is used for dual-booting. As explained in Chapter 2, you can boot to a previous operating system only under the following conditions:

- There must be a previous version of DOS 5.0 or later installed on the system that was not erased during an upgrade installation.

- If you want to be able to run a previous version of Windows, it must be installed in a different directory than where Windows 95 resides.

- The option BootMulti=1 must be present in the MSDOS.SYS file.

WARNING If OSR2 was used to format a drive with the FAT32 file system, no other operating system can dual-boot using that hard drive.

If all of these conditions are met, you can access the previous version by choosing Previous version of MS-DOS from the Startup menu (or by pressing the F4 shortcut key). Several things happen in the system when this option is chosen:

- Files are renamed: CONFIG.SYS and AUTOEXEC.BAT are renamed to CONFIG.WOS and AUTOEXEC.WOS under OSR2 (earlier releases use the extension W40); CONFIG.DOS and AUTOEXEC.DOS are then renamed to CONFIG.SYS and AUTOEXEC.BAT. These files are then renamed back the next time you boot normally to Windows 95.

- The registry is bypassed.

- CONFIG.SYS and AUTOEXEC.BAT are loaded (if they exist).

Modifying the MSDOS.SYS File

With earlier versions of Windows, DOS used two core system files in the initial bootstrap process: IO.SYS provided the system initialization code and then called MSDOS.SYS, which loaded basic system drivers, determined equipment status, and performed other preliminary functions.

With Windows 95, MSDOS.SYS performs a very different function. The tasks handled by MSDOS.SYS in previous versions of DOS have been transferred to IO.SYS, and MSDOS.SYS is now a text file that controls certain

Windows 95 startup options. You can modify these parameters by
changing, or removing lines from MSDOS.SYS.

MSDOS.SYS is a read-only, hidden, system file. Before you can make
changes, you need to modify the attributes of the file. This can be done from
the File Properties dialog box in Windows, or by using the ATTRIB command
from a command prompt. To get to the Windows 95 File Properties dialog
box, navigate to the file you wish to edit, right-click on it, and choose Properties. You can then clear the checkboxes for Hidden and Read Only. Be sure to
change the attributes of MSDOS.SYS back to read-only after you have finished editing. This will keep the file from being changed or deleted accidentally.

A typical MSDOS.SYS file will look something like the one shown in
Figure 3.3.

FIGURE 3.3

An MSDOS.SYS file

```
Msdos.sys - Notepad
File  Edit  Search  Help
;FORMAT
[Paths]
WinDir=C:\WIN95
WinBootDir=C:\WIN95
HostWinBootDrv=C

[Options]
BootMulti=1
BootGUI=1
Network=1
;
;The following lines are required for compatibility with other programs.
;Do not remove them (MSDOS.SYS needs to be >1024 bytes).
;xxxxxxxxxxxxxxxxxxxxxxxxxxxxxxxxxxxxxxxxxxxxxxxxxxxxxxxxxxxxxxxxa
;xxxxxxxxxxxxxxxxxxxxxxxxxxxxxxxxxxxxxxxxxxxxxxxxxxxxxxxxxxxxxxxxb
;xxxxxxxxxxxxxxxxxxxxxxxxxxxxxxxxxxxxxxxxxxxxxxxxxxxxxxxxxxxxxxxxc
;xxxxxxxxxxxxxxxxxxxxxxxxxxxxxxxxxxxxxxxxxxxxxxxxxxxxxxxxxxxxxxxxd
```

WARNING

Incorrect settings in MSDOS.SYS can cause the system not to boot properly.
MSDOS.SYS must be at least 1024 bytes for backward compatibility. This is
why you see all of the x's. There is no limit to how big the file can be—only
how small. Double-check your settings before saving and rebooting the
system.

Table 3.2 shows the command options that can be entered into MSDOS.SYS
and their default values.

mmand	Description
aths] section	
ostWinBootDrv=	Defines the root directory of the boot drive, usually C
VinBootDir=	Specifies the location of the Windows 95 startup files, usually C:\Windows. This location is defined during setup.

[Options] section

AutoScan=	Applies only to OSR2 (Windows 95 version B). Tells Windows 95 whether or not to run ScanDisk after an improper shutdown. The possible values are 1 (default), which notifies the user before running ScanDisk; 2, which runs ScanDisk without notifying the user; and 0, which does not run ScanDisk.
BootDelay=	Specifies the startup delay after "Starting Windows 95" is displayed, in x seconds. The default is 2. This delay allows the user time to press the F8 key to display the Setup menu (or any of the shortcut keys) before the boot continues. BootDelay=0 disables this delay.
BootKeys=	Enables (1) or disables (0) the startup function keys (F8, F5, etc.). The default is 1 (enabled). When set to 0 (disabled), the BootDelay setting is also ignored. Disabling the startup function keys can provide tighter system security by not allowing users to bypass the normal boot process.
BootSafe=	Enables (1) or disables (0) starting the system automatically in Safe mode. The default is 0 (disabled).
BootGUI=	Enables (1) or disables (0) starting the system automatically in the Windows 95 GUI. The default is 1 (enabled). A 0 allows booting to a command prompt with all drivers and the registry loaded. Typing WIN at this command prompt takes you to the GUI.
BootMenu=	Enables (1) or disables (0) automatically displaying the Startup menu without the user pressing F8. The default is 0 (disabled).
BootMenuDefault=	Specifies the default option on the Startup menu when it is displayed. The default is 1, for a normal start.

	Command	Description
TABLE 3.2 *(cont.)* MSDOS.SYS File Commands	**[Options] section**	
	BootMenuDelay=	Specifies how long to display the Startup menu before executing the default menu item, in *x* seconds. The default is 30 seconds.
	BootMulti=	Enables (1) or disables (0) dual-boot capabilities if a previous version of MS-DOS is loaded on the system. The default is 0 (disabled). A 1 allows booting to the previous version by pressing F4 or choosing Previous Version of MS-DOS from the Startup menu.
	BootWarn=	Enables (1) or disables (0) the prompt for a Safe mode startup after a failed boot attempt or a corrupt registry is found. The default is 1 (enabled).
	BootWin=	Enables (1) or disables (0) Windows 95 as the default operating system on bootup. The default is 1 (enabled). A 0 boots to a previous version of MS-DOS by default.
	DoubleBuffer=	Specifies loading a double-buffering driver for SCSI controllers. The possible values are 0, for disabled (default); 1, which allows for double-buffering if the SCSI controller requires it; or 2, which forces double-buffering.
	DrvSpace=	Enables (1) or disables (0) loading DRVSPACE.BIN automatically. The default is 1 (enabled).
	LoadTop=	Enables (1) or disables (0) COMMAND.COM or DRVSPACE.BIN loading at the top of conventional (640KB) memory. The default is 1 (enabled). This should be set to 0 (disabled) if you are using software that uses specific memory settings.
	Logo=	Enables (1) or disables (0) displaying the animated startup screen. The default is 1 (enabled). This may be set to 0 (disabled) to accommodate certain third-party memory managers, or if you prefer to see what is loading and any error messages during the boot process. Pressing the Esc key when the logo screen appears will also do this on a less permanent basis.
	Network=	Allows you to boot in Safe mode with network support if network software is installed. On systems with network software installed, the default is 1 (enabled). The default should be 0 (disabled) on systems without network software installed.

cy Boot Disk

During installation, Windows 95 allows you to create a Startup disk, n is a bootable floppy disk with Windows 95 startup files that can be in troubleshooting many different situations. You can also create a up disk by using the Add/Remove Programs applet in the Control Panel. n you use this disk, the system boots to a command prompt without loading CONFIG.SYS, AUTOEXEC.BAT, or the registry.

The Startup disk contents are listed in Chapter 2 (see Table 2.3). You may want to copy some other files onto the disk that are unique to your system, such as the following:

- CONFIG.SYS, system configuration file

- AUTOEXEC.BAT, system configuration file

- WIN.INI, Windows configuration file

- SYSTEM.INI, Windows configuration file

In addition to these files on your startup disk, you may want to make a backup of your registry files on a second floppy disk. These include the following files:

- SYSTEM.DAT, system registry component for the local hardware

- USER.DAT, system registry component for individual user settings

You can include any other files or drivers that may be helpful in troubleshooting system problems. For example, you may want to add any drivers needed for the CD-ROM drive to function from the command prompt, because you might need to reinstall software from a CD-ROM during troubleshooting. These should go on the startup disk, as the CONFIG.SYS and AUTOEXEC.BAT files may need access to those drivers during the boot sequence.

Here are some situations in which you might want to use the emergency boot disk:

- **System hangs during normal or Safe mode boot:** If the system hangs during boot, especially when booting to Safe mode, the core files may be missing or corrupt. You may also have unresolved hardware conflicts.

- **Unresolved Windows registry error:** When Windows loads, you receive an error message that the registry has become corrupted, and you are asked if you would like to restore from backup. However, after you accept it, the same error message appears multiple times. This means that the registry could not be restored from backup—either the backup files, SYSTEM.DA0 and USER.DA0, are corrupted or they do not exist. In this case, the only way to restore the registry is to boot to a command prompt and reinstall Windows 95.

- **CONFIG.SYS or AUTOEXEC.BAT are corrupted or missing:** If these files are corrupted or missing, certain hardware or software may not load and will not function correctly. If a copy of these files, updated each time you make changes, is on the emergency boot disk, they can be easily restored.

- **You wish to uninstall Windows 95:** This option is available only if you had a previous version of MS-DOS on the computer before Windows 95, and either preserved the Windows 3.*x* files or installed Windows 95 to a unique directory. See Chapter 2 for more information about uninstalling Windows 95.

Starting Windows 95 with Switches

Windows 95 has several command-line switches that can be used with WIN.COM to troubleshoot problems during the boot process. For example, if your problem is resulting from memory address conflicts, you can use the switch win /d:x to force Windows 95 to not use any of the expanded memory area. This is equivalent to the SYSTEM.INI file setting EMMExclude=A000-FFFF.

The command win /switch can be put into the AUTOEXEC.BAT file, and Windows 95 will load with the switches that are present.

The syntax is:

```
win {[/?] [/b] [/w] [/wx] {/d: [f] [m] [n] [s] [v] [x]}}
```

The options are described in Table 3.3.

TABLE 3.3	Option	Action Taken
WIN.COM Switches	/?	Displays a list of available switches
	/b	Logs the startup process in BOOTLOG.TXT, just as if you had chosen the Logged option from the Startup menu
	/w	Restores CONFIG.SYS from CONFIG.WOS (or CONFIG.W40) and AUTOEXEC.BAT (or AUTOEXEC.W40) from AUTOEXEC.WOS and then prompts you to press any key to start Windows 95
	/wx	Restores CONFIG.SYS from CONFIG.WOS and AUTOEXEC.BAT from AUTOEXEC.WOS and starts Windows 95 automatically
	/d:f	Disables 32-bit disk access. This option is useful if you believe that the hard disk may be having problems or if Windows 95 stalls during the boot process.
	/d:m	Starts Windows 95 in Safe mode
	/d:n	Starts Windows 95 in Safe mode with network support
	/d:s	Disables Windows from using the ROM address space between F000:0000 and 1024K for a break point
	/d:v	Tells the ROM routine to handle interrupts from the hard disk controller
	/d:x	Disables Windows from scanning the entire adapter area when looking for used space; equivalent to the SYSTEM.INI setting EMMExclude=A000-FFFF. This may be helpful in troubleshooting upper memory conflicts.

Summary

Understanding the boot sequence is essential to troubleshooting and fixing problems with Windows 95. In this chapter, you learned about the steps in the Windows 95 boot process, which include BIOS bootstrap, master boot record and boot sector, real-mode boot, real-mode configuration, and protected-mode boot. We then discussed the two main ways that you can control the boot process: through the Windows 95 Startup menu (press F8 after the POST) or by editing the MSDOS.SYS file.

The other boot-related topics we covered were the emergency boot, or Startup, disk which you can use to troubleshoot system problems, and the command-line switches that can be used with WIN.COM, which also might be helpful in tracking down problems during the boot process.

Review Questions

1. What is the first step in the Windows 95 boot process?

   A. BIOS bootstrap phase

   B. Master boot record and boot sector phase

   C. Real-mode boot phase

   D. Protected-mode boot phase

2. During what step of the boot process is VMM32.VXD loaded?

   A. BIOS bootstrap phase

   B. Master boot record and boot sector phase

   C. Real-mode boot phase

   D. Protected-mode boot phase

3. What are the two ways Windows 95 allows you to configure the boot process?

   A. The Startup menu

   B. Editing BOOT.INI

   C. Editing IO.SYS

   D. Editing MSDOS.SYS

4. What Startup menu option should you choose to see which real-mode driver(s) might be giving you trouble?

   A. Previous version of DOS

   B. Safe mode with network support

   C. Safe mode

   D. Step-by-step confirmation

5. What Startup menu option should you choose to see which protected-mode driver(s) might be giving you trouble?

   A. Logged (to create BOOTLOG.TXT)

   B. Step-by-step confirmation

   C. Command prompt only

   D. Previous version of DOS

6. What drivers are loaded during a plain Safe mode boot? (Select all that apply.)

   A. Mouse driver

   B. Keyboard driver

   C. Standard VGA device driver

   D. Network drivers

7. What additional files might you want to put on an emergency boot (Startup) disk? (Select all that apply.)

   A. SYSTEM.DAT

   B. CONFIG.SYS

   C. AUTOEXEC.BAT

   D. CD-ROM drivers

8. How can you find out which switches are available with WIN.COM?

    A. Win /?

    B. Win /help

    C. Win /switches

    D. Help /Win

9. What key or key combination do you press to get the Windows 95 Startup menu?

    A. F4

    B. F6

    C. F8

    D. Shift+F4

10. Which MSDOS.SYS parameter will force the "Starting Windows 95" line to display for 4 seconds?

    A. BootDelay=4000

    B. BootDelay=4

    C. None; the default is 4 seconds.

    D. None; you cannot change this option.

11. You can provide tighter security on a Windows 95 client by setting which one of the following parameters?

    A. BootMulti=0

    B. BootMulti=1

    C. BootKeys=1

    D. BootKeys=0

CHAPTER

4

Windows 95 Architecture and Memory

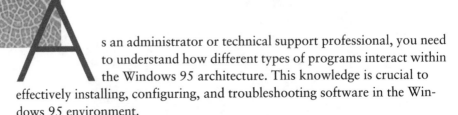

A s an administrator or technical support professional, you need to understand how different types of programs interact within the Windows 95 architecture. This knowledge is crucial to effectively installing, configuring, and troubleshooting software in the Windows 95 environment.

Much of the Windows 95 architecture and memory usage has changed since Windows 3.*x*. In this chapter, we will discuss these changes. The topics covered here include the Intel *x*86 architecture, virtual machines, virtual memory, messaging systems, operating system components (dynamic-link libraries), device drivers, and multitasking (including scheduling). You will also learn how to use some new utilities included with Windows 95 for monitoring and manipulating these new features.

Although the newest version of the Windows 95 certification exam (Exam 70-64) no longer contains objectives directly addressed in this chapter, we have retained this material both for completeness' sake and because subjects covered in this chapter may appear indirectly on the test.

The Intel *x*86 Ring Architecture

T he *x*86 architecture supports multiple levels of processor-provided protection for running programs. These levels are called rings. The transition between rings uses a lot of CPU time and system memory. In order to increase speed and reduce errors, Windows 95 uses only two rings in the *x*86 architecture: Ring 0 and Ring 3. Ring 0 allows a program full access to all system hardware and memory. Each successive ring puts additional limitations on the resources that a program can access.

Many older programs and most MS-DOS-based programs don't take advantage of this ring architecture and are called *real-mode programs*. These real-mode programs also make use of the upper memory areas by installing a memory driver like EMM386. Protected-mode programs make use of the ring architecture and generally resegment the upper memory blocks for their own personal use. Windows 95 segments upper memory by installing the HIMEM .SYS driver.

Ring 0

Ring 0 provides the highest level of program component protection. The microchip itself will protect components running in Ring 0 from writing over each other's resources. Ring 0 components also have the most privileges. They can access all of the system hardware directly and therefore run very quickly. On the other hand, if a program fails while it is running in Ring 0, it can cripple the entire system.

Portions of the core components of Windows 95 (the kernel, user interface, and GDI) run in Ring 0. This gives Windows 95 the fastest possible access to all of the system hardware and leaves entry points for the Ring 3 components to gain access to the various devices through the core components.

Ring 3

There is no processor protection in Ring 3. The resource protection must be provided by the software itself. The Windows 95 operating system provides programs with this protection. Ring 3 also has limited privileges to the hardware.

A Ring 3 program must communicate with a Ring 0 component to execute certain tasks. For example, if a program running in Ring 3 wants to repaint the screen, it must communicate with the GDI (Graphical Device Interface) running in Ring 0 and ask it to repaint the screen. The GDI will then execute the task.

Because of the Ring 3 limitations, software running in Ring 3 cannot cripple the system. If a program in Ring 3 fails, it generally does not affect any other Ring 3 programs running at the same time.

Noncritical system components and all user applications and programs in Windows 95 run in Ring 3.

Virtual Machines

In the old MS-DOS days, programs had direct access to everything in your system. The program that was currently running had exclusive access to all of the system resources. With the advent of multitasking operating systems like Windows 3.*x* and now Windows 95, programs need to share resources. Problems arise when one program needs the same resources as another program. To alleviate these problems, virtual machines (VMs) have been created.

Windows 95 uses virtual machines to fool programs into thinking that they have exclusive access to all system hardware. These virtual machines run in Ring 3 and use a message-passing technique to access memory and hardware. Windows 95 uses messages to ask different components within the interface to do things for it. For example, a program might want the screen refreshed. To do this, the program would send a message to the graphics component and ask it to repaint the screen.

Think of Windows 95 as a resource manager. It keeps track of the hardware and the resources that each running program is using. It also creates a virtual machine in which a running program resides. This virtual machine allows the program running inside of it to think it owns all of the resources. When a program issues a message to a particular device, Windows 95 will intercept that message and then route it to the appropriate device or memory location when that device is not in use by another program. In this way, Windows 95 is managing the system resources, not the individual programs.

All programs in Windows 95 run in virtual machines. Different programs use different types of virtual machines.

Two types of virtual machines exist in Windows 95: a System VM and multiple MS-DOS VMs. These virtual machines are illustrated in Figure 4.1. The following sections highlight the differences between the two types and explain how to track virtual machines running on Windows 95.

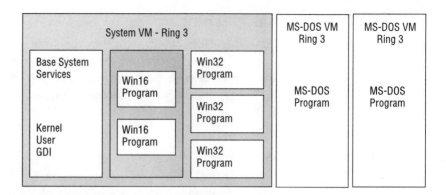

F I G U R E   4.1

All programs in
Windows 95 run
in either the System
VM or an MS-DOS VM.

The System Virtual Machine

The System VM runs in Ring 3 and is broken down into the following components (see Figure 4.1):

- System components (user, GDI, kernel)

- Address space for 16-bit Windows-based programs to share

- Individual address spaces for each running 32-bit program

16-bit Windows Programs

All 16-bit Windows-based programs share a single address space on the System VM. Windows 95 forces 16-bit Windows-based programs to share the same address space and resources for backward compatibility with Windows 3.x. Because of this sharing, it is possible for these 16-bit programs to step on each other's resources. When this happens, you will receive one or more GPF (General Protection Fault) errors. This will cause at least one 16-bit program to fail, and if the resource that caused the GPF was a critical one, all 16-bit programs using that same resource will fail.

Under Windows NT, each 16-bit Windows program can be run in its own separate VM. In Windows 95, each 16-bit Windows program shares the same address space on the System VM.

32-bit Windows Programs

Each 32-bit Windows program has its own address space on the System VM. Because these 32-bit programs don't share their resources, they cannot step on each other.

MS-DOS Virtual Machines

In the past, MS-DOS-based applications could only run one at a time. Because of this, each MS-DOS program expects to have exclusive access to all system resources, and therefore these programs have no concept of sharing resources. For this reason, each MS-DOS-based program runs in its own virtual machine, which Windows 95 manages.

Virtual Machine Tracking

You can track the virtual machines running in Windows 95 using the System Monitor utility. Exercise 4.1 walks you through this process. Figure 4.2 shows an example of the System Monitor's graphical display of virtual machine usage when two MS-DOS windows are open.

Exercise 4.1 assumes that when you installed Windows 95, you chose a Custom setup and then chose all of the options. If you did not do this, you must add the System Monitor to your system. See Appendix B for information about how to install additional Windows 95 components.

F I G U R E   4.2

The System Monitor can track virtual machines in Windows 95. Here, two MS-DOS-based applications are running along with the System VM, for a total of three virtual machines.

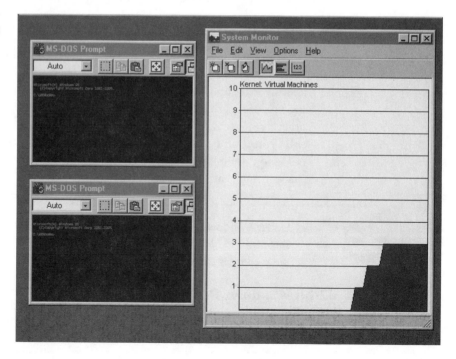

EXERCISE 4.1

Tracking Virtual Machine Usage with System Monitor

1. Select Start ➤ Programs ➤ Accessories ➤ System Tools ➤ System Monitor.

2. Click on the Edit menu and then on Add Item.

3. In the Add Item dialog box under Category, click on Kernel.

4. In the Add Item dialog box under Item, click on Virtual Machines.

5. Click on the OK button.

You should now see a graphical representation of your virtual machine usage. This value should not be changing. To make it change, start some more programs. Remember that only MS-DOS-based programs will open up additional VMs.

6. To open an MS-DOS application, select Start ➤ Programs ➤ MS-DOS Prompt.

Repeat step 6 to open another MS-DOS window.

Virtual Memory

Programs need memory in order to operate. Your computer comes equipped with a finite amount of memory called RAM (random-access memory). In the past, programs could access only the first 640KB of RAM on your system. If you had installed a high memory driver (HIMEM.SYS) in your CONFIG.SYS file, you could access the high memory area or the next 384KB of the first megabyte. This upper memory area was normally used to load system device drivers and TSR (terminate-and-stay-resident) programs like network drivers. These TSRs were loaded here to keep them from using memory in the lower 640KB area that the programs needed.

To access further amounts of RAM above that first megabyte, you needed to install either an Extended Memory Manager (XMS) or an Expanded Memory Manager (EMS) like EMM386.EXE. Under Windows 95, these drivers are no longer needed to access memory over that first megabyte. Windows 95 can also fool your programs into thinking that they have more RAM than is physically installed in your system. It does this by mapping a virtual address space to a page file and then to either physical RAM or a storage file on your hard disk called a *swapfile*. This is all managed by the Virtual Memory Manager (VMM).

Every MS-DOS-based program and 32-bit Windows program receives its own 4GB virtual address space. The 16-bit Windows programs share a single 4GB segment of addresses. This virtual address space allows the VMM to map those addresses to a page table. The page table is like an index card. It keeps track of which programs are using which chunks of memory. The page table is mapped to either physical RAM or to your swapfile.

Since there is a one-to-one relationship between entries in the page table and blocks in memory or in the swapfile, and there is no physical relationship between virtual memory addresses and physical memory addresses except via the page table, you may think that the physical address of a page is potentially changing from moment to moment. This is essentially true; pages may not necessarily be swapped back to their original hard disk location in the swapfile. However, the only way they can be moved is from a swapfile to RAM and then back. They will never be arbitrarily bounced around in the swapfile without a move to RAM first.

Let's walk through an example of what happens when a program makes a call for some memory. Our example is illustrated in Figure 4.3. A 32-bit Windows program needs some memory and makes a call for the memory at address h100, which has been mapped to a location on our page table. That location on our page table then maps to either physical RAM or to a swapfile (in our example it goes to the swapfile). The swapfile is a hard disk file that simulates physical RAM. Memory in Windows 95 is broken down into 4KB blocks called *pages*.

These data pages are what is being mapped between the virtual addresses and your virtual memory. When we have a call for a data page that is not in physical memory (RAM), a page fault occurs. The page fault tells the VMM to load that page from the swapfile into memory. When the system has a page fault, it is reading information from the hard disk rather than memory. Excessive page faulting can result in poor overall performance. To fix this, you should either reduce the number of concurrently running applications or add more RAM to your system. You can use the System Monitor to track page faults, following the steps in Exercise 4.2.

FIGURE 4.3

Virtual memory is broken into virtual address spaces, a page table, a swapfile, and RAM.

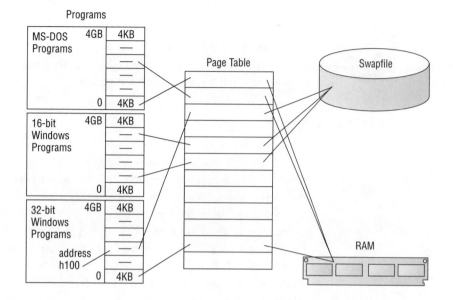

EXERCISE 4.2

Tracking Page Faults with System Monitor

1. Select Start ➤ Programs ➤ Accessories ➤ System Tools ➤ System Monitor.

2. Click on the Edit menu and then on Add Item.

3. In the Add Item dialog box under Category, click on Memory Manager.

4. In the Add Item dialog box under Item, click on Page Faults.

5. Click on the OK button.

6. To simulate page faults, open a few programs. Any programs will do; just make sure to open several. Then check back on the page faults in System Monitor.

Use the System Monitor to track page faults. Excessive page faults usually mean that you need more RAM. The term *thrashing* (or *disk thrashing*) means you are experiencing excessive page faults.

Demand Paging

When the physical RAM becomes full, it will swap some of its data pages out to the swapfile. This process is called *demand paging* or just *paging*. By default, the swapfile in Windows 95 is allowed to grow and shrink as much as the current conditions require. You can alter this setting yourself by adjusting the settings in the Virtual Memory dialog box. The default setting is to let Windows manage the virtual memory. If you choose to alter this setting, you will be adjusting the size of the swapfile. The swapfile is stored on your hard drive as WIN386.SWP and can be altered through the Virtual Memory dialog box, shown in Figure 4.4. Follow the procedure in Exercise 4.3 to change the size of the swapfile.

FIGURE 4.4

You can adjust the size of the swapfile in the Virtual Memory dialog box.

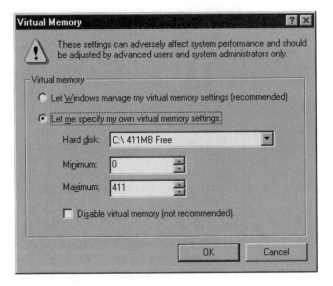

EXERCISE 4.3

Altering Virtual Memory Settings

1. In the Control Panel, double-click on the System icon to open the System Properties dialog box.

2. Click on the Performance tab.

3. Click on the Virtual Memory button at the bottom of this dialog box.

4. In the Virtual Memory dialog box, click on the second radio button to specify your own virtual memory settings, and then adjust the Minimum and Maximum settings.

In general, you want Windows 95 to manage the swapfile for you. You should not alter this setting unless you know what you are doing. You might alter this setting if you need to place the swapfile on a specific hard drive, or if you have limited disk space and want to keep the swapfile at a certain size. Too small a swapfile can severely impact the performance of your system.

You should not put the swapfile on a compressed drive, because this will impact its performance. You want your page swapping to be as fast as possible. You should regularly defragment your drives to allow the swapfile to use contiguous memory; this will also help speed up swapfile access. See Chapter 8 for information about defragmenting your hard drive.

In Windows NT, the swapfile can span multiple drives and is named PAGEFILE .SYS. In Windows 3.*x*, the swapfile was named SPARTPAR.386 and needed to be placed in contiguous memory on a noncompressed drive.

A quick way of navigating to the System Properties dialog box is to right-click on the My Computer icon on your Desktop. A context menu will appear. Click on Properties.

Your system has been designed to use paging to increase your productivity. If you are doing too much paging, however, your performance will degrade. This is called *excessive paging* or *disk thrashing*. Signs of excessive paging include high CPU utilization and large amounts of hard disk activity. If your swapfile is too small, or you don't have much RAM in your system, you may encounter this problem. You can fix this problem by adding more memory to your computer or running fewer programs simultaneously.

Virtual Addresses

Every virtual machine in Windows 95 receives a virtual address space. Each address in this address space points to a memory location where the programs running inside the virtual machine will store and manipulate data. The address space can point to as much as 4GB of memory. The address space is broken into two parts: 2GB for user applications and 2GB for operating system components. Programs use addresses in the virtual address space as follows:

- **0–1MB:** MS-DOS-based programs will use these addresses just as if the programs were really running in an MS-DOS environment. All other programs will ignore these addresses. However, the addresses might be used by any real-mode device drivers that a program loads.

- **1–4MB:** Normally not used. Windows NT loads above these address spaces. To maintain compatibility with NT, Windows 95 and 32-bit programs do not use these addresses either. For backward compatibility reasons, however, 16-bit Windows programs will use these addresses.

- **4MB–2GB:** Used by 32-bit programs. (Some 16-bit Windows programs may also use these addresses.)

- **2GB–3GB:** Used by the DLLs (dynamic-link libraries) and other shared components.

- **3GB–4GB:** Reserved for the operating system. These addresses are generally mapped to Ring 0 components. Most virtual device drivers are loaded into memory at these locations.

Messaging Systems

Windows 95 is an event-driven operating system that uses an asynchronous message-passing model to control program execution. Events like a mouse click cause an interrupt in the system. This interrupt is then converted by an interrupt request handler, or IRQ. The IRQ converts the interrupt into a message, which is then passed to system drivers and waiting programs. A stack of these queued messages is called a *thread*.

Interrupts and IRQs

As you move your mouse across the screen, there will be hundreds of mouse interrupts at IRQ 12. An *interrupt* is simply a request for service. These interrupts will be converted into messages by an interrupt handler. These messages will then be sent to a queue where the messages will be processed. Figure 4.5 shows an example of mouse-generated interrupts. In our example, these "MouseMove" events will be sent to the GDI. The GDI will then process them by repainting the screen with the mouse at the new location. MouseMove messages will also be sent to any running programs. The programs then have the opportunity to process these messages from their queue or ignore them.

FIGURE 4.5

Interrupt handlers convert interrupts into messages, which are then placed into message queues. 16-bit programs share a single queue, or thread; 32-bit programs can have multiple threads.

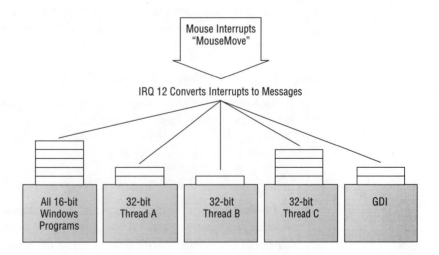

Table 4.1 lists the standard IRQ mappings for a PC.

T A B L E 4.1 IRQ Mappings for PCs				
IRQ 0:	Internal Clock		IRQ 8:	Real-time clock
IRQ 1:	Keyboard		IRQ 9:	Open
IRQ 2:	Open		IRQ 10:	Open
IRQ 3:	COM 2, 4		IRQ 11:	Open
IRQ 4:	COM 1, 3		IRQ 12:	PS/2 mouse
IRQ 5:	Open, LPT2, or sound card		IRQ 13:	Math coprocessor
IRQ 6:	Floppy controller		IRQ 14:	Fixed disk
IRQ 7:	LPT1		IRQ 15:	Open

Queued Messages: Threads

Queued messages are called *threads*. This is an asynchronous messaging system, which means that each thread is processed independently of any other thread. If a program quits reading its messages, it does not affect the other threads. This is a major improvement over the old Windows 3.*x* model, where all programs shared the same queue. This threading affects different program types in different ways.

Threading with MS-DOS–based Programs

MS-DOS-based programs do not use messaging in their design, and therefore don't have a message queue. However, the virtual machine in which an MS-DOS program runs does interact with Windows 95 through threading. An MS-DOS VM usually has two threads.

Threading with 16-bit Windows Programs

All 16-bit Windows programs share a single common thread. Each individual program picks out its personal messages from that stack (see Figure 4.5). If a program quits reading its messages, all of the other 16-bit programs will stop and wait until the program begins reading again or is cleared. This is sometimes called a program *hang*. Windows 95 uses this single-queue design for backward compatibility with Windows 3.*x* programs.

Threading with 32-bit Windows Programs

Each 32-bit program has its own thread and can have multiple threads. Each thread will be processed asynchronously (see Figure 4.5). These multiple threads allow 32-bit programs to run more efficiently than their 16-bit counterparts. The 32-bit programs also have the added advantage of not crashing other programs when they hang or crash.

Operating System Components

We talked about some messages being passed to the operating system components. There are three main components of the operating system:

- **Kernel:** The KERNEL32.DLL and KERNEL.DLL handle functions like file I/O (input/output), program loading and execution, and memory management.

- **User:** The USER32.DLL and USER.DLL handle user input and output. Keyboard, mouse, sounds, and communications are handled here. They also provide you with the Windows interface itself, including such things as icons and standard dialog boxes.

- **GDI:** The GDI32.DLL and GDI.DLL manage all of the graphics and printing in your system.

For speed, modularity, and consistency, Windows 95 implements these components as DLLs, which are modular libraries that can be used by many programs simultaneously. In the GDI, for example, there is a function to repaint the screen. Everything that needs to be done to repaint the screen is handled by that function in the GDI. There are hundreds of these functions stored within each of these DLLs.

The Kernel, User, and GDI DLLs are implemented in both a 32-bit edition and a 16-bit edition in Windows 95. The 16-bit version of the DLLs is included for backward compatibility. These core DLLs are called the Win32 API (Applications Programming Interface). Both Windows 95 and Windows NT are based on the Win32 API.

Windows 95 includes DLLs for networking, multimedia, and OLE functionality as well as many others. To find out about the different functions within
all of these DLLs, get a copy of the Software Developers Toolkit for the
Win32 API, or pick up a Win32 API manual.

Device Drivers

Windows 95 uses *device drivers* to talk with hardware components. A
device driver accepts various commands from the operating system and translates them into hardware-specific commands. This allows for device independence, and means that Windows 95 doesn't need to change when new
hardware is added to the system. A new device driver for the new hardware
will be loaded, and Windows will then talk to that device driver in the same
manner as it did with the old device driver. The driver itself is in charge of
translating the messages from the operating system and making the hardware
understand what Windows is requesting. There are drivers for the system,
keyboard, mouse, communications, and all other pieces of hardware in your
system.

Real Mode versus Protected Mode

Real-mode drivers were created to run in the MS-DOS environment. They are
normally implemented as *.SYS or *.DRV files. Real-mode drivers are loaded
either at boot time, by way of an entry in the CONFIG.SYS file, or at Windows startup, through an entry in the *.INI files. Entries in the CONFIG.SYS
file are always active, which means that they are always using system resources.
Entries in the *.INI files are active only while Windows is running.

Windows NT does not support the use of MS-DOS real-mode device drivers
(*.SYS files).

Protected-mode drivers take advantage of the *x*86 architecture and have
faster access to their devices. They are usually implemented as *.VXD or
*.386 files. Protected-mode drivers are also called *virtual device drivers* or
VxDs. These drivers may be unloaded from memory when not in use. This
frees up more resources for other applications.

Driver Files

Most Windows device drivers are located in the \Windows\System folder and have a .DRV, .386, or .VXD extension. *.DRV files are old 16-bit device drivers. Most of these have been replaced by a more robust and flexible *.386 or *.VXD 32-bit protected-mode driver.

During the Windows 95 setup process, many of the individual *.VXD files are combined into one large file called VMM32.VXD. This speeds loading of Windows 95, since it reads one large file instead of a bunch of smaller ones.

This file is located in the \Windows\System folder. As new virtual device drivers are added to the system, their respective *.VXD files are copied into the VMM32 folder. Once another setup is run, these files will be combined with the others into the VMM32.VXD file. You should have few files in the VMM32 folder, because they are added only when you upgrade drivers or add new hardware to your system.

Real-mode drivers located in the CONFIG.SYS file will be remarked out during the setup process if an appropriate 32-bit protected-mode driver is available. If Windows doesn't have a 32-bit version, or if Windows is unsure about the driver, it will leave that line in the CONFIG.SYS alone.

Protected-mode drivers should be used whenever possible.

Windows Multitasking

Windows 95 is a *multitasking* operating system. This means that many applications can be running at the same time. Multitasking can be broken down into the interaction of processes and threads, and two tasking models: cooperative and preemptive.

Processes

A running application is called a *process*. Processes have the following components:

- Initial code and data
- A memory address space where code and data will be stored
- System resources, including files
- At least one thread

Threads

A process can have one or more *threads*, or *units of execution*. Threads have the following components:

- A stack for use in user mode

- A stack for use in kernel mode

- A processor state, which includes the current instruction

These units of execution tell the different components in Windows 95 what to do. In addition to having multitasking capabilities, Windows 95 is also multithreaded. The 32-bit Windows applications may have more than one thread running at a time. The following sections describe how these threads are maintained.

Monitoring Threads

In a multithreaded environment, it is critical that threads don't overwrite resources being used by other threads. This maintenance is handled by the Windows 95 operating system and the scheduler. The scheduler decides which threads get CPU time.

You can use the System Monitor to monitor threads. Follow the steps in Exercise 4.4 to monitor the number of executing threads.

Thread Priorities

The *priority* of a thread determines when that thread will receive processor time. The higher the priority, the sooner that thread will get a time slice.

Each thread in the system has a base priority. There are 32 priority levels within Windows 95. Threads may have their base priorities changed upward or downward by up to two levels by the scheduler, as explained in the next section. You cannot directly alter a thread's priority other than by making its process (program) a foreground application by giving it the focus, or by making it a background application by minimizing it, or by switching to another running program.

Scheduling

Scheduling determines which thread has use of the processor. Processing time is divided into time slices. There are two scheduling functions within Windows 95: the primary scheduler and the secondary scheduler.

Monitoring Threads with System Monitor

1. Navigate to the \Labs\Threads folder on the CD-ROM that accompanies this book, and run the SETUP.EXE program to install the Threads application. Then select Start ➢ Programs ➢ Threads.

2. Select File ➢ Add a Single Thread. Do this a few times to add several threads. This single 32-bit program now has multiple threads executing.

3. Select Start ➢ Programs ➢ Accessories ➢ System Tools ➢ System Monitor.

4. Select Edit ➢ Add Item.

5. In the Add Item dialog box under Category, click on Kernel.

6. In the Add Item dialog box under Item, click on Threads.

7. Click on OK.

8. Add a few more threads to the Threads program, and see how they affect the display in the System Monitor.

Primary Scheduler   The primary scheduler looks at all of the threads it is presented with and then gives time slices to the thread with the highest priority. If more than one thread has the same priority, the scheduler will give each thread a time slice and then move to the next thread in sequence. After one complete rotation, the scheduler will again evaluate the thread priorities and continue to give out time slices.

Secondary Scheduler   The secondary scheduler is in charge of managing the priorities of the threads. This scheduler will boost priorities of threads that are part of the active window. This makes the system more responsive to the user who is currently using a program in the active window. After a thread gets a time slice, its priority is reduced a level. To prevent the starvation of background programs that have low-priority threads, the scheduler will automatically boost a thread's priority one level at a time until it finally gets some time slices.

Dynamic Priority Adjustment

The secondary scheduler will change the priority of threads over time to smooth the overall performance of Windows 95. A thread's priority may be raised or lowered based on the type of work the thread is doing:

- Threads waiting for user interaction in the foreground get a priority increase. This makes the active program more responsive to the user.

- Threads that have waited voluntarily will get a priority boost.

- Compute-bound threads get their priorities lowered. An example of a compute-bound thread is a calculation from a large, complex spreadsheet.

- All threads will periodically get a priority increase. This prevents lower-priority threads that are using a resource from locking out higher-priority threads that need the same resource.

Priority Inheritance Boosting

Sometimes a low-priority thread will lock a resource that a higher-priority thread needs to continue execution. Since the higher-priority thread is blocked, the low-priority thread will have its priority boosted to the same level as the high-priority thread. The low-priority thread will continue to get time slices at this inherited level until it releases the needed resource. Once the resource has been released, the blocked thread will continue with execution and the low-priority thread will get dropped back to its normal priority level.

Cooperative and Preemptive Multitasking

Now that you understand the concepts of threading and scheduling, let's talk about the cooperative and preemptive multitasking models instituted in Windows 95. Cooperative multitasking is used for backward compatibility with Windows 3.x programs; preemptive multitasking is used for Windows 95.

Cooperative Multitasking

In a *cooperative multitasking* environment, a thread will run until it voluntarily gives up the processor. Each individual program decides when it will stop running a thread. A poorly written Windows 3.x program could tie up the processor, defeating the purpose of multitasking.

In Windows 95, 16-bit programs are cooperatively multitasked. This means that they all share a single thread of execution. If any one 16-bit program fails to relinquish the processor, then the other 16-bit programs will need to wait until it does. That single thread of execution will then be preemptively multitasked with all of the other threads vying for processor time.

Preemptive Multitasking

In a *preemptive multitasking* environment, each thread will get a certain amount of processor time. A single thread will continue to dominate the processor as long as its thread priority is higher than any other thread priority. As explained earlier, thread priorities are managed by the scheduler.

In Windows 95, all 32-bit programs are preemptively multitasked. The 16-bit programs cooperatively multitask among themselves, but their single thread is then preemptively multitasked with all of the other processing threads. Figure 4.6 illustrates how 16-bit and 32-bit programs are multitasked.

FIGURE 4.6

16-bit Windows programs cooperatively multitask sharing a single thread. 32-bit Windows programs can have multiple threads. The scheduler uses preemptive multitasking to determine which thread gets a CPU time slice.

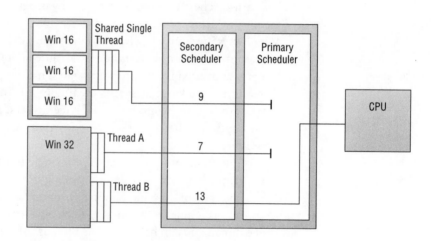

Summary

Windows 95 is a multithreaded, multitasking operating system, which takes advantage of the Intel *x*86 ring architecture. In order to increase speed and reduce errors, Windows 95 uses only Ring 0 and Ring 3. Ring 0 allows a program full access to all system hardware and memory. Noncritical system components and all user applications and programs run in Ring 3.

Windows 95 uses virtual machines to make programs think that they have exclusive access to all system hardware. The virtual machines use a message-passing technique to access memory and hardware. The two types of virtual machines in Windows 95 are a System VM and multiple MS-DOS VMs. A separate memory address space is assigned to each virtual machine running in Windows 95. All non-MS-DOS-based programs run on the System VM in Ring 3. Each MS-DOS-based program receives its own VM in Ring 3. All 16-bit Windows programs share a single memory address space. Each 32-bit Windows program receives its own address space. You can track virtual machine usage with the Windows 95 System Monitor utility.

Memory in Windows 95 is virtualized. By using demand paging with a swapfile, programs can access more memory than is physically in your system. You can track page faults (which occur when there are calls for a data page that is not in physical memory) with the System Monitor.

For speed, modularity, and efficiency, Windows 95 uses DLLs (dynamic-link libraries). These DLLs are referenced by programs through the upper 2GB of memory address space.

Windows 95 uses an asynchronous message-passing model to control program execution. Events like a mouse click cause an interrupt in the system. The interrupt is converted by an interrupt request handler, or IRQ, into a message.

Threads are stacks of messages created by the interrupt handlers. These messages are sent to programs and device drivers. A device driver translates messages into hardware-specific instructions. Programs utilize and generate threads also.

The 16-bit Windows programs share a single thread to their address space and cooperatively multitask using that single thread. Because of this cooperation, it is possible for a 16-bit Windows program to tie up resources and block other 16-bit programs from running. Each 32-bit Windows program has at least one thread and can have multiple threads. All threads in Windows 95 are then preemptively multitasked by the scheduler.

The scheduler is broken into two separate functions. The primary scheduler looks at all thread priorities and gives time slices to the highest priority threads. The secondary scheduler assigns thread priorities, and may adjust these priorities over time.

Review Questions

1. If you open up three MS-DOS–based programs, three 16-bit Windows programs, and two 32-bit Windows programs, how many virtual machines are running?

   A. 8

   B. 3

   C. 4

   D. 2

2. Which of the following is not a core component of the Windows 95 operating system?

   A. Kernel

   B. OSCore

   C. GDI

   D. User

3. You are experiencing disk thrashing. How could you fix this problem? (Select all that apply.)

   A. Add more RAM to your system.

   B. Take your hard disk in for repairs.

   C. Run fewer programs simultaneously.

   D. Move the operating system components to another drive.

4. What area of virtual address space is reserved for the core operating system components?

   A. 0 to 1MB

   B. 1MB to 2GB

   C. 2GB to 3GB

   D. 3GB to 4GB

5. What is the benefit of using a device driver?

   A. It allows for device independence.

   B. It moves a device from one location to another.

   C. It prevents programs from communicating with hardware.

   D. Device drivers aren't available for Windows 95.

6. Virtual device drivers are combined at setup time into a single file called:

   A. VirtDev.VXD

   B. VXD.VXD

   C. VMM32.VXD

   D. Device drivers are not combined.

7. Which one of the following statements is true regarding real-mode and protected-mode drivers?

   A. Real-mode drivers are better than protected-mode drivers because real-mode drivers are always loaded in memory.

   B. Protected-mode drivers are better than real-mode drivers because they can be loaded and unloaded from memory as needed.

C. Real-mode drivers are better than protected-mode drivers because they can be loaded and unloaded from memory as needed.

D. Protected-mode drivers are better than real-mode drivers because they are always loaded in memory.

8. When does a page fault occur?

A. When data was found in RAM

B. When data was found in the swapfile

C. When pages were corrupted

D. When memory was lost

9. Which of the following is not done by the secondary scheduler?

A. Boosting priority levels of all threads periodically

B. Lowering priority levels of compute-bound threads

C. Raising priority levels of threads from the active window

D. Lowering priority levels of threads from the active window

10. Which of the following is true about the primary and secondary schedulers? (Select all that apply.)

A. The primary scheduler looks at all processing threads and gives time slices to the thread with the highest priority.

B. The primary scheduler looks at all threads and can adjust the priority of each processing thread.

C. The secondary scheduler looks at all threads and can adjust the priority of each processing thread.

D. The secondary scheduler looks at all processing threads and gives time slices to the thread with the highest priority.

11. What happens in a cooperative multitasking environment?

    A. Multiple executing threads are given CPU time slices by a scheduling mechanism.

    B. A single thread is shared by all running programs.

    C. Every program receives its own threads.

    D. Threads are given priorities based on how many programs are using them.

12. Which of the following is true regarding multitasking?

    A. Preemptive multitasking means that a scheduler is deciding which threads among many get CPU time slices.

    B. Cooperative multitasking means that a scheduler is deciding which threads among many get CPU time slices.

    C. Windows 3.*x* takes advantage of a scheduler to create a preemptive multitasking environment.

    D. Windows 95 takes advantage of a scheduler to create a cooperative multitasking environment.

13. The relationship between processes and threads can best be described by which of the following?

    A. Threads own multiple processes.

    B. A single process can own multiple threads.

    C. Threads have no relationship to a process.

    D. Threads own a single process.

14. Which of the following is true of threading in Windows 95?

    A. 16-bit programs each have their own thread.

    B. 32-bit programs each have their own thread.

    C. 16-bit programs can have multiple threads.

    D. 32-bit programs can have multiple threads.

CHAPTER

5

Customizing and Configuring
Windows 95

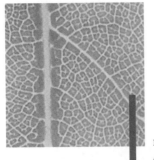

n this chapter, you will learn how to customize and configure Windows 95. Many of the customization and configuration features are new to Windows 95. For example, the Desktop—your starting point—has been simplified yet made very powerful compared with previous versions of Windows. Before you can make adjustments to Windows 95, you need to become familiar with the Desktop and other new features. Our discussion of what's new in Windows 95 includes the following features:

- The Desktop

- The Taskbar

- Control buttons

- Right-mouse clicks

- File finding

- The Help system

- The Recycle Bin

- The document-centered environment

- Performance improvements

- The Display properties

After these topics are examined, the chapter continues with the details of installing new hardware, using and configuring the Taskbar, customizing the Start menu, creating shortcuts, and using the Control Panel. Finally, you will learn how to use the Windows Explorer, the powerful new tool for managing your files and folders.

What's New in Windows 95

Windows 95 is an extremely feature-rich operating system. Virtually every aspect of Windows 95 reflects improvements over Windows 3.1 and Windows for Workgroups. The interface is simplified and improved, granting ease of use for both novice and experienced users. System administrators love the improved networking capabilities. There are thousands of small technical improvements, from sophisticated memory management to Plug-and-Play hardware technology. Windows 95 is a revolutionary step up from the DOS operating system.

The Desktop

Windows 95 has a new look and feel from previous versions of Windows. Windows 95 boots directly when you turn on your computer; you are not required to type a command from the command prompt. (However, there is an option for booting to a command prompt, which will be discussed later in the chapter.)

The most dramatic and obvious change from previous versions of Windows is the Windows 95 Desktop, shown in Figure 5.1. When you first boot up, you see a few icons on the left side of your screen and a Taskbar with a Start button at the bottom of your screen. There is no Program Manager; there are no program groups. Windows 95 has removed the clutter of Windows 3.1 and enhanced the functionality of the Desktop.

The cleaner interface is also more intuitive to use. For example, documents, file folders, and printers can be stored directly on the Desktop. You can then print a document by dragging it to the printer, or file a document by dragging it to a folder. If you want to file a document in a folder that is deeper in your directory structure, you can open My Computer, locate the folder, and then drag the document to it.

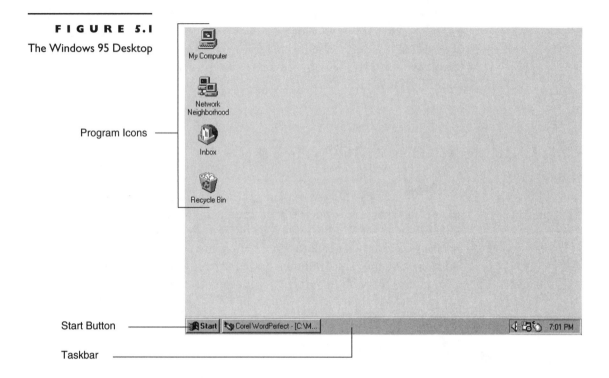

FIGURE 5.1

The Windows 95 Desktop

Program Icons

Start Button

Taskbar

Objects, Actions, and Properties

Microsoft has taken an *object-oriented* approach to the Windows 95 interface. Everything in Windows 95 is considered to be an *object*. Your Desktop icons, documents, folders, Taskbar, Desktop itself, and even your hard drives, mouse, monitor, and keyboard are considered objects. Anytime you want to change one of the characteristics of an object, you change that object's *properties*. If you want to change the wallpaper on your Desktop, you go to the Desktop's properties. If you want to swap the left and right mouse buttons, you change the mouse's properties.

Objects can do different things. For example, an icon can launch a program; a button can find a file. Anything an object does is called an *action*. Working with Windows 95 involves manipulating objects by commanding them to take actions or by changing their properties. Remember, from now on, everything on or about your computer is an object.

The Taskbar

The gray bar at the bottom of the screen is called the *Taskbar*. The Taskbar replaces the Task Manager in previous versions of Windows. Although the Taskbar is located at the bottom of the screen, you can move it to any of the other sides by dragging it with the mouse.

When you click on the Taskbar's Start button, a pop-up menu appears, displaying a list of options, including all of your programs. As you can see in the Taskbar with the Start menu shown below, some of the Start menu items have a small triangle (▶) at the right side. The triangle indicates that item has a submenu, which will appear when you select that item.

Moving among Open Programs

Each time you start a program, that program opens into a separate window. When a new window opens, it will appear on top of (overlapping) the other open windows. Each window will also appear on the Taskbar as a button containing the name of the program. You can have any number of programs (and windows) open at the same time, but you can enter data into only one program (window) at a time. This window is called the *active* window. The active window can be identified by one of three telltale signs:

- The active window is almost always the window on top.

- The active window has a colored title bar (the others are gray).

- The active window button on the Taskbar will look like it is selected, or pressed in.

Figure 5.2 shows an example of the Desktop with several open windows.

Active Window Title Bar

FIGURE 5.2

A Desktop with several open windows, but only one active window

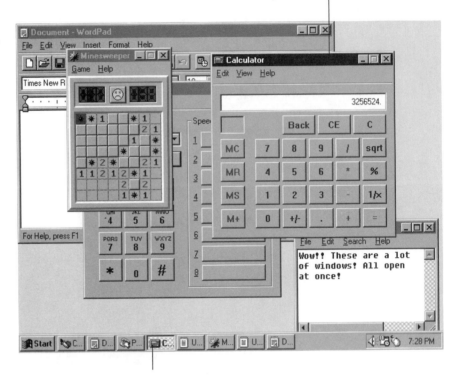

Active Window Button

There are two main techniques for selecting which open program (window) will be active: click on the program's Taskbar button to make that program active, or click on the actual window of the program that you want to be active. Of course, you will not be able to use the latter method if the target window is hidden behind another window or the program is minimized.

You can also move among open windows using the keyboard. Hold down the Alt key and press the Tab key. The first time you press Tab, a box appears displaying an icon for each open program. Press the Tab key repeatedly to move from one icon to another. When you release the Alt key, the selected program will become active.

Taskbar Icons (The Systray)

A clock occupies the far right side of the Taskbar. If you rest the mouse pointer over the clock, or left-click on it, the date is displayed. Double-clicking on the clock allows you to adjust the date and time.

To the left of the clock on the Taskbar, there are several icons. Additional icons may appear and disappear as you are working. For instance, when you start a print job, a printer icon will appear; if you start a fax job, a small fax machine will appear. Most of the Taskbar icons have similar options. Resting the mouse pointer over the icon gives you more information about the function of the icon, and double-clicking on it allows you to change any options associated with it. Right-clicking on an icon displays a pop-up menu with items appropriate to the icon. Keep an eye on the Taskbar and you will always know which programs your computer is running.

Window Control Buttons

Another dramatic change in the Windows 95 interface is the appearance and location of the window control buttons. The control buttons in Windows 3.1 consisted of two arrow buttons on the right side of the title bar and a large dash button on the left. The new control buttons are all on the right side of the title bar, as shown here for the WordPad program.

Figure 5.3 shows a comparison of the Windows 3.1 and Windows 95 buttons.

Maneuvering the Mouse

Windows 3.1 demonstrated to the PC world the wonders of using a mouse to select objects and command the computer. Windows 3.1 used three basic mouse maneuvers, all of which used the left mouse button: the single-click to select an item for future action or to activate a button, a double-click to select an item and launch it, and the drag to change the location of an object. Windows 95 extends your mouse repertoire by adding the right-button click and the right-button drag.

FIGURE 5.3

The Windows 3.1 and
Windows 95 window
control buttons

	Windows 3.1	Windows 95
Minimize	▼	_
Maximize	▲	□
Restore	⬍	⮽
Close	▭	✕

These mouse maneuvers are for the Windows 95 operating environment. Most of the programs that you run under Windows 95 will respond the same way. However, each program might have some special mouse tricks. For example, when working in a Word for Windows document, a double-click selects an entire word and a triple-click selects an entire paragraph.

The Left Mouse Button

In previous versions of Windows, the left mouse button was used almost exclusively. In Windows 95, the left mouse button retains most of its previous functionality. Details for using the left mouse button follow.

Single-Clicking (Selecting)   The left mouse button is considered the "main" mouse button and is used for the majority of your mouse operations. By moving the mouse pointer over an object and pressing the left mouse button once (a maneuver simply called *clicking*), you select that object. Once an object is selected, you can perform any number of actions on that object. You can select more than one object at a time by holding down the Control (Ctrl) key while clicking on different objects. When an object (or objects) is selected, any actions taken will affect that object. For example, if you press the Delete key, everything selected will be deleted. You can select a range of objects (such as files in a list) by clicking on the first object, holding down the Shift key, and clicking on the last object.

The single-click is used to activate any button or menu item, as well as for selecting an object (such as an icon) on your Desktop.

Double-Clicking   To *double-click*, move the mouse pointer over an object and press the left mouse button twice in rapid succession. This action must be rapid so the computer will see it as a double-click instead of two single clicks. You can set the speed at which you must double-click through the Control Panel, as explained later in the chapter. Only icons need to be double-clicked.

Dragging   The technique of *dragging* is used to move an object from one location to another. To drag an object, place the mouse pointer over the object, then press and hold down the left mouse button. While holding down the button, move the mouse pointer. The selected object(s) will move along with the pointer. When the object has reached the final location, release the button. Releasing an object after a drag is called *dropping*.

It is important to point out that dragging can extend beyond a single window or the Desktop. You can use this drag-and-drop technique to copy or move an object (or information) from one window to another. Dragging can also be used to create a "shortcut" to a program file, as explained later in this chapter.

By default, the mouse is configured to be used with the right hand with the user's index and middle fingers placed over the two mouse buttons. In this configuration, the left button is the "main" button. It is possible to reconfigure the mouse so the right button is the main button. This is especially handy for people who use the mouse with their left hand. The technique for swapping these buttons is discussed later in this chapter, in the section about the Control Panel.

The Right Mouse Button

Unlike in previous versions of Windows, the right mouse button is essential to using Windows 95. Learning how to correctly use the right mouse button can save you a tremendous amount of effort. Details on the right mouse button follow.

Right-Clicking   A single-click of the right mouse button displays a pop-up menu. The pop-up menu is *object-sensitive* (or context-sensitive). This means an appropriate pop-up menu is displayed for the object the mouse pointer is over. This menu contains the most likely actions you will take with that object.

These right-button menus are not only available within the Windows 95 environment, but are available within many Windows programs as well. In some cases, you can actually change the items on these pop-up menus or change the order in which they appear.

One of the actions available on the right-click menu is the Open option. This action is the same as double-clicking with the left mouse button. Many people find it easier to right-click and choose Open than to double-click.

Right-Dragging   Dragging with the right mouse button is somewhat different than dragging with the left button. You start by placing the mouse pointer over an object, then hold down the right mouse button while moving the mouse pointer to its destination. The difference is that when you release the right button, a pop-up menu of options is displayed. From that pop-up menu, you can choose the action to be applied to the object. Many users prefer right-dragging files because of the added control.

Finding Files

A very useful feature located on the Start button menu is the Find command, as shown below. You can use this feature to locate a file on your personal computer, a computer on the network, or information on The Microsoft Network (MSN, Microsoft's online service). It is most commonly used to look for a file or a folder.

When you select this option, a three-tabbed dialog box appears, as shown in Figure 5.4. The first tab in the Find dialog box is Name & Location, which is the tab that is most often used. Exercise 5.1 shows the steps for finding a file.

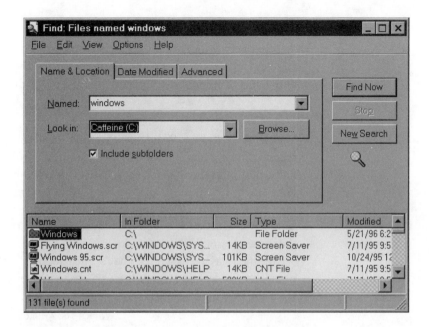

EXERCISE 5.1

Finding a File

1. Select Start ➢ Find ➢ Files or Folders.

2. In the Name & Location tab of the Find dialog box, type the name (or part of the name) of the file you are seeking in the Named text box. (Click on the drop-down arrow next to this text box to see a list of names you have searched for recently.)

3. To tell Windows 95 where to begin looking for your file, click on the drop-down arrow for the Look In text box and select any drive on your system. Alternatively, click on the Browse button to select a folder on a drive. Optionally, check the Include subfolders checkbox.

4. Click on the Find Now button. The dialog box will extend downward to show you a list of all files that match your search information.

5. When you see the file that you want, stop the search by clicking on the Stop button.

Getting Help

Another very noticeable change in Windows 95 is the Help system. You can still get Help using the traditional methods (F1, the Help menu, Help buttons, and ToolTips), but there are a couple of new surprises as well.

What's This?

Within dialog boxes, Windows 95-aware programs provide a "What's This?" feature. Some dialog boxes, like the one shown in Figure 5.5, have a question mark button in the upper-right corner. Clicking on this button activates the What's This? feature for that dialog box and changes the pointer into a question mark pointer. Click this pointer on any element in the dialog box, and a ToolTip-like Help message is displayed. To close the Help message, just click the mouse again.

Another way to view the What's This? feature within a dialog box is to point to an object and right-click. You can then select the What's This? option from the pop-up menu.

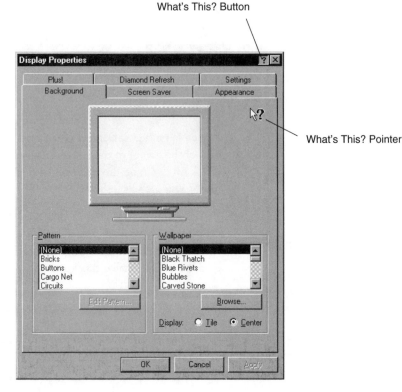

FIGURE 5.5

The Help System's "What's This?" button and pointer

The Help Dialog Box

To get help on Windows 95, click on the Start button on the Taskbar and select Help from the menu. The new Main Help dialog box is displayed. This dialog box has three tabs, labeled Contents, Index, and Find. Each of these tabs gives you a different method of finding the information you need.

The Contents Tab   The Contents tab is similar to the one in previous versions of Windows. Searching for information here is like using the table of contents in a book. Unlike previous versions of Help, the Contents list has multiple levels that can be expanded and collapsed.

The first level of Help topics is very broad and general: How To, Tips & Tricks, Troubleshooting, and so on. Each of these categories of Help can be expanded to give more detailed topics by double-clicking on the book icon to the left of the topic. The book will open, revealing a deeper level of Help topics, as shown in Figure 5.6. The levels will continue to expand until you reach the document level. Double-clicking on a document will open a Help card on your screen and close the Main dialog box. To return to the Help Topics dialog box, click on the Help Topics button at the top of the card.

FIGURE 5.6

The Contents tab of the Help Topics dialog box

The Index Tab   Searching for information using the Index tab is similar to using the index in a reference book. This tab consists of a text box and an alphabetical list of Help topics, as shown in Figure 5.7. To search a particular topic, simply begin typing the first few letters of the topic, and the Help system will take you to that topic and give you a list of subtopics. If you see a topic that you want displayed, double-click on it.

F I G U R E 5.7

The Index tab of the Help
Topics dialog box

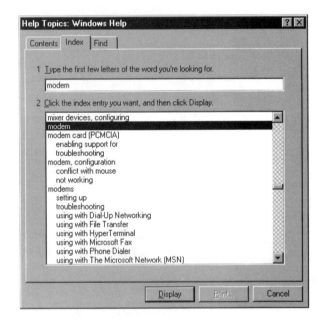

The Find Tab   The Find tab, shown in Figure 5.8, provides a powerful method of seeking information. This tab allows you to search on each word within a Help topic. This can be extremely useful for tracking down information that is not included as a separate Help topic

The first time you use the Find tab, the Help system creates a word list of every word within every topic. The Find Setup Wizard steps you through this process. After the word list has been created, a three-paneled window is displayed. To find information, simply type the word or words you are looking for. The list in the middle shows all of the words that were matched. The list at the bottom shows all of the matching topics for the word you typed. Clicking on a word in the middle list narrows the topic search in the bottom list. Double-clicking on the desired Help page opens it onto your screen.

FIGURE 5.8

The Find tab of the Help Topics dialog box

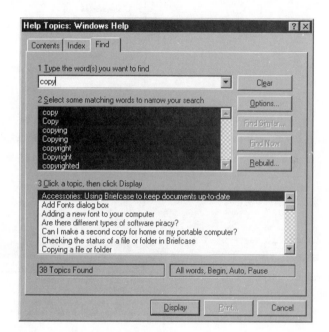

The Help Page

The Help page, or Help card, is a compact window that focuses on the specific Help topic you requested, as shown in Figure 5.9.

As concise as it is, the Help card is packed with tricks and options. For instance, some Help cards have jump buttons that open other cards, as shown in Figure 5.10. The buttons on this card open other Help cards with the actual Help topic. Clicking on a different button changes the Help topic.

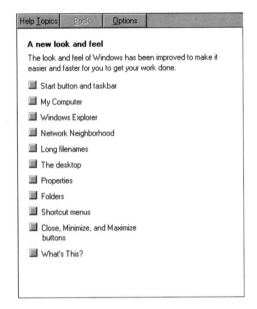

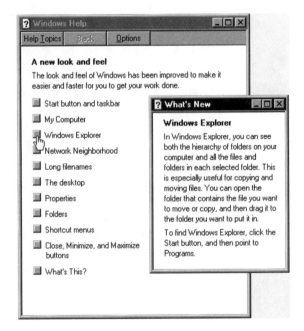

Definition Items   On a Help card, you will often see a word or name in green letters with a dotted underline. These are *definition items*. Clicking on a definition item displays a small box that explains that word, as shown below. Click again, and the box goes away.

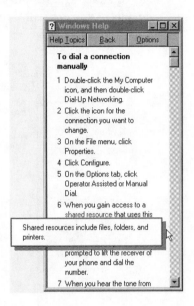

The Help Page Options Menu   Right-clicking on a Help page or clicking on the Options button displays the Options menu for Help, as shown here.

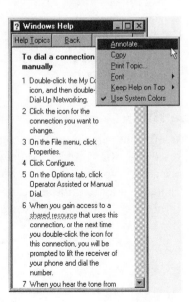

Of the six items listed, two deserve special mention:

- **Annotate:** Opens a small editing window and allows you to write notes or comments about that particular Help topic. These annotations are stored along with the Help topic for future viewing. If a Help topic has an annotation, a small green paperclip is displayed in the upper-left corner, as shown here.

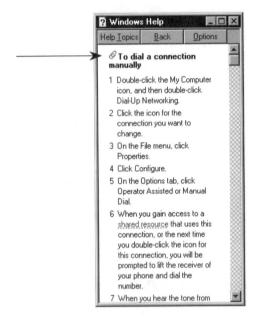

- **Keep Help on Top:** Keeps the Help card on top of the current application. This is very handy for reading the topic while working in an application.

The Recycle Bin

In previous versions of Windows, when you deleted a file, it was gone. If you discovered that you deleted the wrong file (something very easy to do considering the cryptic nature of eight-character filenames), you could take your chances with the Undelete feature in Windows for Workgroups 3.11, or use a third-party utility like the Norton Utilities.

Windows 95 is much more forgiving. Instead of deleting a file, Windows 95 simply moves it to the Recycle Bin. The Recycle Bin resides on your Desktop. Double-clicking on it will list all the files you have deleted since the Bin was last emptied. If you've accidentally deleted a file, open the Recycle Bin. Simply click on the file to select it and choose Restore from the File menu (or right-click on the file and choose Restore). The file will be restored to where it was when you deleted it.

There is one caveat, however. If you are deleting files in order to free up hard disk space, you must then empty the Recycle Bin before that space is freed. Simply sending a document to the Recycle Bin does not free up hard disk space. To empty the Recycle Bin, either right-click on the Recycle Bin icon and choose Empty Recycle Bin, or open the Recycle Bin and choose Empty Recycle Bin from the File menu.

If you want to delete an item and bypass the Recycle Bin, hold down the Shift key while deleting. Also, you can remove the confirmation warning and allocate how much hard drive space the Recycle Bin is allowed to use by right-clicking in the Recycle Bin and choosing Properties.

A Document-Centered Approach

Previous versions of Windows all took an *application-centered* approach to using a computer. Under this old approach, the computer's primary role was to run programs, which in turn created files or documents. With Windows 95, Microsoft turned this idea upside-down, making the primary function of a computer the creation of documents. Documents—whether they are letters, contracts, spreadsheets, graphic images, or multimedia presentations—are the final product in corporate computing. Windows 95 starts with the end in mind.

The Documents Menu

One of the major conceptual changes to Windows 95 was to switch the focus from working with programs to working with documents. Users should be able to open a document directly from the Desktop, without needing to launch an application first. Windows 95 makes it easier than ever to select a document and launch that document with the application that created it. Every time you create or revise a document, Windows 95 keeps track of it and places a shortcut to it on the Documents menu. Up to 15 documents can be retained in the Documents menu. To open a recently used document, just click on the Start button, move the mouse to the Documents menu, and select the document from the submenu, shown here.

Windows 95 will launch the correct program with your document retrieved, ready to edit.

Clearing the Documents Menu

The Start menu remembers the last 15 documents the user has used most recently and lists them on the Documents menu. By selecting a document from the Documents menu, you can launch the program that created the document, with that document on the screen. This is much faster than locating and starting the program, and then locating and opening the document.

You can clear the contents of the Documents menu by clicking on the Clear button in the Start Menu Programs tab of the Taskbar Properties dialog box. Clearing this menu does not delete the documents. It just clears a list of shortcuts stored in a special folder. Once you begin opening or creating documents after clearing the menu, the Documents menu once again starts remembering the last 15 documents that you used.

You can clear individual documents from the Documents menu by using the Windows Explorer. The shortcuts displayed on the Documents menu are stored in the C:\Windows\Recent folder. Use the Explorer to open this folder, and then delete any document shortcuts that you do not want to display on the Documents menu (using Windows Explorer is explained later in the chapter). Deleting the shortcut in the Recent folder does not delete the document itself.

Long Filenames

At last! Ever since the dark old days of DOS 1.0, PC users have been forced to save their files using the cryptic 8.3 naming standard. Finally, with Windows 95 you are permitted long names for files and folders, and you can even use spaces. However, there are still a few restrictions. Filenames must be 255 or fewer characters, including spaces. If you start a name with one or more spaces, Windows 95 will throw them away. The following is a list of forbidden characters: / \ : * ? " > < |.

There is one catch when using long filenames (LFNs). The programs you run under Windows 95 must be long filename-aware. Otherwise, the program will see only short filenames. When Windows 95 uses a long filename to create an 8.3 filename (or *alias*), it uses only the first six characters, dropping any spaces, then adds a tilde (~) and a sequencing number beginning with 1. For example, the long filename *My Budget for 1999* would become *MYBUDG~1*. The three-character filename extension, which is placed on the file by the application that created it, is retained. If the sequencing is forced past single digits, the sixth character in the long filename is sacrificed to make room for the double-digit number.

Here are some examples of how long filenames are truncated:

Long Filename	8.3 Filename
My Budget for 1997.doc	MYBUDG~1.DOC
My Budget for 1998.doc	MYBUDG~2.DOC
My Budget for 1999.doc	MYBUDG~3.DOC
My Budget for 2000.xls	MYBUDG~1.XLS

You can disable the tilde in long filenames, which is explained in Chapter 6. Chapter 8 includes information about how long filenames work on servers and problems you may encounter with long filenames.

Performance Enhancements

Aside from the cosmetic changes, Windows 95 has acquired some impressive performance enhancements that make a dramatic impact. For example, Windows 95 printing performance has been changed to provide both faster printing and far greater control over the printing environment. In addition to being able to access printers from within your applications, you can also access a printer from the Start button, or create a shortcut directly on your Desktop. (See Chapter 13 for details about Windows 95 printing.)

Windows 95 also provides a way for different users of the same computer to each have an individualized Desktop and custom environment. Windows 95 offers a very straightforward and simple way for each user to create a personal user profile. When that user logs on to the computer, his or her profile is downloaded. (See Chapter 14 for more information about user profiles.)

Many of the most important changes are not visible to the user. These are changes to the technology itself. The most notable of these changes is the transition away from the 16-bit MS-DOS environment to a full 32-bit windowing environment. Previous versions of Windows were more like a shell wrapped around the DOS core, extending its capabilities, rather than being a fully integrated operating system. While it's true that Windows 95 starts with an MS-DOS kernel, the environment is immediately able to leap from that limited 16-bit shell to a fuller, richer 32-bit environment. (See Chapter 4 for details about the Windows 95 architecture.)

Using and Configuring the Taskbar

The new Windows 95 Taskbar is easily the most powerful and useful tool in this new computing environment. At first glance, you might think the Taskbar is simply a replacement for the old Task Manager. In fact, the Taskbar has taken on the roles of the Task Manager, the Program Manager, and a few other tools as well. Here, we will discuss the many roles of the Taskbar as well as special techniques for getting the most from this powerful tool.

The surest path to mastering the Taskbar is not by reading about it, but by using it. With this goal in mind, this section includes several exercises using the Taskbar's special techniques and configuration options.

Displaying Multiple Programs

As you already know, every time you open a new program, a program button appears on the Taskbar; you can quickly switch from one program to the next by clicking on a button. But what if you wanted to display two or three programs side-by-side on your Desktop? The Taskbar can help you out with this as well. Right-clicking on the Taskbar and selecting either Tile Horizontally or Tile Vertically from the pop-up menu, as shown here, automatically sets your programs up for perfect viewing.

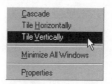

Tiling is a useful option. It automatically sizes and positions the program windows for optimal viewing, as you can see in Figure 5.11. This technique is especially handy for copy and paste actions between programs. However, some programs have a fixed-size window and will not tile quite as neatly.

FIGURE 5.11

Two vertically tiled windows

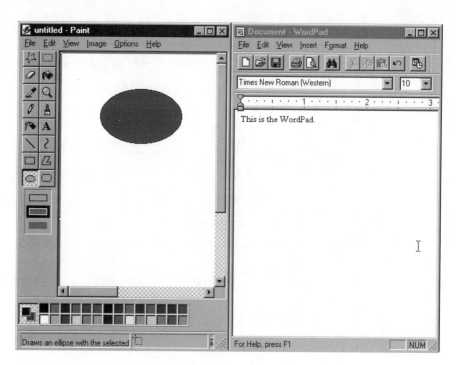

When right-clicking on the Taskbar, it is important to place the pointer over an unoccupied section of the bar. If the pointer is over a program button when you click, the pop-up menu will apply to that program and not the Taskbar. Finding an unoccupied area becomes more difficult as you open more and more programs. However, there is usually a vacant area close to the clock which works nicely.

The Taskbar has another good trick. Sometimes it is important to be able to get to your Desktop quickly. The Taskbar can assist you with this, even if you have several windows open.

Follow the steps in Exercise 5.2 to see how to use these Taskbar options.

EXERCISE 5.2

Tiling and Minimizing Programs Using the Taskbar

1. To launch the WordPad program, select Start ➢ Programs ➢ Accessories ➢ WordPad. The WordPad program opens with a blank word processing document. Type a few words in WordPad.

2. To launch the Paint program, select Start ➢ Programs➢ Accessories ➢ Paint. The Paint program opens with a blank graphics document. Draw a circle or another design on your canvas.

3. The two programs overlap. To tile them on the screen, right-click on the Taskbar and choose Tile Vertically. The two windows are now tiled, with each taking half the screen. They are divided vertically.

4. To copy an image from the Paint program, in the Paint window choose the rectangular Select tool in the upper right of the tool palette. Drag a rectangle around your image. Right-click on the selected area and choose Copy.

5. To paste the image into your WordPad document, click anywhere in the WordPad to activate it, right-click in the editing area, and choose Paste.

6. To copy text from WordPad, select all or some of the text you have written. Right-click on the selected text and choose Copy.

7. Click anywhere in the Paint program to activate it, right-click in the drawing area, and choose Paste. The text from your WordPad document is now part of your drawing.

8. To see how fixed-size windows are tiled, launch the Calculator program (select Start ➢ Programs ➢ Accessories ➢ Calculator).

9. Right-click on the Taskbar and choose Tile Horizontally. Notice that the Calculator doesn't tile in the same way as the other windows.

10. Right-click on the Taskbar and choose Tile Vertically. Because the Calculator has a fixed size, it will not fit neatly into a tiled Desktop.

11. Minimize the Calculator.

12. Right-click on the Taskbar and choose Tile Horizontally. The windows tile nicely. Minimized programs do not participate in tiling.

13. Click on the Calculator button on the Taskbar and restore it to the screen. You should have three programs running.

14. Right-click on the Taskbar and choose Minimize All Windows. Every open window is minimized down to the Taskbar, revealing the Desktop below.

15. To restore all of the programs to their original location on the Desktop, right-click on the Taskbar and choose Undo Minimize All. All of the windows are restored to their original size and position.

Configuring the Taskbar

The more programs you open, the more crowded the Taskbar becomes. As more programs line up on the Taskbar, the buttons get smaller so the Taskbar can accommodate them all. Eventually, the buttons get so small that you can't read which program is on which button. Fortunately, the Taskbar is completely customizable. You can configure the Taskbar to accommodate more programs with full-sized buttons, following the procedure in Exercise 5.3.

EXERCISE 5.3

Changing the Taskbar Height

1. Select Start ➤ Programs ➤ Accessories ➤ Notepad. Repeat this until you have eight copies running along with the Paint program, Calculator, and WordPad, which you opened in Exercise 5.2. (If these programs are not still open, launch them now.) Notice that the buttons on the Taskbar become smaller with each program you open.

2. Move the mouse pointer down to the top edge of the Taskbar. When the pointer makes contact with the edge, the pointer will turn into a double-headed arrow, as shown below.

3. Drag the edge of the Taskbar toward the center of the screen. The Taskbar gets taller and the buttons grow to fill in the new space, as shown below.

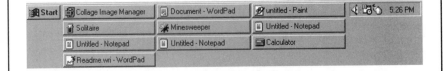

4. Move the mouse pointer to an empty place on the Taskbar.

EXERCISE 5.3 (CONTINUED FROM PREVIOUS PAGE)

5. Drag the Taskbar to any of the sides of your Desktop. The Taskbar fits nicely in a vertical orientation as well as a horizontal one, as shown below.

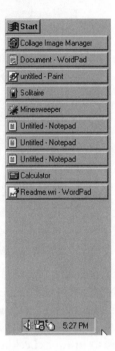

6. Practice widening the Taskbar in its new location.

7. To close one of the open programs, right-click over its program button on the Taskbar and choose Close.

8. Close the remaining open programs using the same method.

Changing Taskbar Properties

You can change the Taskbar properties in the same way that you change the properties of other objects: right-click (on a vacant area of the Taskbar) and choose Properties. The Taskbar Properties dialog box is shown in Figure 5.12.

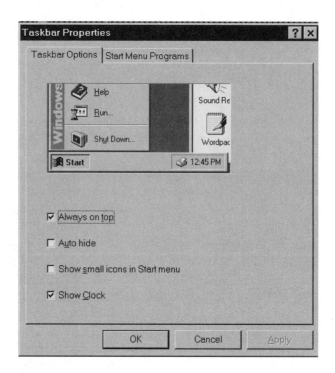

Notice that the Taskbar Properties dialog box has two tabs: Taskbar Options and Start Menu Programs. The Start Menu Programs tab is used to customize the Start menu, as explained in the next section. The Taskbar Options tab consists of four checkboxes below a sample Taskbar. The sample Taskbar shows you how the different options will affect the Taskbar without actually applying them. The checkboxes work as follows:

- **Always on top:** This option is active by default. It controls whether a window can appear on top of the Taskbar. If Always on top is selected, any window that is moved to the bottom of the screen appears behind the Taskbar. This ensures that the Taskbar is always available. It is recommended that this option be left active.

- **Auto hide:** This option increases your working area. Activating it causes the Taskbar to shrink down to a thin gray line at the bottom of the Desktop. It stays out of the way until you touch that gray line with the pointer; then the Taskbar reappears.

- **Show small icons in Start menu:** Activating this option causes the Start menu to display smaller icons. This has no great advantage other than making the Start menu more compact.

- **Show Clock:** This option is active by default. Removing the check removes the clock display from the Taskbar.

Customizing the Start Menu

The Start menu is the direct route to all of the features and programs on your computer. Windows 95 allows you to completely customize and configure this powerful feature to suit your individual needs. All customization of the Start menu is done from the Start Menu Programs tab of the Taskbar Properties dialog box, shown in Figure 5.13.

FIGURE 5.13

The Start Menu Programs tab of the Taskbar Properties dialog box

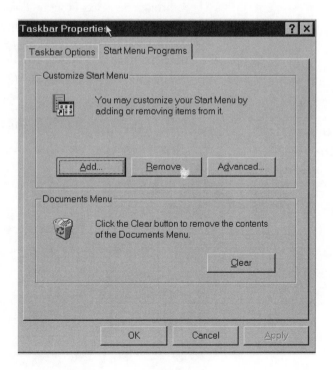

The Start Menu Programs tab is divided into two sections. The upper section lets you add or remove programs from the Start menu. The lower section lets you clear the documents from the Documents menu, as explained earlier in this chapter.

The Advanced button in the Customize Start Menu section launches the Windows Explorer program at the Start menu folder level. The Windows Explorer is the most powerful file management and navigation feature in Windows 95. You can use the Explorer to completely rearrange the structure and contents of your Start menu. You can also use it to make programs self-start when you boot up your computer by adding shortcuts to the Startup folder. We'll discuss the Windows Explorer in detail later in this chapter.

Adding Items to the Start Menu

When you click on the Add button in the Customize Start Menu section of the Start Menu Programs tab, the Create Shortcut dialog box appears, as shown in Figure 5.14. From here, you can pick a program to add to the Start menu. Then, through the Select Program Folder dialog box, shown in Figure 5.15, you can place the shortcut for the program in an existing folder or create a new folder for it. Finally, you specify the name for the program that will appear on the Start menu, through the dialog box shown in Figure 5.16. Exercise 5.4 shows the procedure for adding a program to the Start menu.

FIGURE 5.14

The Create Shortcut dialog box

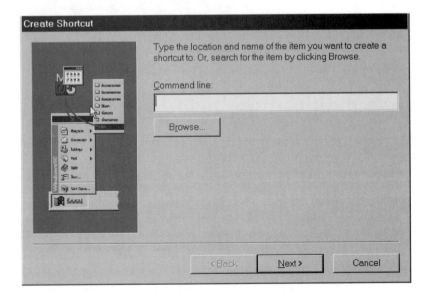

FIGURE 5.15

The Select Program
Folder dialog box

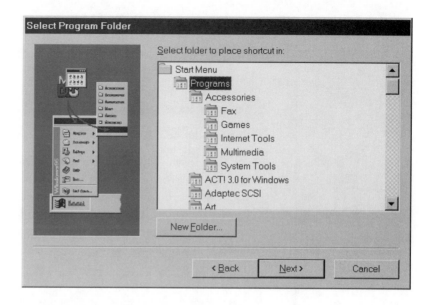

FIGURE 5.15

The Select Program
Folder dialog box

FIGURE 5.16

The Select a Title for the
Program dialog box

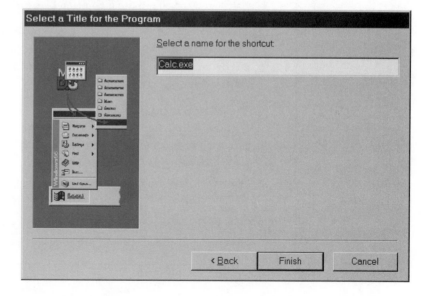

FIGURE 5.16

The Select a Title for the
Program dialog box

EXERCISE 5.4

Adding a Folder and Program to the Start Menu

1. Right-click on the Taskbar and choose Properties.

2. Select the Start Menu Programs tab.

3. Click on the Add button to display the Create Shortcut dialog box (Figure 5.14).

4. Click on the Browse button. (Optionally, if you know the location of the program, you can type it in the Command Line text box.) The Browse dialog box displays all of your first-level folders on the C: drive. In this example, we'll add the Calculator program, which resides in the Windows folder.

5. Double-click on the Windows folder to open it.

6. Use the scrollbar to locate the program CALC or CALC.EXE. A small calculator icon will be next to the filename. Click on the Calculator file to select it, then click the Open button. The full path to the Calculator appears in the Command Line box.

7. Click on the Next button. The Select Program Folder dialog box (Figure 5.15) is displayed. The folder area shows the current folders already on the Programs menu. You can place the Calculator shortcut in an existing folder or create a new folder. Let's create a new folder.

8. The folder you create will be nested inside of whichever folder is selected. To put your new folder inside the Programs folder, make sure the Programs folder is selected and click on the New Folder button. A new folder is created with the default name Program Group (1). The name is highlighted, which indicates that it is ready for renaming.

9. Type in the name for your new folder as you want it to appear on the Start menu. For this example, use your first name for the folder name.

---

10. Press the Enter key or click on the Next button. You have created and named a new folder on the Start Programs menu. All that's left to do is select a title for the shortcut you have created. The Select a Title dialog box is on the screen.

11. In this dialog box, type a name for the shortcut as it will appear on the menu. The name should be brief yet descriptive. Let's name the shortcut Calculator. The default name, Calc.exe, is highlighted and ready for renaming (Figure 5.16). Type the word **Calculator**.

12. Either press the Enter key or click on the Finish button to complete the process.

13. Click on the OK button at the bottom of the Taskbar Properties dialog box to close it.

14. To test your handiwork, click on the Start button and go to the Programs menu. When the submenu expands, you should see the folder you created with your first name on it. Move the pointer to that folder. When it opens, you should see the Calculator shortcut you created.

When you place a program on the Start menu, you are not changing the location of that program, nor are you making a copy of that program. You create a *shortcut*, or pointer to the program, which will launch it. Shortcuts are discussed in more detail later in this chapter.

Removing Items from the Start Menu

Removing a program from the Start menu is even faster and easier than adding one. Removing programs involves only one dialog box instead of three—the Remove Shortcuts/Folders dialog box, shown in Figure 5.17. Follow the steps in Exercise 5.5 to remove a program from the Start menu.

FIGURE 5.17

The Remove Shortcuts
Folders dialog box

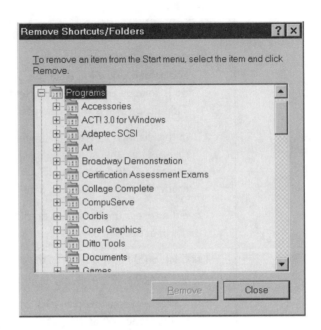

EXERCISE 5.5

Removing a Program from the Start Menu

1. Right-click on the Taskbar and choose Properties.

2. Select the Start Menu Programs tab.

3. Click on the Remove button. The Remove Shortcuts/Folders dialog box (Figure 5.17) appears.

4. Scroll down the list of folders until you find the one you created for the shortcut (the folder with your first name, created in Exercise 5.4).

5. Double-click on your folder to open it. The Calculator shortcut is displayed beneath the folder.

6. Select the Calculator shortcut, click on the Remove button, and confirm the deletion.

7. Select the folder you created earlier. Remove it from the Programs menu.

8. Close both the Remove Shortcuts/Folders and the Taskbar Properties dialog boxes.

If you remove the folder that contains your shortcut first, this removes the shortcut as well. We used two separate steps in Exercise 5.5 to reinforce the shortcut-inside-the-folder concept as well as to demonstrate that you can perform more than one remove operation without reopening the dialog box.

Creating Shortcuts

Shortcuts are an extremely powerful tool for increasing efficiency. You can create a shortcut to any object or resource on your computer or on the network. A shortcut is a special instruction to launch an object (program, file, printer, and so on). Shortcuts are usually stored on your Desktop, but they can be stored in folders as well. In fact, the Start button's menu is completely made up of shortcuts.

There are three main techniques for creating shortcuts: with the Shortcut Wizard, through My Computer, or with the Find feature. These are described in the following sections.

As you work more with Windows 95, you will discover several other ways of creating shortcuts. For example, right-clicking on an object in a folder displays a pop-up menu. Create Shortcut is usually an option. Also, right-dragging an object usually displays a Create Shortcut option.

Using the Shortcut Wizard

When you use the Shortcut Wizard, you need to know the full command line (command name) of the program, unless the path to the program is contained in the path statement. Figure 5.18 shows the first screen presented by the Shortcut Wizard. Follow the steps in Exercise 5.6 to create a shortcut using the wizard. In this exercise, you will add a shortcut for the Calculator program.

Notice the small arrow in the lower-left corner of your shortcut's icon. That arrow identifies the icon as a shortcut. It's important to realize that the shortcut is not a copy of the program, but a pointer to the program. If the shortcut is deleted, the program is not affected.

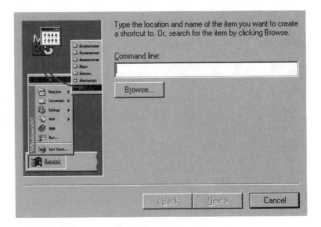

EXERCISE 5.6

Creating a Shortcut Using the Shortcut Wizard

1. Right-click in an empty space on your Desktop and select New ➤ Shortcut to start the Shortcut Wizard. It begins with the Create Shortcut dialog box (Figure 5.18).

2. In the Command Line text box, type **C:\WINDOWS\CALC.EXE** (the Calculator program is usually stored in the Windows folder). Alternatively, you can click on the Browse button, then double-click on the Windows folder, select the Calc program, and click on the Open button.

3. Press the Enter key or click on the Next button.

4. You must now name the shortcut. The name "calc" is placed in the Shortcut Name text box and highlighted, ready for editing. Type **My Calculator** and press the Enter key or click on the Finish button. The new shortcut appears on your Desktop with the name My Calculator.

5. Double-click on your new My Calculator shortcut. The Calculator should open on your Desktop.

6. Close the Calculator.

Using My Computer to Create a Shortcut

Another way to create a shortcut is through the My Computer window. This also requires you to know the full command line for the program. Exercise 5.7 shows how to use this method, again using the Calculator program in the example. We'll discuss the other functions available through My Computer later in this chapter, in the section about Windows Explorer.

EXERCISE 5.7

Creating a Shortcut Using My Computer

1. Double-click on the My Computer icon on your Desktop. A window opens displaying all the storage devices on your computer.

2. Double-click on your C: drive icon. This opens a window displaying all of the folders and files in the highest level of your C: drive. (This window should not be maximized. If it is, click on the Restore button to make it a floating window.)

3. Use the scrollbars to locate the Windows folder. Double-click on the Windows folder. This opens a window displaying the contents of that folder.

4. Use the scrollbars to locate the Calculator program. It will be shown as either CALC or CALC.EXE, depending on how your machine is set up. You will see the Calculator icon next to the name. If the calculator is not installed, either use a different program or refer to Appendix B on installing new components to Windows 95.

5. Click on the Calculator icon once to select it. Drag the Calculator icon outside the window and drop it on your Desktop.

6. A new shortcut is automatically created with the name Shortcut to Calc. Double-click on the new shortcut to check it, then close the Calculator.

7. To rename the shortcut, right-click on it and choose Rename from the pop-up menu. The shortcut's name will be highlighted, ready for you to type the new name. Type: **My Other Calculator** and press the Enter key. Each shortcut must have a unique name.

Using the Find Feature to Create a Shortcut

In order to use the shortcut-creation methods already discussed, you need to know the location of the target program. An alternative is to use the Find feature to locate the program, then create a shortcut to it. Exercise 5.8 shows how to create a shortcut (once again, for the Calculator) using this method.

EXERCISE 5.8

Creating a Shortcut Using Find

1. Select Start ➤ Find ➤ Files or Folders. The Find All Files dialog box appears.

2. In the Named text box, type the name of the Calculator program: **CALC.EXE**.

3. Press the Enter key or click on the Find Now button to start the search. The Find window expands, displaying the Calculator program. (If you had typed only **calc** in the text box, the list would show every file with *calc* in the name.) If necessary, use the scrollbars to locate the Calculator program. It will have a Calculator icon next to it.

4. Click on the Calculator icon once to select it, then drag the icon out of the Find window and onto your Desktop. A new shortcut to the Calculator is created.

5. Close the Find All Files dialog box.

Deleting a Shortcut

A shortcut is just another object on your Desktop. It can be moved, copied, or deleted just like anything else. One easy way to delete it is to select it and press the Delete key. Another simple method is by dragging it to the Recycle Bin. Deleting a shortcut does not affect the target program or the other shortcuts in any way. Follow the steps in Exercise 5.9 to delete two of the shortcuts you created in the previous exercises.

Assigning Shortcut Keys

Creating shortcuts on your Desktop is a great way to work more effectively. You can increase your efficiency even more by assigning a keystroke to your shortcut. Not only are shortcut keys faster, they save you from needing to minimize several windows just to get to your shortcut icon.

EXERCISE 5.9

Deleting Shortcuts

1. Select one of your new shortcuts by single-clicking on it.

2. With the shortcut selected, press the Delete key on your keyboard. The Confirm File Delete dialog box appears.

3. Press the Enter key or click on the Yes button. The shortcut has been sent to the Recycle Bin.

4. Select another shortcut and drag it until it is directly on top of the Recycle Bin, then drop it. Confirm the deletion.

You can assign a keyboard key combination to your shortcut through the Shortcut tab of the Shortcut Properties dialog box, shown in Figure 5.19. Follow the steps in Exercise 5.10 to assign the Ctrl+Alt+C keystroke to the Calculator shortcut you created in a previous exercise (one shortcut should remain; you deleted two of the three in Exercise 5.9).

FIGURE 5.19

The Shortcut tab of the Shortcut Properties dialog box

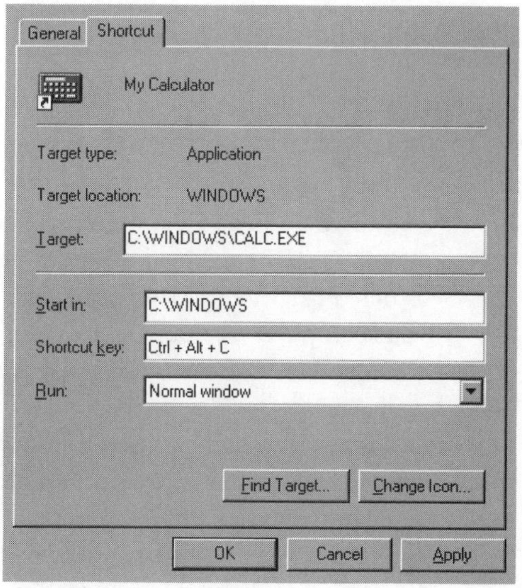

EXERCISE 5.10

Assigning a Keystroke to a Shortcut

1. Right-click on the shortcut called My Calculator, which you created earlier, and select Properties from the pop-up menu. The Shortcut Properties dialog box appears.

2. Click on the Shortcut tab (Figure 5.19).

3. Click on the text box labeled Shortcut Key. The flashing insertion point should be visible in the text box.

4. Press the C key on your keyboard. The keystroke Ctrl+Alt+C is automatically entered in the text box. You can add any letter or number after Ctrl+Alt.

5. Click on the OK button to assign the keystroke and close the dialog box.

6. To test your new shortcut key, hold down the Ctrl key and the Alt key together, and tap the C key. The Calculator should open onto your Desktop.

The Control Panel and Property Sheets

Windows 95 is extremely customizable. These changes can be as simple as changing the date and time on your computer's clock, or as complex as deleting software from your hard drive. When you change the way part of your computer works, you are changing an object's properties. For example, when you change the options for your mouse, you are changing the mouse's properties.

There are usually at least two ways to change an object's properties. If you can see an icon that represents an object, such as the speaker on your Taskbar, you can right-click on the object and choose Properties from the pop-up menu. Another way to change properties is to go to the Control Panel.

The Control Panel is a collection of almost all of the customizable objects on your computer. To open the Control Panel, click Start ➤ Settings ➤ Control Panel. The Control Panel displays a list of customizable objects, similar to the one shown in Figure 5.20.

FIGURE 5.20

The Control Panel

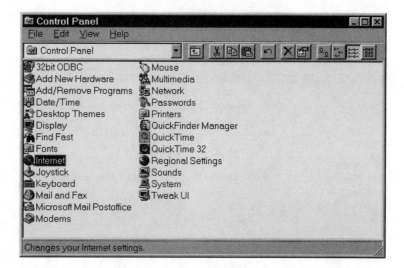

You may have different applets than those shown here. Applications may add icons to the Control Panel.

The Properties dialog boxes (also called *property sheets*) for the various Control Panel objects are self-explanatory and easy to use. The following are the main Control Panel applets:

- **Add New Hardware:** Installs hardware drivers, either by having Windows 95 automatically search for new hardware or by specifying what hardware you have

- **Add/Remove Programs:** Installs additional software and uninstalls applications. You can also make a Startup disk from here.

- **Date/Time:** Changes the date or time on your computer

- **Display:** Changes your display settings, such as color and resolution. (See the end of this chapter for details.)

- **Fonts:** Lists, installs, and removes fonts from your system

- **Internet:** Changes Internet Explorer options

- **Mail and Fax:** Changes e-mail and fax settings. (See Chapter 19 for details.)

- **Modems:** Installs, configures, and tests modems. (See Chapter 17 for details.)

- **Mouse:** Changes the mouse settings

- **Multimedia:** Controls settings for different multimedia items. (See Appendix D for details.)

- **Network:** Controls network settings. (See Chapters 10, 11, and 12 for details.)

- **Passwords:** Changes passwords and configures user profiles and remote administration. (See Chapters 11, 14, and 16 for details.)

- **Printers:** Installs, removes, and configures printers. (See Chapter 13 for details.)

- **System:** Shows hardware configurations (with Device Manager) and contains various performance and troubleshooting options. (See Chapter 21 and Appendix C for details.)

The following sections discuss two of the most common changes users make through the Control Panel: setting mouse options and changing the date and time.

Changing the Mouse Properties

Double-clicking on the mouse icon in the Control Panel displays a Mouse Properties dialog box, or the Mouse Control Panel, similar to the one shown in Figure 5.21. Selecting a tab displays different options within the tab's category.

The mouse properties shown here are for a Microsoft PS2 mouse with a wheel. Your mouse or other pointing device might have different features.

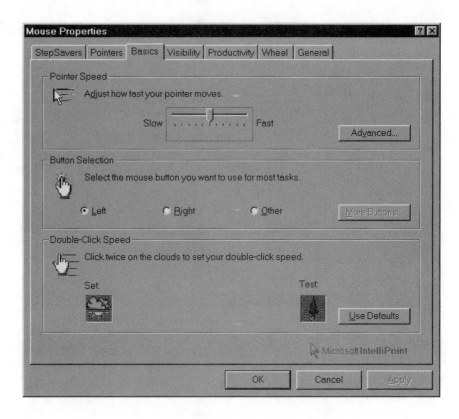

Changing Mouse Pointers

The standard mouse pointers that are the default in Windows 95 work just fine. However, if you want to add a little flair to your pointing, you can choose from several different pointers that are included with the program. These choices are listed on the Pointers tab of the Mouse Properties dialog box, as shown in Figure 5.22.

From this tab, you can select which pointers are used for various mouse actions. You can select a scheme of mouse pointers by using the Scheme drop-down list at the top of the dialog box. New schemes can be purchased or downloaded over the Internet.

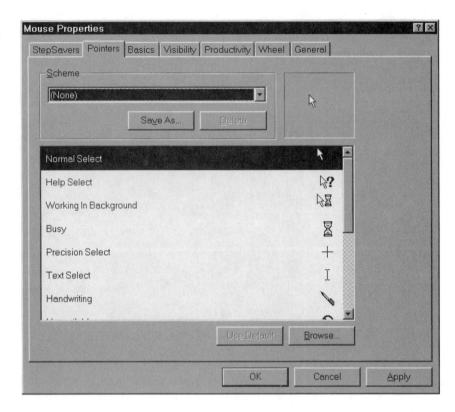

Another alternative is to assign different pointers to the various actions individually. By changing each pointer individually, you create your own custom pointer scheme which can be saved. Follow the steps in Exercise 5.11 to change your mouse pointers.

EXERCISE 5.11

Creating a Mouse Pointer Scheme

1. Select Start ➢ Settings ➢ Control Panel.

2. Double-click on the Mouse icon to display the Mouse Properties dialog box (Figure 5.21).

3. Select the Pointers tab (Figure 5.22).

4. In the pointers selection area, select the pointer action you wish to change, then click on the Browse button.

5. From the Browse dialog box, select the pointer you wish to use for the action, then click on the Open button.

6. Repeat steps 4 and 5 until you have set all of the pointers you wish to use.

7. Click on the Save As button.

8. In the Save Scheme dialog box, type in a name for your new pointer scheme, then click on OK.

9. Click on OK to close the dialog box and save your changes.

Changing the Time and Date Properties

The time and date properties can be changed from the Taskbar or the Control Panel window. To change these properties from the Taskbar, double-click on the digital clock at the end of the Taskbar. To change them from the Control Panel, double-click on the Date/Time icon. Both methods bring up the Date/Time Properties dialog box (or Control Panel), which displays a clock face and a calendar, as shown in Figure 5.23.

At the top of the Date portion of this dialog box, there is a drop-down list for selecting the month and a scrollbox for selecting the correct year. When these are changed, the calendar portion changes, displaying the correct dates and days of the week. Click on the date to set the internal calendar setting on your computer.

The right side of the dialog box displays an analog clock face and a digital counterpart. Use the digital display to set the correct time. You can drag over the displayed time to select it, or click on the portion of the display (hours, minutes, seconds, AM/PM) that you want to change. Clicking on the up or down arrow changes the time. (Clicking on the analog clock face does not change the time.)

The bottom of the dialog box displays your time zone. To change the time zone, click on the Time Zone tab to see the dialog box shown in Figure 5.24.

FIGURE 5.23

The Date/Time
Control Panel

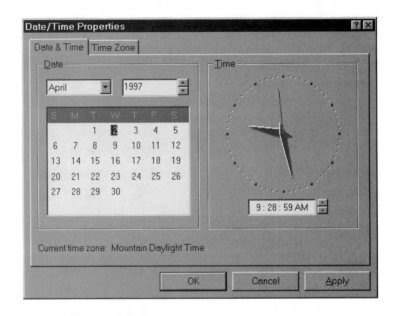

FIGURE 5.24

The Time Zone tab of the
Date/Time Properties
dialog box

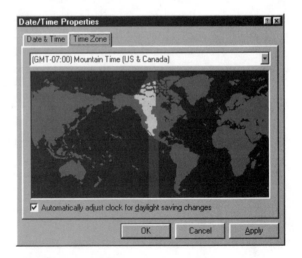

The drop-down list at the top of the dialog box lets you select your time zone. The map in the middle of the display uses a highlighted band to indicate the selected zone. You can use the drop-down list or click on the map directly to change the current time zone. At the bottom of the dialog box is a checkbox for selecting Daylight Savings time. When this feature is active, you are prompted to change the time on the days when Daylight Savings time is invoked or revoked. By default, the Daylight Savings box is active.

The Windows Explorer

When designing Windows 95, the programmers had many design goals. Among them was to create a file browser that was intuitive and easy to learn, so that novice computer users could master this browser easily. On the other hand, the design team realized that experienced computer users would want a very powerful tool for their file management chores. They quickly found that these two design goals were in many ways incompatible. The powerful file management tools were not intuitive to new users, and the intuitive browsers seemed cumbersome to the veterans.

To resolve this dilemma, they created a file browser that operated in two different modes. The default mode is simple and nonthreatening. To use it, a user just double-clicks on the My Computer icon, and a window displays all of the computer's resources. Double-clicking on a resource (the C: drive, for example) opens another window displaying folders and documents. More experienced users could launch the browser with a right-click and use a more powerful, double-pane window.

The design team scored a great success with this "Two Tools in One" approach. The new Windows 95 file browser is called the Windows Explorer. However, when using it in the novice mode, one is said to be using the Open window; in the advanced mode, it is called the Explorer window. We'll examine the Open window first, and then move on to the Explorer window.

Note that you can choose to install the 'Active Desktop' when you install Internet Explorer 4.0. The active desktop basically links your desktop to the browser, and is covered in Chapter 20.

Using the Open Window

Opening the Open window is the default action when you double-click on My Computer, Network Neighborhood, Recycle Bin, or any file folder icon. Opening any of these objects displays a clean and uncomplicated window, which is simple to understand. Figure 5.25 shows the Open window displayed after double-clicking on the My Computer icon.

FIGURE 5.25

Browsing My Computer in the Open window

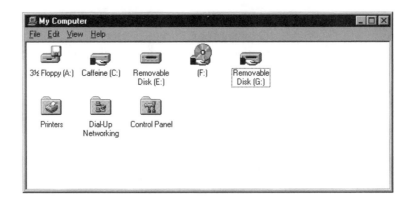

Opening My Computer displays icons representing the storage devices on your computer as well as folders for your printers and the Control Panel. To browse any object in the window, simply double-click on the object. A new window opens, displaying the contents of that object. Double-clicking on an object in the new window opens yet a third window, and so on. Each new window takes you one level deeper into your file folder structure. To move backward through the structure, simply close the top window.

Follow the steps in Exercise 5.12 to browse your C: drive and the Windows folder using the Open window.

EXERCISE 5.12

Browsing with the Open Window

1. Double-click on the My Computer icon. The Open window displays the contents of My Computer. Notice that My Computer appears on the title bar.

2. Double-click on the C: drive icon. A new window opens, displaying the contents of the C: drive. Use the scrollbars to scroll through the contents of the C: drive and locate the Windows folder.

3. Double-click on the Windows folder. A new window opens, displaying the files and folders contained in the Windows folder. Notice that the name of the folder you are browsing appears on the title bar.

4. Double-click on any of the file folders in the Windows folder. Notice that every time you open a new folder, a new window opens.

5. Click on the Close button. The current folder window closes, leaving the previous window open, displaying the contents of the Windows folder.

6. With your Windows folder open, click on the View menu at the top of the Open window. Select items on the View menu to see how they change the display.

Changing the View

You have several useful options available to help you view your folders more comfortably. The default view setting displays the contents of your folders with large icons arranged alphabetically from right to left. Folders are always grouped together, followed by documents.

The View menu lets you choose from four views:

- **Large Icons:** Displays files and folders with large, easy-to-see icons. The folders are grouped at the top of the window and are displayed alphabetically, from left to right. The files are grouped below the folders and are also alphabetized from left to right.

- **Small Icons:** Reduces the size of the icons, allowing the window to display more information in the same space. Folders and files are still grouped and alphabetized from left to right.

- **List:** Uses the small size icons, but alphabetizes folders and files from top to bottom

- **Detail:** Lists folders and files alphabetically from top to bottom and includes important details like file size and modification date. The Detail view also allows you to sort the folder by any detail category. To sort by a category, click on the category title button at the top of the column. Clicking a second time will reverse the sort.

Adding a Status Bar and Toolbar

The View menu also gives you the option of adding a Status bar and a toolbar to the Open window. The Status bar, when active, displays the number of objects in the window or the number of objects selected in the window. The toolbar is a row of buttons that ease the use of the Open window's options. Figure 5.26 shows an Open window with the toolbar and Status bar displayed. To activate either of these features, click on the View menu, then click on the feature.

F I G U R E 5.26

The Open window
with the Status bar and
toolbar displayed

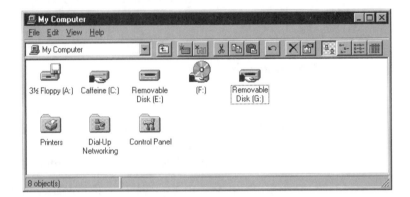

When you activate the toolbar feature, you may need to widen the Open window to display all of the toolbar buttons.

Arranging Icons

The View menu has a couple of other options for organizing the way your files and folders are displayed. The Arrange Icons option lets you organize or sort the contents of a folder by name, type, size, or date. You can also choose Auto Arrange, which will automatically arrange new icons in the scheme you have chosen. The Line Up Icons option straightens up any overlapping items in the window. This is the fastest way to unclutter a messy window.

Setting View Options

The final choice on the View menu is Options. Selecting Options displays a dialog box with three tabs: Folder, View, and File Types.

The Folder Tab   The Folder tab, shown in Figure 5.27, changes the number of windows that will open as you browse the folders on your system. By default, a new window opens each time you open a folder by double-clicking. Many users like this method of browsing. However, you end up with a lot of open windows.

F I G U R E 5.27

The Folder tab of the View Options dialog box

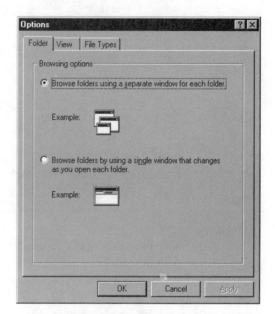

The other browsing choice, for a single window, opens only one window. When you open a second or a third folder, the window changes to display the contents of the open folder. This technique has the advantage of keeping your screen and your Taskbar less cluttered. If you want to move back up through your folders, use the Up One Level button on the toolbar or press the backspace key.

The View tab   The View tab in the Options dialog box, shown in Figure 5.28, instructs Windows 95 to show all files or to hide files of certain file types (hiding files is the default). The types of files that are hidden are system files that Windows 95 or your application programs use internally. These files are hidden by default to prevent new users from accidentally deleting or moving them. Deleting or moving any of these files could cause your computer to malfunction. Unless you are an experienced user and need to see these files, it is recommended that you keep them hidden.

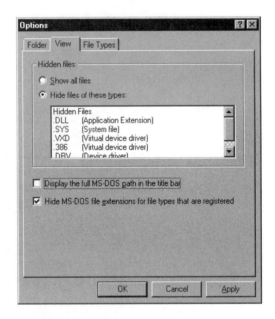

The View tab also has two checkboxes. The first box displays the full MS-DOS path in the title bar of the Open window. This is a good way of keeping track of your location as you browse your file folder structure.

The second checkbox hides MS-DOS extensions for the file types that are registered. These file types are files that you created with your various application programs. For example, when you create a file using the Windows 95 Notepad, that filename automatically gets a .TXT extension. Files created with the Windows Paint program get a .BMP extension. These filename extensions let Windows 95 know which program created each file. That way, when you open a file by double-clicking on it, the correct program is launched with the file. If you organize your files well, you should not need to see the extension. The registered file types appear on the File Types tab, discussed next.

Hiding registered file types has another advantage. When you create a file without launching an application first (discussed later), you almost always need to change the default filename Windows 95 assigns to the new file. If your registered file extensions are displayed, you must include the correct extension when renaming the file. If you type in the wrong extension, you'll be disappointed when you try to open that file. If your registered file extensions are hidden, they are protected from change and do not need to be included when renaming a file.

The File Types Tab   As explained in the previous section, when you create a new file in an application program and give the file a name, that filename automatically receives an extension. The extension identifies the file as being created by a certain application. For example, Microsoft Word files automatically receive a .DOC extension. Windows 95 calls these filename extensions *file types*. These file types are registered automatically when an application is installed on your computer.

The File Types tab of the Options dialog box, shown in Figure 5.29, displays a list of the file extensions and the application programs associated with them. From this tab, you can change the application association and add or delete any file type. You can also change the icon that is displayed next to a filename.

FIGURE 5.29

The File Types tab of the View Options dialog box

File types are only registered automatically if the application is written for Windows 95. Installing older, Windows 3.1 programs will not automatically register file extensions. If you want these files to launch a program, you need to register the file types manually in the File Types tab of the View Options dialog box.

The Explorer Window

As elegant and simple as the Open window is, experienced computer users are sometimes frustrated by its lack of power. For those who want more, Windows 95 provides the Windows Explorer. Although similar to the Open window, the Windows Explorer displays much more information on the screen and is packed with powerful file management tools.

There are several ways to launch the Windows Explorer. For many users, choosing Start ➤ Programs ➤ Windows Explorer is the preferred method. Another, faster way is to right-click on the My Computer icon and select Explore. Others prefer to create a shortcut on their Desktop. Using the right-click method, the Windows Explorer displays information in a two-pane window, like the one shown in Figure 5.30.

FIGURE 5.30

The Explorer window

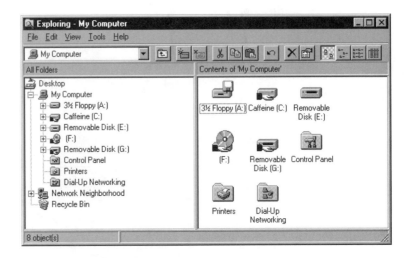

The pane on the left is the Navigation pane. Through the Navigation pane, you can explore all of the resources on your computer. The right pane is the Contents pane. The Contents pane displays the contents of whatever is selected in the Navigation pane. Also notice that the Windows Explorer already has the Status bar and toolbar active.

Follow the steps in Exercise 5.13 to investigate and use the different parts of the Explorer window.

EXERCISE 5.13

Using the Explorer's Navigation and Contents Panes

1. If you have not already done so, close all of the open windows. Launch the Windows Explorer by right-clicking on the My Computer icon on your Desktop. The Explorer two-pane view displays all resources on your Desktop.

In the Navigation pane, you should see small plus signs and minus signs. A plus sign next to an object signifies that the object can be expanded to show more depth. A minus sign next to an object means that object is currently expanded. Notice the minus sign next to My Computer.

2. Click on the minus sign. The objects under My Computer are hidden, showing only the program objects directly on your Desktop. The minus sign becomes a plus sign.

3. Click on the plus sign. This expands My Computer, revealing your storage devices and system folders.

4. Click on the plus sign next to your C: drive. All of your first-level file folders are displayed below the C: drive icon. The plus sign becomes a minus sign.

It is important to notice that clicking on plus or minus signs does not select any folder or object; it only shows or hides any nested levels. If an expanded level is longer than the Navigation pane can display, a scrollbar will appear on the pane's right side.

5. If necessary, use the scrollbar to scroll through the folders until you can see the Windows folder.

6. Click on the Windows folder once. The Windows folder icon changes to resemble an open file folder and the name of the folder is highlighted. You have selected the Windows folder. Notice that single-clicking the folder did not expand it.

---

7. Double-click on the Windows folder. Double-clicking on the folder expanded it; it's the same as clicking on the folder's plus sign. (Double-clicking on the Windows folder a second time would collapse it.)

With the Windows folder selected and expanded, notice the Contents pane. The Contents pane displays the same folders you see expanded on the Navigation pane. This makes sense, because those folders are contained in the Windows folder. The Contents pane also displays the files in the Windows folder. If there are more objects than will fit in the Contents pane, a scrollbar is displayed.

Notice the Status bar at the bottom of the Explorer. It reports how many objects are in the Windows folder, how much storage space the folder occupies, and how much free disk space still exists on the drive. The toolbar spans the top of the Explorer window.

8. Move your mouse pointer to the four buttons on the right side of the toolbar. These four buttons control the view of the Contents pane. The four views are the same as in the Open window, described in the "Changing the View" section earlier in this chapter. Experiment with the four view buttons.

Using the File Management Tools

Understanding the Explorer window is the key to using the powerful file management tools available in Windows 95. Now that you've explored the Navigation and the Contents panes of the Explorer window, we'll focus on managing the files and folders that make up the bulk of your computer's storage capacity.

Creating New Folders and Files

Most paper-based filing systems use a filing cabinet. The filing cabinet has several drawers, and each drawer holds several file folders. Documents are placed into these file folders in some organized fashion.

We use the filing cabinet as a metaphor or a model when organizing the documents (files) on a computer. Consider each drive on your computer as a drawer in a filing cabinet. Your floppy drive, the A: drive, is the A: drawer, your C: drive is the C: drawer, and so on. Each drawer holds file folders, which in turn hold files. The only real difference is that in your electronic filing cabinet, you can nest file folders inside of other file folders. This allows you to create a deep and well-organized file folder structure.

You can select a folder in the Navigation pane and then create a new folder beneath it by right-clicking on the Contents pane and choosing New ➣ Folder.

Follow the steps in Exercise 5.14 to create several new file folders within the Explorer window. The first folder will be a first-level folder (the top level), named Level 1. The other folders will be second level or lower folders nested within the Level 1 folder. (Folders nested in this manner are sometimes called *parent folders* and *daughter folders*.) Then you will create a few sample documents in the Level 1 folder.

EXERCISE 5.14

Creating New File Folders and Documents

1. Launch the Windows Explorer (right-click on the My Computer icon on your Desktop) and select your C: drive in the Navigation pane. If necessary, expand the C: drive by clicking on the plus sign next to the C: drive icon. Make sure the C: drive icon is selected.

2. Select File ➣ New ➣ Folder. A new file folder appears in the Contents pane with the name New Folder. The name is highlighted and ready for renaming.

3. Type the name **Level 1** and press the Enter key. (Yes, it's okay to use a space—see the section on long filenames.) You should see the Level 1 folder in the Contents pane as well as the Navigator pane.

4. Click on the Level 1 folder in the Navigator pane to select it. The Contents pane should be empty. Every new folder you create will be attached to whatever is selected at the time of creation. When creating a nested folder, make sure to start with the correct folder selected. Make sure the Level 1 folder is selected in the Navigator pane.

---

5. Select File ➤ New ➤ Folder and type **Level 2** to create a nested folder. The new folder appears in the Contents pane. In the Navigator pane, the Level 1 folder has acquired a plus sign, indicating a folder is nested within it. Click on the Level 1 plus sign to reveal the new folder.

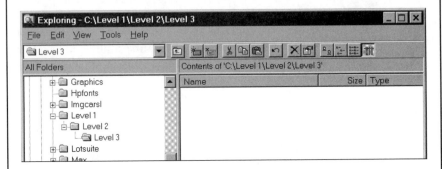

6. Use the same method to create a Level 3 folder nested within your Level 2 folder. You now have a basic file folder structure that should look like the example shown above.

7. In the Navigator pane of the Explorer, select the Level 1 folder. (The Contents pane contains only the Level 2 folder.)

8. From the menu at the top of the window, select File ➤ New ➤ Text Document. Type in the name **Document 1** and press the Enter key. You have just created a blank text document named Document 1 in the Level 1 folder.

9. Using the same method, create seven more (for a total of eight) blank documents in the Level 1 folder. The documents don't need to be text documents—any type will do. Name them Document 2 through Document 8.

Your eight new documents should be displayed in the Contents pane. Notice that they are displayed in the Contents pane only, not in the Navigator pane.

By default, filename extensions are hidden from view. Hiding the filename extensions allows you to name a document without including the extension. If you have changed this to show filename extensions, you must type the correct file extension when you are naming a document. For example, if you have chosen to view (and thus be able to edit) your extensions, you must type the extension .TXT at the end of a text document in order to keep it as a text document. To change your current setting, select View ➤ Options ➤ View from the menu at the top of the Explorer window.

Moving and Copying Files

You can move a file from one folder to another by dragging and dropping it. To move more than one file at a time, use the Ctrl-click or Shift-click to select them first, and then drag-and-drop them together.

Follow the steps in Exercise 5.15 to move documents from the Level 1 folder to the Level 3 folder.

EXERCISE 5.15

Moving Documents

1. The three file folders that you created earlier should be displayed in the Explorer's Navigation pane. The Level 1 folder is selected, displaying your documents in the Contents pane. Select the List View button from the toolbar.

2. Select Document 1. Drag Document 1 from the Contents pane into the Navigation pane until it is directly over the Level 3 folder and drop it. Document 1 has been moved from the Level 1 folder to the Level 3 folder.

3. Select the Level 3 folder to confirm that Document 1 has been moved. Then return to the Level 1 folder.

4. Select Document 2 from the Contents pane. Press and hold down the Ctrl key on your keyboard while you select Document 4 and Document 7. Then release the Ctrl key. The three documents will remain selected. Place the mouse pointer over any of the three selected documents, drag them to the Level 3 folder, and drop them.

EXERCISE 5.15 (CONTINUED FROM PREVIOUS PAGE)

5. Select Document 3 from the Contents pane. Press and hold down the Shift key on your keyboard while you select Document 8, and then release the Shift key. All of the documents are selected. Drag the group to the Level 3 folder and drop them. All of the documents have been moved from the Level 1 folder to the Level 3 folder.

6. Select the Level 3 folder and view the Contents pane.

An easy mistake to make is accidentally trying to move a file into the same folder that it is already in. If this happens, you will receive an error message stating that the source and destination names are the same. Click on the OK button and try again.

Copying files leaves the original in its current folder and places an exact duplicate in another folder. To activate the Copy feature, hold down the Ctrl key while dragging and dropping the document. You can copy several documents at the same time by holding the Ctrl key down while selecting documents, and keeping it down while you drag-and-drop. To select a contiguous group of files, hold down the Shift key while selecting them. Then release the Shift key and hold down the Ctrl key while dragging and dropping them.

When copying documents using the Ctrl key, be sure to drop the documents in the destination folder before releasing the Ctrl key. Releasing the Ctrl key too soon will cancel the copy operation.

Moving and Copying Folders

The techniques you have learned for copying and moving files work for folders as well. When you move a folder, the entire contents of the folder, including all documents and nested folders, will go with it. When copying a folder, you create a copy of every document and nested folder as well. You can use these techniques to copy files or entire folders from one drive to another.

Follow the steps in Exercise 5.16 to copy and move folders in the Navigation pane of the Windows Explorer.

EXERCISE 5.16

Moving and Copying Folders

1. In the Navigation pane, select the Level 3 folder. Drag the Level 3 folder up to the Level 1 folder and drop it. The Level 3 folder and its documents are now nested directly in the Level 1 folder.

2. Select the Level 3 folder in the Navigator pane. Hold down the Ctrl key, drag the Level 3 folder to the Level 2 folder, and drop it. You now have two Level 3 folders with identical files in each.

3. Place a blank, formatted floppy disk in your A: drive. Select the Level 1 folder in the Navigation pane. Drag the Level 1 folder toward the top of the Navigation pane. If necessary, the Navigation pane will automatically scroll up. When your A: drive is visible, drop the folder on that drive. The entire file folder structure, complete with all of the documents, is copied to your floppy drive.

Note that when you copy a folder or file to another drive, you do not need to hold down the Ctrl key. Copying is automatic when dragging folders or documents from one drive to another.

 When you select a document or a file folder, click on the icon rather than the name. Sometimes, clicking on the name will open the Rename feature by mistake.

Display Improvements in Windows 95

Users frequently take advantage of their ability to change the way things look in Windows. Windows 95 adds increased flexibility and functions for configuring the display.

Windows 95 addresses many of the problems of Windows 3.1 display drivers by providing enhanced functionality and easier customization and setup. Benefits of the new display driver support include the following:

- The mini-driver architecture supports video display drivers written by independent hardware vendors (IHVs). This improves support for the range of products offered by IHVs and provides more stable and reliable drivers.

- The system adds support for new features, including the ability to change video resolution "on the fly" without restarting Windows 95.

- The Windows 95 Setup program can automatically detect the video display adapter installed in the PC and install the appropriate Windows 95 display driver (Plug and Play).

- If you need to change the display adapter or monitor type, Windows 95 will supply a list of compatible devices for you to choose from. This reduces the risk of damaging your hardware by choosing an incompatible driver.

- The system has more support for laptop users with docking stations. Windows 95 provides video driver support between the video card in the portable computer and the video card in the base unit by automatically switching between them.

- If a video driver fails to load or initialize when the system starts, Windows 95 will default to a generic VGA video driver. Users can fix the problem from within Windows 95.

- Display properties are consolidated in the Display Control Panel. This allows easy customization of the colors, wallpaper, screen saver, and display adapter settings from a single location.

- The system includes support for new generations of hardware and device functionality, such as Energy Star Monitors (which can power down to save energy), and detection of monitor properties, such as the maximum resolution supported. Some monitors include an Optimal setting, which adjusts the display to cover the entire screen.

Configuring the Display

From the Display Control Panel, you can configure the following:

- Display and monitor type or driver
- Video resolution on the fly without restarting Windows 95
- Color palette
- Font size to increase or decrease magnification
- Color schemes and text styles for all screen elements, including dialog boxes, menus, and title bars
- Screen savers, with options for using passwords and customization
- Energy-saving features of your monitor (if applicable)
- Background pattern and wallpaper, with options to edit the pattern and choose custom bitmaps
- Graphics hardware settings

To quickly access the display properties, right-click on the Desktop, then choose Properties.

Changing the Color Palette, Resolution, and Font Size

The Settings tab of the Display Properties dialog box, shown in Figure 5.31, allows you to configure several display properties. If you are using a Plug-and-Play-compliant display adapter and driver that support on-the-fly changes, you will not need to restart the computer for the changes to take effect. Otherwise, Windows 95 will prompt you to restart the computer.

Microsoft supplies a simple utility that is really a shortcut to the Settings tab of the Display Properties dialog box. QUICKRES.EXE creates a small icon on the Taskbar next to your clock. This utility is found in the Windows 95 Resource Kit and in the Power Toys package.

FIGURE 5.31

The Settings tab of the
Display Properties
dialog box

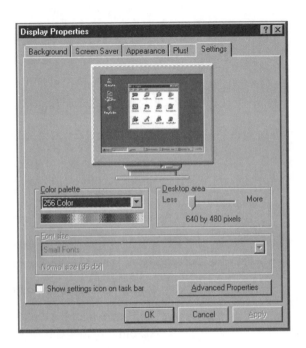

The following are the options on the Settings tab:

- **Color palette:** Specifies the number of colors displayed for your display adapter. The color palette has four choices: 16 colors, 256 colors, High Color (16 bit), or True Color (24 bit). More colors equal more memory required on the video card. More colors at higher resolutions equal even more required memory.

- **Desktop area:** Increases or decreases the amount of information on your screen. The higher the number of pixels for the display, referred to as *resolution*, the smaller everything appears on your screen. Again, your type of monitor or display adapter determines whether you can change this setting.

- **Font size:** Allows you to set the magnification of the font size used by the Desktop, similar to the zoom capabilities of word processors. You can increase the displayed size of affected areas for the text in the client window, icons, icon titles, and the spacing between icons. This setting also affects the text in window titles, menus (including the Start menu), and dialog boxes. Typically, the selections available are Small Fonts, Large Fonts, and Other for custom settings.

The trade-off with text size on the screen is real estate. The bigger the displayed text, the smaller the size of your "lot." For example, when the setting is Large Fonts, a 14-inch monitor at 640 × 480 resolution can display 20 lines of text—less than a third of a page. However, when the setting is Small Fonts, the same size monitor at 800 × 600 resolution can display 31 lines of text.

As you change the color palette or Desktop area, notice how the display on the sample monitor models your options before you apply your changes. This capability has been referred to as *What You See Before You Get It* (WYSBYGI).

Changing the Driver and Monitor Type

Not only are the video display adapters more stable and reliable in Windows 95, they are also automatically detected and installed during setup. Microsoft achieved this by developing many display drivers with the cooperation of all major display controller IHVs. This ensures broad display support for the range of products offered by vendors such as ATI Technologies, Cirrus Logic, Diamond Technologies, and others. This mini-driver architecture support for display drivers also results in improved graphic performance over Windows 3.1.

When Windows 95 is installed, the Setup program attempts to determine what type of video display adapter is installed in your computer by examining the chip set on your video adapter. It will often display a generic video chip type (such as S3 compatible) for your display adapter. It will also attempt to match your video resolution and color depth from your previous version of Windows, if you are upgrading.

If you need to change the driver or monitor type, click on the Advanced Properties button in the Settings tab of the Display Properties dialog box to get to the Change Display Type dialog box, shown in Figure 5.32.

From the Adapter tab, you can go to the Select Device dialog box, shown in Figure 5.33, and choose a manufacturer and model for your device.

Follow the steps in Exercise 5.17 to change the display driver.

Some monitors can be damaged by incorrect display settings. Carefully check the manual for your monitor before choosing a new setting. You can also reduce the risk by choosing the Show compatible devices option and selecting one of those choices only.

F I G U R E 5.32

The Adapter tab of the
Advanced Display
Properties dialog box

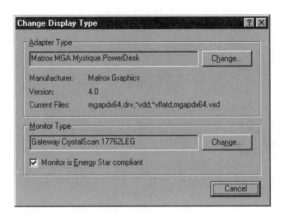

F I G U R E 5.33

The Select Device
dialog box shows video
drivers that come with
Windows 95.

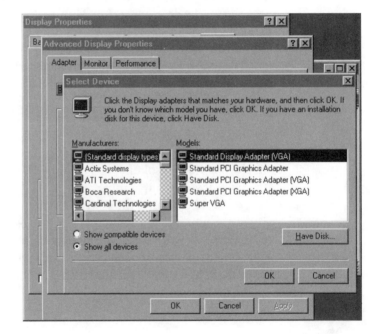

NOTE Depending on the version of Windows 95 you're using, your screens may look slightly different than the ones shown here. Although there may be slight differences in their appearance, the procedures for using them are the same.

EXERCISE 5.17

Changing the Display Driver

1. Go to Control Panel ➤ Display.

2. Click on the Settings tab.

3. Click on the Advanced Properties button.

4. In the Adapter tab of the Advanced Display Properties dialog box, click on the Change button to get to the Select Device dialog box (Figure 5.33).

5. Select the manufacturer and model for your adapter. If you don't see your manufacturer, you can always select Standard display types.

6. Click on OK and then close the dialog box. (Select Cancel if you don't want to save your changes.)

7. When Windows 95 prompts you to restart your computer for the settings to take effect, select OK.

Refining the Display's Appearance

The default scheme for colors and fonts is okay, but it assumes the worst hardware. Windows 95 allows you to make a number of improvements in how your Desktop and the objects on it look.

The strengths and limitations of your video card, video driver, and monitor combination are reflected in the range of choices you have in the Settings tab of the Display Properties dialog box. Within the limits of your settings for the number of colors and the magnification of text, you have the ability to make further refinements. These refinements are made in the Appearance tab of the Display Properties dialog box, shown in Figure 5.34.

The top part of the tab shows a mock display of typical windows and Desktop objects. When you click an object in this part of the dialog box, the description in the Item text box changes to reflect the name of that object. You can change the color, size, font style, font size, and font color associated with the selected Desktop object.

The Items drop-down box lists 18 Desktop objects, 12 of which are displayed in the mock Desktop window at the top of the Appearance tab. The other items, such as Horizontal and Vertical Icon Spacing, do not appear in the mock window and must be selected from the list.

FIGURE 5.34

The Appearance tab of the Display Properties dialog box

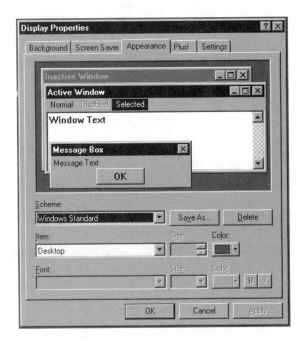

 You can change the appearance of other Desktop objects by editing the registry directly or by using tools (such as Power Toys) that edit the registry for you. See Chapter 6 for information about editing the registry.

Using Schemes

A complete collection of attributes is referred to as a *scheme*. Windows 95 comes with 28 predefined schemes. These schemes are more comprehensive than those that came with Windows 3.1. Not only do they include color settings, but they also set sizes, font styles, font sizes, and font colors as well. To see how a predefined scheme looks, choose it from the Scheme drop-down list in the Appearance tab. The scheme will be displayed in the mock Desktop above.

The changes you make to the attributes of the Desktop objects are saved in the unnamed "current" scheme. If you choose a predefined scheme, you will lose any modifications you have made to it unless you name the scheme. When you want to save a scheme, click on the Save As button and type in the new name.

You can also add your own schemes or modify pieces of the predefined schemes. Be sure to save your modifications with a new name so you do not overwrite the predefined names.

Setting Screen Saver Options

Windows 95 comes with predefined screen savers, as well as energy-saving features. You can also buy additional screen savers from third-party software developers or create your own. Another great place to get schemes is to download them from Web sites (one of our favorites is www.winfiles.com). You set screen saver options from the Screen Saver tab of the Display Properties dialog box, shown in Figure 5.35.

Click on the Screen Saver drop-down to display a list of the built-in screen savers, as well as any others that you have installed. The Settings button allows you to customize the settings for a specific screen saver. The options include speed, density, number of lines or curves, colors, and other settings. As in the other tabs of the Display dialog box, you can see your choices in the mock display at the top part of the dialog box before applying them. The selected screen saver will appear when you click on the Preview button.

Check the Password protected box if you want to assign a password with the screen saver to protect the machine from unauthorized use. Then the screen saver will not clear from the screen unless the correct password is entered. The Wait setting specifies how much time will elapse before Windows 95 displays the selected screen saver or password dialog box.

F I G U R E 5.35

The Screen Saver tab of
the Display Properties
dialog box

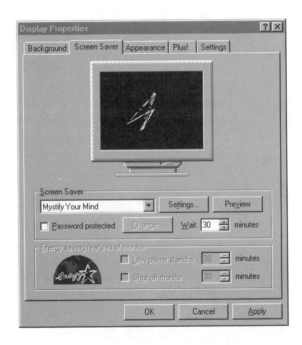

The options in the Energy saving features of monitor section of the dialog box will be available if your hardware supports this feature. The display monitor is typically one of the most "power-hungry" components of a computer. Using the options in this section, you can set an amount of time to elapse after the screen saver has displayed before the monitor goes into low-power standby mode and before the monitor shuts off. To take advantage of these power-efficient features, both your display adapter and monitor must meet the Energy Star specifications.

For more information about the Energy Star program, go to the EPA's Web site at www.epa.gov/energystar.html.

Setting Background Options

Windows 95 comes with built-in patterns and wallpaper designs. Like screen savers, patterns and wallpaper are available from third-party vendors, and you can also create your own. The pattern and wallpaper options are on the Background tab of the Display Properties dialog box, shown in Figure 5.36.

From the Pattern list, you can choose a pattern, such as bricks, daisies, or tile, for your Desktop. The pattern will appear in the color selected in the Appearance tab. Click on the Edit Pattern button to change the density of the pattern.

FIGURE 5.36

The Background tab of
the Display Properties
dialog box

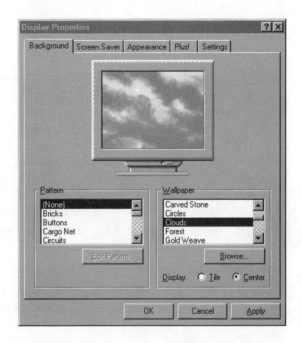

Choosing from the Wallpaper list puts that selection on your Desktop. A wallpaper choice overrides a pattern; typically you choose one or the other, but not both. Click on the Browse button if you want to select other bitmap files to be used as wallpaper. The tab also offers two options for the display of your wallpaper:

- **Tile:** Displays multiple copies of the wallpaper. This style looks good with small pictures.

- **Center:** Displays a single copy of the wallpaper in the center of the Desktop. This style works well with a large picture.

If you're using Internet Explorer 3.x or 4.x, you can hang up new wallpaper by right-clicking on any Web page and choosing the Set As Wallpaper option. This trick lets you turn any picture from a Web page into your Windows Desktop wallpaper.

The Plus! tab allows you to alter the way icons and wallpaper appear on the Desktop. See Chapter 8 for information about installing and using the Microsoft Plus! software.

Troubleshooting Display Problems

Users love to change both the colors and resolution of their screens, which can cause problems if the wrong settings are chosen. Display-related problems can involve anything from small irregularities on the screen to system failure. Windows 95 will let you select a wrong driver, although it tries to help by showing you just the compatible drivers. The following sections suggest some ways to troubleshoot display-related problems.

Even though this area is not specified in the objectives, you will probably have questions on the test about troubleshooting display drivers.

A good resource for diagnosing display-related problems is the Hardware Conflict troubleshooting aid in the online Help.

Starting in Safe Mode

As explained in Chapter 3, starting the system in Safe mode changes the driver to the standard VGA mode (640 × 480 pixels, 16 colors). This method is generally used if the display does not work correctly:

- Restart the computer, and then press F8 when the "Starting Windows 95" message appears.

- Choose Safe Mode from the Startup menu.

If this resolves the display problem, then you know that the display driver may be involved. Try reinstalling the driver or replacing it with an upgraded driver. If, after rebooting, you are still having problems, try changing the performance settings, as described in the next section.

Changing Graphics Performance Settings

If Safe mode system startup did not solve the problem, you can try adjusting the graphics hardware acceleration feature. You can do this from the Performance tab of the System Control Panel. Follow the steps in Exercise 5.18 to use this technique to discover if your problems are related to the display adapter.

EXERCISE 5.18

Changing the Graphics Hardware Acceleration

1. Go to Control Panel ➤ System.

2. Click on the Performance tab.

3. In the Advanced Settings section at the bottom of the dialog box, click on the Graphics button. This displays a dialog box with a slider control, as shown below.

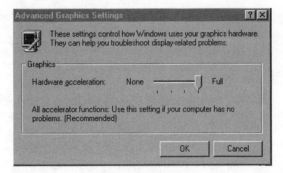

4. Drag the slider across the notches, from None to Full (the default) and read the description that appears for each of the four settings:

■ **None:** Turns off the acceleration setting. This can be used to correct problems if your computer frequently stops responding to input, or has other severe problems. This setting adds SafeMode=2 in the Windows section of WIN.INI, which removes all driver acceleration support.

■ **Basic:** Use this setting to correct more severe problems such as unexpected errors in applications. This setting prevents some bit block transfers from being performed on the display card and disables memory-mapped I/O from some display drivers. This adds SwCursor=1 and Mmio=0 to the Display section of SYSTEM.INI, and SafeMode=1 to the Windows section of WIN.INI.

EXERCISE 5.18 (CONTINUED FROM PREVIOUS PAGE)

- **Most:** Use this setting to correct problems with the mouse pointer. This disables hardware cursor support in the display driver by adding SwCursor=1 to the Display section of SYSTEM.INI.

- **Full(All):** Turns on all graphics hardware acceleration features that are available in the display driver.

5. To save your changes, choose OK twice. (Select Cancel if you don't want to save your changes.)

6. Restart Windows 95 for the setting to take effect.

Changing to a VGA Display Driver

If an error occurs during the display adapter initialization, the computer may stop responding. This problem may occur if you changed the resolution from the default setting to 1024 × 768 pixels, 256 colors. If your video card is an accelerator card instead of nonaccelerated SVGA (which is what the higher setting is designed for), then that could be causing the problem. Restart the computer and change your display driver to VGA.

To choose the VGA display driver, restart the computer in Safe mode (by pressing F8 when you see the "Starting Windows 95" message) and change the adapter from the Display Control Panel (see Exercise 5.17). You will need to click on the Show all devices button, and then choose Standard display types in the Manufacturers list and Standard Display Adapter (VGA) in the Models list (see Figure 5.33, earlier in the chapter). If you want to use a higher-resolution display driver, consult your display adapter manufacturer for the correct driver to choose.

If you installed DirectX support (Microsoft's new multimedia API set), you may experience incompatibility problems with older applications or display adapters. These incompatibilities happen almost exclusively with the display driver part of DirectX. There is not much you can do to resolve DirectX driver incompatibilities except check for new versions of the display driver from your manufacturer. See Appendix D for more information about DirectX.

Using the Keyboard Instead of the Mouse

As users become more familiar with Windows 95, they often notice that using the mouse for every action slows down their work. For a user who is comfortable with the keyboard, there are many keyboard shortcuts available. These keyboard shortcuts are not only for speed typists and computer gurus; it is wise for everyone to know a few.

Table 5.1 lists the most commonly used actions usually performed with a mouse and their keystroke counterparts.

T A B L E 5.1 Keystrokes for Common Actions	**Action**	**Keystrokes**
	Minimize a program window	Alt+Spacebar Minimize
	Minimize a document window	Alt+Minus Minimize
	Maximize a floating program window	Alt+Spacebar Maximize
	Maximize a floating document window	Alt+Minus Maximize
	Resize a floating program window	Alt+Spacebar Size (use arrow keys to resize; press Esc or Enter when finished)
	Resize a floating document window	Alt+Minus Size (use arrow keys to resize; press Esc or Enter when finished)
	Move among open programs using the icon box	Alt+Tab
	Move among open programs directly	Alt+Esc
	Move through a dialog box	Tab
	Activate a drop-down list in a dialog box	Arrow
	Mark a radio button or checkbox	Spacebar
	Close a program window	Alt+F4
	Close a document window	Ctrl+F4

	Action	Keystrokes
T A B L E 5.1 (*cont.*) Keystrokes for Common Actions	Activate the Start menu	Ctrl+Esc or Windows button
	Rename the selected item	F2
	Start Find Files or Folders	F3
	Drop the folder selection in Explorer	F4
	Refresh	F5
	Open Properties dialog box	Alt+Enter
	Cut a selected item	Ctrl+X or Shift+Delete
	Copy a selected item	Ctrl+C
	Paste	Ctrl+V or Shift+Insert
	Undo	Ctrl+Z

Summary

Windows 95 is an extremely feature-rich operating system. Virtually every aspect of Windows 95 reflects improvements over Windows 3.1 and Windows for Workgroups.

The interface has been simplified by the use of the Desktop and Taskbar. Windows 95 is a revolutionary step away from the DOS operating system, and understanding the new interface is essential to the computer support professional. While the new interface might seem confusing at first, soon the power and flexibility of the Windows 95 interface is guaranteed to win almost everyone over.

In this chapter, you learned about the object-oriented approach of Windows 95, and how this approach is reflected in the new Desktop. We reviewed the new features, including the Taskbar, right-click menus, the file-finding feature, the improved Help system, and the Recycle Bin for storing deleted files. We also discussed the document-centered approach taken by Windows 95.

Then we explained how to customize and configure Windows 95, including setting up new hardware, configuring the Taskbar, customizing the Start menu, using the Control Panel, and creating shortcuts. We then talked about the new Windows Explorer and its file management tools.

Windows 95 includes many new display customization and configuration options. Plug-and-Play support makes it easy to install display devices. The Display Control Panel organizes all the display-related options in a single location. From there, you can change driver and monitor settings. You can also set colors, resolution, and font size, as well as the colors and sizes used for individual Desktop items. The Display Control Panel also contains settings for screen savers, patterns, and wallpaper.

Because the display is so often changed, knowing how to troubleshoot display-related problems is essential. This chapter presented some troubleshooting techniques, including Safe mode booting, adjusting graphics performance settings, and changing to a VGA display driver.

Review Questions

1. What are the new names for directories and files?

   A. Directories and documents

   B. Directories and folders

   C. Folders and files

   D. Folders and documents

2. What is the name of the new program that lets you see folders and files?

   A. Windows Explorer

   B. File Manager Plus

   C. Browser

   D. Folder Manager

3. What feature prevents novice users from changing document associations?

    A. Locking Explorer to Read-Only Mode

    B. Locking the taskbar

    C. Hiding file extensions

    D. Hiding long filenames

4. The Taskbar can be moved to which side of the Desktop? (Select all that apply.)

    A. Top

    B. Right

    C. Left

    D. Bottom

5. What is the name of the main working area in Windows 95?

    A. The screen

    B. The Temp folder

    C. The Windows folder

    D. The Desktop

6. What is the new focus for managing your work in Windows 95?

    A. Documents

    B. Applications

    C. Date of files

    D. Name of user

7. What new feature of Windows 95 allows you to undelete files?

   A. The Trash Can

   B. The Undo command

   C. The Undelete utility

   D. The Recycle Bin

8. Which mouse button is used in Windows 95?

   A. The left mouse button

   B. The right mouse button

   C. Both mouse buttons

   D. Neither mouse button—keyboard commands are the main way of doing things.

9. How many characters can a long filename have in Windows 95?

   A. 8.3

   B. 254

   C. 255

   D. 512

10. Which of the following long filenames are valid? (Select all that apply.)

   A. This is a valid filename

   B. This.is.a.valid.filename

   C. This_is_a_valid_filename

   D. Thisisavalidfilename

11. How does Windows 95 ensure backward compatibility with earlier versions of MS-DOS and applications?

    A. Windows 95 autogenerates a valid 8.3 filename.

    B. Windows 95 operates in "MS-DOS 6.22 compatibility mode."

    C. The previous version of MS-DOS is run side-by-side with Windows 95.

    D. Windows 95 does nothing special to ensure compatibility.

12. If using the correct video driver, Windows 95 helps protect you from fatal configuration errors by which of the following?

    A. By not allowing you to choose a display property your video adapter does not support

    B. By handling all video card configurations for you

    C. By automatically updating video drivers when you connect to the Internet

    D. By automatically testing your video card when the screen saver is running

13. What is the default setting of the graphics hardware acceleration feature?

    A. Basic

    B. None

    C. Full

    D. Most

14. If starting the system in Safe mode solves your display problem, what may have caused the problem?

   A. Bit block transfers were being prevented from performing on the display card.

   B. Mouse pointer settings were incorrect.

   C. The display driver is incorrect.

   D. Choices A and C

15. Unexpected errors in applications can be due to which of the following? (Select all that apply.)

   A. Memory problems

   B. Display problems

   C. Bad coding in the application

   D. Hard drive problems

16. In order to troubleshoot your graphics card, the setting for hardware acceleration should be set to:

   A. Basic

   B. None

   C. Full

   D. Most

17. In order to see all possible choices for video card drivers, you should pick which option when choosing a new driver?

   A. Show Compatible Devices

   B. Have Disk

   C. Show All Devices

   D. Show All Device Choices

CHAPTER

6

The Registry

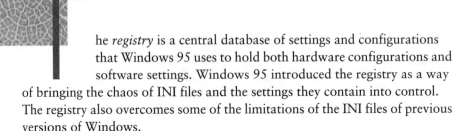

he *registry* is a central database of settings and configurations that Windows 95 uses to hold both hardware configurations and software settings. Windows 95 introduced the registry as a way of bringing the chaos of INI files and the settings they contain into control. The registry also overcomes some of the limitations of the INI files of previous versions of Windows.

Most users will seldom, if ever, need to worry about the registry, let alone edit it directly. As an administrator or technical support professional, understanding and being able to troubleshoot and edit the registry is vital to your success as a "miracle worker."

The registry is used by almost every aspect of Windows 95:

- **Hardware:** Stores Plug-and-Play data

- **Applications:** Store settings, paths, and DLL information

- **Device drivers:** Store settings, versions, and filenames

- **Operating system:** Tracks installed software, drivers, settings, and associations

Although INI files worked well in the past, their limitations quickly became evident. However, INI files are important to understand, not only because the registry solves most, if not all, of the limitations of INI files, but also because Windows 95 still supports INI files for backward compatibility.

This chapter begins with a review of INI files, and then moves on to registry-related topics: using the Registry Editor program, registry components, backing up and restoring the registry, modifying the registry, and troubleshooting registry problems.

Understanding INI Files

Both the operating system and applications previously stored their information in the SYSTEM.INI file, the WINDOWS.INI file, or any other INI file they chose. Types of information stored in INI files included paths, DLLs and their paths and versions, settings that the user had saved, and various drivers and their configurations. Finding and changing values in the INI files were extremely difficult, if not impossible. However, users and administrators quickly found that editing the INI files manually was not only possible, but sometimes the only way a problem could be fixed, or advanced functionality could be addressed.

Limitations of INI Files

For simple purposes, the INI files were adequate, but the limitations of INI files soon became apparent when more than one user wanted to use a computer. INI files could hold only a single value for any variable, which meant that every user on a particular system shared the same settings. In order to share a computer, and have users with different settings, elaborate batch files were necessary. These batch files would copy an individual's version of the INI files into the Window's directory before that user loaded Windows.

Also, INI files did not provide a built-in way of allowing administrators to troubleshoot and edit them remotely. Administrators would almost always need to physically visit a computer to diagnose and fix problems with INI files and settings. INI files were also limited to 64KB in size, which usually wouldn't bother the common user. Users who installed a lot of software might find problems later, however, as they couldn't add any more entries to their INI files.

One of the most important limitations that administrators would face daily was that there were few standards for INI files, and software companies could pretty much do their own thing. INI files were never guaranteed to be consistent, which meant that wise users would back up their INI files before attempting to edit them.

INI Files under Windows 95

INI files are still used by, and acceptable to, Windows 95 for compatibility reasons. This is because 16-bit programs may not know to save their settings in the registry.

The SYSTEM.INI and WINDOWS.INI files are still present in Windows 95, and settings in those files can affect the way Windows 95 behaves. If Windows 95 was installed on top of an older version of Windows 3.*x*, most settings from the SYSTEM.INI, WINDOWS.INI, CONTROL.INI, and PROGMAN.INI files were migrated to the registry. Some settings, however, were left in the SYSTEM.INI, WINFILE.INI, and WINDOWS.INI files for backward compatibility.

Viewing and Editing INI Files

You can see and edit the old INI files by running the System Configuration Editor (Sysedit), shown in Figure 6.1. Exercise 6.1 shows the steps for viewing and editing the INI files. We will add a line to WIN.INI that will start Solitaire when Windows 95 boots.

F I G U R E   6.1

Using Sysedit to view and edit INI files

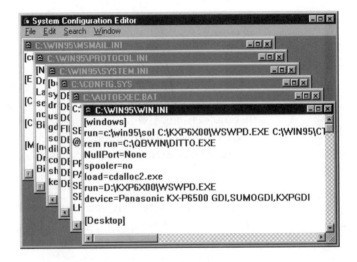

EXERCISE 6.1

Examining INI Files with Sysedit

1. Select Start ➤ Run to open the Run dialog box.

2. Type **SYSEDIT** and click on OK. Your INI files and the AUTOEXEC.BAT and CONFIG.SYS files will open (Figure 6.1).

3. Make the WIN.INI window active.

4. Look for a RUN command.

   ■ If there already is a RUN command, add a space to the current command and add the path to the Solitaire program, such as C:\WIN95\SOL.

   ■ If there are no RUN entries, add **RUN=** and the path to the Solitaire program, such as RUN=C:\WIN95\SOL (as shown in Figure 6.1).

5. Close the System Configuration Editor, saving WIN.INI when prompted.

6. Reboot and see if Solitaire loads.

7. After you get Solitaire to load automatically, you will probably want to return to the System Configuration Editor and remove the RUN command.

Using the Registry Editor

Normally, the registry works in the background, tracking configurations and settings that the user makes. Occasionally, you may need to look at the registry and possibly edit it directly, in order to provide advanced functionality and customization of Windows 95. The Registry Editor (Regedit) is the program that is used to examine and edit the registry.

By default, the Registry Editor does not appear on either the Desktop or anywhere in the Start menu. The Registry Editor is installed if Windows 95 was installed from CD-ROM—the floppy disk version of Windows 95 does not contain the Registry Editor.

If you do not have the Registry Editor on your machine, it may be because you have a version of Windows 95 that was installed from floppies. If that is the case, refer to Appendix B for details on adding software to Windows 95.

After you start the program called Regedit, you will see the entire registry opened by default—all six keys will appear. You can search the registry for keys, text strings, or numeric data. If you know what key or value you are looking for, the Find feature of the Registry Editor is invaluable. As you can see in Figure 6.2, the Registry Editor is made up of the menu bar; the left pane, which shows what section or subkey of the registry you are looking at; the right pane, which shows the contents of the section or subkey (it will be blank until you open a key by clicking on the + symbol); and the status bar, which tells you what part of the registry you are looking at. Follow the steps in Exercise 6.2 to start the Registry Editor and find a value.

FIGURE 6.2

The Registry Editor

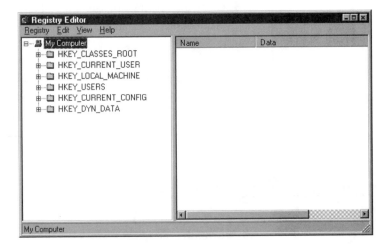

Although the Registry Editor is easy to use, the main drawback to using it is that it doesn't check any changes you make for their effect on Windows 95 or your applications. It is all too easy to change or delete something vital, and not even know it! You should always back up the registry before attempting to directly edit it.

EXERCISE 6.2

Finding Registry Values with Regedit

1. Select Start ➢ Run to open the Run dialog box.

2. Type **REGEDIT** and click on OK. The Registry Editor will open, and the six keys will be visible (Figure 6.2).

3. Select Edit ➢ Find to get to the Find submenu.

4. Type in the key or value you are looking for (try **background**).

5. It may take a few seconds, but the Registry Editor should find the key and display its associated value.

Components of the Registry

The registry uses a very organized and flexible system to store a lot of information. The following sections describe how the registry is organized, the types of values it contains, and the registry files.

Registry Organization by Keys

The registry is organized into six different sections, or *keys*. Some keys have to do with hardware configurations; others deal with software and configurations that the user may have set. There are six main keys:

- **Hkey_Local_Machine:** Hardware settings

- **Hkey_Current_Config:** Hardware profiles

- **Hkey_Classes_Root:** Associations and file linkings

- **Hkey_Dyn_Data:** Hardware settings in RAM for fast access

- **Hkey_Users:** Software settings for all users

- **Hkey_Current_User:** Software settings for the current user

These keys can contain subkeys that help organize data according to category or user. The following sections describe each main key and the major subkeys.

The registries of Windows 95 and Windows NT look very similar on the outside, but they share few specific settings within the registry. The six general keys are about the same, with computer-specific information held in Hkey_Local_Machine and user information held in Hkey_Users. In Windows NT, the name of the editor is REGEDIT32.EXE, although REGEDIT.EXE can also be used. Specific keys and values will be different, and just because a setting works in one operating system doesn't mean it will work in the other one.

The Hkey_Local_Machine Key

The Hkey_Local_Machine key holds the hardware settings for the computer, such as IRQs, network cards, video devices, and other hardware-specific information. It also holds settings that are common for all users, such as local printers, protocols, and computer identifications. Figure 6.3 shows this key displayed in the Registry Editor.

FIGURE 6.3

The Hkey_Local_
Machine key

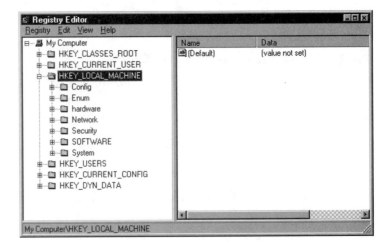

All users who log on to this computer will use the settings from this registry key. The following are brief descriptions of the Hkey_Local_Machine key's subkeys.

The Config Subkey   The Config subkey tracks different hardware configurations that the computer may need. For example, if a laptop is used by itself and at a docking station, there would be two configurations: one for undocked mode and one for docked mode. Each configuration would appear in the Control Panel, under the System icon, under the Hardware Profiles tab, as shown in Figure 6.4. And each would have a corresponding entry in the Config subkey, as shown in Figure 6.5.

FIGURE 6.4

The Hardware Profiles tab of the System Properties

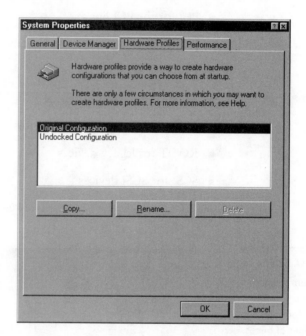

FIGURE 6.5

The Config subkey in the registry contains entries for each hardware profile.

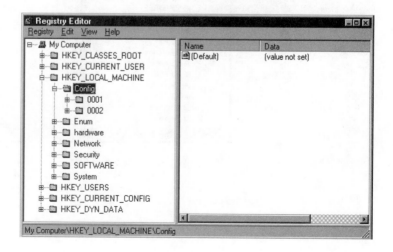

The Enum Subkey   The Enum subkey contains information about hardware devices and bus enumeration that Windows 95 uses to build and store the hardware tree. Different types of buses and their keywords in the registry include the following:

- BIOS for BIOS-supported devices

- ESDI for hard drives

- PCI for the PCI bus

- ISAPNP for the Plug-and-Play bus

- FLOP for the floppy interface

- Monitor for monitor devices

- Network for the network devices

- ROOT for legacy devices

- SCSI for SCSI devices

Figure 6.6 shows the Enum subkey entries.

FIGURE 6.6

The Enum subkey in the registry contains entries for different types of buses.

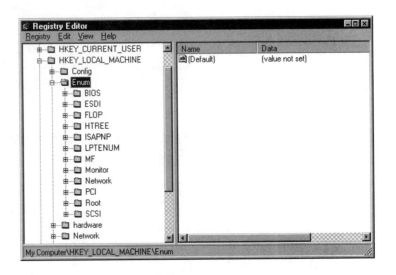

The Software Subkey   The Software subkey contains information about all software that is compatible with the registry, as shown in Figure 6.7. All 32-bit software should register itself in this subkey, and some 16-bit software may also enter values into the Software subkey. Whether software registers itself in the registry is up to the programmers of the software. If an application either doesn't register itself at all, or registers itself in a way you don't agree with, there is not much (if anything) you can do about it.

FIGURE 6.7

The Software subkey in the registry contains entries for registry-compatible software.

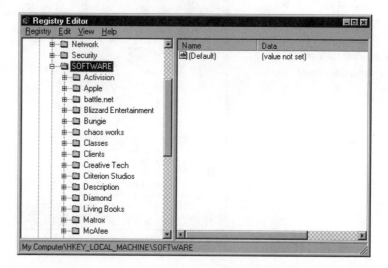

Applications will use this information to store their configurations and paths, and any preferences the user may set. This key may be changed by the applications as options are selected, preferences changed, and setups reconfigured.

The Classes subkey under the Software heading contains the OLE and extension information that Windows 95 needs to function. The Hkey_Classes_Root key points to this subkey.

The Description subkeys under the Software heading are usually associated with particular manufacturers, and contain information specific to their products.

Data within these subkeys should be edited only with the help of technical support from that particular software company.

The System Subkey   The System subkey contains configuration information that Windows 95 uses on startup and that helps determine how the various pieces of Windows 95 interact with each other.

The Control subkey under the System heading contains startup parameters, as well as printing engine parameters, as shown in Figure 6.8.

F I G U R E 6.8

The Control subkey under the System subkey contains entries for startup parameters.

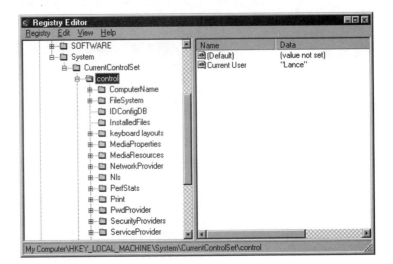

The Services subkey contains information that the various pieces of Windows 95 use to determine how and in what order the various device drivers and services will load.

The Hardware Subkey   The Hardware subkey holds information about the CPU and serial ports. You should never need to edit it manually.

The Network Subkey   The Network subkey holds information about the username and what server (if any) the user is logging on to. The best way to edit this key is through the Network Control Panel applet.

The Security Subkey   The Security subkey is where the server name and type are stored when User level security is configured. (User level security is covered in Chapter 11.) Like the Network subkey, the Security subkey should be changed through the Network Control Panel rather than edited directly.

The Hkey_Current_Config Key

The Hkey_Current_Config key is a just a pointer that refers back to the current configuration being used, which is stored in the Config subkey of Hkey_Local_Machine. Figure 6.9 shows this key displayed in the Registry Editor. This key is used to track hardware profiles and changes that might occur on a regular basis with the hardware.

FIGURE 6.9

The Hkey_Current_
Config key

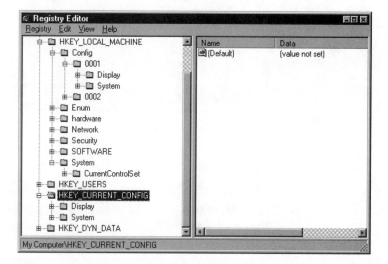

The Hkey_Classes_Root Key

The Hkey_Classes_Root key deals with OLE and associations that accompany file extensions. Figure 6.10 shows this key displayed in the Registry Editor. Windows 95 uses these settings for shortcuts and parts of the user interface.

Windows 95 is highly dependent on correct file associations, and uses this key to help keep track of how all the pieces and files of Windows 95 interact and work together. This key ensures that when you double-click on a file, the correct application automatically opens it.

The Hkey_Dyn_Data Key

The Hkey_Dyn_Data key resides in RAM for fast access, and contains information about hardware devices, including Plug-and-Play devices. The Config Manager subkey deals with hardware configurations, and the PerfStats subkey maintains statistics for network components.

FIGURE 6.10

The Hkey_Classes_
Root key

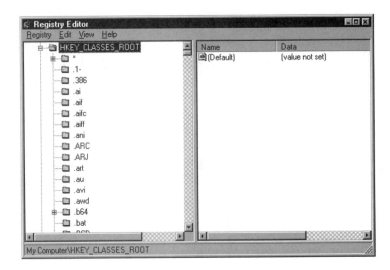

The Hkey_Users Key

The Hkey_Users key has the configurations for all of the users who have ever used the system, as well as default user settings. Hkey_Current_User points back to this key to the corresponding user who is currently logged in. Because you frequently look at and make changes to the Hkey_Current_User key (to ensure that your changes are made to the correct user), details about the Hkey_ Users key are covered in the next section.

The Hkey_Current_User Key

The Hkey_Current_User key points to the specific subkey of the user contained in Hkey_Users who is logged in at the present time. Figure 6.11 shows this key displayed in the Registry Editor.

If there is ever a conflict between subkeys in Hkey_Current_User and Hkey_ Local_Machine, the settings in Hkey_Current_User will override those of the Hkey_Local_Machine. The Software subkey is especially prone to this effect, because it exists in both keys.

FIGURE 6.11

The Hkey_Current_
User key

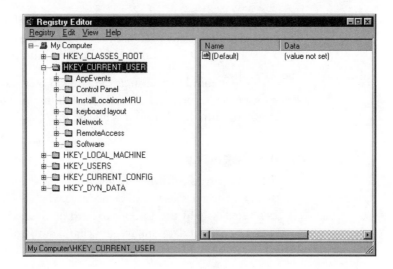

This is one of the more important keys, because it holds settings for the current user. You will usually be in one of the subkeys when you are diagnosing or fixing problems.

- **AppEvents subkey:** Contains sound file and theme settings for Windows 95

- **Control Panel subkey:** Contains Control Panel settings, including settings that may have been stored in the WINDOWS.INI and CONTROL .INI files in older versions of Windows

- **Install LocationsMRU subkey:** Tracks most recently used installation paths. You can change the default location of the Windows 95 Source files in Hkey_Local_Machine\Software\Microsoft\Windows\ CurrentVersion\Setup\SourcePath

- **Keyboard Layout subkey:** Contains the keyboard layout. This setting should be changed only by using the Keyboard Control Panel applet

- **Network subkey:** Contains information about recent and persistent network connections

- **RemoteAccess subkey:** Contains information about any remote-access connections that have been defined by the user

■ **Software subkey:** Contains software configuration information that is unique to this particular user. Sometimes software may register itself in both the Hkey_Local_Machine key and in the Hkey_Current_User key.

Keep in mind that settings that are in Hkey_Local_Machine are available to everyone who uses the computer, while settings found in Hkey_Current_User apply to only the user who is logged in.

Values in the Registry

Registry entries consist of a value that has a name and some data associated with it. The entry itself can be no larger than 64KB, although the entire registry is limited only by the amount of hard drive space available. There are two generic types of data: binary and character. Figure 6.12 shows these two types of data displayed in the Registry Editor.

FIGURE 6.12

Binary and character data in the registry

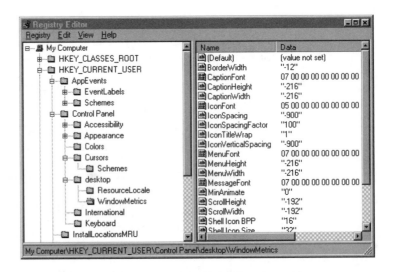

DWORD values are also binary values. Binary data is represented by the 0111100 in the icon. Character data is denoted by the *ab* in the icon.

Files Comprising the Registry

Although the registry is logically one database, it has been physically divided into two files for ease of administration and use:

- **USER.DAT:** User-specific settings

- **SYSTEM.DAT:** System-specific settings

The only real drawback to splitting up the registry is that you need to back up both files in order to have a complete backup of the registry.

Usually, both files are in the Windows directory, but Windows 95 allows the USER.DAT file to be placed on a server in a user's home directory so that user's unique settings are available from whatever Windows 95 machine he or she may log on to. This is called a *roaming profile*, which is covered in more detail in Chapter 14.

Backing Up and Restoring the Registry

Because the registry contains all of the settings for your computer, it is essential that it does not become corrupt or erased. Because the registry is constantly being changed and added to by applications and hardware configurations, it is more likely to become corrupted or damaged than other, more static, files on your computer. By backing up the registry, you can ensure that the latest changes and configurations can be restored in case of corruption or damage.

Another reason you may want to restore your registry to an earlier state is if an application installs incorrectly, thus damaging your registry.

The designers of Windows 95 realized that the registry is extremely important, and programmed Windows 95 to automatically back up the registry. You can also manually back up the registry to further ensure recoverability.

Automatic Registry Backup

Windows 95 is smart enough to automatically back up the registry whenever the machine is booted. USER.DAT is backed up to USER.DA0, and SYSTEM.DAT is backed up to SYSTEM.DA0. On a typical computer, USER.DAT is about 200KB, and SYSTEM.DAT is about 1.3MB.

USER.DAT, USER.DA0, SYSTEM.DAT, and SYSTEM.DA0 are all hidden, system, read-only files located in the Windows directory. If you want to copy these to a disk by hand, you will probably need to do a safe boot-command prompt only, and copy the files from a command prompt.

Manually Backing Up and Restoring the Registry

You can use the Regedit command to back up and to restore the registry manually while within Windows 95. The Regedit program is contained on the Windows 95 Startup disk, so that if the registry becomes corrupted, it can be restored.

To export the registry to an ASCII text file, enter this command at the command prompt:

Regedit /e *file.txt*

To overwrite the current registry with the file that you indicate, use this command at the command prompt:

Regedit /c *file.txt*

Follow the steps in Exercise 6.3 to run the command that will back up your registry, and then open your backup file to see what it looks like.

EXERCISE 6.3

Backing Up the Registry from a Command Prompt

1. Start a command prompt by selecting Start ➤ Programs ➤ MS-DOS Command Prompt.

2. Type **REGEDIT /e regback.txt**. This backs up your registry to a file called regback.txt.

3. Type **EDIT regback.txt**. This calls up the editor and allows you to look at the backup file.

4. When you are finished looking around, close the editor (press Alt+F, then choose Exit) and command prompt (type **EXIT**).

WARNING If you ever have to restore the registry (using the Regedit /c command) from a previous backup that was made using the Regedit /e command, be aware that the file is not checked by the system before it is restored in place of your current registry. Make sure that the file you are restoring is a complete, bug-free text version of the registry, because it completely overwrites (and does *not* merge with) your old registry.

Backing Up and Restoring the Registry with CFGBACK

The Windows 95 Resource Kit comes with a program named CFGBACK.EXE (Configuration Backup) that can be used to back up and restore the registry. CFGBACK.EXE allows you to have up to nine different backups of your registry, and tracks the date of your backups as well. You can pick any of your backups to restore from.

Figure 6.13 shows the Configuration Backup window. To back up your registry, specify a name for your backup and click on the Backup button. To restore the registry, highlight one of your backups and click on the Restore button.

For more details about backing up and restoring individual pieces of the registry, see the section on troubleshooting the registry, later in this chapter.

FIGURE 6.13

Using CFGBACK to back up the registry

Configuration Backup

Use this application to create a backup of your system registry configuration or to restore a previously backed up configuration.

Selected Backup Name :

backup3

List of Previous Backups :

backup1
backup2

Date Backed Up :   2/4/97

Backup

Restore

Delete

Help

Exit

Modifying the Registry

As you use Windows 95 and your applications, the registry is constantly being added to and changed. Applications will add subkeys to the registry when you install them, and each will change its particular settings when you change settings within the application. Adding new hardware to the computer will also cause changes as configurations and driver information are written to the registry.

WARNING   Under most circumstances, you should not change registry entries directly; instead, you should rely on your applications to edit the registry as needed.

Microsoft
Exam
Objective   **Perform direct modification of the registry as appropriate by using Regedit.**

There are two basic ways to modify the registry:

- Make changes within an application, and let the application modify the registry. All 32-bit programs should keep their settings in the registry, but some are specifically designed to change the way Windows 95 works. The Control Panel and Power Toys (a freeware program from Microsoft) are examples of such programs.

- Edit the registry directly (manually). This requires knowledge of the exact subkey and value you want to edit, and the value you need to change it to.

There are times when you may need to edit the registry directly. The first reason you would edit the registry is to add functionality to Windows 95 (see Exercise 6.4) or change the way Windows 95 works (see Exercises 6.5, 6.6, and 6.7). Another common reason to edit the registry directly is when you are troubleshooting—either replacing a deleted section or changing bad values in an existing subkey.

Windows 95 allows the registry to be administered and edited remotely. Chapter 16 provides details on how to do this.

Using Programs to Modify the Registry

Many changes that you make in Windows 95 are best made using the Control Panel. Applets exist for changing items like your mouse and cursors, as well as all of your networking components. The Control Panel and its applets are covered in Chapter 5.

Other programs that let you change how Windows 95 works are available. For example, Microsoft's Power Toys for Windows 95 contains a useful applet called Tweak UI, shown in Figure 6.14. This applet allows you to modify the interface of Windows 95.

FIGURE 6.14

The Tweak UI applet

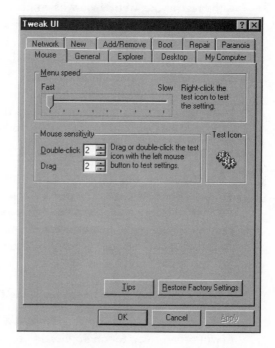

Power Toys is a set of applets, which Microsoft has released into the public domain for convenience (but doesn't support in any way). You can download Power Toys from the Microsoft Web site at www.microsoft.com. Some of the registry changes presented in the next exercises in this chapter can be made by using the Power Toys utility rather than by using the Registry Editor.

Using the Control Panel is the safest way to make changes to the registry. Similarly, all the changes you can make through the Tweak UI applet are also possible by directly editing the registry, but using this type of application is a much safer way of modifying the interface.

Using the Registry Editor to Modify the Registry

As mentioned earlier in the chapter, the Registry Editor lets you directly edit the registry, as well as view its contents. With the Registry Editor, you can make real-time edits of keys and values in the registry. Just be sure to always double-check your edits for accuracy, because the Registry Editor has no safeguards built into it to check for bad data.

You may need to edit the registry in order to get Windows 95 to behave exactly as you want. For example, you may want to disable the tilde (~) in autogenerated 8.3 names or speed up the menus. These and some other useful registry entries are described in the following sections.

We will be using the Registry Editor to modify the registry directly in the upcoming exercises. Make sure you carefully read and understand the exercises before attempting them. And be sure to have a current backup of the registry before attempting any direct modifications! We want to stress that you should back up your registry before trying these exercises—just in case you make a mistake in editing.

Adding a Viewer for Unregistered Files

Whenever you try to open a file that Windows 95 does not have registered, it will prompt you for an application to open the file with. You can adjust the registry so that an option to open the document with Notepad appears when you right-click on the document.

Follow the steps in Exercise 6.4 to edit the registry so that Open With Notepad appears as a pop-up menu option, both when you right-click on an unknown file type and when you Shift+right-click on known file types. To do this, you need to add a key named Open With Notepad, and another new key below that, named Command, as shown in Figure 6.15.

EXERCISE 6.4

Adding a Default Application for Opening Files

1. Start the Regedit program.

2. Open the Hkey_Classes_Root\Unknown\Shell subkey.

3. To add a new key, select Edit ➢ New ➢ Key. Type **Open With Notepad** as its name.

4. To add a new key below that called Command, open your new key. Then choose Edit ➢ New ➢ Key.

5. Right-click on Default in the right pane and select Modify.

6. Change the value for the command to match the path for Notepad, and add %1 after Notepad; for example, change it to C:\Win95\ Notepad.exe %1 (Figure 6.15).

7. To test the change, close the Registry Editor and return to the Desktop.

8. Create a new file with the extension of XYZ (an unregistered extension).

9. Right-click on the file to display the pop-up menu.

10. Choose your new Open With Notepad option, as shown below. Notepad should open the file.

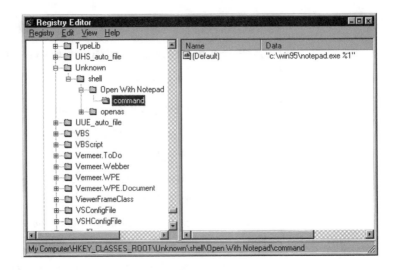

Disabling the Tilde in Long Filenames

When Windows 95 truncates a long filename to make an 8.3 name, the default
is to use the first six characters and a tilde (~). You can have Windows 95 not
use tildes by making a change to the registry. This is accomplished by adding a
new value, as shown in Figure 6.16. Follow the steps in Exercise 6.5 to disable
the tilde in shortened filenames.

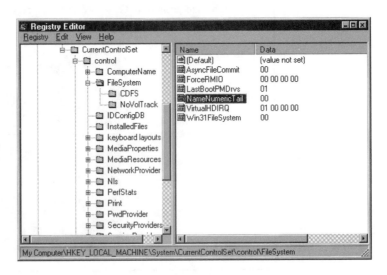

EXERCISE 6.5

Disabling the Tilde in Truncated Filenames

1. Start the Regedit program.

2. Open the Hkey_Local_Machine\System\CurrentControlSet\Control subkey.

3. Open the FileSystem subkey. Right-click on FileSystem.

4. Choose New ➢ Binary Value and enter **NameNumericTail**.

5. Double-click on the new value and type **0,** and then choose OK. The value will show as four zeros, some spaces, and two zeros: 0000 00 (Figure 6.16).

6. Test the change by closing the Registry Editor and going to the Desktop.

7. Create a new file with a long filename (longer than eight characters).

8. Examine the properties of the file. You should see that the 8.3 (MS-DOS) name does not contain any tildes.

WARNING

Many 32-bit applications also use the 8.3 file and folder names, and expect the tilde (~) to be present. Turning off the ~ may cause certain applications (including the Plus! pack from Microsoft) to not function correctly

TIP

You can see short filenames from either the DOS prompt, or by examining the properties of a file.

Making a change in the registry to disable the tilde (~) in truncated filenames affects only files created after this change. Any old files will still have the tilde in the 8.3 name.

Disabling Windows Animations

Windows 95 animates the minimizing and maximizing of windows to help users visualize where their work has gone. On slower machines, the animations may be so slow as to be distracting. You can disable animations by editing the registry and adding a value, as shown in Figure 6.17. Follow the steps in Exercise 6.6 to disable these animations.

FIGURE 6.17

Adding a value to disable animations

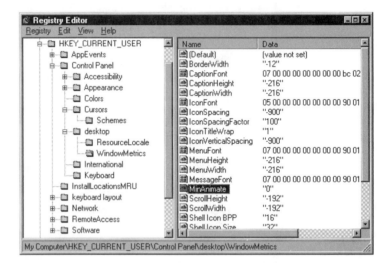

Disabling Windows Animations

1. Start the Regedit program.

2. Open the Hkey_Current_User\Control Panel\Desktop\Windows-Metrics subkey.

3. Add a new string value called **MinAnimate** with a value of **0** for no animations (Figure 6.17). Later, to turn animations back on, you can change this value to 1 by highlighting it and choosing Modify.

4. Restart Windows 95.

Increasing the Speed of Menus

Whenever you click on the Start button, the first level of menus pop up. As you move your mouse over the different menu items, the submenus will pop up. The default speed of pop-up menus from the Taskbar is usually too slow for most people. This is another change you can effect by editing the registry and adding a value, as shown in Figure 6.18. Follow the steps in Exercise 6.7 to adjust the speed of the pop-up menus so they will appear much more quickly.

FIGURE 6.18

Adding a value to speed up menus

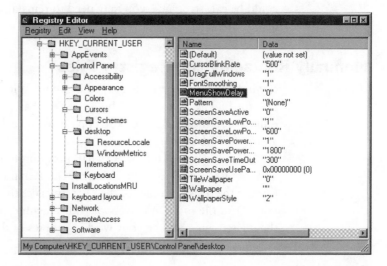

EXERCISE 6.7

Increasing the Speed of the Taskbar's Pop-Up Menus

1. Start the Regedit program.

2. Go to the Hkey_Current_User\Control Panel\Desktop subkey.

3. Add a new string value called **MenuShowDelay**.

4. Highlight the new value and select Modify.

5. Set the value from 0 to 10, with 0 being the fastest (Figure 6.18).

6. Restart Windows 95.

Troubleshooting the Registry

There are many aspects to troubleshooting the registry, such as backing up the entire registry, exporting certain sections of the registry, importing either the entire registry or certain parts, and printing the registry to help pinpoint differences between subkeys and between computers. If you have planned ahead and have a current backup of the registry, a corrupt registry file is no more than an inconvenience. If you have no backups, a failure of your registry could be catastrophic—you may need to reinstall applications and even Windows 95 itself.

Manually Replacing the Registry Files

If you have a corrupt registry, you can boot Windows 95 in Safe mode by hitting the F8 key as it starts to boot. Choose Safe Mode—command prompt only. There should be a backup copy of your registry files called USER.DA0 and SYSTEM.DA0.

You will need to run the ATTRIB program to reset the flags on the *.DAT and *.DA0 files so you can rename them. Rename the *.DAT files to *.BAK (in case the backup copies of the registry make things worse), and then rename the *.DA0 file to *.DAT. Reboot your machine, and your backup copies of the registry will now be your working copies of the registry.

Your *.DA0 files are a backup of your *previous* registry (when you booted). They do not reflect any changes you have made in the current session of Windows 95.

Exporting the Registry

There are two reasons that exporting the registry might help you in troubleshooting problems:

- If you are prepared for (or expecting) trouble, you can export the registry in order to have a current backup.

- You can export the subkey in question from a computer that works, and import it into the computer that is having problems.

The registry can be exported in its entirety by using the /e switch with the Regedit command from the command prompt, as explained earlier in the chapter.

Creating a Startup Disk

Windows 95 comes with a feature that allows you to create what is called a *Startup disk*. The option is on the Startup Disk tab of the Add/Remove Programs Properties dialog box, shown in Figure 6.19. The Startup disk Windows 95 creates contains several programs that you can use to help recover from disasters that may prevent Windows 95 from booting. One of the files that is copied onto the disk is Regedit. Follow the steps in Exercise 6.8 to make a Startup disk.

FIGURE 6.19

Creating a Windows 95 Startup disk

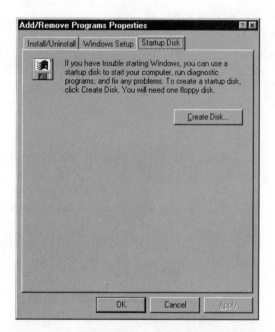

EXERCISE 6.8

Making a Startup Disk

1. Obtain a blank, formatted floppy disk.

2. Go to Control Panel ➢ Add/Remove Programs.

3. Go to the Startup Disk tab (Figure 6.19).

4. Insert the Windows 95 CD if prompted.

5. When the Startup disk is completed, check out the files on the disk. Regedit should be there, along with other utilities.

Exporting the Registry from the Registry Editor

You can also export the registry from within the Registry Editor by selecting Registry ➢ Export. You are then presented with the Export Registry File dialog box, which includes a choice of exporting the entire registry or just a part of the registry. Figure 6.20 shows this dialog box with an export range specified.

When you export the registry, Windows 95 writes the saved file as an ASCII text file. If necessary, you can edit the file before importing it back in.

F I G U R E   6.20

Exporting a piece of the registry

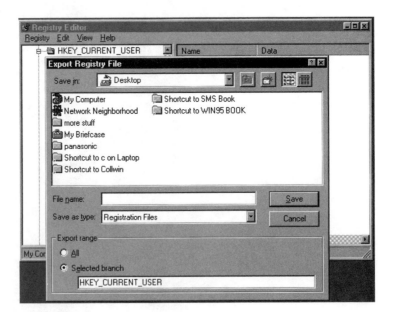

Importing a Copy of the Registry

There are two basic ways to import into the registry using Regedit. The first is called *real-mode editing* because you do it at a command prompt. The second way to use Regedit is by selecting the Import command from the Registry Editor.

Real-Mode Editing

The Regedit program has command-line switches that allow you to easily back up and restore the entire registry. As mentioned earlier, Regedit /e will back up the registry to an ASCII file.

If you are lucky enough to have a backup of the registry that has been created this way, you can also restore the registry from a command prompt. The command is:

Regedit /c *name_of_backup_file*

The /c switch replaces the entire contents of the registry with the file you specify. You may need to run Regedit from a floppy disk if Windows 95 has been damaged badly.

Importing the Registry from the Registry Editor

From within the Registry Editor, you can import either the entire registry or a select piece of the registry by choosing Registry ➤ Import Registry File.

If you import just pieces of the registry, it adds to your current registry. This is extremely helpful when you are replacing pieces of the registry that have been deleted by mistake, or when you are adding the same variable time after time. In order to import a piece of the registry, it must have been exported first, or be an ASCII file created by hand.

Printing the Registry

You may want to print parts of the registry to have a hard copy of your settings, as well as to better understand the format of the registry. Printing the registry is also useful in troubleshooting, because you can compare printed subkeys of two computers (one that is working and one that is not).

To print the registry from within the Registry Editor, select Registry ➤ Print. Just as when you are exporting the registry, you will be given a choice of printing the entire registry or only certain keys.

If you print the entire registry you may be looking at 100 or more pages!

Summary

The registry represents a dramatic change in the way configuration information is kept compared to older versions of Windows. The limitations of old INI files have been overcome with the registry, although Windows 95 still supports INI files for backward compatibility.

The registry contains settings for both hardware and software, and is very flexible. It is composed of various keys, subkeys, and values. Multiple subkeys can be kept under each key, allowing for multiple configurations for both hardware and users. This allows Windows 95 to natively support hardware and user profiles.

The registry can be backed up and restored by various methods. Windows 95 keeps an automatic backup in the files USER.DA0 and SYSTEM.DA0. The Registry Editor or Configuration Backup (CFGBACK) program in the Windows 95 Resource Kit can also be used to back up and restore the registry.

The best way to make changes to the registry is to use the appropriate program, which is usually a Control Panel applet. However, sometimes the only way to make a program or Windows 95 behave the way you want is to make changes directly to the registry. The registry can be edited directly by using the Registry Editor (Regedit), but extreme caution should be used, because modifications are not checked for compatibility by the editor.

Finally, the chapter covered techniques for troubleshooting the registry, including backing up all or parts of the registry, importing registry information, and printing a copy of the registry.

Review Questions

I. What is the name of the registry key that holds user settings?

A. Hkey_Local_Machine

B. Hkey_Users

C. Hkey_Dyn_Data

D. Hkey_Current_Config

2. What is the name of the registry key that holds Plug-and-Play settings?

   A. Hkey_Local_Machine

   B. Hkey_Users

   C. Hkey_Dyn_Data

   D. Hkey_Current_Config

3. What is the name of the registry key that holds generic hardware information?

   A. Hkey_Local_Machine

   B. Hkey_Users

   C. Hkey_Dyn_Data

   D. Hkey_Current_Config

4. What is the name of the registry key that holds hardware profile information?

   A. Hkey_Local_Machine

   B. Hkey_Users

   C. Hkey_Dyn_Data

   D. Hkey_Current_Config

5. What is the name of the registry file that holds system settings?

   A. USER.INI

   B. USER.DAT

   C. SYSTEM.DAT

   D. SYSTEM.INI

6. What is the name of the registry file that holds user settings?

   A. USER.INI

   B. USER.DAT

   C. SYSTEM.DAT

   D. SYSTEM.INI

7. What are the two types of data that a registry value can hold?

   A. Binary

   B. Time

   C. Date

   D. Character

   E. Integer

8. What is the name of the registry editor for Windows 95?

   A. REGEDT32.EXE

   B. REGISTRY EDITOR.EXE

   C. REGEDIT.EXE

   D. REGISTRY.EXE

9. What is the name of the backup registry file that is automatically created and contains user-specific information?

   A. USER.DA0

   B. USER.BAK

   C. SYSTEM.BAK

   D. SYSTEM.DA0

10. What is the name of the backup registry file that is automatically created and contains system information?

   A. USER.DA0

   B. USER.BAK

   C. SYSTEM.BAK

   D. SYSTEM.DA0

11. Which of the following methods allow you to back up the registry? (Select all that apply.)

   A. Regedit /e

   B. Regedit ➤ Registry ➤ Export Registry File

   C. The Configuration Backup (CFGBACK) utility

   D. Copying your SYSTEM.DAT and USER.DAT files to a disk

12. Which of the following methods allow you to restore the registry? (Select all that apply.)

   A. Regedit /c

   B. Regedit ➤ Registry ➤ Import Registry File

   C. The Configuration Backup (CFGBACK) utility

   D. Overwriting your SYSTEM.DAT and USER.DAT files with previous versions

CHAPTER

7

Running Applications

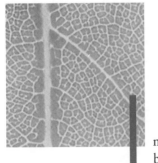

n this chapter, we will discuss how different types of applications behave and interact in the Windows 95 environment. We will begin by explaining General Protection Faults and nonresponding programs, and how to deal with them. Then we will discuss how system resources (user, GDI, and kernel) are used and subsequently returned to the system. Although Windows 95 is considered a 32-bit operating system, it still uses some 16-bit code for processing. We will look at why it still uses 16-bit code and how that might affect your applications.

We round out the chapter with a section on setting up Program Information Files (PIFs), which allow MS-DOS-based programs to coexist with Windows programs. You will learn about the options for customizing your PIFs for individual MS-DOS programs so that they run more efficiently.

A quick review of virtual machines, messaging, and multitasking will help you to better understand how running applications interact. See Chapter 4 for details about Windows 95 architecture and memory usage.

General Protection Faults

An understanding of what causes General Protection Faults (GPFs) and how to deal with them can be very beneficial to the systems administrator who must spend time troubleshooting these problems. A GPF occurs when a program violates the integrity of the system. This often happens when a program tries to access memory that is not part of its memory address space. The GPF is a defense mechanism employed by the operating system. When a program attempts to do something that could corrupt the operating system, the operating system halts the program before it can do any damage.

Let's take a look at how the different types of programs handle GPFs in Windows 95.

GPFs in MS-DOS–Based Programs

If an MS-DOS–based program fails, only that program is affected. This is because the MS-DOS program is running in its own virtual machine. A Windows 95-style GPF message will be displayed to the user, indicating that the program failed. When you click on the OK button in the GPF dialog box, the MS-DOS program will be terminated along with the virtual machine in which it was running.

If you click on the Details button, you will get the stack dump. A *stack dump* is the information stored in the system registers at the time the program crashed. This information is generally useful only to the person who wrote the program.

GPFs in 16-Bit Windows Programs

When a 16-bit Windows program fails, the operating system will again issue a GPF dialog box indicating the failed program. This dialog box will have the old Windows 3.*x*-style dialog box with a Close button and an Ignore button. After you select the Close button, you will see the Windows 95 GPF dialog box.

Since all other 16-bit programs share the same address space, they will be halted until the 16-bit program that caused the GPF is cleared. Once the program is cleared, the other 16-bit applications should be able to continue reading their messages in the thread and continue to operate normally. The failed program generally will not return its resources back to the operating system. This is because of the shared address space and shared thread. To return resources, you must close all 16-bit Windows-based programs.

GPFs in 32-Bit Windows Programs

When a 32-bit Windows-based program fails, it does not affect any other programs. This is because each 32-bit program receives its own virtual address space.

You will see the Windows 95 GPF dialog box. When you click on the OK button, Windows 95 will remove that failed program and return its resources back to the operating system.

GPFs in Device Drivers

You might encounter a GPF with a driver program. Since drivers can access hardware directly and run as part of the base operating system, it is a good idea to take a GPF with a driver very seriously.

Driver failures can affect the ability of the entire operating system to continue functioning properly.

Nonresponding Programs

Nonresponding ("hung") programs are still running, but they are not responding to the system. "Program hangs" can happen for many reasons. Your 16-bit programs can hang when they do not have access to the message queue. This can be caused by a poorly written program that doesn't voluntarily share resources with other 16-bit programs, or if a GPF occurs and hasn't been cleared. Your 32-bit programs can be hung when a resource they need is being used by some other program.

If any program hangs while it is using a critical resource, any other program that needs that resource will be hung also. The hung program will need to be restarted so that the other programs can continue execution.

This is a nice upgrade from Windows 3.*x*, where you were required to restart the entire Windows 3.*x* operating system.

Hung MS-DOS–Based Programs

When an MS-DOS–based program hangs, you need to do a local restart of the program. To run a local restart, press the Ctrl+Alt+Del key combination (press all three keys at the same time). This will bring up the Close Program dialog box, shown in Figure 7.1.

As you can see, there are several choices that you can make. If you choose End Task, it will immediately shut down the selected program. If you choose Shut Down, it will shut down all active programs and close Windows 95. The Cancel button cancels this window without changing anything. Occasionally, when you click on the End Task button, the program doesn't respond to the End Task messages being sent to it. After a few seconds, a secondary dialog box will pop up, giving you two options: End Task and Wait, or End Task and Cancel,as shown in Figure 7.2. The title bar for the End Task dialog box will display the application's title bar. In Figure 7.2, notice that we are trying to end the Microsoft Excel - Tax Liability program. If you choose Wait, the program will wait for a few seconds and try to end the hung application again. If you choose End Task from this dialog box, it will override whatever the hung application is doing (or not doing) and close it down. If you choose Cancel, the End Task will be ignored and you will return to Windows.

FIGURE 7.1

The Close Program
dialog box

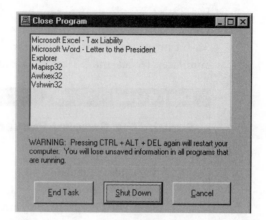

FIGURE 7.2

The End Task dialog box

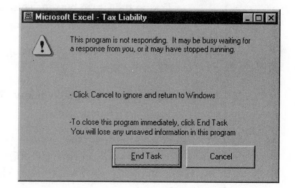

Hung 16-Bit Windows Programs

When 16-bit Windows programs hang, they might not release control of the thread or other system resources. This will cause all other 16-bit programs to hang also.

You should do a local restart (Ctrl+Alt+Del) and terminate the hung program. After termination, the other programs should resume operating normally, because they again have access to their messages in the thread.

Hung 32-Bit Windows Programs

If a 32-bit Windows program hangs, you can terminate it with a local restart. This should not affect any other running programs, because the 32-bit program has its own threads and doesn't share them. Exercise 7.1 simulates 16-bit and 32-bit program hangs and GPFs.

EXERCISE 7.1

Simulating General Protection Faults and Program Hangs

1. We will first simulate a 16-bit Windows GPF. Navigate to the \Labs\ Crash16 folder on the CD-ROM that accompanies this book, and run the SETUP.EXE program to install the Crash16 application. Then select Start ➢ Programs ➢ Crash16.

2. Click on the Crash button. This forces the program to create a GPF, and the Windows 3.x GPF dialog box appears.

3. Select Close from the GPF dialog box. You now see the Windows 95 GPF dialog box.

4. Select Close from the Windows 95 GPF dialog box. This terminates your Crash16 program.

5. Let's do the same thing with a 32-bit application. From the \Labs\ Crash32 folder on your CD-ROM, run the SETUP.EXE program to install the Crash32 application. Then select Start ➢ Programs ➢ Crash32.

6. Click on the Crash button. This forces the program to create a GPF, and you see only the Windows 95 GPF dialog box.

7. Choose Close to terminate your Crash32 program.

8. Now let's simulate a program hang in the 16-bit Windows environment. Open Crash16, and then open a second instance of Crash16. We will call these App A and App B, respectively. From App A, click on the Hang button.

9. App A has now been hung. Note that the other 16-bit application (App B) is hung also. This is because they are sharing the same thread, and App B cannot get to its messages in the thread because of App A. To resolve this problem, press Ctrl+Alt+Del to open the Task Manager dialog box.

10. In the list of running applications, you should see Crash16 (Not Responding). Click on that line, and then choose End Task. This pops up another dialog box indicating that the program is still not responding. Click on End Task again. Once you have done this, App B will begin running again because it can now read the thread.

11. Close App B.

12. Follow the same procedures outlined in steps 8 through 10 for Crash32. You will find that App B continues to run despite App A's hung status.

Resource Usage in Windows 95

In Windows 3.*x*, you may have had problems with Out of Memory errors. This was caused by both memory leaks in those 16-bit programs and the resource architecture of Windows 3.*x*. Because 16-bit programs share the same memory address space, this can still happen in Windows 95, especially if you have 16-bit programs that crash. Losing all of your resources while using 32-bit programs is much more difficult. Remember, every 32-bit Windows program gets its own separate address space and system resources.

Let's take a look at how and when system resources (user, GDI, and kernel) are used and returned to the system.

- **MS-DOS-based programs:** When an MS-DOS program is terminated, all of the resources it was using, as well as the virtual machine it was running in, are returned to Windows 95.

- **16-bit Windows programs:** These programs may use resources that the operating system doesn't know about. They might also share resources used by other 16-bit programs. Because of this, when a 16-bit program is closed, its resources will not be returned to the operating system. This can eventually cause an Out of Memory error. To fix this error, close all 16-bit programs. Resources used by 16-bit programs will be returned after all 16-bit applications are closed. This will include any orphaned resources that were once attached to a 16-bit program. This was done for backward compatibility.

- **32-bit Windows programs:** Resources used by 32-bit programs can be tracked in their entirety by the operating system. When a 32-bit application is closed, it will return all resources.

Resources returned to the system may not affect your resource counts. This is due to the fact that Windows 95 will cache frequently used and shared resources. This allows programs in Windows 95 to start up and run more quickly.

Resource Architecture

Windows 95 is considered a 32-bit operating system, but it still uses a lot of 16-bit code at the system level. This was done for several reasons. One reason is that 32-bit code takes up more memory than an equivalent amount of 16-bit code. Windows 95 was built for efficiency. Many functions don't need the larger 32-bit memory areas. For example, would you rent an 18-wheel tractor trailer to move a one-bedroom apartment? Probably not. A smaller truck would be much more efficient and cost-effective.

Also, in certain instances, 16-bit code runs faster than 32-bit code. Compatibility with existing programs is another reason that Windows 95 still uses 16-bit code fragments.

Under normal circumstances, a 32-bit program cannot use 16-bit code, and vice versa. Think of them as two different languages. To translate between these languages and get the benefits outlined above, Windows 95 employs a procedure called *thunking* in which the code is redirected and translated from one version to the other.

Here is how 16-bit and 32-bit code is used in Windows 95 system components:

- **User interface:** The user interface in Windows 95 is almost totally written in 16-bit code. This was done to keep this component as small and fast as possible.

- **GDI:** The GDI (Graphical Device Interface) uses a fairly even mix of 16-bit and 32-bit code. The GDI will use 16-bit code when compatibility is necessary. It will use 32-bit code for speed or when precise floating-point measurements are necessary (such as rendering a high-resolution graphic). See Chapter 4 for more information about the GDI.

- **Kernel:** The kernel uses all 32-bit code. When a program makes a call to a 16-bit procedure, that call is thunked to the 32-bit version. See Chapter 4 for more information about the kernel.

16-bit versus 32-bit Code

There are different rules for using 16-bit and 32-bit code. For example, 16-bit code is non-reentrant. This means that while a particular thread is using a 16-bit piece of code, no other programs can be using that same 16-bit piece of code. 32-bit code does not have this problem because it is reentrant, which means that many threads can be processing the same procedures at the same time.

Windows 95 uses a Win16Mutex flag to indicate to other programs that this particular 16-bit section of code is currently in use. This blocks other programs from using that same procedure. If a program hangs and the Win16Mutex flag is set, you must perform a local restart on the hung program, which will then release the Win16Mutex flag. An interesting side effect of the Win16Mutex flag is that a 32-bit program that uses a 16-bit code fragment could be hung by other programs that are trying to use the same 16-bit code fragment.

Since the kernel uses only 32-bit code, it cannot be blocked by the Win16-Mutex flag.

Tracking Resource Usage

You can track resource usage using the Resource Meter. Select Start ➤ Programs ➤ Accessories ➤ System Tools ➤ Resource Meter. This will place the Resource Meter icon on your Taskbar. Right-click on the icon (it should look like three horizontal bars) and choose Details. You should see a dialog box similar to the one shown in Figure 7.3.

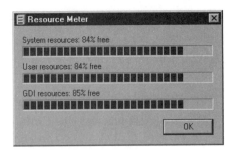

FIGURE 7.3

The Resource Meter
monitors the System,
User, and GDI resources.

Configuring Program Information Files for MS-DOS Programs

Windows-based programs keep information about resources and memory in their headers, which allows them to coexist with other running Windows applications. MS-DOS-based programs were designed to use whatever resources were in the system. For MS-DOS-based programs to comfortably coexist with Windows programs, they need to have a header information file. This file is called a Program Information File, or PIF.

Microsoft ✓ Exam Objective

Establish application environments for Microsoft MS-DOS® applications.

If an MS-DOS-based application doesn't have its own PIF, Windows will use the DEFAULT.PIF file for it. DEFAULT.PIF has default settings that work with most MS-DOS-based programs. A PIF is really a configuration header file for the MS-DOS virtual machine. You can customize PIFs for individual MS-DOS programs so that they will run more efficiently. The following sections describe how to customize a PIF for a particular MS-DOS program.

PIF Customization Options

When you complete a customized PIF, the PIF itself will be stored in the same folder where the MS-DOS file is located. It will also have the same eight-character filename, followed by .PIF. For example, if your MS-DOS file is C:\Games\ DOOM.EXE, then your PIF file would be: C:\Games\DOOM.PIF.

You use the property sheets of an MS-DOS-based program to customize its PIF. Property sheets can be accessed by right-clicking on the MS-DOS program's .EXE or .COM file and then selecting Properties from the pop-up menu. The Properties dialog box is divided into several tabs. In the following sections, we will go through each tab's features. At the end of this section, you will be able to customize your own PIF (Exercise 7.2).

The General Tab

The General tab of the DOS Properties dialog box, shown in Figure 7.4, shows general-purpose information about the MS-DOS program. It includes the file's location, size, PIF name, creation date, modification date, last accessed date, and file attributes.

FIGURE 7.4

The General tab of the DOS Properties dialog box

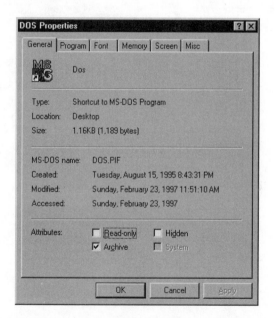

You can modify the following file attributes from this screen:

- **Read-only:** When this attribute is set, the file becomes Read-only. This means that the file cannot be overwritten or accidentally deleted.

- **Archive:** Some programs use this attribute to decide whether or not the program should be backed up.

- **Hidden:** This attribute will hide the file from view. You will not be able to use the file unless you know its exact filename.

- **System:** This attribute normally will be disabled. When it is checked, it means that this file is required for use by the system. This file will also be hidden automatically. You should not delete system files.

The Program Tab

The Program tab of the DOS Properties dialog box, shown in Figure 7.5, is used to specify how this MS-DOS program will start up. The first line shows the program or shortcut name.

F I G U R E 7.5

The Program tab of the
DOS Properties dialog box

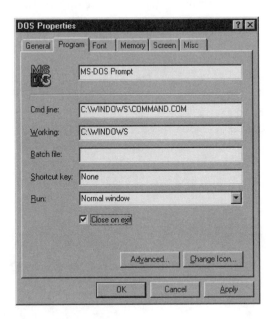

The following options are available on the Program tab:

- **Cmd line:** Allows you to type the path and command needed to start an MS-DOS application. You can enter any information on this command line, including command-line parameters that the program might need to run.

- **Working:** Allows you to specify a working directory. The working directory is where the MS-DOS program will store its data. Normally, the working directory is the same as the directory where the MS-DOS program is stored. The path statement you place here can be a UNC name for a network location. For example, your MS-DOS program may reside in: C:\Games\Doom, but you might want to store data associated with that program on the network at \\MainServer\Games\DoomData.

- **Batch file:** Allows you to specify a batch file that will run before the MS-DOS program starts. This is a nice way to start a terminate-and-stay-resident (TSR) program that the MS-DOS program might need. You might also use this to log on to a network server that the MS-DOS program will pull data from.

- **Shortcut key:** Allows you to specify a shortcut key to start this application. The shortcut keys will be reserved for the entire system; no matter where you are, if you hit that shortcut key, this program will start executing.

Be careful when you assign shortcut keys, because they are reserved for the entire system and will overwrite any other shortcut keys that have been created within applications. For example, if you assign the shortcut key Ctrl+C to an MS-DOS application, you will no longer be able to use that shortcut to copy selected information to the clipboard.

- **Run:** A list box that allows you to change the default window that the MS-DOS program will start in. Your choices are Normal window, Minimized, and Maximized. The Normal window opens up a full-screen MS-DOS window. Minimized will start the program and then run it minimized on your Taskbar. Maximized will place the program in an MS-DOS window, which will take up roughly three-quarters of your screen.

You can force a normal full-screen MS-DOS window into a smaller MS-DOS window on your desktop and vice-versa by pressing Alt+Enter.

- **Close on exit:** If you run the MEM command from an MS-DOS command prompt, it will write data to the MS-DOS screen about the current memory configurations and then close the window before you have a chance to read it. To avoid this problem, make sure that the Close on exit checkbox is not selected. This will force the MS-DOS window to stay open until you close it by clicking on the X in the upper-right corner.

■ **Change Icon:** Allows you to change the icon shown for the MS-DOS program you are creating this PIF for. Normally, you will see the MS-DOS icon with your filename listed below it.

■ **Advanced:** Most MS-DOS programs will run without your ever needing to make the modifications available when you click on the Advanced button. The Advanced options are discussed next.

Advanced Program Settings When you click on the Advanced button in the Program tab of the DOS Properties dialog box, the Advanced Program Settings dialog box appears, as shown in Figure 7.6.

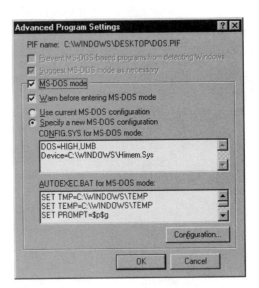

The following settings are available in this dialog box:

■ **Prevent MS-DOS-based programs from detecting Windows:** Some MS-DOS programs can detect whether or not they are running within a Windows virtual machine or in the native MS-DOS environment. Many of these programs will issue an error message telling you that they cannot be run from Windows. Selecting this option will prevent those programs from detecting that they are running in a Windows virtual machine.

- **Suggest MS-DOS mode as necessary:** Allows Windows to decide whether or not the MS-DOS program will run best from a Windows virtual machine or in the native MS-DOS environment. If the program does require the native MS-DOS environment, Windows will automatically run a wizard to create a custom icon that you can select to run the program.

If the program needs to run in the native MS-DOS environment and the Suggest MS-DOS mode as necessary option is not selected, the program may run poorly or could fail completely. Some MS-DOS programs, like flight simulators and graphic design programs, are resource-intensive and should be run only in MS-DOS mode. If you are having problems with an MS-DOS application crashing when running in a window, switch it to MS-DOS mode.

- **MS-DOS mode:** Forces the program to be run in the native MS-DOS environment. It does this by unloading the Windows 95 Desktop. You will see the normal Windows 95 shutdown screens. Once Windows 95 is unloaded, the program will reboot your system, and then run in the MS-DOS environment.

- **Warn before entering MS-DOS mode:** Displays a warning message when Windows 95 is about to shut down and restart in MS-DOS mode.

- **Use current MS-DOS configuration:** Forces the MS-DOS program to use the current AUTOEXEC.BAT and CONFIG.SYS files to load environment settings for the MS-DOS program about to start.

- **Specify a new MS-DOS configuration:** Allows you to specify AUTO-EXEC.BAT and CONFIG.SYS settings for your program.

- **Configuration:** Brings up a checklist of items that can be added to your CONFIG.SYS and AUTOEXEC.BAT programs, as shown in Figure 7.7. The checklist is nice because you don't need to remember all of the syntax to properly set up these files. Just click on a choice, and it will be added.

When you specify a new MS-DOS configuration, you can also copy and paste settings from a DOS boot disk. This will essentially replace the need for your boot disk, and is especially useful when your program needs specific DOS drivers or other TSRs to be loaded.

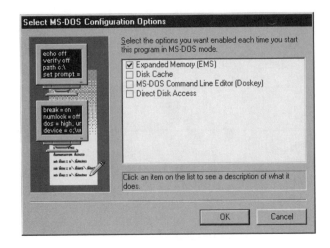

The Font Tab

The Font tab of the DOS Properties dialog box, shown in Figure 7.8, allows you to specify what font type you want your MS-DOS window to display.

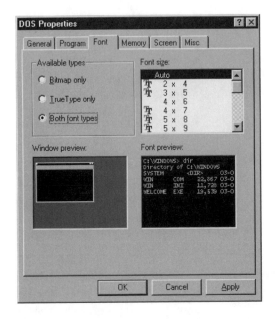

Bitmap fonts take up more space than TrueType fonts. Bitmap fonts are saved as bitmap images; every font size must be rendered and saved as a bitmap image.

TrueType fonts are stored as a set of instructions on how to render the image. As each TrueType letter is rendered, the instructions are modified appropriately. This is similar to following a cookie recipe. The recipe might call for one egg and one cup of sugar for 10 cookies. To make 100 cookies, you would increase all the recipe specifications 10 times (that is, use 10 eggs and 10 cups of sugar). Some printers don't support TrueType fonts and require bitmap fonts to be downloaded to them.

You can also alter the font size. The Auto setting will adjust the size of the font based on the size of the window in which it will be displayed.

You will find it much more convenient to view MS-DOS windows if you leave the Font size setting to Auto. This is especially true if you resize an MS-DOS window.

The Memory Tab

The Memory tab of the DOS Properties dialog box, shown in Figure 7.9, is used to adjust how the different types of memory available to an MS-DOS program should be used.

The following options are available on the Memory tab:

- **Conventional memory:** Conventional memory is considered the first 1MB of memory: 640KB of conventional memory and 384KB of high memory. Within the Conventional memory area, the following items can be modified:

  - The Total box indicates how much conventional memory is set aside for this program. In most cases, the Auto setting will be best.

  - The Initial environment box is used to set aside some conventional memory for use by the COMMAND.COM MS-DOS interpreter and variable settings like PATH statements in an AUTOEXEC.BAT file.

If you increase the Initial environment amount, you will decrease the amount of conventional memory set aside for this program.

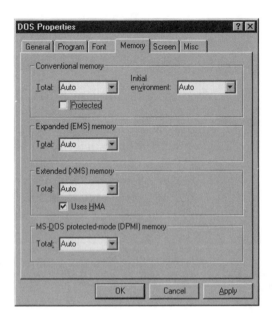

- The **Protected** checkbox can increase the memory protection for your application. When this checkbox is selected, the memory set aside for this program will not be swapped to a swapfile. This can impact the performance of your entire system.

- **Expanded (EMS) memory:** Specifies the maximum amount of expanded memory to allocate to this program. The numbers are in kilobytes. If you set this to Auto, no limit is imposed on the program.

Older MS-DOS programs have difficulty with large amounts of expanded and extended memory. If this is the case, try setting the values of the Expanded Memory and Extended Memory options to 8192 or 8MB.

- **Extended (XMS) memory:** Specifies the maximum amount of extended memory to allocate to this program. The numbers are in kilobytes. If you set this to Auto, no limit is imposed on the program.

- **Uses HMA:** Specifies whether or not the program will use the High Memory Area. This option is ignored if the MS-DOS application is already using the HMA.

- **MS-DOS protected mode (DPMI) memory:** Specifies the maximum amount of DPMI memory to allocate to this program. The numbers are in kilobytes. Setting this value to Auto allows Windows to choose limits based on current system configuration settings.

If you have a DEVICE=C:\DOS\EMM386.EXE NOEMS parameter in your CONFIG.SYS file, Windows cannot provide you with DPMI memory. You can use the RAM parameter with *x* =*mmmm-nnnn* statement to allocate enough space in upper memory for Windows 95 to create an EMS page frame for your DPMI memory.

The Screen Tab

The Screen tab of the DOS Properties dialog box, shown in Figure 7.10, is used to determine how the MS-DOS program will start up, such as whether it will be in a full screen or a window, have toolbars, and so on.

FIGURE 7.10

The Screen tab of the DOS Properties dialog box

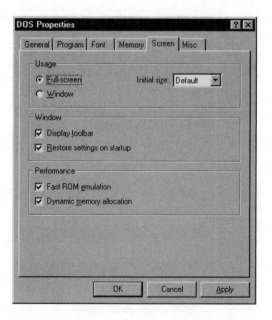

The following options are available on the Screen tab:

- **Usage:** Determines how the MS-DOS application will be viewed. Within the Usage area, the following items can be adjusted:

- The Full-screen setting specifies that the program runs in a full screen. This uses the least memory and CPU cycles and is used to run many graphics-based MS-DOS programs. This is faster for graphical applications because the processor doesn't need to re-render an image into a smaller version that would be displayed in a Window.

- The Window setting specifies that the application should run in a window. This makes it easier to share information with other Windows programs through cut-and-paste operations. This is used primarily with text-based applications.

- The Initial size setting specifies a certain number of lines to display on the screen when you start this program. Many programs will override this setting and set it back to the default.

- **Window:** Modifies how the MS-DOS window will be displayed.

  - The Display toolbar option adds a toolbar to the MS-DOS window. The toolbar has features like Cut and Paste buttons.

  - The Restore settings on startup checkbox resets all the changes you have made after the program finishes executing. This includes things like position, font, and window size.

- **Performance:** Affects the way MS-DOS windows use video drivers.

  - The Fast ROM emulation option allows the system to emulate video ROM drivers while in protected mode. This allows the system to write to the screen faster. If your program is having difficulty writing text to the screen or other video problems, try disabling this option.

  - The Dynamic memory allocation option allows the program to hold memory for video display. This is useful for programs that switch between text and graphics modes, such as when a word processing program switches from text view to a print preview. If this option is not set, the memory needed to switch displays must be reallocated every time you switch modes.

If you want to ensure that there is always enough memory for Windows 95 to correctly display this program, be sure that the Dynamic memory allocation option is not selected.

The Misc Tab

The Misc tab of the DOS Properties dialog box, shown in Figure 7.11, is the catchall for the options that didn't fit neatly into the other categories. This includes things like shortcut keys and mouse interaction.

FIGURE 7.11

The Misc tab of the DOS Properties dialog box

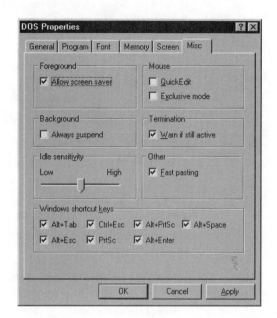

This tab includes the following options:

- **Foreground:** When the Allow screen saver checkbox is selected, the Windows 95 screen saver will be allowed to display even when the MS-DOS program is running in the foreground. When deselected, the screen saver will be prevented from running when the MS-DOS application is in the foreground.

- **Mouse:** Affects how the mouse is used within an MS-DOS window.

  - The QuickEdit option allows the mouse to be used to highlight text within the MS-DOS window. This should not be used when the MS-DOS application itself supports a mouse.

- The Exclusive mode option confines the mouse within the MS-DOS window. This can be useful with programs that lose mouse synchronization between the MS-DOS window and the Windows 95 environment.

- **Background:** The Always suspend option forces the MS-DOS application to pause when it has been minimized or placed in the background.

- **Termination:** The Warn if still active choice displays a dialog box warning you that the MS-DOS application is about to close when you try to close it. This will give you a chance to cancel the program termination and save any work you might have forgotten to save from the MS-DOS application. This is especially useful if the MS-DOS application opens up sensitive files. If the MS-DOS application terminates, those files may become corrupted.

- **Idle sensitivity:** Determines when the system suspends a program. A program will be suspended after a certain length of inactivity. This can be caused by the program waiting for some user input. This slider control is useful when a program is using the math coprocessor. Even though the program is running (using the math coprocessor), Windows 95 might think it is idle.

- **Other:** Fast pasting allows pasting from the Windows 95 clipboard into the MS-DOS-based program. If you are having trouble doing this, try deselecting this option.

- **Windows shortcut keys:** When these shortcut key options are selected, you can use them within the MS-DOS window. The keystrokes themselves will bypass the MS-DOS program and be sent directly to Windows 95. If you need to have the MS-DOS program receive any of the keystrokes, deselect the appropriate option.

Configuring a PIF for an MS-DOS Program

Now that you know about all the properties you can set for your MS-DOS programs, you are prepared to create a PIF. Follow the steps in Exercise 7.2 to configure a PIF. For this exercise, we will use the MS-DOS Prompt program, which is stored in the Programs folder beneath the Start Menu folder, as shown in Figure 7.12.

EXERCISE 7.2

Configuring a PIF

1. To get to the Windows Explorer, select Start ➣ Programs ➣ Explorer.

2. From the Explorer, "drill down" (either double-click on the folders in the left partition of the window or click on the + symbols next to the folders in the left partition) to the Start Menu folder.

3. You should see the Programs folder. Click on the Programs folder in the left partition. You should see the contents of this folder (Figure 7.12).

4. Right-click on the MS-DOS prompt and choose Properties. You should now see the General tab displayed (Figure 7.4).

5. Click on the different tabs to see the information displayed.

6. If you want further detail on any option, click on the question mark in the upper-right corner of the Properties dialog box, and then click on the option you are interested in.

7. When you are finished configuring the PIF for the MS-DOS prompt, close the Properties dialog box.

FIGURE 7.12

Contents of the Programs folder

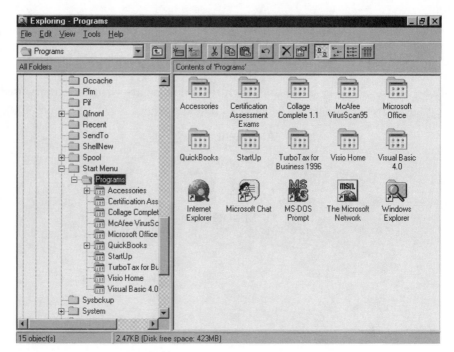

Summary

In this chapter, we discussed how different types of applications behave and interact in the Windows 95 environment. Because 16-bit Windows programs cooperatively multitask and share a single thread of execution, they can step on each other's resources. They are also less efficient than 32-bit programs, which don't share address space and can have multiple threads of execution. Because of this sharing, 16-bit resources are not returned to the system until all 16-bit Windows applications are terminated.

GPFs are also handled differently for these different types of programs. When a 16-bit program is hung or crashed, it will hang all of the other 16-bit programs. MS-DOS programs just terminate. The 32-bit Windows programs also terminate, but generally don't hang other running applications.

There are still portions of 16-bit code in the Windows 95 operating system. This was done for speed and backward compatibility. The Win16Mutex flag is used to keep different programs from trying to use the same non-reentrant 16-bit procedures.

MS-DOS-based programs use PIF files to configure the virtual machine in which they run. There are many options that can be changed from the DOS Properties dialog box, including window type, font size, and toolbars, as well as behind-the-scenes instructions, like memory management features.

Review Questions

1. Which of the following are virtual machines used in Windows 95? (Select all that apply.)

   A. System VM

   B. Core VM

   C. W95 VM

   D. MS-DOS VM

For the next three questions, please use the following scenario: You have three 16-bit applications, a 32-bit application, and two MS-DOS-based applications running.

2. If one of the 16-bit applications is hung, how many programs altogether will be hung, including the hung application?

    A. 1

    B. 2

    C. 3

    D. 5

3. If one of the 32-bit applications has hung, how many programs altogether will be hung, including the hung application?

    A. 1

    B. 2

    C. 3

    D. 5

4. If an MS-DOS application has a GPF, how many programs will be affected, including the crashed MS-DOS application?

    A. 1

    B. 2

    C. 3

    D. 5

5. You want to run a batch file to log on to a network server before your MS-DOS application runs. What is the easiest method to accomplish this?

   A. Build a shortcut to the batch file and to the MS-DOS program; double-click on the batch shortcut first, and then run the MS-DOS program.

   B. Go to a command prompt and run the batch file before running the MS-DOS program.

   C. Add the batch file to the Batch File parameter in the property sheet for the MS-DOS program.

   D. You don't need to run the batch file because Windows 95 will automatically detect that the MS-DOS program needs access to the server and will log you in.

6. Your MS-DOS program is named FOO.EXE. You create a PIF file for your MS-DOS program. What is the name of the PIF file?

   A. MS-DOS.PIF

   B. PIF.EXE

   C. DEFAULT.PIF

   D. FOO.PIF

7. In the Working parameter of an MS-DOS property sheet, you specify C:\TEMP. What will be placed in the C:\TEMP directory, if anything?

   A. Output files used by your MS-DOS program

   B. The files used by Windows 95 to track program performance

   C. The .INI files used by all the Windows programs running at the same time your MS-DOS program is running

   D. There will never be anything stored here.

8. You are editing a document in Microsoft Word. You highlight a line of text and press Ctrl+C to copy it to the clipboard, when suddenly your MS-DOS application starts up. What could cause this?

A. You have the OLE functionality of Microsoft Word linked to your MS-DOS program.

B. You have chosen Ctrl+C as a shortcut for your MS-DOS-based application.

C. Ctrl+C always starts up the last used MS-DOS program.

D. This is a glitch in the computer system and should never happen.

9. When you are in your MS-DOS program, you want to be able to press Alt+Tab to switch to another running application. How could you enable this feature?

A. In the Misc tab of the MS-DOS property sheet, click on the Alt+Tab checkbox.

B. You don't have to do anything—this functionality always exists for MS-DOS applications.

C. This is not an available feature and can't be implemented.

D. You must edit the registry in order to do this.

CHAPTER

8

Managing Disk Resources and Utilities

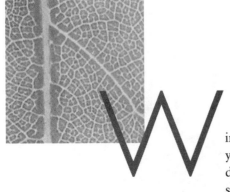

indows 95 has many built-in utilities for managing your hard drive and files. Support for 32-bit disk drivers has also been enhanced from previous versions of Windows.

This chapter begins with a discussion of the disk drivers supported by Windows 95 and how to troubleshoot problems with your disk drivers. Then it covers long filename support, as well as how to troubleshoot problems with long filenames. Then you'll learn about the integrated tools and utilities, including the disk compressor, disk defragmenter, disk-error checker, and backup and restore programs. Finally, we'll cover all the other disk-management tasks, such as partitioning the hard drive, formatting floppy drives, managing the hard drive cache, and optimizing your cluster size.

Windows 95 Disk Drivers

To understand how Windows 95 handles requests to and from the hard disk, you need to understand the driver architecture, as well as the advantages of 32-bit disk drivers. As explained in Chapter 4, device drivers are the software that Windows 95 uses to communicate with the hardware. Drivers are a "middleman" of sorts—they interpret commands from Windows 95 and pass the commands along to the hardware.

Like other types of device drivers, disk drivers can be categorized by being real mode (16-bit) or protected mode (32-bit). Protected-mode drivers are used by Windows 95 and Windows NT. Protected-mode drivers are usually superior in both their stability and performance compared to real-mode drivers (created to be used in the MS-DOS environment). The term *protected* comes from the fact that applications can be protected from each other, so if one application locks up, it does not affect other applications.

Windows 95 uses 32-bit disk drivers that have been enhanced over the 16-bit versions used in earlier version of Windows. The new disk drivers are capable of supporting large hard drives (LBA mode drives). They also have real-mode (16-bit) versions that can be enabled for compatibility.

Types of Devices and Drivers

The types of disk drives supported by Windows 95 are listed in Table 8.1. Table 8.2 lists the bus adapters that Windows 95 supports.

T A B L E 8.1 Disk Drives Supported by Windows 95		
	Disk Drive	**Description**
	ESDI	A standard from IBM for hard drives
	IDE	The new standard for most hard drives based on the MFM and RLL standard
	IDE-LBA	A mode where the motherboard BIOS translates drive parameters to maintain compatibility because IDE drives that are larger than 512MB have a hard time being recognized by both software and hardware
	Ultra-IDE or Ultra-DMA (UDMA)	This new standard for IDE drives doubles the theoretical throughput of the hard drive from 16.67 Megabits per second to 33.33 Megabits per second. You will need both a UDMA hard drive and a UDMA controller to take advantage of UDMA.
	MFM	The old standard for hard drives—rarely seen anymore
	SCSI	A standard that allows greater flexibility than IDE (but at a higher cost)
	SCSI 2	The newer SCSI standard that offers (among other things) faster data transfers
	Hardcard	This was a popular and easy way to add an additional drive to your computer. It featured a controller and hard drive on a full-sized card. These are not seen as much anymore.

	Bus Adapter	Description
TABLE 8.2 Bus Adapters Supported by Windows 95	EISA	An early standard for a 32-bit bus
	PCI	The current 32-bit standard for desktops
	PCMCIA (PC Card)	The current standard for laptops
	ISA	The old 16-bit standard
	MCA (Microchannel)	A 32-bit standard from IBM
	RLL	A hard drive standard that squeezed 50% more drive space from MFM drives with the same physical drive. This technology has been incorporated into the IDE standard.
	VLB	A 32-bit standard especially good for fast video cards, mostly used for 486 computers
	AGP	A 32-bit standard which stands for Advanced Graphics Port— a new standard for high-end video cards

Windows 95 uses a 32-bit virtual file allocation table file system (VFAT) as the primary file system. VFAT is enabled by default and cannot be turned off. VFAT handles all disk requests, and operates in protected (32-bit) mode. It communicates with both 32-bit disk drivers (preferred) and with 16-bit disk drivers (for compatibility). Note that OSR2*x* supports FAT32, which is a newer File Allocation Table that will be discussed below.

IDE Devices and Drivers

Windows 95 provides protected-mode (32-bit) drivers for IDE disk drives. The Windows 95 drivers support up to two IDE controllers in a computer. The drivers also support IDE CD-ROM drives.

Although Windows 95 supports large hard disks that use an LBA scheme (for drives over 512MB), primary and logical partitions are limited to 2GB each, unless you are using the latest version of Windows 95 (Windows 95B).

You will need either OSR2 (Windows 95B) or a driver from the motherboard manufacturer to take full advantage of the latest IDE specification, Ultra-IDE.

SCSI Devices and Drivers

Windows 95 provides 32-bit driver support for SCSI, which earlier versions of Windows did not. Windows 95 includes drivers for some of the most common SCSI manufacturers, such as Adaptec and Future Domain, as well as others.

The SCSI drivers included with Windows 95 also support common SCSI specifications, such as Advanced SCSI Programming Interface (ASPI) and Common Access Method (CAM).

Floppy Devices and Drivers

Windows 95 provides a protected-mode (32-bit) driver for the floppy drive. This means that all of the advantages of protected mode (multitasking, performance, and reliability) are now available when using or formatting floppy disks.

Removable Media Drivers

Most removable media have new protected-mode drivers. Windows 95 supports floppy drives, CD-ROM drives, and other removable media, such as Iomega's Zip and Jaz drives. Windows 95 allows you to lock the media so it cannot be ejected during your session. Windows 95 also supports software-controlled ejection of your media.

Improved support for docking stations has also been added. Windows 95 can detect when your docking status has changed, and can work in *hot docking* (where the computer is on when docking or undocking) or *cold docking* (where the computer is turned off before docking or undocking). Windows 95 can even help resolve hot undocking problems by asking the user to save files that would be lost after the undocking.

Troubleshooting Windows 95 Disk Drivers

Windows 95 sometimes has problems with older hard drives and controllers. There are several things you can do to troubleshoot a disk driver problem. Most of the solutions entail turning off features of Windows 95 so that it operates in an older, more compatible mode.

Microsoft ✓ *Exam* *Objective*

Diagnose and resolve file system problems.

There are also times when you might want to disable certain features of Windows 95, including some features of the 32-bit disk drivers, even when they are working correctly, because they are not what the user wants. For instance, users may want to disable the write-behind cache because they have been losing data during power outages (or just when the user turns the power off without shutting down Windows 95 properly).

Disabling the 32-Bit Mode Drivers

Some older hard drive controllers or older motherboards may have a difficult time using 32-bit drivers. If this is the case, you can set Windows 95 to disable 32-bit mode operation to the hard drive. You can disable the 32-bit mode drivers through the Troubleshooting tab of the File System Properties dialog box, shown in Figure 8.1. Exercise 8.1 shows the steps involved.

FIGURE 8.1

Disabling the 32-bit disk drivers

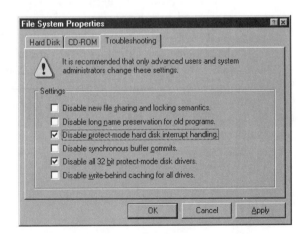

EXERCISE 8.1

Disabling the 32-bit Mode Drivers

1. Go to Control Panel ➤ System and choose the Performance tab.

2. Click on the File System button at the bottom of the dialog box.

3. Choose the Troubleshooting tab in the File System Properties dialog box.

4. Select the two checkboxes to disable 32-bit mode: Disable all 32 bit protect-mode disk drivers and Disable protect-mode hard disk interrupt handling (Figure 8.1). This will cause 16-bit drivers to be used.

Installing old DOS drivers directly in the CONFIG.SYS or AUTOEXEC.BAT file can sometimes automatically "trip" the switches in this troubleshooting exercise.

Disabling the Write-Behind Cache

Earlier versions of DOS introduced the concept of a *hard drive cache*, which is used to read data into RAM before the CPU requests it, hoping that the CPU can get the data from the cache instead of the hard disk.

DOS 6.0 introduced the *write-behind cache* as an extension of the read cache. A write-behind cache fools applications by writing their changes into RAM, and then flushing the changes to the hard disk eventually. The application will behave as if the data had been written, when the data is actually in volatile RAM. If the computer is turned off for any reason before the data is flushed to disk, the data is gone. Write-behind caching is a default feature of Windows 95 that was designed with performance (not safety) in mind.

Exercise 8.2 shows you how to disable the write-behind cache.

EXERCISE 8.2

Disabling the Write-Behind Cache

1. Go to Control Panel ➢ System and choose the Performance tab.

2. Click on the File System button at the bottom of the dialog box.

3. Choose the Troubleshooting tab in the File System Properties dialog box (Figure 8.1).

4. Select Disable write-behind caching for all drives. Now only the read cache is enabled.

Long Filenames

As explained in Chapter 5, Windows 95 has added the ability to save files with names up to 255 characters long.

Although filenames can be 255 characters long, the entire path of a file can only be 260 characters.

Spaces in filenames are now supported as well. All 32-bit programs should be able to recognize, use, and save files with long filenames.

Microsoft ✓ *Exam* *Objective* | **Diagnose and resolve resource access problems.**

Older 16-bit programs use the older file system API, which does not recognize long filenames. For compatibility purposes, Windows 95 constructs an 8.3 name whenever a long filename is saved. See Chapter 5 for some examples of how Windows 95 truncates long filenames.

When Windows 95 truncates a long filename to make an 8.3 name, the default setting uses the first six characters and then a tilde (~). You can configure Windows 95 to not use tildes by making a change to the registry. Exercise 6.5 in Chapter 6 shows how to disable the tilde. You can see the 8.3 names from the MS-DOS prompt or by viewing the properties of a file.

Once you start using long filenames, you will wonder how you ever got along with just the 8.3 convention. The only problems you will probably face will be exchanging files with people not on Windows 95 (they will see the 8.3 alias) and using applications or utilities that don't recognize the long filenames. The following sections describe how long filenames work on servers and problems you may encounter with long filenames.

Long Filenames on Servers

Windows 95 can save files with long filenames on networks if the servers support long filenames. Microsoft's Windows NT versions 3.5 and higher support long filenames natively. Novell's NetWare needs to have support for OS/2 installed before Windows 95 can use long filenames on the server.

If you have DOS clients on the network, they will see the long filename files as 8.3 files. Macintosh clients will see the long filename if it is less than 34 characters (the Macintosh limit). Otherwise, the Macintosh client will see the 8.3 name.

Problems Associated with Long Filenames

You may come across programs, such as applications, backup programs, or utilities, that don't recognize long filenames. Another problem you may encounter with long filenames is that they take up more directory entries, thus limiting the number of files that may be stored in a root directory. The following sections discuss these issues and suggest how to troubleshoot and fix problems.

Programs That Don't Recognize Long Filenames

The main category of programs that won't recognize long filenames are older, 16-bit programs. These programs will show only the 8.3 alias for both folders and files when you go to open or save a file. The solution to this problem is quite simple—upgrade to the 32-bit, Windows 95 version of the software.

Older backup programs may not recognize long filenames. If you use older backup programs, or programs that are not certified to work with Windows 95, you will probably be able to back up your files, but only the 8.3 names will be saved. If you do restore your files and find you have only 8.3 names, there is no way to fix the problem—the long filenames will be permanently gone.

Older versions of utility programs such as Norton Disk Utilities and PC Tools are not compatible with Windows 95. These older disk utilities will not only report errors when they encounter long filenames, but may also cause long filenames and even data files to be erased.

Make sure that any backup or utility program you run under Windows 95 has been certified for Windows 95.

The 512 Directory Entry Limit in Root Directories

A file is normally allocated 11 spaces (one directory entry) for the filename. Long filenames work by being assigned one directory entry for every 11 spaces of the filename. For example, if the long filename is composed of 23 to 33 characters, it takes three directory entries, and so on.

By default, the root of any volume is limited to 512 directory entries. Under DOS, that would mean that you were limited to 512 files in the root directory, no matter how much hard drive space you had left. Under Windows 95, if each file is taking five directory entries (names of 45 to 55 characters on average), then there are only enough directory entries for a little more than 100 files. The solution is either to use shorter names for files in the root directory, or keep as few files as possible in the root of any volume.

Turning Off Long Filenames

If you have an application that is incompatible with long filenames, you can temporarily disable long filenames, run your application, and re-enable long filenames again. You can also disable long filenames on a permanent basis.

To temporarily back up and remove long filenames, you can run the LFNBK utility, which copies all of the long filenames out to a file, and then renames the files to match their 8.3 aliases. Exercise 8.3 shows the steps for backing up your old filenames, deleting them, and then restoring your saved filenames.

WARNING

It is recommended that you just read through Exercise 8.3, or perform the steps on a non-critical computer. LFNBK is an advanced utility, and should be run only by people with a very good working knowledge of Windows 95.

EXERCISE 8.3

Backing Up, Deleting, and Restoring Long Filenames

1. Go to Control Panel ➤ System and choose the Performance tab.

2. Click on the File System button at the bottom of the dialog box.

3. Choose the Troubleshooting tab in the File System Properties dialog box (Figure 8.1).

4. Check the Disable long name preservation for old programs option.

5. Close all applications and files.

6. At a command prompt, type **LFNBK /b** *drive*, where *drive* is the drive you want the long filenames removed from. LFNBK will back up the long filenames to a file on the root of the drive called LFNBK .DAT, and will remove long filenames from your drive by renaming all your files to their 8.3 aliases.

7. Restart your computer and run the application that is incompatible with long filenames.

8. At a command prompt, type **LFNBK /r** *drive*, where *drive* is the drive you want to restore long filenames to.

9. Return to the Troubleshooting tab of the File System Properties dialog box and uncheck the Disable long name preservation for old programs option.

10. Restart your computer.

If your directory structure changes for any reason (such as defragmentation, adding and deleting folders, and so on), the LFNBK.DAT file will no longer precisely correspond to your drive, and your long filenames cannot be restored.

To permanently disable long filenames, you need to first remove long filenames using the LFNBK /b option. You can also use the Scandsk /o option to remove long filenames. You will then need to go to the registry in the Hkey_ Local_Machine\System\CurrentControlSet\Control\FileSystem and set the Win31FileSystem value to 1 (see Chapter 6 for more information about modifying the registry). After your next reboot, your file system will be that of the old DOS.

Disk Compression

Disk compression has been around for many years. Some early versions of disk compression required that a hardware compression board be installed in the computer, while others were software-based.

The primary benefit of using disk compression is that you can store more on a hard drive. The two disadvantages of using compression are a speed decrease and a chance for the entire drive to become corrupted. With prices of hard drives dropping rapidly over the last couple of years, compression makes more sense for computers that are hard to upgrade to larger hard drives (such as laptops) than for computers easily upgraded (such as desktops).

Microsoft ✓ *Exam Objective*

Manage hard disks. Tasks include:

- Disk compression
- Partitioning

Windows 95 supports and comes with software-based, real-time compression of volumes and disk drives. By using compression, you can gain anywhere from 10 to 100 percent or more free disk space. Windows 95 has new protected-mode compression drivers, but is also backward-compatible with older compression programs from Microsoft. Because compression is now an integral part of Windows 95, both the paging file and Windows 95 itself can be kept on a compressed drive.

WARNING

Drives compressed under Windows 95 are unavailable to both OS/2 and to Windows NT. If you are dual-booting Windows 95 and NT, you should not use compression.

Windows 95 is compatible with DOS compression programs, including DBLSPACE and DRVSPACE. Windows 95 replaces the DBLSPACE.BIN or DRVSPACE.BIN files in the root directory with ones that it can unload, so that the 32-bit version (DBLSPACX.VXD) can be loaded.

The version of compression that comes with Windows 95 is fully integrated into the operating system. This means that registry files, page files, and system files can all reside on a compressed drive. Compressed drives can hold long filenames, and can be cached by Vcache.

Compressing a Drive

When you compress a drive, you are actually taking the contents of an entire drive and putting them into one large file. The file is called a compressed volume file (CVF). The CVF usually has a filename such as DRVSPACE.000 or DBLSPACE.000. DRVSPACE.000 appears if Windows 95 reads an older compressed drive, and DBLSPACE.000 appears when Windows 95 reads a newer compressed drive or creates a new one.

Microsoft ✓ *Exam* *Objective*

Tune and optimize the system. Tools include:

- Disk Defragmenter
- ScanDisk
- DriveSpace

When you compress a drive, the CVF is stored on the host drive, which is the original drive. The host drive letter is then changed to a higher letter, usually H:. Programs see the compressed drive normally, but Windows 95 is actually compressing and decompressing files into and out of the CVF (which is on the H: drive) and displaying the uncompressed files as the C:. You can choose to hide the host drive, which is a good option for users with less experience; they will have less chance of damaging or deleting the CVF.

WARNING

It is absolutely essential that the CVF is not modified or edited by hand. Doing so could cause the entire compressed volume to become corrupt.

Compressing a Floppy Disk Drive

Compressing a drive under Windows 95 is a simple process. When you run the DriveSpace program and choose to compress a drive, it will show you before and after compression information, as shown in Figures 8.2 and 8.3. Follow the steps in Exercise 8.4 to compress a floppy disk drive. If you don't have DriveSpace installed, refer to Appendix B for information on installing additional software to your Windows 95 installation.

FIGURE 8.2

Confirming the compression

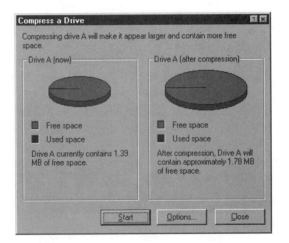

F I G U R E 8.3

Post compression
status screen

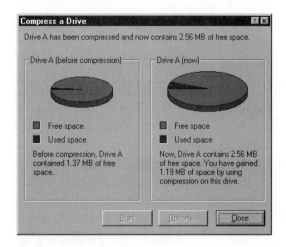

Compressing a Hard Disk Drive

The steps in Exercise 8.4 will also work on your hard drive, but you should
back up any critical data before compressing or decompressing a hard drive. If
you are compressing a hard drive, you can choose to compress the entire
volume or just a part of the volume. Windows 95 will prompt you for a size to
make the new drive, as shown in Figure 8.4.

F I G U R E 8.4

Choosing the size of the
compressed volume

EXERCISE 8.4

Compressing a Floppy Disk

1. Format a floppy disk, or find one that still has some room on it.

2. Select Start ➢ Run and type **drvspace**, or go to Start ➢ Programs ➢ Accessories ➢ System Tools ➢ DriveSpace. (If you have Microsoft Plus! installed, you can also go to the Properties dialog box for your floppy and choose the Compression tab.)

3. From the DriveSpace menu, highlight the floppy drive and choose Drive ➢ Compress. DriveSpace will then show you the estimated size of your new drive, and ask you to confirm before it actually does the compression (Figure 8.2).

4. Click on the Start button to start the compression.

5. After compressing your floppy, you should get a status screen, reporting on the compressed floppy drive (Figure 8.3).

6. Click on the Close button to close the window.

The Microsoft Plus! Software

Windows 95 is limited to compressing volumes 512MB or smaller. If you install Microsoft Plus!, not only do you get support for volumes up to 2GB, but you have several new options for compression such as Hipack and Ultrapack. If you have Microsoft Plus! installed, you can go to the Properties dialog box for your floppy and choose the Compression tab, shown in Figure 8.5.

> If you are going to use compression under Windows 95, using the Plus! software is highly recommended.

As you copy data to your new drive, you can check the status of your compressed files on the Compression tab of the drive's Properties dialog box, as shown in Figure 8.6. If there are many uncompressed files, you can run Compression Agent manually. Click on the Run Agent button in the Compression tab to see the Compression Agent dialog box, shown in Figure 8.7. You can either cause compression to happen with your current settings or you can change your compression settings.

F I G U R E 8.5

The Compression tab for
a floppy drive, with
Microsoft Plus! installed

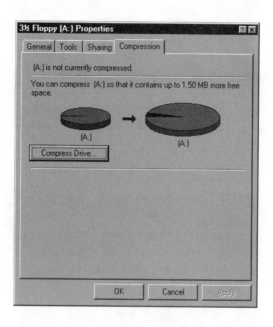

F I G U R E 8.5

The Compression tab for
a floppy drive, with
Microsoft Plus! installed

F I G U R E 8.6

Checking the status of
your compressed volume

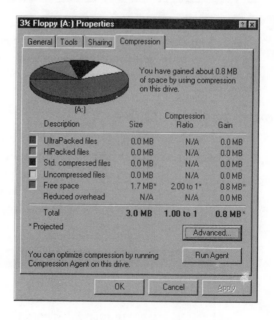

FIGURE 8.7

Running Compression
Agent manually

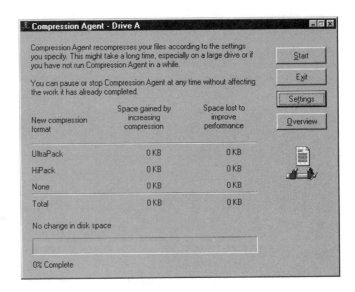

The Compression tab exists only if the Plus! software was installed. Compression Agent also comes with the Plus! software. If you don't have Plus! installed, you can still get compression ratios—you just need to start DriveSpace manually by choosing Accessories ➢ System Tools.

Decompressing a Drive

You may want to decompress your drive at some future date. Windows 95 supports nondestructive decompression of the hard drive. When you run DriveSpace and choose the Uncompress option, you will see before and after uncompression status screens, similar to the compression status screens (Figures 8.2 and 8.3). In Exercise 8.5, we will decompress the floppy you compressed in Exercise 8.4.

EXERCISE 8.5

Decompressing a Drive

1. Make sure your disk (floppy or hard drive) is large enough to hold the files it may contain after it has been decompressed by checking the Properties dialog box for your disk. Make sure that used space is less than the capacity of your drive after decompression.

---

2. Select Start ➤ Run and type **drvspace**, or go to Start ➤ Programs ➤ Accessories ➤ System Tools ➤ DriveSpace. (If you have Microsoft Plus! installed, you can go to the Properties dialog box for your floppy and choose the Compression tab.)

3. Highlight the drive you want to decompress and choose Uncompress. Windows 95 will show an Uncompress screen, with estimates for how much free space your drive will have after uncompressing it.

4. Click on the Start button to begin the decompression process.

5. After successfully uncompressing your drive, you will see a final status screen, with your new used and free space for that drive.

6. Click on the Close button to close the window.

Disk Fragmentation

Over time, you may find your computer doesn't perform as fast as it once did. *Fragmentation* of your files may have occurred. Fragmentation is a natural phenomenon that can easily be fixed.

Fragmentation happens as files are deleted and their space is used by new files. When files are saved, they are saved in sequential order on your hard drive. If a 10MB file is being saved, it will use free space as it finds it, not bothering to look for a contiguous 10MB spot it can use. By being scattered all over the hard drive, the file is harder to find and put back together, and may take double the number of hard drive revolutions compared to the amount it would take if it were contiguous.

Defragmenting the Hard Drive

Windows 95 includes a disk defragmentation program. The default settings will defragment your drive both by making sure that files are stored in contiguous clusters and by consolidating free space so defragmentation is less likely to happen in the future. The defragmentation program will also run ScanDisk to check for errors before defragmenting.

Tune and optimize the system. Tools include:

- Disk Defragmenter
- ScanDisk
- DriveSpace

The defragmentation program is available from the Tools tab of any drive's Properties dialog box, as shown in Figure 8.8. You can go to the Advanced Options dialog box, shown in Figure 8.9, and change the way the defragmentation program will work, but the default options are probably the best. You can also see a graphical display of the defragmentation process, as shown in Figure 8.10. In Exercise 8.6, we will run the defragmentation program and look at the advanced options as well as the graphical display.

Of the three options for defragmenting your hard drive, the Full defragmentation takes the longest time, but will move all of your files and folders to the front of your hard drive, consolidating empty space at the back of the drive. The Defragment files only option defragments your files, but doesn't consolidate the free space throughout the drive, thus making it more likely that fragmentation will happen in the future. The Consolidate free space option is the quickest option, but simply consolidates existing free space into one lump, and doesn't defragment existing files. This option would be good if you were planning on installing new software, but probably won't do anything to speed up existing software.

If you have installed the Microsoft Plus! software (which contains additional applications and utilities for Windows 95), the disk defragmentation program (along with other programs) is scheduled to run automatically by a Plus! application called System Agent. System Agent, and how to add, change, and delete Plus! tasks, is covered later in this chapter.

FIGURE 8.8

The Disk
Defragmentation
dialog box

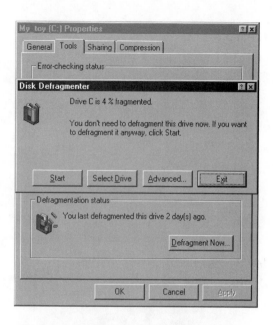

FIGURE 8.9

The Advanced Options
dialog box

FIGURE 8.10

Disk defragmentation in progress

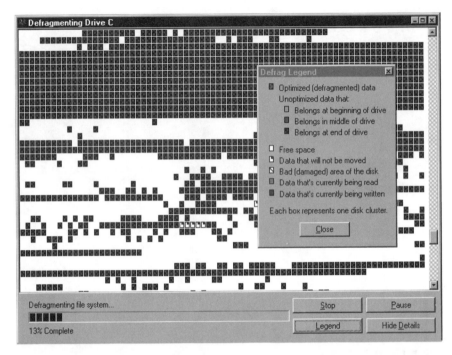

EXERCISE 8.6

Defragmenting a Hard Drive

1. Go to the Properties dialog box for any drive and choose the Tools tab. From there, choose the Defragment Now button (Figure 8.8). The disk defragmenting program will analyze your hard drive and suggest defragmentation if it is needed.

2. Click on the Advanced button to see how you can change the way defragmentation works (Figure 8.9). The default settings are recommended.

3. Start the fragmentation process, even if it is not recommended, by clicking on the Start button.

4. While your disk is defragmenting, click on the Show Details button to get a graphical representation of your drive. Then click on the Legend button to see the Defrag Legend box (Figure 8.10).

5. After defragmentation is complete, close the window.

Checking for Disk Errors Using ScanDisk

Although there is no software fix for your hard drive if the drive is failing because of physical defects, there are some problems that occur on a hard drive that can be repaired with software. Windows 95 comes with a program called ScanDisk, which can diagnose and fix many problems with either floppy drives or hard drives.

Microsoft ✓ *Exam* *Objective*

Tune and optimize the system. Tools include:

- Disk Defragmenter
- ScanDisk
- DriveSpace

Common Disk Problems

Several things can happen to files on your hard drive that might make them unusable. Some problems are easily fixed; others can be very serious. Here are some occurrences that could cause problems on your drive:

- **Crosslinked files:** This can happen when two or more files have become confused as to where their data resides. The crosslinked files both point to the same data area, as illustrated in Figure 8.11. This is one of the more serious errors, because one of the two files no longer points to the correct data area, and will probably not be recoverable.

FIGURE 8.11

Crosslinked files

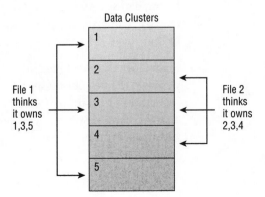

Data Clusters

1
2
3
4
5

File 1 thinks it owns 1,3,5

File 2 thinks it owns 2,3,4

- **Bad spots:** These can occur on either a floppy disk or hard drive and prevent programs or data files from working correctly. Bad spots can happen naturally because of wear and tear on a drive, or can be caused by scratching the surface of a floppy by touching it, or of a hard drive by the drive head hitting the platter (usually because of dropping or banging the drive while in use). Bad spots can sometimes be read, and the data moved to a good spot, but sometimes a bad spot will be completely inaccessible. If the latter happens, the affected file is probably unrecoverable.

- **Lost clusters:** These appear when data areas have not been correctly identified as either in use or available for use by a new file. Lost clusters cannot be used for files until their status is resolved. Lost clusters can either be correctly identified as deleted, or can be recovered as files in case something valuable was in those clusters. This is usually the least damaging problem that you will encounter on your hard drive.

Fixing Problems Using ScanDisk

ScanDisk can fix all three of these problems. As with any kind of troubleshooting, success is never guaranteed, but ScanDisk has a relatively good chance:

- **Fixing crosslinked files:** Since ScanDisk can't tell which crosslinked file is the original and which one got attached by mistake, by default it fixes crosslinked files by taking the crosslinked data area and attaching it to both files. One of your files will be good, while the other one will be corrupted. You can have ScanDisk copy the crosslinked data to both files, delete both files, or ignore any crosslinked errors by using the Advanced button.

- **Fixing bad spots:** Files that happen to be on bad spots can sometimes be read by ScanDisk, and moved to a safe area. The bad area is then marked so that future files will not try to save there.

- **Fixing lost clusters:** Lost clusters can either be erased or saved as a file. If you save the lost cluster as a file, you can later look at the file and see if it contains any data that you still need. Seldom, if ever, do these files contain anything of use. You can choose either option by using the Advanced button.

The ScanDisk program is available from the Tools tab of the drive's Properties dialog box, as shown in Figure 8.12. Click on the Advanced button while in ScanDisk if you want to configure how ScanDisk will run, and how it will deal with any errors it may find. Figure 8.13 shows the ScanDisk Advanced Options dialog box. In Exercise 8.7, we will run ScanDisk to check the C: drive for errors.

FIGURE 8.12

Starting ScanDisk

FIGURE 8.13

The ScanDisk Advanced
Options dialog box

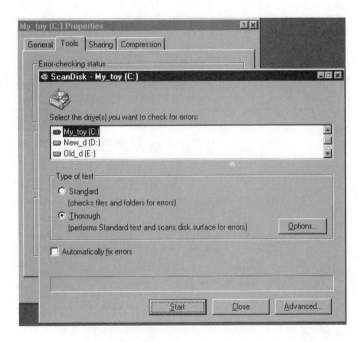

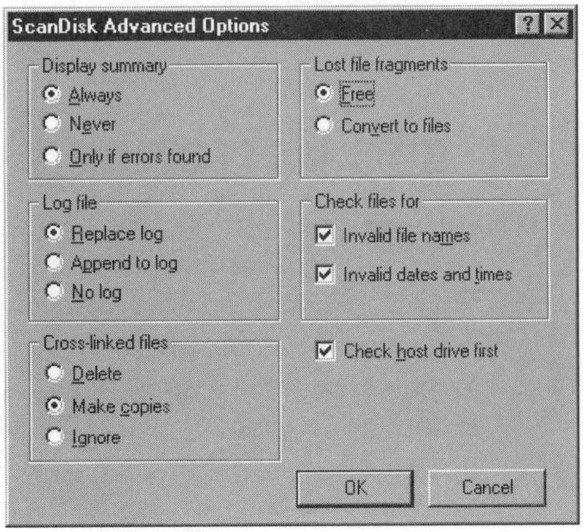

EXERCISE 8.7

Checking a Drive for Errors with ScanDisk

1. Go to the Properties dialog box for the C: drive, choose the Tools tab, and select Check Now from the Error-checking status section of the dialog box (Figure 8.12).

2. Click on the Advanced button to see the default options (Figure 8.13). Click on Cancel to go back to the main ScanDisk dialog box.

3. If you are in a hurry, choose Standard for the type of test and check the Automatically fix errors checkbox. If you have a while, choose the Thorough test and deselect Automatically fix errors.

4. Wait for ScanDisk to finish. If there are any errors, ScanDisk will automatically fix them (if selected) or it will prompt you on how to fix them.

5. If you selected a Thorough test, ScanDisk will check your current files, and will then check the entire hard drive for bad spots—this takes a while.

6. When ScanDisk is finished, close its information box.

If you have installed the Microsoft Plus! software, the System Agent automatically schedules ScanDisk to run at regular intervals. The System Agent is covered later in the chapter.

Backing Up and Restoring Data

Today's hardware has become so reliable that people expect it to work forever. When a hard drive fails, it is usually catastrophic, because most people don't expect hard drives to fail anymore and are not prepared when they do. Viruses are another reason to back up your data, because certain viruses can cause data loss. Data can also be lost because of accidental or malicious deletions by users.

Back up data and restore data.

Windows 95 includes a backup and restore program that lets you easily back up and restore files on your hard drive. Although there are many different programs you could use to back up your hard drive, the program that comes with Windows 95 has the advantage of being able to save long filenames; other programs may not preserve long filenames if they are not certified for Windows 95.

Installing Backup Hardware and Software

Before you can use the Backup program you will need to install your hardware and software.

Install and configure backup hardware and software. Hardware and software include:

- Tape drives
- The Backup application

The Backup application supports backing up to a wide variety of hardware devices. You can back up to floppy disks, other hard disks, a network drive, or a tape drive. Tape drives are probably the hardest type of devices to install, but they offer an inexpensive backup solution so they are in wide use.

Because the Backup program can back up to network drives, if you need to reinstall Windows 95 you can back up all of your data to the network, reinstall Windows 95, and then restore your data. Backing up to a network drive is also useful if your hard drive outgrows your tape drive.

Installing Tape Devices

There are three generic categories of tape drives: those that work with Windows 95 software, those that install their own software, and those that won't work under Windows 95 at all.

Native Windows 95 Tape Drives   Native Windows 95 tape drives are few and far between. The help files for the Backup program list compatible tape drives, which mostly consist of QIC 40, 80, and 3010 tape drives. These types of tape drives have become relatively obsolete in recent years. If you had one of these tape drives, it probably connected to the floppy controller, or through the parallel port. The Backup program should detect these tape drives automatically when it starts. You can force a scan for compatible tape drives by going to Tools ➤ Redetect Tape Drive from within the backup program.

Third-Party Tape Drives   Most newer tape drives come with their own software. Newer tape drives are capable of backing up 10GB of data, and cost only $300 or so. Some tape drives and the software they come with can simulate a (very slow) hard drive, in that you can drag and drop files onto the tape drive to do your backups.

Incompatible Tape Drives   Older tape drives may not even be compatible with Windows 95. For example, a local computer store was going out of business and had an 850MB tape drive for about $12! When I asked about compatibility, I found out that it only worked under MS-DOS, and wouldn't even work in DOS mode in Windows 95. Needless to say, I didn't buy it.

Installing the Software

When you install the backup software, you have two choices as to how your computer will be backed up.

- The Backup program allows you to make local backups.

- Backup agents allow a network server to back up your computer.

Installing the Backup Program   Installing the Backup program is done via the Add Software applet in the Control Panel. The Disk Tools category contains only one entry—that of the Backup program. After you install the Backup program you will be able to run it from Start ➤ Programs ➤ Accessories ➤ System Tools ➤ Backup.

Installing Backup Agents   Windows 95 comes with native agents for Arcada and Cheyenne backup programs. By installing these agents, you allow a network server (with a really big tape drive) to back up your computer to the network. Of course, your network server will need to be running the appropriate backup application (Arcada or Cheyenne) in order to use the agent installed on your computer.

You install the backup agents by going to Control Panel ➤ Network ➤ Add ➤ Service. You will see both Arcada Software and Cheyenne Software listed; choose the appropriate agent to install. After you install the agent, it loads automatically when you boot Windows 95. Note that there may be newer versions of the agents supplied with the latest versions of Arcada and Cheyenne software.

Backing Up Your Data

The Windows 95 Backup program was designed to be easy to use. The Backup program can back up to any valid device, including floppies, hard drives, tape drives, removable media (such as ZIP drives), or network drives. When you start the Backup program, you are asked to choose the files you want to back up, as shown in Figure 8.14. In Exercise 8.8, we will create a backup directory and back up the Windows 95 cursors to it.

FIGURE 8.14

Marking a folder for backup

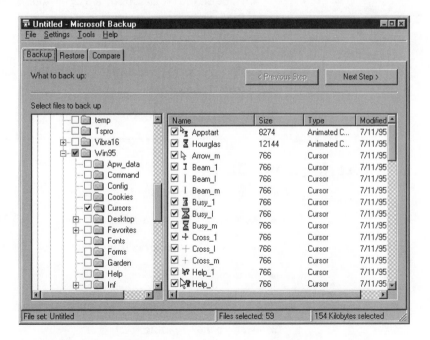

In order to back up the registry, you need to choose to back up the folder and subfolders where Windows 95 is installed.

EXERCISE 8.8

Backing Up Data

1. Create a folder on your C: drive called Backups.

2. Start the Backup program by going to the Properties dialog box of the C: drive and choosing Backup Now from the middle pane. The Backup Wizard will start, allowing you to select what you want to back up.

3. Open the C: drive and go to your Windows 95 directory. You should find a Cursors folder. Click on the Cursors folder to mark it for backup (Figure 8.14). (If you don't have a Cursors folder, see Appendix B for information about how to install additional cursors with Windows 95.)

4. Click on the Next button, and open your C: drive. Highlight the Backups folder you created in step 1.

5. Click on Start Backup.

6. Give the backup set a name (such as **test**). After a few seconds, the backup should finish.

7. Close the window.

Restoring Your Data

There are several reasons you may need to restore data:

- Accidental erasure or editing of data

- Malicious erasure or editing of data

- Viruses

- Failure of a hard disk

- Archive data loading

There are several questions to ask yourself before you can restore your data:

- Do I have a valid backup?

- Have I solved the problem that is requiring me to restore my data?

- Where do I want to restore my data to?

If you don't have a valid backup, you may need to send your hard drive to a professional repair service. This can get quite expensive—one client spent over $9,000! (They did get their data back, however). If you have a valid backup and you have fixed your problem, then restoring your data is relatively simple.

To restore your data, run the Backup program and choose the Restore tab, shown in Figure 8.15. You can select to restore to the same drive and directory, or you can specify a different drive and directory to restore to. If you suffer a complete failure of your hard drive, but you have a backup on tape, you will need to reinstall Windows 95 and then use the restore program to restore your drive the way it was.

FIGURE 8.15

Choosing files to restore

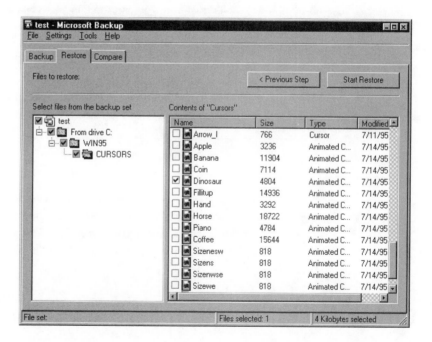

In Exercise 8.9, we will rename one of the cursor files we backed up in Exercise 8.8. We will then restore from our backup, which will let us recover the file we renamed.

EXERCISE 8.9

Restoring Files

1. Go to the C:\Windows95\Cursors folder and rename the Dinosaur animated cursor to something else (like **T-REX**).

2. Start the Backup program by selecting Start ➢ Programs ➢ Accessories ➢ System Tools ➢ Backup.

3. Choose the Restore tab. Open the C: drive and highlight your Back-ups directory. The backup set you saved in Exercise 8.8 should show up. If you cannot find your backup, repeat Exercise 8.8.

4. Highlight your backup set and choose Next.

5. Open your backup set and deselect everything.

6. Scroll down until you find the Dinosaur animated cursors. Put a check in the appropriate box (Figure 8.15).

7. Click on the Start Restore button. After a few seconds, the restore process should finish successfully.

8. Go back to your Cursors folder and make sure the Dinosaur cursors are back (you may need to refresh with F5).

WARNING

The Backup program that is included with Windows 95 is not compatible with any earlier versions from DOS such as the Windows 3.1 Backup. If you have backup files that were made with a DOS version of a backup program, you will not be able to restore those with Windows 95.

Other Disk-Management Tasks

Windows 95 includes other tools and utilities that help you manage your hard drive and files. The major tasks and tools required for each are detailed in the following sections.

Windows 95 comes with an application that tracks files as you delete them. When deleting files from within Windows 95, the files are not actually deleted, but are moved to a special directory called Recycle Bin. The Recycle Bin is covered in Chapter 5.

Using System Agent for Plus!

If you have installed Microsoft Plus!, there is an additional program that is installed called System Agent. System Agent can be used to run programs on a pre-set schedule. Running the ScanDisk and Disk Defragmenter programs is scheduled by default when you install System Agent.

You can add, edit, or delete scheduled tasks by opening System Agent (you don't technically start System Agent; it is always running in the background). Figure 8.16 shows System Agent's schedule for the ScanDisk program. Clicking on the Change Schedule button in this Properties dialog box brings up the dialog box shown in Figure 8.17. Follow the steps in Exercise 8.10 to open System Agent, look at what tasks have been scheduled, and add a new task.

F I G U R E 8.16

Looking at
scheduled tasks

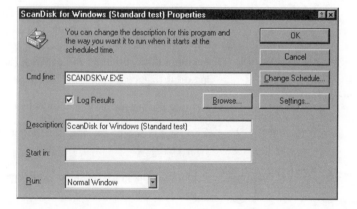

System Agent does not come with Windows 95—it must be purchased as part of the Plus! software. If you don't have the Plus! software installed, you will not be able to perform Exercise 8.10.

FIGURE 8.17

Scheduling a time for
your task

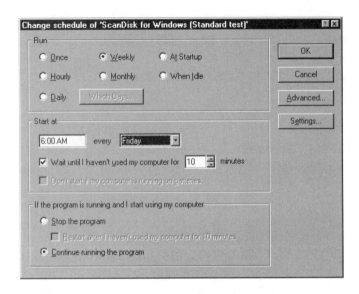

EXERCISE 8.10

Using the System Agent

1. Open System Agent by selecting Start ➢ Programs ➢ Accessories ➢ System Tools ➢ System Agent.

2. Examine the properties of ScanDisk (Standard test) by double-clicking on it (Figure 8.16).

3. Change the schedule of ScanDisk by clicking on the Schedule button.

4. Choose a different day and time (Figure 8.17) and choose OK to save your changes.

5. Add a new program by selecting Program ➢ Schedule a New Program, as shown below.

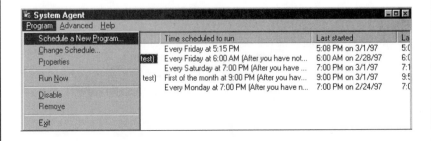

6. In the Cmd Line box of the Properties dialog box, enter the appropriate path for the Solitaire program (usually C:\WIN95\Sol.exe).

7. In the Change schedule dialog box, choose Daily and type **7:00 PM** in the Start at box.

8. Once you are satisfied that it works, delete the task by highlighting the task in the System Agent and choosing Program ➤ Remove, as shown below.

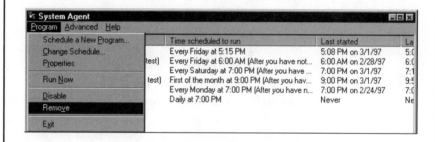

Disk Partitioning

Before you can format a hard drive, it must be partitioned. The original version of Windows 95 allows a maximum size for primary and logical partitions of up to 2GB each.

Microsoft ✓ **Exam Objective**

Manage hard disks. Tasks include:

- Disk compression
- Partitioning

There are three types of partitions you can make using the Fdisk utility: primary, extended, and logical. Each of these partition types is described in detail in the following sections.

Primary Partition

The first partition you create on a hard disk is almost always a primary partition. A primary partition is required to be bootable in DOS. This is generally how the C: drive is partitioned. Older versions of DOS (5.0 and earlier) would allow only one primary partition per hard drive, but DOS 6.0 and higher permit up to four.

Extended and Logical Partitions

An extended partition can hold logical partitions within it, and these can be formatted as separate drives. Extended partitions exist because of the limitations that older versions of DOS (5.0 and earlier) had on the number and sizes of partitions. Older versions of DOS would allow only two partitions: one primary and one of another type. Older versions of DOS also would allow partitions of only 30MB or less. If you had a hard drive that was 80MB, and were not using extended partitions, you could have only 60MB of your hard drive in use (30MB on each of the two allowed partitions).

Extended partitions can fill the remainder of the space left after the primary partition is created. Within the extended partition, logical drives can be created (each adhering to the 30MB size restriction).

By using logical partitions within extended partitions, DOS can get around its limitations of number of partitions (two—the primary and extended) and size of partition. Size restrictions affect only primary and logical partitions, so the extended partition can be as large as is needed to fill the hard drive.

We still have a size restriction of 2GB, so being able to use primary, extended, and logical partitions is still useful. Figure 8.18 shows a typical hard drive, with a primary partition (C:) and an extended partition that has been divided into a D: and an E: by using logical partitions.

FIGURE 8.18

Disk Partitions

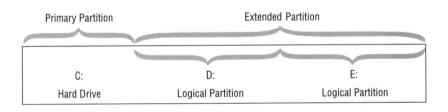

Partitioning a Disk with Fdisk

Windows 95 does not provide a graphical partition manager. You must still use the DOS-based partition manager called Fdisk, shown in Figure 8.19. When you choose to display the partition information, you'll see a screen similar to the one shown in Figure 8.20. Fdisk also allows you to change your current hard drive, as shown in Figure 8.21. In Exercise 8.11, we will use Fdisk to look at the disk partition on the drive.

FIGURE 8.19

The Fdisk menu

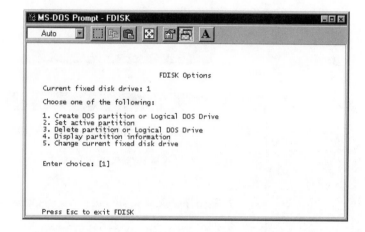

FIGURE 8.20

Fdisk partition information

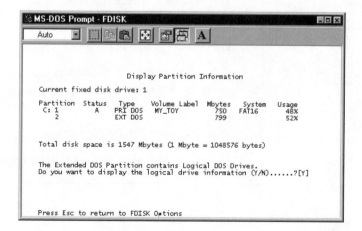

FIGURE 8.21

Choosing a hard drive to change

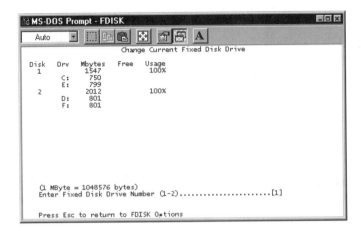

EXERCISE 8.11

Looking at Partitions with Fdisk

1. Open a DOS screen by selecting Start ➢ Programs ➢ MS-DOS Prompt.

2. Type **Fdisk**. You should see the FDISK Options screen (Figure 8.19).

3. Choose 4. Display partition information.

4. From the information screen (Figure 8.20), press Y to see your logical drive partitions (if applicable).

5. Press the Escape key when you are finished looking.

6. If you have more than one hard drive, go back to the main menu and choose 5. Change current fixed disk drive. The next screen will show your hard disks (Figure 8.21).

7. Repeat steps 3–6 for each drive.

8. Press Escape when you are finished looking around.

Any changes you make with Fdisk will destroy all of your data on that partition. To nondestructively change your partitions, use a product like Partition-Magic from PowerQuest Corporation (the company's Web site is www .powerquest.com).

Formatting Drives

Before a floppy or hard drive can be used, it must be formatted. You can format a drive from a DOS prompt, or use the Windows 95 Format feature, shown in Figure 8.22. The options in the Format dialog box let you do a quick format (which reformats just the header part of the disk), make a system disk (equivalent to the old SYS command or FORMAT /s command), or do a full format (equivalent to the FORMAT command). In Exercise 8.12, we will format a floppy using the mouse.

WARNING

Formatting a disk using the /s switch is not the same as running the Sys command on a disk. The Format c: /s command creates a system disk, but also reformats the drive, completely wiping out all data that was on the drive. The Sys c: command will also copy the system files onto a disk, but will do it non-destructively, by moving files around to make room for the system files.

FIGURE 8.22

The Windows 95
Format dialog box

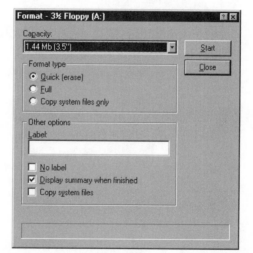

EXERCISE 8.12

Formatting a Floppy

1. Insert a floppy that it is safe to format (no essential data is on the disk).

2. Go to My Computer.

3. Highlight the floppy and right-click on it.

> **EXERCISE 8.12 (CONTINUED FROM PREVIOUS PAGE)**
>
> **4.** Choose Format from the pop-up menu.
>
> **5.** You will be presented with the Format dialog box, which lets you choose how to format the disk (Figure 8.22). Choose Quick Format.
>
> **6.** In a few seconds, the disk will be formatted.
>
> **7.** Close the Format dialog box.

Managing the Hard Drive Cache

A caching program uses RAM to store information to and from the hard drive, so that the CPU can get the information from RAM instead of from the hard drive. When caching is enabled, the CPU checks the cache for any data it might need. If the data is in cache, it can be quickly grabbed by the CPU. If the data is not in cache, the CPU will read the data from the hard drive, as shown in Figure 8.23. Because RAM is rated in nanoseconds, and hard drives in milliseconds, it is easy to see that using RAM to temporarily cache data can significantly speed up access to data on the hard drive.

FIGURE 8.23

A hard drive cache

Running Vcache

Windows 95 uses a new 32-bit program called Vcache to manage the caching of data from the hard drive. You can adjust the size of Vcache to increase performance if you have enough RAM for your applications. There is also a setting that affects the way your computer reserves memory for use. You can set your computer for the role it plays: as a server, workstation, or laptop. These settings are located on the Hard Disk tab of the File System Properties dialog box, shown in Figure 8.24. In Exercise 8.13, we will look at the Vcache settings and the role of your computer.

FIGURE 8.24

Adjusting Vcache

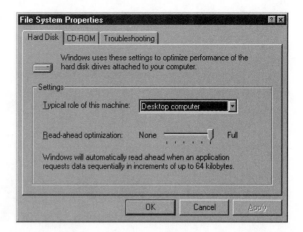

EXERCISE 8.13

Adjusting the Size of Vcache and Setting the Role

1. Select Control Panel ➤ System ➤ Performance ➤ File System ➤ Hard Disk tab.

2. Choose the role that your computer will function as most of the time (probably Desktop computer).

3. Adjust Vcache to its maximum size by sliding the Read-Ahead Optimization slider to the right to the Full setting (Figure 8.24).

4. Click on OK to close the dialog box and save your changes.

Running CDFS

You must set the size of the CD-ROM cache separately from the size of the hard drive cache. Caching is built into the CD-ROM driver, which is called CDFS. This keeps the CD-ROM and hard drive from competing with each other, and increases performance. The CD-ROM cache settings are located on the CD-ROM tab of the File System Properties dialog box, shown in Figure 8.25. Follow the steps in Exercise 8.14 to adjust this cache's settings.

If you need to use a real-mode driver (a 16-bit driver) for your CD-ROM, you must use SMARTDRV (a 16-bit caching program) to cache your CD-ROM.

FIGURE 8.25

Adjusting the
CD-ROM cache

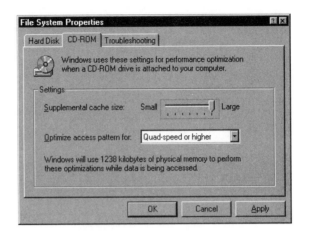

EXERCISE 8.14

Adjusting the Size of the CD-ROM Cache

1. Select Control Panel ➢ System ➢ Performance ➢ File System ➢ CD-ROM tab.

2. If you have 16MB or more of RAM, adjust the size of the cache to its largest size (Figure 8.25). If you have 8MB of RAM, adjust the size of the cache to about the halfway point. If you have less than 8MB, go get some more RAM!

3. Make sure the speed setting is also correct for your CD-ROM.

4. Click on OK to close the dialog box and save your changes.

Optimizing Your Cluster Size

Hard drives are organized by sectors, with clusters as groups of sectors. The cluster is the smallest size that a file uses when it is saved; clusters can't be subdivided between files.

The FAT file system that is used to format floppy disks and hard drives has been with us since DOS 1.0. It was never intended for huge partitions such as those we are seeing now. Because DOS and Windows 95 must remain backward-compatible with older versions of DOS, newer operating systems (including Windows 95) must find ways to extend the operating system while adhering to the restrictions of previous versions of DOS. DOS and Windows 95 overcome the FAT's limitations in the size of partitions by increasing the size of each cluster as the partition grows bigger. This older way of partitioning drives is referred to as FAT16.

Size of Partition	Size of Clusters in FAT16
1–15 MB*	4KB
16–127MB	2KB
128–255MB	4KB
256–511MB	8KB
512–1023MB	16KB
1024–2047MB	32KB

*The FAT for 1-15 MB partitions is a 12-bit FAT. All others are 16-bit FAT.

As you can see, when partitions become bigger, the cluster size also becomes bigger. Anytime a file is saved, it uses at least one cluster, so files saved on large partitions have more wasted space than those on smaller partitions. In other words, a file that contains only one sentence still takes 32KB if saved on a partition larger than 1023MB.

The FAT32 Solution

Microsoft's response to the problem of large cluster sizes has been to release a version of Windows 95 that fixes the problem by supporting partitions up to 8GB with a cluster size of only 4KB and supports a maximum volume size of 2 terabytes (TB)! This new FAT scheme is called FAT32.

Size of Partition	Size of Clusters in FAT32
1–512MB	FAT16 is used
513MB–8GB	4KB
8GB–16GB	8KB
16GB–32GB	16KB

The only problem is that FAT32, which comes with Windows 95B (OSR2), is no longer backward-compatible with DOS or with some third-party utilities that were compatible with the original version of Windows 95.

FAT32 partitions are not visible to NT 4.0 or MS-DOS, but will be visible to Windows NT 5.0.

Follow the steps in Exercise 8.15 to determine which version of Windows 95 you have, and then to determine if your drives have been partitioned with OSR2.

Just because you have OSR2 doesn't necessarily mean you have the benefit of decreased cluster size. Use Exercise 8.15 to determine your partition status. If your hard drive was partitioned and formatted with non-OSR2 Fdisk and format, your partitions will be in the old FAT16 style. You need to make a startup disk with OSR2, delete your old partitions, make new partitions using the OSR2 startup disk, and reinstall Windows 95.

EXERCISE 8.15

Determining If OSR2 Partitioned Your Drives

1. Select Control Panel ➤ System.

2. Look for a system version (4.00.950). If you have a B after the number, you have Windows 95B (OSR2). Continue with the steps below to see if your drives have been partitioned with OSR2.

3. Run ScanDisk on your drive (see Exercise 8.7).

4. At the status screen shown at the end of the procedure, note the allocation unit size, as indicated below.

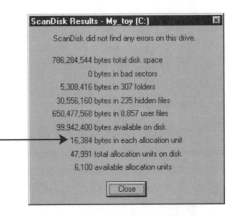

> **EXERCISE 8.15 (CONTINUED FROM PREVIOUS PAGE)**
>
> **5.** If the bytes per allocation unit (cluster) are greater than 16,000 or 32,000 bytes (as in the drive shown here), your drive was probably partitioned using an older version of DOS (FAT16). If your bytes per allocation unit are around 4000 (and you have a drive bigger than 512MB), your drive was partitioned with OSR2.

Summary

Windows 95 has various programs and utilities to help you manage your hard drive and files. New protected-mode drivers support almost any kind of hard drive and CD-ROM.

The chapter began with a summary of the types of disk drives and bus adapters supported by Windows 95. You then learned how to troubleshoot disk driver problems by disabling features such as 32-bit mode drivers and the write-behind cache.

Our next topic was long filenames and how to handle problems associated with them. These include programs that don't recognize long filenames and the 512 directory entry limit in root directories. You learned how to turn off and restore long filename support.

Next, we covered the built-in tools for managing disk resources:

- Compression is now natively supported by Windows 95. Run the DriveSpace program and choose to compress a drive. You are limited to 512MB or smaller when using compression, unless you have installed the Plus! pack.

- The defragmentation program is available from the Tools tab of any drive's Properties dialog box.

- ScanDisk is the main utility used to fix minor problems on your hard drive.

- The Backup program provides a quick and easy way to back up and restore both the registry and files. Files can be backed up to tape or to a local or network drive.

The final sections of the chapter described how to accomplish other disk-management tasks:

- Fdisk is used to partition a drive.

- Format is used to format a drive.

- A new 32-bit program called Vcache is used to manage the caching of data from the hard drive.

- Caching is built into the CD-ROM driver, which is called CDFS.

- A new FAT scheme called FAT32 supports partitions of up to 8GB with a cluster size of only 4KB.

Review Questions

1. What is the name of the program that can fix minor errors on your hard drive?

   A. Format

   B. Fdisk

   C. ScanDisk

   D. Vcache

2. What is it called when files get scattered over a hard drive?

   A. Compression

   B. Corruption

   C. Clustering

   D. Fragmentation

3. What is the name of the new 32-bit caching piece of Windows 95?

   A. Format

   B. Fdisk

   C. ScanDisk

   D. Vcache

4. Windows 95 includes a native anti-virus program.

   A. Yes, but only on the CD-ROM version of Windows 95.

   B. Yes, but you have to pay for it before you can install it.

   C. Yes, but it only comes with OSR2.

   D. No.

5. Windows 95's Backup program is backward-compatible with older DOS versions of backup and restore.

   A. True

   B. False

6. Creating smaller partitions may be a more efficient way of formatting your hard drive.

   A. Yes, because files take up less room on your disk.

   B. Yes, because the hard drive works faster.

   C. Yes, because the hard drive spins less often, saving wear and tear.

   D. No, there is no difference.

7. The long filename "This is a company memo about the party for.1998.doc" would have which 8.3 name created for it?

   A. This is .doc

   B. Thisis~1.199

   C. Thisis~1.doc

   D. Thisisal.doc

8. Disabling the write-behind cache is done with which program?

   A. Control Panel ➤ System

   B. Control Panel ➤ Devices

   C. Control Panel ➤ Drives

   D. My Computer ➤ Properties of the Drive

9. You can restore deleted files in Windows 95 due to which program?

   A. Vcache

   B. Recycle Bin

   C. Trash Can

   D. Undelete

10. Which program can be used to schedule tasks such as ScanDisk and Disk Defragmenter in Windows 95?

    A. My Computer ➤ Properties

    B. Shortcuts

    C. System Agent

    D. The AT command

11. You purchase a 6GB drive, but can only create 2GB partitions on it. Why?

    A. Your motherboard needs a BIOS upgrade.

    B. You installed Windows 95 as an upgrade to MS-DOS 5.0.

    C. You are running the original version of Windows 95.

    D. You haven't set the master/slave settings on the hard drive correctly.

12. You use the format c: /s switch to recover from a virus. What will happen to your data on the c: drive?

   A. The data will be fine.

   B. The data will be completely gone.

   C. Your data will be OK but you will have to reinstall Windows 95.

   D. Windows 95 will be OK but your data will be gone.

13. How can you configure the Backup program so that you won't have to change tapes as often? (Select all that apply.)

   A. Buy the new QIC-250 type tapes.

   B. Use compression.

   C. Back up to a network drive.

   D. Back up only data files.

14. Which advanced option would you choose for defrag.exe in order to gain the most speed from your computer?

   A. Full defragmentation

   B. Consolidate free space only

   C. Optimize defragmentation

   D. Defragment files only

15. Which advanced option would you choose if you were only worried about increasing the speed of your current applications?

   A. Full defragmentation

   B. Consolidate free space only

   C. Optimize defragmentation

   D. Defragment files only

16. A user calls and says they can't create any folders on their C:\ even though they still have over 500MB free. What could be the cause?

A. They have too many long file and folder names already on C:\.

B. They are using a 16-bit program to create the folder.

C. They need to defragment their hard drive, then it will work.

D. They need to create folder names that are 8.3 or less on the C:\.

CHAPTER

9

The Networking Components of
Windows 95

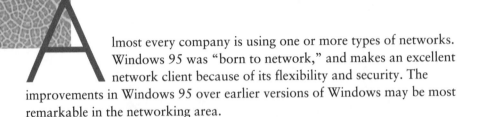

lmost every company is using one or more types of networks. Windows 95 was "born to network," and makes an excellent network client because of its flexibility and security. The improvements in Windows 95 over earlier versions of Windows may be most remarkable in the networking area.

Although there are not a lot of objectives directly addressed in this chapter, the Windows 95 test is heavily weighted with networking questions. A thorough understanding of networking is essential not only to passing the test but for successfully using Windows 95 in real life!

This chapter begins with an overview of the major network protocols that Windows 95 supports. Next, it describes the network architecture of Windows 95, explaining how it corresponds with the OSI (Open Systems Interconnection) reference model. Then you will learn how Windows 95 can function as a network client or server. Finally, it introduces the Network Neighborhood, which provides easy access to network resources.

If you are fairly new to networking, you probably want to review *MCSE: Networking Essentials Study Guide* (published by Sybex) for a complete, in-depth look at networking protocols, configurations, and implementations.

The Protocols—A Quick Overview

etworks must use some kind of protocol to communicate. The three major protocols that Windows 95 supports are TCP/IP (Transmission Control Protocol/Internet Protocol), IPX/SPX (Internetwork Packet Exchange/Sequenced

Packet Exchange), and NetBEUI (NETBIOS Extended User Interface). Support for DLC (Data Link Control) and NETBIOS (Network Basic Input/Output System) is also available. Here is a brief overview of these protocols, which are each discussed in more detail in later chapters:

- **TCP/IP:** This protocol is popular for many reasons, including its open design, its nonproprietary heterogeneous support, and the Internet. TCP/IP, and how it is installed and configured on a Windows 95 computer, is covered in Chapter 10. Suffice it to say that every network administrator needs to be at least familiar with, if not an expert in, TCP/IP.

- **IPX/SPX:** This is a proprietary protocol that Novell developed for use in its NetWare networks. In the past, Microsoft called its compatible protocol NWLink; now it is called by the very inventive name "IPX/SPX compatible protocol." Almost every application that works with, and expects, NetWare's IPX/SPX will also work with Microsoft's IPX/SPX compatible protocol. In order to communicate with NetWare servers, the IPX/SPX compatible protocol must be installed. Installing and configuring IPX/SPX are covered in Chapters 11 and 12.

- **NetBEUI:** This protocol was developed by IBM for small interoffice networks. NetBEUI has severe limitations, because it was designed for no more than 254 nodes and can't be routed. Interoffice mail may be a good analogy for NetBEUI: Interoffice mail is quick and cheap inside your company, but if an envelope is put in the regular mail bin, there is no way of delivering it, since it has no address (other than the person's name) on it. This protocol is almost never used as a regular protocol, but can be useful as a dial-up protocol, which is covered in Chapter 18.

- **DLC:** This protocol must be used in conjunction with another protocol—TCP/IP, IPX/SPX, or NetBEUI. DLC is used to communicate with IBM mainframe computers and Hewlett-Packard (HP) JetDirect adapters.

- **NETBIOS:** This is not a protocol per se, but is a specification that protocols and applications can be designed to support. IPX/SPX adds support for NETBIOS via TSRs (terminate-and-stay-resident programs), but Microsoft's IPX-compatible protocol, TCP/IP, and NetBEUI come with native NETBIOS support. Microsoft's networking, as well as many applications, requires NETBIOS support in order to function correctly. Chapter 11 discusses NETBIOS in more detail.

The Network Architecture of Windows 95

Networking is a very complex matter. Fortunately, it can be broken down into smaller parts to make it easier to understand.

The OSI model is one of the most prevalent models used to break down networking. First we will review the OSI model, and then we will match the Windows 95 components to their respective layers. This approach will help you understand how Windows 95 implements networking and where the various pieces fit.

The OSI Model

There are several different ways of looking at networking, just as there are several ways of looking at building a house. The OSI model is presented here because it is a popular and well-defined model for breaking down networking into more manageable pieces.

Just as a set of blueprints for a house can be read and used by any competent contractor, the OSI model provides a blueprint for networking that can be (and usually is) followed (to one degree or another) by most major software and hardware companies. If you build a house, you should be able to hire any plumber subcontractor and any electrician subcontractor, and your plumbing and electricity should be installed to standard specifications and function as you expect. The OSI model, and the standards built around it, has the same goal: that is, you should not be forced into using equipment from a particular manufacturer—you should be able to use software and hardware from any company and make them communicate. (It's a nice idea in theory, but sometimes you can still get tied to a proprietary solution.)

The OSI model, developed by the ISO (International Standardization Organization), is a conceptual framework used to describe how to connect any combination of devices for purposes of communication. Although there are other networking models developed by other organizations, the OSI model is the standard for network layered architecture and the most widely accepted model for understanding network communications. The OSI model does not perform any functions in the communication processes; this work is done by the appropriate software and hardware. The model's purpose is to define the tasks that need to be done and which protocols will handle those tasks.

The OSI model has seven layers:

- **Application:** The layer that the user's applications communicate with. This layer consists of API (Application Programming Interface) calls that applications can make. Its purpose is to allow transparent access to operating system or networking functions. For instance, an application shouldn't need to know which protocol or brand of network card is being used, as long as that protocol or card is compatible with Windows 95.

- **Presentation:** The layer that is responsible for translating the input from the application (and thus the user) into a form that can more easily be transmitted across the network. ASCII and EBCDIC are two methods of translating the alphabet into bits and bytes. This layer is also responsible for data encryption and compression.

- **Session:** The layer that is in charge of the big picture. It makes the overall networking session happen by synchronizing and sequencing the elements (packets) in a network connection. This layer also deals with any errors that are not the network's or a protocol's fault (such as running out of paper), makes sure that the transmission is complete, and ensures that appropriate security measures are taken during the connection.

- **Transport:** The layer that makes sure that the packets are delivered correctly. This layer is where the connection is made for the TCP and SPX protocols.

- **Network:** The layer that is in charge of addressing the packets so they are delivered to the correct network. Network routers work at this level. Routers examine the destination network address and pass the packet along on its way.

- **Data Link:** The layer that consists of the driver for the network card. This layer, often split into two sub-layers called the Data Link and MAC (Media Access Control) layers, helps watch for errors in the transmission and conversion of signals, and is responsible for delivering packets between computers without errors. Network bridges function at this layer. A bridge put in between two segments of the same network will examine each packet, and if the destination is on the other side of the bridge, it will let it pass; otherwise, the bridge keeps the traffic local.

- **Physical:** This layer consists of the network card, which is in charge of translating bits and bytes to and from electrical impulses. Network repeaters operate at this level. Their job is to boost the network signal (without doing any analysis on the signal).

One way to help remember the OSI model layers (and their order) is the saying **A**ll **P**eople **S**eem **T**o **N**eed **D**ata **P**rocessing.

Data is passed from applications down through the layers of communications until it reaches the network card and cabling system. It is then transmitted back up the network layers until it reaches the appropriate application on the receiving side. Figure 9.1 illustrates communication through the OSI model's layers.

FIGURE 9.1

Communication through the OSI model's layers

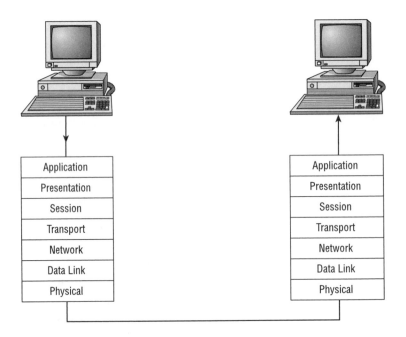

Windows 95 and the OSI Model

Microsoft presents its networking components in a model that is similar to the OSI model. The OSI layers, corresponding Microsoft layers, and Windows 95 implementation are shown in Figure 9.2.

FIGURE 9.2

The OSI and Microsoft models, and the respective Windows 95 implementations

OSI Layers	Microsoft Layers	Windows 95 Implementation
Application	Application Interface	Win32 WinNet APIs / Win32 Print APIs
Presentation	Network Providers	WinNet16 / NetWare/Windows
Session	File System Interface	IFS Manager
Transport	Redirectors and Services	Redirector/Services
Network	Transport Driver Interface	NETBIOS / Windows Sockets
Data Link	Transport Protocols	TCP/IP / IPX/SPX / NetBEUI
Physical	Device Driver Interface	NDIS 3.*x* / ODI / NDIS 2.*x*

This figure shouldn't be taken too literally, because the layers don't match exactly with each other due to differences in definitions.

Microsoft's model includes the following seven layers:

- **Application Interface:** Like the OSI model's Application layer, this layer is where the API calls are made by user applications. Windows 95 provides APIs for file access as well as printing.

- **Network Providers:** Like its OSI model counterpart, this layer translates the API calls into a language that other computers can understand. Windows 95 has support for 16-bit networking calls (for compatibility), as well as 32-bit providers for Microsoft, NetWare, and other servers.

- **File System Interface:** This layer provides a "railroad switch" function—it figures out whether a request can be fulfilled locally or needs to come from across the network. The IFS (Installable File System) manager is the Windows 95 component that fulfills this role. Windows 95 was designed so that resources look the same whether they are local or across the network.

You can see how the transparency of network access works in Windows 95 by going into Network Neighborhood and showing the resources on your machine (something that Windows for Workgroups couldn't do). Network Neighborhood is discussed later in the chapter.

- **Redirectors and Services:** Redirectors function when Windows 95 acts like a client, and services are used when Windows 95 is acting like a server or providing a function on the network. Redirectors and services are discussed in more detail in Chapters 11, 12, and 13.

- **Transport Driver Interface:** This layer allows applications, redirectors, and services to communicate via NETBIOS or socket connections. (NETBIOS is discussed in Chapter 11.) The Transport Driver Interface ensures that applications have transparent access to network resources.

- **Transport Protocols:** This layer is where TCP/IP, IPX/SPX, and/or Net-BEUI are implemented.

- **Device Driver Interface:** This layer is where the software driver that comes with the network card operates. Windows 95 can use drivers written to the ODI (Open Data-link Interface, for NetWare) specification, but ODI drivers are real-mode (16-bit). Microsoft uses the NDIS (Network Driver Interface Specification) standard for network card adapters.

There are four versions of NDIS for Windows: Version 2.0, real-mode (16-bit), is the lowest type usable by Windows 95; Version 3.0, protected mode (32-bit), is the lowest type usable by Windows NT 3.x; Version 3.1, protected mode, adds Plug and Play for Windows 95; and Version 4.0 adds PPTP (Point-to-Point Tunneling Protocol) and better network monitor support, and better network monitoring for Windows NT 4.0.

Windows 95 as a Client

Windows 95 excels as a networking client. In order to understand your options when installing client software for Windows 95, it is important to know how networking works for both Novell and Microsoft networks.

Microsoft
✓ *Exam*
Objective

Install and configure the network components of a client computer and server.

There are various new features in Windows 95 that offer a compelling reason to upgrade from earlier versions of MS-DOS or Windows 3.*x* software. Windows 95 also works very well in mixed environments; it can easily handle two or more different types of servers concurrently.

Windows 95 Networking Features

Windows 95 has many more networking features than earlier versions of Windows, including the following:

- **Graphical, standardized way of making networking changes:** All networking functions can be changed from one spot—the Network Control Panel. Using the Network Control Panel to make changes is much easier than using the methods available in previous versions of Windows. Use of the Network Control Panel is covered in Chapters 10, 11, and 12.

- **Simultaneous client connections to dissimilar servers:** Although Windows 3.*x* could connect to different types of networks, it wasn't designed from the ground up for networking, and conflicts often resulted. With the appropriate software, Windows 95 can connect to both NetWare and Microsoft servers.

- **Plug-and-Play support for network adapters:** Windows 95 adds this support, which makes installing and configuring network cards easier. The procedures for installing and configuring network cards are discussed in Chapters 11 and 12.

- **Automatic reconnection of lost connections:** Windows 95 will attempt to reconnect if a connection is broken. Often, the user doesn't even know the connection was broken and reestablished.

- **Client-side caching of network data:** Windows 95 uses Vcache (the new protected-mode cache program) to cache data from the network to increase performance. Vcache is discussed in Chapter 8.

- **Long filename support:** Long filenames can be stored on both Microsoft and NetWare servers. NT servers automatically save long filenames. NetWare servers need the OS2 support enabled, as explained in Chapter 12.

- **Support for user profiles and system policies:** User profiles allow more than one user to save user settings on a computer. System policies allow administrators to enforce rules on the network. User profiles are covered in Chapter 14, and system policies are the topic of Chapter 15.

- **Real-mode (16-bit) network driver support:** Windows 95 can use older real-mode (16-bit) drivers if 32-bit ones are not available. This will affect performance, but at least the drivers will function. Real mode versus protected mode is explained in Chapter 4.

- **Protected-mode (32-bit) network driver support:** Windows 95 can use all protected-mode drivers for network connectivity. In this mode, networking components use no conventional memory. This allows DOS programs that are run under Windows 95 to have much more conventional RAM than they would have under DOS.

Communicating with Servers

Novell NetWare servers communicate using a language called NCP (NetWare Core Protocol). This language is spoken by both the NetWare clients and servers. When you install the Client for NetWare Networks, you are enabling Windows 95 to communicate (using NCP) with NetWare servers, as illustrated in Figure 9.3. See Chapter 12 for details on networking with NetWare servers.

Microsoft servers communicate using a language called SMB (Server Message Block). By installing the Client for Microsoft Networks, you enable Windows 95 to communicate with Microsoft (Windows NT) servers, as illustrated in Figure 9.4. See Chapter 11 for details on networking with NT servers.

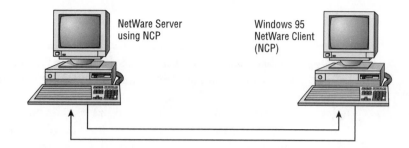

NetWare Server
using NCP

Windows 95
NetWare Client
(NCP)

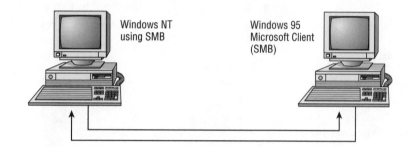

Windows NT
using SMB

Windows 95
Microsoft Client
(SMB)

Windows 95 is flexible enough to have both client languages (NCP and SMB) installed at the same time. This allows Windows 95 to simultaneously communicate with both NetWare and Microsoft servers, as illustrated in Figure 9.5.

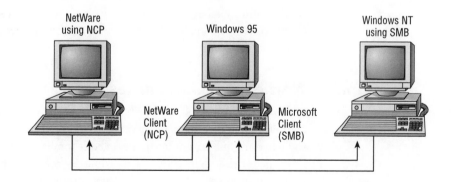

NetWare
using NCP

Windows 95

Windows NT
using SMB

NetWare
Client
(NCP)

Microsoft
Client
(SMB)

Using SMB or NCP is independent of which network protocol is in use. SMB and NCP are used at a higher level of the OSI model (the Application layer); protocols are used at a lower level (the Data Link layer).

Another way to allow Windows 95 to communicate with both NetWare and Microsoft servers is to have both servers speak a common language, and install just one client on Windows 95. A product from Microsoft called File and Print Services for NetWare (FPNW) makes this possible. With this product installed, Windows NT servers speak the NCP language as well as their own native SMB language, as illustrated in Figure 9.6. See Chapter 12 for more information about File and Print Services for NetWare.

FIGURE 9.6

Windows 95 using a NetWare client to communicate with both NetWare and NT servers

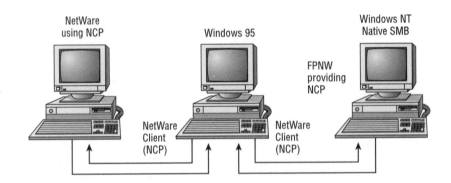

Getting Windows 95 to communicate with other types of servers (such as Banyan Vines) is basically done in the same way. By installing the appropriate client software, you allow Windows 95 to communicate with almost any server.

Computer Names and Usernames

Because Microsoft follows the NETBIOS specifications, and all Windows 95 computers could possibly be servers as well as clients, *all* computers are required to have a unique computer name, even if they are participating only on a NetWare network (where names are ordinarily required only for servers). Computer names must be unique, and they can be up to 14 characters long.

If your computer name is not unique, upon booting your computer you will get an error message stating that networking services have not been started because of a duplicate computer name. You will need to either change your computer name or find the duplicate and change that computer name.

Usernames don't need to be unique. However, any pop-up message or notification will be sent to all users who are logged in as the target recipient.

Accessing Resources with UNC

UNC (Universal Naming Convention) is a NETBIOS specification that lets you easily specify the computer and shared resource you want to access. The format of a UNC is:

\\Server\Shared_Resource

Here is a typical command:

```
Net Use S: \\Server\Shared Folder
```

This would connect the S: to the shared folder, and whenever the S: is used, it would actually be the shared folder. For example, if you typed **DIR S:**, you would get a directory listing of the shared folder.

Connecting a drive via a UNC is like mapping a drive under NetWare.

Most applications are now UNC-aware; that is, you can use a UNC where you would normally use a local drive and directory (when saving files, inputting the path to new software, and so on).

Windows 95 as a Server

Besides functioning as a client, Windows 95 can also function as a server, allowing others to connect to shared drives or shared printers.

Such an arrangement is called a *peer-to-peer network*, illustrated in Figure 9.7. Windows 95 can perform both client and server functions simultaneously, but larger networks tend to have dedicated servers for security and performance reasons. However, small offices may have neither the budget nor the need for a dedicated server. Windows 95 operates as a peer-to-peer server when it uses Share level security (the default). Windows 95 can also act like a dedicated server when it uses User level security. Both of these security options are discussed in Chapter 11.

FIGURE 9.7

A peer-to-peer network

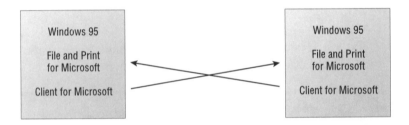

Windows 95 can be installed as either a Microsoft or a NetWare server—not both. Only Windows NT can simultaneously be both a Microsoft and NetWare server (by using File and Print Services for NetWare to provide NCP support).

You can have Windows 95 share its resources as a Microsoft server by installing file and printer sharing for Microsoft Networks, as illustrated in Figure 9.8. This allows both folders and printers to be shared. Installing and configuring sharing are covered in detail in Chapter 11.

For Windows 95 to act like a NetWare server, you need to install file and printer sharing for NetWare Networks, as shown in Figure 9.9. This allows NetWare clients to use the server's folders and printers. The major restriction is that a NetWare server must already be in place on the network before you can set up a Windows 95 server. Details on installing and configuring the service are in Chapter 12.

F I G U R E 9.8

File and printer
sharing installed for
Microsoft networks

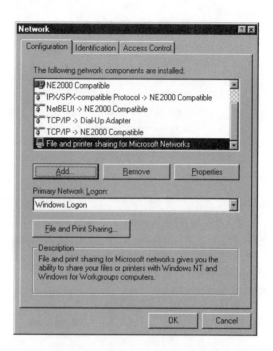

F I G U R E 9.9

File and printer
sharing installed for
NetWare networks

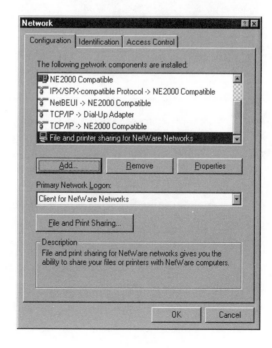

The Network Neighborhood

The Network Neighborhood in Windows 95 introduces an integrated way of looking at network resources as if they were merely an extension of your local computer's resources. The Network Neighborhood presents network resources from a hierarchical viewpoint, starting with the domain or workgroup you are a member of. Network Neighborhood can be found on the Desktop. If you have the Explorer open, the Network Neighborhood is shown at the same level as My Computer, as you can see in Figure 9.10. You can view other domains or workgroups by choosing Entire Network.

FIGURE 9.10

The Network Neighborhood in Explorer

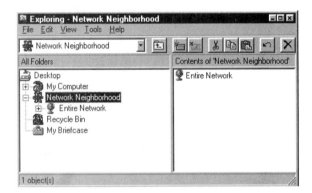

 In order to see Microsoft servers, you need the Microsoft client installed (covered in Chapter 11). To see NetWare servers, you need the NetWare client installed (covered in Chapter 12).

The Network Neighborhood's context menu (which appears when you highlight the Network Neighborhood and right-click) has the following options:

- **Open:** Presents the servers in your domain or workgroup in a folder format. You can then open a server to see the shared folders available.

- **Explore:** Presents the network in an Explorer fashion, and also shows My Computer and the Recycle Bin.

- **Find Computer:** Bypasses the browser, and allows you to see the server you are searching for, regardless of the state of the browsing service. This command is very valuable, because sometimes servers do not register themselves with the browser service, which is responsible for maintaining the Network Neighborhood lists.

- **Map Network Drive:** Lets you connect a drive letter to a shared folder on the network. The drive letter will then appear in My Computer. This is the same as using the Net Use command from a DOS prompt.

- **Disconnect Network Drive:** Lets you disconnect a drive letter from a network folder.

- **Create Shortcut:** Makes a shortcut to the Network Neighborhood. You can also make shortcuts to a server or a shared folder by right-dragging the server or folder to your Desktop and choosing Create Shortcut.

- **Rename:** Lets you rename the Network Neighborhood.

- **Properties:** Brings up the Network Control Panel (same as selecting Control Panel ➤ Network).

Summary

Windows 95 comes with full IPX/SPX, NetBEUI, and TCP/IP protocol support, which makes hooking it to existing networks, and to the Internet, a breeze. This chapter provided a brief introduction to the use of these protocols. They are covered in more detail in the following chapters.

Understanding the process of networking will help you in both supporting and troubleshooting Windows 95 systems. As you learned in this chapter, the OSI model was developed to break networking down into its basic components. Analyzing networking functions based on the OSI model is a popular way to help isolate functions and understand how networks work. Microsoft has a networking model similar to the OSI model. Windows 95 networking components match up well to the OSI model.

Windows 95 can function as a network client in Novell NetWare, Microsoft, and other types of networks, and can do it simultaneously and without any conflicts. Configuring Windows 95 as an NT client is discussed in Chapter 11. Configuring Windows 95 as a NetWare client is covered in Chapter 12.

Windows 95 can also act like a server, allowing either Microsoft or NetWare clients access to its resources. Windows 95 can be a server for only one type of network at a time. Configuring Windows 95 as a Microsoft network server is covered in Chapter 11. Installing NetWare server support is described in Chapter 12.

Whatever type of network you are connected to, the Network Neighborhood provides easy access to available resources. The Network Neighborhood presents network resources in a hierarchical structure, starting with your domain or workgroup.

Review Questions

1. Which Microsoft layer talks to the network card?

   A. Device Driver Interface

   B. Physical Driver Interface

   C. Transport Driver Interface

   D. Session Driver Interface

2. Which is *not* a protocol that Windows 95 supports?

   A. IPX/SPX

   B. Frame0

   C. NetBEUI

   D. TCP/IP

3. Which NDIS specification was designed for Windows 95?

A. NDIS 2.0

B. NDIS 2.1

C. NDIS 3.0

D. NDIS 3.1

4. Does Windows 95 support autoreconnect for both Windows NT and NetWare environments?

A. Yes, for both environments.

B. No, only for the Windows NT environment.

C. No, only for the NetWare environment.

D. No, for neither environment.

5. What does UNC stand for?

A. Universal Network Convention

B. Universal Naming Convention

C. Universal NETBIOS Convention

D. Universal NetWare Convention

6. Microsoft servers communicate natively with which language?

A. NCP

B. MMP

C. BTT

D. SMB

7. Can Windows 95 be both a Microsoft and a NetWare client simultaneously?

  A. Yes, it can be both.

  B. No, it can only function as a Microsoft client.

  C. No, it can only function as a NetWare client.

  D. No, it can do both, but not simultaneously.

8. Can Windows 95 be both a Microsoft and NetWare server simultaneously?

  A. Yes, it can be both.

  B. No, it can function only as a Microsoft server.

  C. No, it can function only as a NetWare server.

  D. No, it can function as one or the other, but not both simultaneously.

9. Which type of name must be unique? (Select all that apply.)

  A. Computer names

  B. User names

  C. Workgroup names

  D. Domain names

10. Which protocols can cross routers (under normal conditions)? (Select all that apply.)

  A. TCP/IP

  B. NetBEUI

  C. IPX/SPX

  D. AppleTalk

11. What new feature of Windows 95 lets you see network resources?

   A. My Computer

   B. Network Resources

   C. Network Servers

   D. Network Neighborhood

12. If Sue, Katie, and Linda are in the same workgroup, how would they see each other's computers?

   A. Network Neighborhood ➤ Entire Network

   B. Network Neighborhood (all computers in their workgroup are visible by default)

   C. Network Neighborhood ➤ Scan for Workgroup Computers

   D. Network Neighborhood ➤ Find Computers in My Workgroup

13. What pieces of software would be required to connect to Windows NT as a client, share your printers to other Microsoft clients, and connect to a NetWare 3.12 computer? (Select all that apply.)

   A. Microsoft Client for NetWare

   B. Microsoft Client for Microsoft

   C. File and printer sharing for Microsoft

   D. File and printer sharing for NetWare

CHAPTER

10

TCP/IP on Windows 95

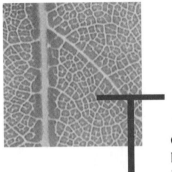

TCP/IP (Transmission Control Protocol/Internet Protocol) has become one of the most (if not the most) widely used protocols in today's computing environments. Its popularity is due to many things, including its availability on almost every hardware platform, its support of open standards, and the explosion of the Internet. TCP/IP allows the operation of various network applications, from FTP clients to Web browsers.

TCP/IP is the oldest of the popular networking protocols used today. This chapter begins with some background on the development of TCP/IP. It then explains the IP addressing scheme and subnets. Then you will learn how to install TCP/IP and Dial-Up Networking, and how to configure TCP/IP.

A Brief History of TCP/IP

Originally developed in 1969 for the Department of Defense Advanced Research Project Agency (ARPA), TCP/IP was part of a resource-sharing experiment called ARPANET. The original motivation was to design a communications protocol that could be implemented independently of the various existing hardware systems the government possessed. This would allow these systems to exchange data, regardless of their hardware makeup.

Eventually, ARPANET and the network infrastructure provided by the National Science Foundation (NSFNET) grew into the worldwide community of networks now known as the Internet. Because ARPA provided the standards for the protocol free of charge to government agencies and universities, there was further development of the protocols. The public universities became great contributors to the development of TCP/IP. Many of the higher-level protocols for such things as e-mail (SMTP), newsgroups, printing, and file transfer (FTP) came from those working in the universities.

The initial fuel for this growth began when TCP/IP was included with Berkeley Standard Distribution (BSD) Unix, and it has been a standard feature of Unix almost ever since. Now TCP/IP can be found in just about every other operating system, from Macintosh to mainframes to Windows. The most explosive growth, however, has come with the development of HTTP (Hypertext Transfer Protocol) for the sharing of HTML (Hypertext Markup Language) documents, which has evolved into the Internet's World Wide Web.

One of the features of TCP/IP that make it popular in its use across hardware platforms and software vendors is that it's an "open" protocol—*open* meaning that not just one organization has input into its design. Ideas for its improvement can be offered via documents called Requests for Comments (RFCs). There have been more than 2000 RFCs submitted to date that, directly or indirectly, define the current standards for TCP/IP.

RFCs can be submitted to the Internet Activities Board (IAB), where they will be debated, considered, and assigned a priority level or classification that determines whether they should be used for future implementations. There are five possible classifications: Required (must be used for TCP/IP hosts), Recommended (encouraged but not required), Elective (optional—agreed upon but not in wide use), Limited Use (not recommended for general use), and Not Recommended (not meeting any usage requirements).

IP Addresses

Unlike IPX or NetBEUI, TCP/IP requires each node or host to be assigned a unique address to participate on the network. This can require much more administrative work than other protocols, because each host (which includes desktop computers, printers, routers, and any other device that needs to communicate on the network) needs to have an address assigned to it. The address, commonly referred to as an *IP address*, looks similar to this:

131.107.2.200

An IP address is a 32-bit address, where each of the four numbers presented is actually an octet, or contains 8 bits of data. For example, the above address is actually:

10000011.01101011.00000010.11001000

or four 8-bit numbers (octets). Because this binary format is not easily read by humans, it is converted into decimal format as first shown.

In determining IP addresses, there are several factors to consider:

- Class of address

- Address uniqueness

- Restricted addresses

IP Address Classes

The class of address, along with the subnet mask (explained later in the chapter) determines which part of the IP address is used for network identification (net ID) and which part is used for host identification (host ID). Although there are five address classes defined, only three can be used for host addressing: Class A, Class B, and Class C.

> The first octet in the address determines whether an address is a Class A, B, or C address.

Table 10.1 provides a summary of the properties for each class of address. They are discussed in more detail in the following sections.

	Address Class	Range of Network IDs	Number of Networks	Hosts per Network
TABLE 10.1 IP Address Class Summary	Class A	1–126	126	16,777,214
	Class B	128–191	16,384	65,534
	Class C	192–223	2,097,152	254

Class A Addresses

Class A addresses allow the most hosts, and so they are typically owned by very large organizations (like IBM). They use only the first octet for the net ID. The other three octets are available for host addressing. Also, the high-order bit is always set to zero in the first octet for Class A addresses. For example, the first octet looks something like this:

```
01010111
```

Because a Class A address always has the first bit in the octet set to zero, this limits the range of Class A addresses to 1 through 127. However, since the address 127 is reserved for diagnostic purposes, 126 is actually the last available Class A address.

In the Class A address example shown here, if you convert the octet to decimal, you get 87. So, the net ID is 87.0.0.0, leaving the last three octets available for host IDs. This allows for 16,777,214 hosts, which is far more than you could use for a single network. However, one large address can be split up into several smaller ranges of addresses to be used on different network segments, or *subnets*. Subnets are explained later in this chapter.

This separation between net ID and host ID in an IP address helps define the subnet mask. In this example of a Class A address, because the first octet is taken to identify the network, it is "masked out" from being used for host IDs. The default subnet mask with a Class A address is 255.0.0.0, signifying that the first octet is unavailable for host IDs.

Class B Addresses

Class B addresses allow for fewer overall hosts because they use the first two octets for the net ID. The second octet is part of the net ID, but this doesn't matter as far as determining the class of address. In a Class B address, the first two high-order bits in the first octet are always 10. For example, the first two octets look something like this:

10000011.01101011

This limits the range of Class B addresses to 128 through 191. In the example shown here, if you convert the two octets to decimal, you get 131.107. So, the net ID is 131.107.0.0, leaving the last two octets 0.0 available for host IDs. This allows for 65,534 hosts on a Class B address. Also, since there are two octets available for the net ID, there are 16,384 possible Class B addresses, instead of only 126 as with Class A addresses.

The default subnet mask for a Class B address is 255.255.0.0, since the first two octets are masked out from being used as host IDs.

Class C Addresses

Class C addresses are the smallest address class because the first three octets are used for the net ID, leaving only the last octet for host IDs. Again, only the first octet is looked at to determine class of address, although the first three octets make up the net ID. In a Class C address, the first three high-order bits in the first octet are always 110. For example, the first three octets look something like this:

11011010.10101010.00000101

This limits the range of Class C addresses to 192 through 223. In this example, if you convert the three octets to decimal, you get 218.170.5. So, the net ID is 218.170.5.0, leaving only the last octet .0 for host IDs. This allows for only 254 hosts on a Class C address. However, since there are three octets available for the net ID, there are 2,097,152 possible Class C addresses.

The default subnet mask for a Class C address is 255.255.255.0, because these octets are used for the net ID and are unavailable for use as host IDs.

Class D and E Addresses

Class D and E addresses are not used for host IDs, which means that the network administrator will never use them. They are used for only multicasts and broadcasts. These are generic addresses used to contact groups of computers.

A *broadcast* is a transmission that is sent to all hosts indiscriminately. This is usually done in an attempt to locate or identify a specific host.

Multicasting is a bit more selective than broadcasting since it is usually dealing with a specific group instead of the network at large. For example, Windows Sockets applications can join a multicast group in order to participate in a wide-area conference.

Both types of transmissions are handled by software at a lower level. Class D addresses range from 224 through 254 (multicast). Class E addresses use 255 (broadcast only).

IP Address Restrictions

IP addresses must be unique for every host on the network. This means that there must be a unique combination of net ID and host ID for every host. Also, every host on the same network segment must have the same net ID.

This is because local communication is established through a series of broadcasts that are for that network only. These broadcasts will not cross a router (which connects the different networks). So, if a host with the same net ID is across a router, it will never be reached. (In TCP/IP terminology, *router* and *gateway* mean the same thing.)

A host address cannot be 255 because 255 is a broadcast address. For example, 255.255.255.255 is broadcast for all hosts on all networks, regardless of the local net ID. But 131.107.255.255 is a broadcast address only for the local network of 131.107.0.0. Therefore, a host on this network would never use this address as its unique IP address.

As a rule, neither the net ID nor host ID part of the IP address can have all ones or all zeros. If you follow the established range of network IDs for the addresses of Class A, B, and C, you will not run into this on the net ID side.

If you are on a private network that will never connect to the Internet, you can choose your own class of address and net ID to use for your network, and no one else will care. However, if you are planning to connect to the Internet someday, you will need to have an address assigned to you that will not conflict with the existing addresses on the Internet. Internet addresses are assigned by InterNIC; see the note below for more details.

If you're planning on using TCP/IP, it's a good idea to have your addresses assigned by InterNIC. Even if you're not going to connect to the Internet initially, if there is a possibility that you may want to connect to it in the future, let InterNIC assign the addresses. Then you won't need to deal with reassigning all the host IP addresses on your network. You can reach InterNIC by e-mail at info@internic.net, at the Web site www.internic.net, or by phone: (703) 742-4777.

Besides the address itself, there are two other important components in host IP address configuration: the subnet mask and default gateway. The subnet mask is absolutely essential, but the default gateway can be optional, depending on your network.

Subnets and Subnet Masks

Before studying subnet masks, it is important to understand what a subnet is. Simply put, a *subnet* is a network segment. However, from an IP perspective, it is a segment in a multiple-segmented network that has been given a net ID derived from a "parent" net ID. For example, in Figure 10.1, a Class B parent net ID of 131.107.0.0 is the assigned address and has been subnetted into smaller networks.

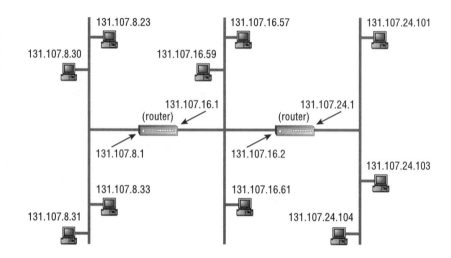

In the example in Figure 10.1, there are three subnets connected by routers:

- 131.107.8.0

- 131.107.16.0

- 131.107.24.0

Since the parent address has been subnetted, it is no longer used as a single network; but all the subnets together are the network of 131.107.0.0.

The subnet mask used determines how many subnets have been created. Whatever the subnet mask is, it must be the same for all the subnets created, even though they will each have their own unique net IDs. The subnet mask not only determines what part of the IP address belongs to the host (host ID) and what part belongs to the network (net ID), it also determines what is local or remote to a subnet.

Each subnet must be connected by a router (or gateway) to the other subnets in order to communicate.

Using AND to Determine Local or Remote Hosts

When a host tries to reach another host, it must first determine if the destination host is local (on the same subnet) or remote. To determine this, IP ANDs the subnet mask with the host's own address when TCP/IP is initialized.

ANDing simply means combining binary values to get a result. In ANDing, 1 and 1 equals 1. Any other combinations such as 0 and 1, or 0 and 0, equal 0.

For example, in Figure 10.1, if host 131.107.24.103 tries to reach host 131.107.24.101, the binary value for the subnet mask 255.255.248.0 is ANDed with the binary value of the initiating host's IP address to come up with a result:

131.107.24.103	10000011.01101011.00011000.01100111
AND	
255.255.248.0	<u>11111111.11111111.11111000.00000000</u>
Result	10000011.01101011.00010000.00000000
131.107.24.101	10000011.01101011.00011000.01100101
AND	
255.255.248.0	<u>11111111.11111111.11111000.00000000</u>
Result	10000011.01101011.00010000.00000000

The result is saved for later comparison. When the host needs to reach another host, the IP address of the destination host is ANDed with the subnet mask of the originating host. In this case, the results match—IP knows the hosts are local to each other, or in other words, on the same subnet. If the results are different, the destination host is remote, and the originating host needs to use its default gateway to find the appropriate subnet.

Defining Subnet Masks

The default subnet masks for each class of address are as follows:

Class A: 255.0.0.0

Class B: 255.255.0.0

Class C: 255.255.255.0

This assumes default values and that there is no subnetting being done. When you need to make subnets, the default values must be modified.

There are several benefits to defining custom subnet masks:

- You can connect different topologies, such as Ethernet and Token Ring.

- You can overcome limitations on hosts per network (for example, Ethernet allows only 1024 hosts per network).

- You can divide up the network to reduce traffic.

- You can create separate networks for organizational purposes.

To define a custom subnet mask, you should first decide how many subnets are needed. Then convert this number to binary. For example, with a Class B address, the default mask is 255.255.0.0. The octet to be modified is the third one, since it is the first available one. If you need 12 subnets, you would convert 12 to binary, which is 1100. In this case, it takes four binary bits to represent the number of subnets desired:

128	64	32	16	8	4	2	1	
0	0	0	0	1	1	0	0	=12

These bits are then moved to the high-order position:

128	64	32	16	8	4	2	1
1	1	0	0	0	0	0	0

and then all set, or turned to one. (In our example we started with four bits, two of which were 1s and two of which were 0s. When all get set, we end up with four 1s.)

128	64	32	16	8	4	2	1	
1	1	1	1	0	0	0	0	=240

Then convert this number back to decimal, and this is your mask value. The mask then becomes 255.255.240.0 to support the desired 12 subnets.

Now that the subnet mask is defined, the individual subnet net IDs need to be defined from the parent net ID. This mask was defined with four bits, so all the possible combinations of four bits (minus all the one and all the zero combinations) will give us the valid net IDs:

~~00000000 = 0~~	**0110**0000 = 96	**1100**0000 = 192
00010000 = 16	**0111**0000 = 112	**1101**0000 = 208
00100000 = 32	**1000**0000 = 128	**1110**0000 = 224
00110000 = 48	**1001**0000 = 144	~~11110000 = 240~~
01000000 = 64	**1010**0000 = 160	
01010000 = 80	**1011**0000 = 176	

This gives 16 combinations, but the all zeros at the beginning are thrown out, and all the ones at the end are thrown out—for 14 usable subnets. This is as close as you can get to the desired 12 subnets. Using the Class B net ID 131.107.0.0 as an example along with the above combinations, the subnet net IDs are now defined as follows:

1) 131.107.16.0	8) 131.107.128.0
2) 131.107.32.0	9) 131.107.144.0
3) 131.107.48.0	10) 131.107.160.0
4) 131.107.64.0	11) 131.107.176.0
5) 131.107.80.0	12) 131.107.192.0
6) 131.107.96.0	13) 131.107.208.0
7) 131.107.112.0	14) 131.107.224.0

Now that the net IDs have been defined, the next step is defining the ranges of each subnet. This can be determined easily. Using subnet 1 (131.107.16.0) as an example, its range of host addresses starts at 1 and goes until it runs into the beginning of subnet 2:

1) 131.107.16.0: range of host IDs: 131.107.16.1–131.107.31.254

2) 131.107.32.0: range of host IDs: 131.107.32.1–131.107.47.254

3) 131.107.48.0: range of host IDs: 131.107.48.1–131.107.63.254

and so on...

While this process works, it can be cumbersome, especially if you subnet out to the fifth through eighth bits, where the number of possible combinations runs from 30 through 254. Table 10.2 simplifies the whole process. The values shown in the table are the only possible combinations for subnet masks and the number of subnets you can have.

Bits	1	2	3	4	5	6	7	8
Mask	—	192	224	240	248	252	254	255
Number of subnets	—	2	6	14	30	62	126	254
Starting net IDs	—	64	32	16	8	4	2	1

T A B L E   10.2

Summary of Subnet Mask Values

Here's how to use the table for the previous example of needing 12 subnets. First, you can see that 12 is not a number of subnets directly available; 14 is the closest number. The necessary mask then is 240.

The associated starting net ID in this case is 16. To get the subnet net IDs and ranges, just use this as the beginning subnet ID and increment by it for the subsequent net IDs. For example, 131.107.0.0 with a mask of 240 starts the first subnet at 16, and every subsequent subnet is incremented by 16 from there:

131.107.**16**.0

131.107.**32**.0

131.107.**48**.0

until the 14 subnets have been defined. Using this method, the ranges are the same as those shown earlier.

It may also be necessary to keep in mind how many host addresses are needed for each subnet. For example, suppose that you have a Class B address and you need to split it into as many subnets as possible while still allowing for at least 500 hosts per subnet. How far out can it be subnetted? This also can be tedious to calculate. Instead, refer to Table 10.3, which summarizes the number of host IDs available per subnet according to class of address and the number of bits used in your subnet mask.

TABLE 10.3	Bits	1	2	3	4	5	6	7	8
Hosts per Subnet	Class A	—	4,194,302	2,097,150	1,048,574	524,286	262,142	131,070	65,534
	Class B	—	16,382	8,190	4,094	2,046	1,022	510	254
	Class C	—	126	30	14	6	2	—	—

The Default Gateway

The *default gateway* is the way out of a subnet. It is the router that connects one subnet to another so that hosts can communicate with hosts on other interconnected networks. The default gateway has its own IP address, which the hosts on its subnet must know to use.

When a host determines that a destination host is not local, it sends its data to its configured default gateway. The router then refers to its route table to determine if it has a direct connection to the destination network or if it must send the data on to another router that can deliver the data to the destination host.

TCP/IP Installation

Installing TCP/IP on Windows 95 is relatively simple. The software comes on the CD-ROM—there is nothing extra you will need.

Microsoft ✓ ***Exam Objective***

Install and configure the network components of a client computer and server.

Install and configure network protocols. Protocols include:

- NetBEUI
- IPX/SPX-compatible Protocol
- TCP/IP
- Microsoft DLC
- PPTP/VPN

Installing TCP/IP in Windows 95

You can add a protocol through the Network Control Panel, as shown in Figure 10.2. Windows 95 offers TCP/IP as a choice in the Select Network Protocol dialog box, as shown in Figure 10.3. Follow the steps in Exercise 10.1 to install TCP/IP.

FIGURE 10.2

The Select Network Component Type dialog box

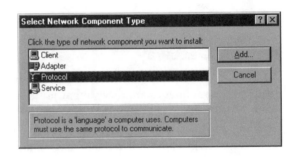

FIGURE 10.3

The Select Network Protocol dialog box

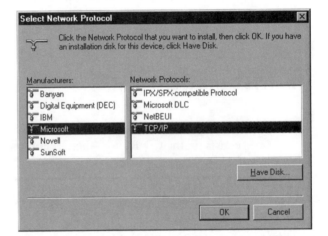

If you already have TCP/IP installed and you want to practice reinstalling it, remove TCP/IP first. If you are not using DHCP (Dynamic Host Configuration Protocol), you should record your settings so you can reenter them later.

EXERCISE 10.1

Installing TCP/IP

1. In the Control Panel, double-click on the Network icon to open the Select Network Component Type dialog box (Figure 10.2).

2. Click on Add, select Protocol, and click on Add again. This brings up the Select Network Protocol dialog box (Figure 10.3).

3. Select Microsoft in the list of Manufacturers.

4. Select TCP/IP in the list of Network Protocols.

5. Click on OK. Windows will prompt you for the location of the Windows 95 distribution files.

6. Indicate the location of the files. After Windows 95 finishes copying files, you will be prompted to restart your computer, as shown below.

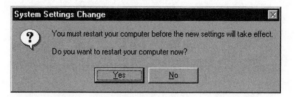

7. Click on Yes to reboot your computer and have the changes take effect.

Installing and Using SNMP

SNMP (Simple Network Management Protocol) is a component of the TCP/IP suite that can be used to get information from devices and software and to send commands to those same devices and software. SNMP also allows you to monitor additional items, such as TCP/IP traffic, using System Monitor.

Although SNMP is not listed in the objectives for the 70-64 test, you will likely get a question or two that mentions SNMP.

Installing SNMP is not intuitive in Windows 95. To install the Windows 95 SNMP agent, go to Control Panel ➤ Network ➤ Add ➤ Service ➤ Have Disk. For the path name, type or browse to **CD-ROM\Admin\Nettools\SNMP**. You should see the Microsoft SNMP agent listed. After you install the agent you will have to reboot Windows 95 to have it take effect.

Although the Windows NT SNMP agent can be configured from the GUI, the Windows 95 agent must be configured by directly editing the registry. There are three configurations you may want to set for SNMP:

- **Communities:** This sets up a group of computers of which this computer is a member. Only those in the community can query the SNMP agent.

- **Permitted Managers:** This specifies TCP/IP or IPX/SPX addresses of those permitted to manage this computer. If no specific address is configured, all potential managers have access to this computer.

- **Trap Destination:** This specifies to which computer error and other types of messages (called traps) are sent.

The registry key that needs to be edited is Hkey_Local_Machine\System\CurrentControlSet\Services\SNMP\Parameters\TrapConfiguration.

Using TCP/IP Utilities

There are several utilities and applications that are installed with TCP/IP that can help with diagnostic functions:

- **WinIPCfg:** A GUI utility for verification of IP settings, such as IP address, subnet mask, default gateway, WINS server address, MAC address, DHCP server address, and DHCP lease status

- **PING:** For verification of configuration and connections

- **Tracert:** For verification of the route taken to reach another host

- **Route:** For viewing or editing a local route table

- **NetStat:** For viewing protocol statistics and connections

- **FTP:** A command-line FTP client

- **Telnet:** A GUI Telnet client

Microsoft
✓ ***Exam***
Objective

Diagnose and resolve connectivity problems. Tools include:

- WinIPCfg
- Net Watcher
- Troubleshooting wizards

The Winsock interface (version 1.1) will automatically be available, so it is not necessary to install a third-party Winsock utility such as Trumpet. It may be necessary to open the TCP/IP property sheet and fill in the IP address information manually, as discussed in the "TCP/IP Configuration" section later in this chapter, if DHCP is not configured on the network.

Dial-Up Networking Installation

If the only available connection is dial-up, it is also necessary to install Dial-Up Networking. You can install Dial-Up Networking in one of two ways: by using the Internet Connection Wizard or through the Control Panel.

Microsoft
✓ ***Exam***
Objective

Configure a client computer to use Dial-Up Networking for remote access.

Configure a Windows 95 computer to access the Internet.

Using the Internet Connection Wizard

When you double-click on the icon labeled The Internet on the Windows 95 Desktop for the first time, Windows 95 will step you through creating a specific dial-up connection to an ISP (Internet service provider). You must already have an account with that ISP.

Although it does not come with Windows 95 (unless you have version B or have installed the Service Pack), you can download Microsoft's Internet Explorer from Microsoft's Web site (www.microsoft.com).

The options presented to you depend on the version of Internet Explorer you have. With version 3.0*x*, you will be presented with the setup options shown in Figure 10.4.

Internet Explorer versions 3.0*x* and 4.0*x*, and the Internet, are covered in more detail in Chapter 20.

FIGURE 10.4

Running Internet Explorer 3.0*x* for the first time

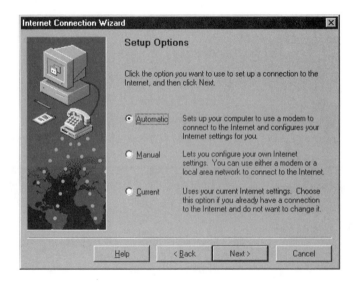

If Dial-Up Networking is already installed, you will see a Connect To dialog box appear when you start Internet Explorer. You can use your current settings, or choose Make New Connection to define settings for a new phone number.

Adding Dial-Up Networking from the Control Panel

To add Dial-Up Networking from the Control Panel, double-click on the Add/ Remove Programs icon, and then choose the Windows Setup tab. Choose the Communications option, and then click on the Details button, as shown in Figure 10.5. In the next dialog box, click on the checkbox for Dial-Up Networking, and then click on OK. Fill in the path to the Windows 95 distribution files, and Windows 95 will install Dial-Up Networking.

F I G U R E   10.5

The Windows Setup tab of the Add/Remove Programs Properties dialog box

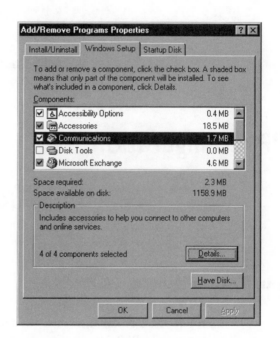

Using Dial-Up Networking

Once installed, Dial-Up Networking appears in the My Computer group on the Desktop, as shown in Figure 10.6. Double-click on this icon to define new Internet or other dial-up connections. You can now run Internet tools and applications from the workstation. See Chapter 18 for more information about using Dial-Up Networking.

FIGURE 10.6

Dial-Up Networking on
the Desktop

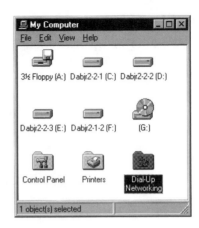

TCP/IP Configuration

After you've installed TCP/IP, you can configure it manually through its property sheet (accessed from the Network Control Panel), or you can use DHCP (Dynamic Host Configuration Protocol) to configure it automatically. The following sections describe both methods.

Manually Configuring TCP/IP

The TCP/IP Properties dialog box allows you to manually enter IP address parameters. You can also enter the subnet mask, DNS servers, WINS servers, and other TCP/IP settings. Figures 10.7, 10.8, and 10.9 show the IP Address, WINS Configuration, and DNS Configuration tabs of the TCP/IP Properties dialog box.

Use the period (.) to move between octets (within an address) and the Tab key to move to a new address or field.

After you've set TCP/IP properties, you can check your configuration by running the WinIPCfg program and clicking on the More Info button. Figure 10.10 shows an example of this program's IP Configuration dialog box.

FIGURE 10.7

FIGURE 10.7

The IP Address tab of the TCP/IP Properties dialog box

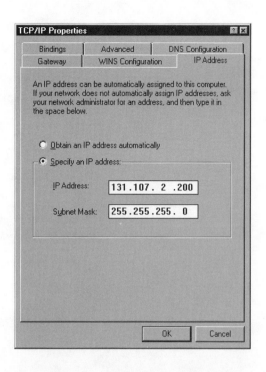

FIGURE 10.8

The WINS Configuration tab of the TCP/IP Properties dialog box

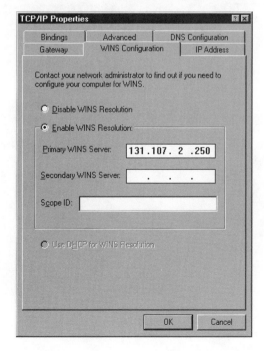

F I G U R E 10.9

The DNS Configuration
tab of the TCP/IP
Properties dialog box

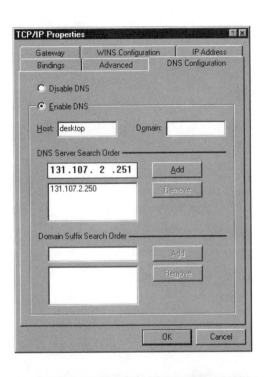

F I G U R E 10.10

Using WinIPCfg to
check your TCP/IP
settings

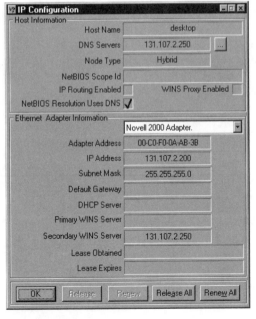

Follow the steps in Exercise 10.2 to manually set TCP/IP addresses, and then check your configuration settings.

WARNING If you already have TCP/IP installed, you should carefully record your settings so you can reset them after the exercise. If you are using DHCP, you can just reset Windows 95 to use DHCP; you won't need to record any other settings.

EXERCISE 10.2

Manually Configuring TCP/IP

1. Go to Control Panel ➢ Network.

2. Highlight TCP/IP and choose Properties (or right-click on Network Neighborhood and choose Properties).

3. Choose the IP Address tab. Enter **131.107.2.200** for the IP Address and **255.255.255.0** for the Subnet Mask (Figure 10.7).

4. Choose the WINS tab and enter **131.107.2.250** for the Primary WINS Server (Figure 10.8).

5. Choose the DNS Configuration tab and enter **desktop** for the Host, and **131.107.2.250** and **131.107.2.251** for the addresses (Figure 10.9).

6. Choose OK to save your changes.

7. Restart Windows 95.

8. Select Start ➢ Run and type **WINIPCFG**.

9. Click on the More Info button and check your settings against what you entered (Figure 10.10).

Using DHCP to Configure TCP/IP

DHCP was developed to help with the administration of TCP/IP. DHCP allows for centralization of TCP/IP management. Instead of an administrator needing to individually configure each host with its IP parameters, this configuration can be done automatically with a DHCP server.

Although Microsoft has been one of the first to implement DHCP, it was not developed by Microsoft. Like the other TCP/IP protocols, DHCP was developed through RFCs. DHCP is defined in RFCs 1533, 1534, 1541, and 1542. It is an extension of the Bootp protocol (RFC 951), which automatically assigns IP addresses to diskless clients.

The DHCP server can assign an IP address, a subnet mask, a default gateway, and a WINS server address to hosts. A client needs to specify that it will use DHCP instead of being manually configured with IP information. In Windows 95, this is done via a radio button in the TCP/IP Properties dialog box. Follow the steps in Exercise 10.3 to set up TCP/IP to use DHCP for automatic configuration.

EXERCISE 10.3340

Enabling Automatic Configuration Using DHCP

1. Go to Control Panel ➢ Network.

2. Highlight TCP/IP and choose Properties.

3. Choose Obtain an IP address automatically, which is the top radio button in the IP Address tab (Figure 10.7).

4. Restart Windows 95.

The DHCP server software can run only on Windows NT Server (not Windows 95 or Windows NT Workstation). Once the server software is installed, an icon called DHCP Manager is added to the NT Administration Tools group. This is the interface for administrators to define the pool of IP addresses. DHCP clients (those that receive an IP address from the DHCP server) can be any of several operating systems, including Windows 95. Refer to *MCSE: Windows NT 4 Server* for more information about installing and configuring DHCP.

There is a four-step process for a host to receive IP configuration through DHCP:

1. The DHCP client boots up and broadcasts a DHCP Discover message looking for a DHCP server.

2. Any DHCP server that received the broadcast responds with a DHCP Offer (which includes the IP address of the offering server). This message also has the IP address being offered.

3. The client broadcasts a DHCP Request for the first offer received (in a case where multiple servers responded with offers) to accept.

4. The DHCP server broadcasts a DHCP Acknowledgment to confirm the assignment.

The address is assigned on a lease basis (usually somewhere between 72 and 96 hours, but this can be changed by the administrator). When half of the lease time expires, the client renews the lease to full time again. In this way, the lease will never run out unless the client could not find the server to renew, or the client was shut down and could not renew.

Using WINS for NETBIOS Communication

WINS (Windows Internet Name Service) is another NT Server service that helps lower administrative overhead. WINS is an enhanced NETBIOS Name Server (NBNS) designed by Microsoft to perform two main tasks:

- To help eliminate broadcast traffic associated with resolving NETBIOS names over TCP/IP

- To help facilitate NETBIOS communication between subnets

Most of the applications that are native to Windows and Windows NT (such as File Manager and Explorer) are NETBIOS-based. One of the requirements for a NETBIOS session to be established is that each side has a NETBIOS name to reference. In Windows, this is accomplished by assigning a computer name. The computer name is a NETBIOS name that can be used to establish a NETBIOS session.

When running over TCP/IP, an IP address is also required for communication. This means that a NETBIOS name must be resolved to an IP address. This can be done by means of a broadcast (which works only if the computers are on the same subnet), a WINS server, or a local LMHOSTS file (which is an ASCII file that has computer names listed along with their IP addresses) that has been configured at each host.

To configure a host to be a WINS client in Windows 95, the client needs to have the IP address of the WINS server. This can be done either manually by entering the address by hand (as in Exercise 10.2) or automatically by using DHCP (as in Exercise 10.3).

WINS works dynamically by registering computer names and IP addresses of clients as they boot up and become active on the network. Since each WINS client knows the IP address of the WINS server, it can communicate directly with a WINS server to register its computer name and IP address instead of using a broadcast. When a WINS client needs to resolve a computer name to an IP address, such as when a net use \\computer\share is used, the WINS client sends a direct request to the WINS server (again saving the broadcast traffic) for the IP address of the requested computer name.

Summary

TCP/IP is an open protocol that was jointly developed and enhanced over time by the Internet community through a series of documents called RFCs. It is a routable protocol that is used for connecting dissimilar hardware platforms and for connecting to the Internet. There are also many other protocols commonly associated with TCP/IP for higher-level functions such as e-mail and file transfer.

There are three classes of IP addresses available for networking: Class A, Class B, and Class C. Each of these varies in the number of hosts and networks supported. Custom subnet masks can be used to alter the number of networks and host addresses available for an address.

Windows 95 provides a 32-bit TCP/IP protocol and built-in dial-up connectivity software. It also comes with several TCP/IP utilities and applications, including PING, WinIPCfg, and a Web browser.

DHCP and WINS can be used to ease administrative overhead on a TCP/IP network. DHCP is used to automatically configure hosts with IP settings. WINS is used to provide a dynamic, centralized database for resolving NETBIOS names to IP addresses.

Review Questions

1. What was the first operating system to include TCP/IP?

   A. BSD Unix

   B. Macintosh System 1.0

   C. IBM DOS

   D. Amiga DOS

2. Which type of document contains the standards for TCP/IP?

   A. DOCs (Documentation Files)

   B. RFCs (Requests for Comments)

   C. IPREQs (TCP/IP Requests)

   D. TCP/IP Specifications

3. How many bits long is an IP address?

   A. 8 bits

   B. 16 bits

   C. 32 bits

   D. 64 bits

4. What is the largest class of IP address?

   A. Class A

   B. Class B

   C. Class C

   D. Class D

5. 127.118.175.211 is a valid IP address.

    A. True, this is always a valid address.

    B. True, but only if you are not connected to the Internet.

    C. False, there are too many digits.

    D. False, the 127 range is reserved.

6. What are the three main components of an IP address?

    A. Address itself

    B. Subnet mask

    C. DHCP server

    D. Default gateway

7. With a subnet mask of 255.255.255.0, are the two addresses 106.108.10.50 and 106.108.11.51 located on the same subnet?

    A. Yes.

    B. No, the subnet makes them different networks.

    C. No, the address of 106 is reserved for Internet addresses only.

    D. No, the address of 106.108 is for loopback purposes.

8. With a subnet mask of 255.255.0.0, are the two addresses 106.108.10.50 and 106.108.11.51 located on the same subnet?

    A. Yes.

    B. No, the subnet makes them different networks.

    C. No, the address of 106 is reserved for Internet addresses only.

    D. No, the address of 106.108 is for loopback purposes.

9. What subnet mask would give you at least 15 subnets for the net ID of 160.108.0.0?

A. 255.255.248.0

B. 255.255.255.0

C. 255.255.240.0

D. 255.255.0.0

10. With the subnet mask from question 9 (above), what is the first subnet net ID?

A. 160.108.1.0

B. 160.108.255.0

C. 160.108.8.0

D. 160.108.16.0

11. How can you find out what IP address has been assigned to you by DHCP in Windows 95?

A. Use the WinIPCfg utility.

B. Use the PING utility.

C. Use the TCPIP utility.

D. Use the IPCONFIG utility.

12. Which two software components in Windows 95 are necessary to allow you to use your Web browser on the Internet from a LAN?

A. DHCP

B. Windows Sockets

C. TCP/IP protocol

D. Router

13. If you can see computers on your LAN, but cannot access the Internet, which networking configuration would you probably suspect is bad?

A. DNS

B. TCP/IP Address

C. Subnet Mask

D. Default Gateway

14. Which software component helps prevent duplicate TCP/IP addresses?

A. DHCP

B. WINS

C. DNS

D. HTTP

15. Windows 95 can function as which type of server using software from Microsoft? (Select all that apply.)

A. DHCP

B. WINS

C. DNS

D. HTTP

16. Refer to Figure 10.1. For the computer with the address of 131.107.8.31, what would you enter as the default gateway?

A. 131.107.8.31

B. 131.107.8.1

C. 131.107.16.1

D. 131.107.8.33

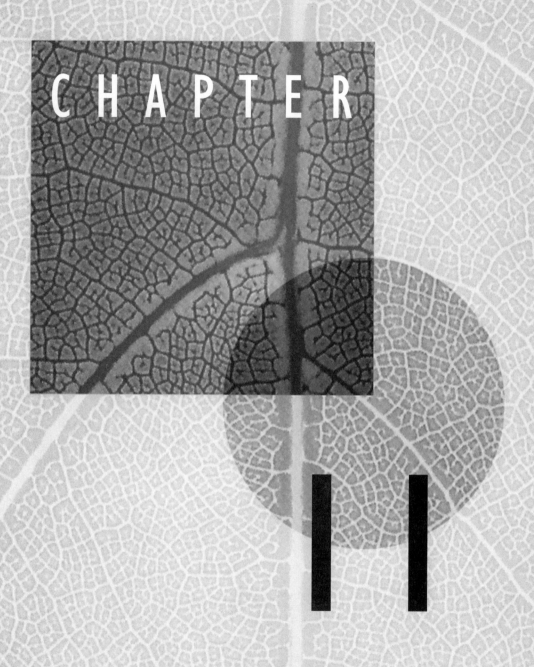

CHAPTER

11

Networking with Microsoft Servers

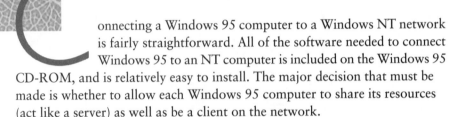

Connecting a Windows 95 computer to a Windows NT network is fairly straightforward. All of the software needed to connect Windows 95 to an NT computer is included on the Windows 95 CD-ROM, and is relatively easy to install. The major decision that must be made is whether to allow each Windows 95 computer to share its resources (act like a server) as well as be a client on the network.

As explained in Chapter 9, when computers act as both clients and servers they form a peer-to-peer network. Peer-to-peer networks are great for small offices (such as a dentist's or doctor's office), but with more than about six to eight computers, keeping track of all of the shares and passwords on the network can get rather confusing and time-consuming. After a network grows to ten or more machines, companies often find it easier to dedicate one computer to being a server (even if it can still do client functions), and let the rest of the clients be just plain clients.

In this chapter, you will learn how to install and configure the Client for Microsoft Networks software so that Windows 95 can connect to Windows NT servers. You will also learn how to allow a Windows 95 computer to share its resources. We will discuss setting up shares and selecting a security level. Finally, we'll cover the network browsing service, which allows users to see the shared resources on the network. Windows 95 can act as a browser client and/or browser server.

Windows NT Client Installation

Microsoft servers communicate using a language called SMB (Server Message Block). By installing the Client for Microsoft Networks, you enable Windows 95 to communicate with Microsoft (Windows NT) servers.

Microsoft
✓ **Exam**
Objective

Install and configure the network components of a client computer and server.

There are several steps involved in installing the client software for Windows NT:

- Check licensing agreements to ensure legality.

- Install the network card and drivers.

- Install the client software.

- Configure the network card.

- Configure the protocols.

- Configure the client software.

Each of these steps is explained in the following sections.

Licensing the Client

By purchasing Windows 95, you have bought a license to use it on a single computer, but not necessarily on a network. If you connect the Windows 95 computer to an NT server, you will need to make sure you have a Client Access License (CAL) for each client attached.

There are two different client licensing schemes:

- **Per Server:** Licenses are purchased with the Windows NT Server package. These allow a certain number of simultaneous connections to that server.

- **Per Seat:** Licenses are purchased for each client that needs to connect to NT servers. These licenses allow the client to connect to any NT server on the network.

When you buy additional licenses, you usually just get a piece of paper that proves you are legal, in case of an audit.

For more information about the licensing schemes, see *MCSE: NT Server Study Guide*, published by Sybex.

Installing a Network Card and Driver

The first step in installing network support in Windows 95 is to install the physical card in the computer. If the card is an older, legacy card (its settings are made by jumpers and/or switches), you should make a note of its settings. If the card is a Plug-and-Play variety, Windows 95 should be able to automatically detect and configure the card to the correct settings.

Microsoft
✓ Exam
Objective

Diagnose and resolve hardware device and device driver problems. Tools include:

- MSD
- Add/Remove Hardware Wizard

If Windows 95 can auto-detect the card, it may install the driver automatically. You can force Windows 95 to search for new hardware by starting the Add New Hardware Wizard from the Control Panel and selecting Yes, as shown in Figure 11.1.

FIGURE 11.1

Searching for new hardware

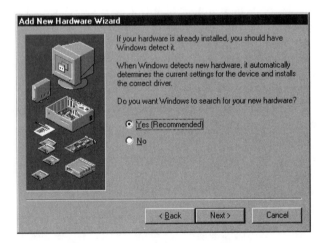

If Windows 95 doesn't install the driver automatically, you will need to install it manually. Start the Add New Hardware Wizard from the Control Panel, and click on the No button to tell Windows 95 not to try to detect the device. Windows 95 displays a list of hardware devices for which it has drivers, as shown in Figure 11.2. If your network card has a newer driver on a disk, click on the Have Disk button, and insert the driver disk that came with your network card. Windows 95 will install the driver from the floppy disk.

F I G U R E   11.2

Installing a network driver manually

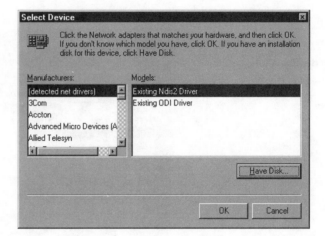

Installing the Client Software

By installing the client software, you allow Windows 95 to see and connect to Windows NT servers.

You install the software through the Network Control Panel. First choose to add a client, as shown in Figure 11.3. Then pick the type of client from the Network Control Panel's Select Network Client dialog box, as shown in Figure 11.4. Follow the steps in Exercise 11.1 to install the Client for Microsoft Networks software.

If you already have the Client for Microsoft Networks software installed and you would like to practice reinstalling it, remove it and then follow the steps in Exercise 11.1.

FIGURE 11.3

Adding a new client

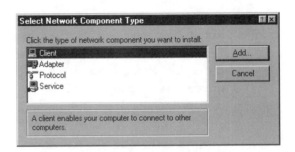

FIGURE 11.4

Choosing the Client for
Microsoft Networks

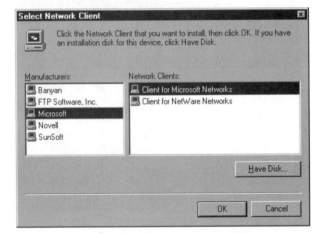

EXERCISE 11.1

Installing the Client for Microsoft Networks

1. Go to Control Panel ➤ Network and choose Add.

2. Highlight Client and choose Add (Figure 11.3).

3. Highlight Microsoft in the list of Manufacturers.

4. Highlight Client for Microsoft Networks in the list of Network Clients (Figure 11.4).

5. Click on OK.

6. Reboot Windows 95.

Configuring the Network Card

Windows 95 should detect and install the correct drivers for your network card. Every device connected to your computer needs to be assigned a unique IRQ, I/O port, and memory address (if used):

- **IRQ or interrupt:** This is like a doorbell that devices use to get the attention of the CPU. Every device needs a unique IRQ or your accessories may not be able to talk to the CPU. IRQs range from 0 to 15. IRQs 5, 10, 11, and 12 are commonly used for accessories.

- **I/O port:** This is like a doorway that data travels through to get to and from the CPU. Every device needs a unique I/O port assigned to it. The I/O port ranges are from 200 to 3E0. I/O ports 210, 220, 300, and 310 are often used by accessories.

- **Memory address:** This is like a waiting room outside the CPU. Older network cards (especially older Token Ring cards) may require a memory address, which must then be excluded from the range that Windows 95 is using (see Chapter 3 for switches to use to exclude memory addresses from Windows 95). CC00 to FF00 is a common range that accessories use (if they need one).

If more than one device is assigned a particular setting, you will need to resolve the conflict before Windows 95 will work properly.

How you change the settings of your network card depends on whether it is a Plug-and-Play card or a legacy (jumpered or set by software) card. If it is a Plug-and-Play card, you should be able to change its settings in Device Manager by going to the property sheet for the card and choosing Change Setting, as shown in Figure 11.5. After you reboot, the card should be set to the new settings.

Device Manager is one of the best utilities included in Windows 95, because it allows you to see, troubleshoot, and control your hardware settings. To open Device Manager, go to Control Panel ➤ System and choose the Device Manager tab. See Chapter 21 and Appendix C for more information about using the Device Manager.

FIGURE 11.5

Changing network card
settings in Device
Manager

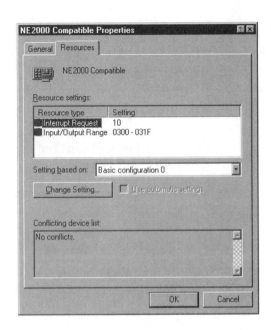

If your card is a legacy card, you will need to power off the computer and
then change the jumpers or switches on your card or use a software setup program (sometimes called *softset)* to the new settings. When you are finished,
turn on your computer and start Windows 95, and then make the changes in
Device Manager. Reboot for the changes to take effect.

Configuring Protocols

Although the default settings for the protocols work almost all of the time,
you can change many of the settings for each of the protocols. If you have
more than one protocol installed, you can designate one as your default protocol. You should designate the protocol you use the most often as the default
protocol, since it will be slightly faster than the other protocols.

Setting your default protocol is also important because certain applications
(like Microsoft's System Management Server, SMS) will use only the default
protocol for certain network communications.

Microsoft
✓ **Exam**
Objective

Install and configure network protocols. Protocols include:

- NetBEUI
- IPX/SPX-compatible Protocol
- TCP/IP
- Microsoft DLC
- PPTP/VPN

Configuring IPX/SPX

There are only a couple of settings you may need to change on a regular basis when using the IPX/SPX protocol: selecting the frame type and enabling NET-BIOS support.

The most important setting to check when using the IPX/SPX protocol on an Ethernet network is the frame type. There are four basic frames that can be run under Ethernet:

- Ethernet 802.2

- Ethernet 802.3

- Ethernet_II

- Ethernet_Snap

Microsoft's IPX/SPX default frame selection is Automatic, which means that Windows 95 will try to determine the frame type being used and match itself to that. If a frame cannot be determined, it will default to 802.2 (which is the default for NetWare 3.12 and higher).

You can also control which protocol is connected to which network adapter. This is often referred to as the network bindings. The default setting is for all protocols to be bound to all adapters. You may wish to change this for performance or security reasons. For example, if you have two network adapters, one that connects to your LAN and one that connects to the Internet, by unbinding TCP/IP from your LAN adapter you can prevent hackers on the Internet from accessing your LAN.

Each protocol and adapter will have a tab that will list the bindings for that particular component. If you make changes, you will probably have to reboot to have those changes take effect.

If you were using IPX/SPX from Novell and had different frame types on two computers, the two computers would not see each other at all. When you are using Microsoft's version of IPX/SPX, if the wrong frame type is selected the computers may still connect, but the communication will be extremely slow. You also may be able to see servers with different frames, even though Windows 95 is using only one, because a server is routing, or converting, to the other frame type. For best performance, you should run the same frame type on all your computers.

The Automatic setting will bind to only the first frame it finds. If you have multiple frames on your network, Windows 95 may bind to the wrong one. If you have servers with various frame types, you should specify the frame for the client software so it will see the correct servers. The Frame Type setting is on the Advanced tab of the IPX/SPX Compatible Protocol Properties dialog box, as shown in Figure 11.6. Follow the steps in Exercise 11.2 to set the frame type manually.

FIGURE 11.6

Setting frame types manually

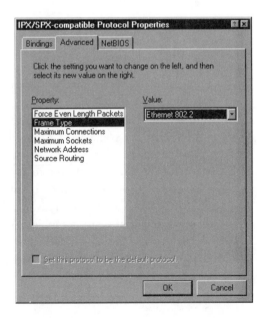

EXERCISE 11.2

Setting the Frame Type Manually

1. Go to Control Panel ➤ Network.

2. Highlight IPX/SPX and choose Properties.

3. Choose the Advanced tab.

4. Choose Frame Type.

5. Change the Value from Automatic to Ethernet 802.2 (Figure 11.6).

6. Click on OK.

7. Reboot Windows 95.

Another parameter you may need to set is whether to support NETBIOS over IPX/SPX. NETBIOS is a specification that some programs require in order to work on a network. The documentation for the network application should specify which protocol(s) are supported, and if NETBIOS support is required. Older network applications often require NETBIOS support; newer applications seldom do. If you have applications that require NETBIOS support, you will need to select the option. This setting is on the NetBIOS tab of the IPX/SPX-compatible Protocol Properties dialog box, as shown in Figure 11.7. Follow the steps in Exercise 11.3 to enable NETBIOS support.

EXERCISE 11.3

Enabling NETBIOS Support

1. Go to Control Panel ➤ Network.

2. Highlight IPX/SPX and choose Properties.

3. Choose the NetBIOS tab.

4. Check the I want to enable NetBIOS over IPX/SPX box (Figure 11.7).

5. Click on OK.

6. Reboot Windows 95.

FIGURE 11.7

Enabling NETBIOS
support

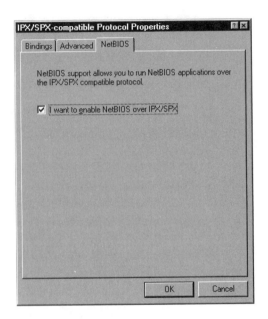

Configuring TCP/IP

Installing and configuring TCP/IP are covered in detail in Chapter 10. Your configuration choices are whether to use DHCP (Dynamic Host Configuration Protocol) to dynamically assign addresses and subnet masks or to manually assign addresses and subnet masks. The addresses of DNS servers, WINS servers, and default gateways can also be assigned manually or by DHCP.

Configuring NetBEUI

NetBEUI parameters will rarely, if ever, need to be changed. Changing these settings affects only real-mode NetBEUI. The protected mode NetBEUI parameters are dynamically adjusted by Windows 95.

Remember, NetBEUI can handle only up to 254 nodes, and NetBEUI packets cannot cross a router. Although this protocol is rarely used as a regular protocol, it can be useful as a dial-up protocol, as explained in Chapter 18.

There are only two parameters that can be changed for real-mode NetBEUI: maximum sessions and NCBs (Network Control Blocks). These settings are on the Advanced tab of the NetBEUI Properties dialog box, as shown in Figure 11.8.

FIGURE II.8

Real-mode NetBEUI
parameters

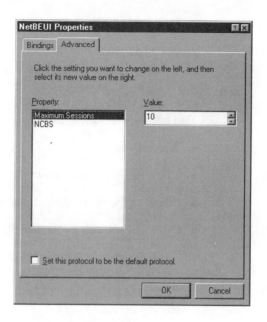

Configuring the Client

Several options can be configured for the client software, including protocols which are bound to the network card and which client (NetWare, NT, or another client) software will be the primary one (the one that Windows 95 loads and logs in to first). These settings are usually set during installation of the computer, when the client is first set up, and rarely need to be changed.

Microsoft ✓ ***Exam*** ***Objective***	**Configure a Windows 95 computer as a client computer in a Windows NT network.**

An item that may need to be changed on a regular basis (if the security policy of the server requires it) is the user password. Windows 95 will cache usernames and passwords that you use to connect to various shared resources so it can automatically reconnect to those resources after you log in. You may want to disable the password cache for security reasons (this will be shown in Chapter 15).

Choosing a Primary Network Logon

Windows 95 keeps a local database of usernames and passwords. If you are logging on to a domain or another type of server, you must choose whether to have Windows 95 first log you in to the domain and then the local computer, or first log in to the local computer and then the domain.

You have the following choices for primary logon:

- Windows logon

- Client for Microsoft Networks (if installed)

- Client for NetWare (if installed)

- Other clients such as Banyan Vines or DECNET (if installed)

You should set the client that you use most often as your primary client. Some features of Windows 95 (such as roaming user profiles, described in Chapter 14) work only if the Client for Microsoft Networks is set as the primary client.

If security is not an issue, in order to keep Windows 95 from prompting you for a password, set Primary Network Logon to Windows Logon, and make your password blank. Although this is not secure, it is convenient.

The Primary Network Logon setting is on the Configuration tab of the Network Control Panel, as shown in Figure 11.9. Follow the steps in Exercise 11.4 to choose your primary logon.

Logging into an NT Domain

Another logon option you have is whether you log in to a workgroup or a domain. If you choose to log in to a domain, you must already have an account on that domain (usually created by a network administrator).

A workgroup is a loose association of computers that has no central database of users, groups, or passwords. A domain has one or more Windows NT servers acting as controllers. Each controller has a copy of a user database and can validate logon requests.

F I G U R E 11.9

Choosing a primary
network logon

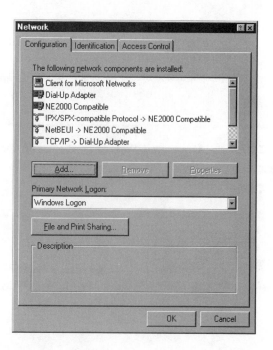

EXERCISE 11.4

Changing Your Primary Network Logon

1. Go to Control Panel ➢ Network.

2. From the Primary Network Logon drop-down list, choose where
you want to log on first. Select Windows Logon for a peer-to-peer
network (Figure 11.9), or Client for Microsoft if you log in to an NT
domain.

3. Click on OK.

4. Reboot Windows 95.

The benefit of logging in to a domain is that once you are validated, you
should never need to enter your username and password again (during your

session) to access resources on the network. The controllers on the domain create an access token when you log in, and that token is used by all the servers in the domain. It is much like getting your ticket stamped at an amusement park and being able to go on any of the rides (because you have been authenticated at one of the ticket windows).

Microsoft ✓ **_Exam_** **_Objective_**

Develop an appropriate implementation model for specific requirements. Considerations include:

- Choosing a workgroup configuration or logging on to an existing domain

---

The option to log on to a Windows NT domain is in the Client for Microsoft Networks Properties dialog box, as shown in Figure 11.10. Follow the steps in Exercise 11.5 to set up Windows 95 to log on to an NT domain.

FIGURE 11.10

Setting Windows 95 to log on to an NT domain

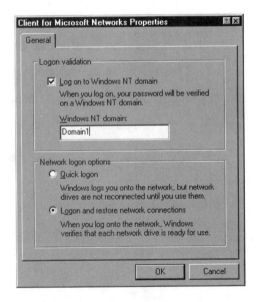

Setting Windows 95 to Log On to an NT Domain

1. Go to Control Panel ➤ Network.

2. Highlight Client for Microsoft Networks and choose Properties.

3. Put a checkmark in the Log on to Windows NT domain box.

4. Type the name of the domain in the text box. If you don't currently have a real domain, enter **Domain1** (Figure 11.10).

5. Click on OK.

6. Reboot Windows 95.

Changing Your Password

You can change both your Windows 95 local password and your NT password from the Passwords Properties dialog box, shown in Figure 11.11. Windows 95 will also allow you to change other passwords, such as those for screen savers, from the same Properties dialog box.

FIGURE 11.11

The Password Properties
dialog box

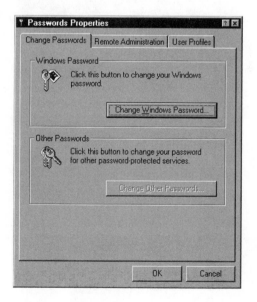

Exercise 11.6 shows the steps for changing the Windows NT domain and screen saver passwords.

EXERCISE 11.6

Changing Your Passwords

1. Go to Control Panel ➤ Passwords.

2. Click on Change Windows Password (Figure 11.11).

3. In the Change Windows Password dialog box, select the Microsoft Networking (to change your NT domain password) and the Windows Screen Saver boxes, as shown below.

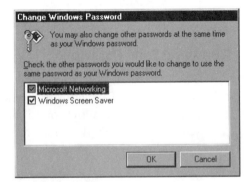

4. Click on OK.

5. In the next dialog box, change your password by typing the old one once, and the new one twice, as shown below.

6. Click on OK.

7. Reboot Windows 95 to use your new password.

Password Caching

Windows 95 can cache, or remember, the usernames and passwords with which you connect to shared resources. While convenient, caching passwords poses a security risk if the password file is de-encrypted. The caching of passwords happens if you select the Reconnect at Logon box when using a network resource. When you log in to Windows 95, the system uses the cached passwords to automatically reestablish all the drive connections you had the last time you logged off.

WARNING   The password encryption that comes with the standard Windows 95 is easy to break. Download the new version at Microsoft's Web site (www.microsoft .com) for added security, or turn off password caching.

Password caching can be disabled by using a system policy. See Chapter 15 for more information.

Sharing Resources as a Server

Windows 95 computers can have an additional service installed that allows them to share resources and act like Windows NT file and print servers. Allowing users to share their resources does make sharing information more convenient, but it is also makes more work for those who maintain and administer the network and is a lot less secure. You now have many administrators to train and supervise, instead of just a few. Problems can arise if users share their drives incorrectly and sensitive information gets out, or if users have too many rights and delete the wrong files.

Microsoft ✓ *Exam* *Objective*

Create, share, and monitor resources. Resources include:

- Remote
- Network printers
- Shared fax modem
- Unimodem/V

Many smaller companies love the fact that they don't need a dedicated, expensive computer in order to share a few files and printers. Larger companies tend to have more resources for both hardware and administrators, and usually don't allow users to share their local resources on the network. Restrictions can be enforced with system policies, which are discussed in Chapter 15.

When all is said and done, Windows 95 is a great PC operating system and network client, but it's much better to leave the role of a server to Windows NT or NetWare.

The following are the steps to setting up and managing shared resources:

- Choose a security model (Share level versus User level).

- Install file and printer sharing for Microsoft Networks.

- Configure file and printer sharing.

- Create shared resources.

- Modify shared resources.

These steps are discussed in detail in the following sections.

Choosing a Security Model

There are two types of security systems that Windows 95 can use to share resources: Share level and User level.

Microsoft ✓ *Exam* *Objective*	**Assign access permissions for shared folders. Methods include:** • Passwords • User permissions • Group permissions

The way you create and modify shared resources depends on whether you set Share level or User level security.

You will need to reset sharing of all your resources if you switch between the two security types. When you switch, Windows 95 will turn off sharing of all folders and printers. There is no way for Windows 95 to convert rights from one scheme to another, so it doesn't even try.

Share Level Security

Share level is the same as it is in Windows for Workgroups; that is, a password is assigned to a shared resource when the shared resource is created. This is the default level of security.

With Share level security, if a user knows the passwords, he or she can access the resources, even if the original owner did not intend that particular user to have access to those shared resources.

Using Share level security has the advantages of being easy and fast. However, it has the following disadvantages:

- It is not secure.

- Specific users cannot be blocked.

- The passwords can be discovered.

- There is no centralized control (central Information Systems is no longer in charge).

- Changing passwords requires informing all intended users.

Share level security is the default security setting for the sharing service for Microsoft networks.

User Level Security

Because of the limitations of Share level security, Microsoft added a more advanced option in Windows 95 that is much more secure. The User level system bases its security on an existing server of some sort: either a Windows NT computer (NT Workstation, NT Server, or a domain controller) or a NetWare server. After a new share is made, existing users or groups are then given rights to the share. This means that you must have some kind of server in place before you can switch to User level security.

User level security has the following advantages:

- Rights can be assigned to a user or group.

- It allows centralized control of users and groups.

- It's more flexible than Share level (custom rights can be assigned).

There are a few disadvantages of using User level security, however:

- Some kind of server must be in place.

- It's more complex than Share level.

- A live network connection to the server must be maintained when assigning rights and shares.

You can switch to User level security when you configure sharing services, as described later in the chapter.

Installing File and Printer Sharing for Microsoft Networks

A Windows 95 computer can have many different client pieces installed simultaneously, but it can have only one sharing service installed at a time. Installing file and printer sharing is quite easy. This is a network service, which you can install from the Network Control Panel, as shown in Figure 11.12.

F I G U R E   11.12

Adding file and printer sharing for Microsoft Networks

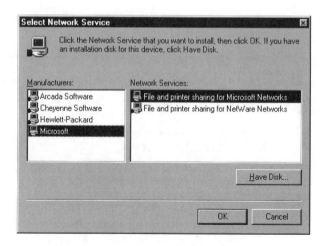

Another way to access the network configuration dialog box is by right-clicking on Network Neighborhood and selecting Properties.

Follow the steps in Exercise 11.7 to install the sharing service for Microsoft Networks.

EXERCISE 11.7

Installing File and Printer Sharing for Microsoft Networks

1. Go to Control Panel ➢ Network.

2. Choose Add in the Select Network Component Type dialog box (shown earlier in Figure 11.3).

3. Highlight Service and choose Add.

4. Highlight Microsoft and choose File and printer sharing for Microsoft Networks (Figure 11.12).

5. Click on OK.

6. Reboot Windows 95.

Configuring File and Printer Sharing for Microsoft Networks

The major decision when configuring file and printer sharing is which security model to use. If you are in a workgroup, without any central server, Share level security is probably your best (if not only) option. If you have a central server (either NetWare or NT), User level security is probably the better option. In either case, the mechanics of sharing resources is the same, but the security options are different.

You will need to designate a workgroup for your Windows 95 computer to be a member of. A workgroup is simply a collection of computers that appear together, by default, when Network Neighborhood is opened. Normally, you can select Entire Network to browse computers outside of your workgroup, unless there is a system policy in place that prevents you from browsing outside of your workgroup (policies are covered in Chapter 15).

Changing the Security Model

As explained earlier, the default security model is Share level, which allows you to put passwords on shared resources. User level is more secure, and is thus preferred if users will be allowed to share their resources. Before you can change to User level, you need a server (either NetWare or NT) in place.

You switch to User level security through the Access Control tab of the Network Control Panel, as shown in Figure 11.13. If you set User level to an NT server that is not a domain controller, you will need the server name. If you set User level to an NT domain, you will need the domain name. Exercise 11.8 shows the steps for switching the security model to User level, based on an NT domain.

FIGURE 11.13

Changing to User level security

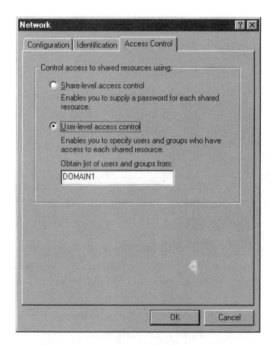

EXERCISE 11.8

Switching to User Level Security

1. Go to Control Panel ➤ Network.

2. Choose the Access Control tab.

> **EXERCISE 11.8 (CONTINUED FROM PREVIOUS PAGE)**
>
> **3.** Select User-level access control.
>
> **4.** Enter the name of the NT server or domain. Use **Domain1** if you don't have a real domain to use (Figure 11.13).
>
> **5.** Click on OK.
>
> **6.** Reboot Windows 95.

To switch back to Share level, follow the steps in Exercise 11.8 to return to the Access Control tab, and select Share-level access control.

The process of creating shared folders is similar for both Share level and User level security settings, but the types of security settings you can pick are different. The following sections describe the procedures for sharing folders and managing shares for both Share level and User level sharing. Sharing printers and printer security are covered in Chapter 13.

Creating Shares Using Share Level Security

When you share a folder using Share level security, you have three basic security options:

- **Read-Only:** Allows users on the network to see and run applications in that folder, and to see and open files

- **Full:** Allows all of the above rights, plus gives users the rights to modify and delete programs and files, and to create new files

- **Depends on Password:** Allows you to set different passwords for Read-Only and Full access. You then give the appropriate password to users based on which rights you want them to have.

WARNING   If you select Read-Only or Full access, users don't need to use a password; in that case, the shares are wide open to any and all users on your network—even those who have not been authenticated by any server!

These options are listed on the Sharing tab of a folder's Properties dialog box, as shown in Figure 11.14.

Follow the steps in Exercise 11.9 to share a folder and set the security parameters using passwords.

FIGURE 11.14

Setting up a new share
with Share level security

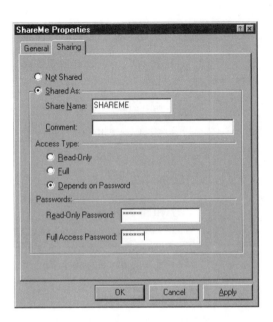

EXERCISE 11.9

Creating a Share Using Share Level Security

1. Create a folder called ShareMe.

2. Highlight the folder and right-click. Sharing should appear in the pop-up menu, as shown below, if you installed the Sharing service correctly (see Exercise 11.7).

3. Select Sharing to display the Sharing tab of the ShareMe Properties dialog box.

4. Select the Shared As button.

5. As the Share Name, leave the default name SHAREME, or enter another name.

Note that if your share name ends with a $ (dollar sign), the share will be hidden from the browser. The only way to connect to this share will be to use the Map Network Drive command and type in the UNC.

6. Select Depends on Password.

7. Enter **Readme** in the Read-Only Password box.

8. Enter **Fullcontrol** in the Full Access Password box (Figure 11.14).

9. Retype the passwords when prompted, as shown below.

10. Click on OK to save your new share.

11. You should now see the folder with a hand under it, signifying it is shared, as shown below.

You can check all of your shares by going to the Network Neighborhood. Under your computer name, all the shares should be listed.

Creating Shares Using User Level Security

When you share folders with User level security, you are able to grant rights to users or groups. The Sharing tab of the shared folder's Properties dialog box (Figure 11.15) looks different than one that has Share level security, as shown in Figure 11.14.

FIGURE 11.15

Setting up a new share with User level security

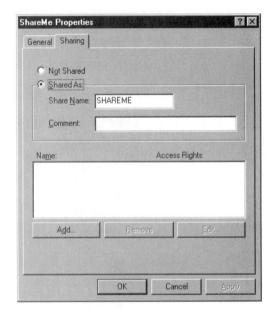

The rights you can grant are Read Only, Full Access, or Custom, as shown in Figure 11.16. You can grant rights to users or groups from the domain, or to The world, which is all users on the network.

If you choose Custom, you can set individual rights, as shown in Figure 11.17. These include the following:

- **Read Files:** Allows the user to open or run files or applications

- **Write to Files:** Allows the user to edit existing files

- **Create Files and Folders:** Allows the user to create new files or folders

- **Delete Files:** Allows the user to delete files or folders

- **Change File Attributes:** Allows the user to change file or folder attributes

- **List Files:** Allows the user to show files and folders

- **Change Access Control:** Allows the user to change security settings

FIGURE 11.16

Assigning rights using User level security

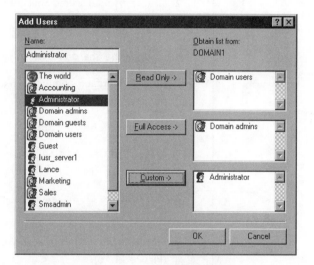

FIGURE 11.17

Assigning custom security rights

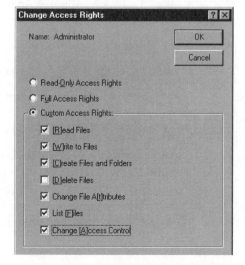

Follow the steps in Exercise 11.10 to create a new share using User level security and assign rights to users and groups.

EXERCISE 11.10

Creating a Share Using User Level Security

1. Make sure you are using User level security (see Exercise 11.8).

2. Create a folder called ShareMe.

3. Select the ShareMe folder, right-click on it, and choose Sharing.

4. Choose the Shared As button.

5. Leave the default name of SHAREME as the Share Name or enter a different name (Figure 11.15).

6. Click on the Add button.

7. In the Add Users dialog box, highlight the Domain users group and click on the Read Only button.

8. Highlight the Domain admins group and click on the Full Access button.

9. Highlight the Administrator user and click on the Custom button (Figure 11.16).

10. Click on OK. The Change Access Rights dialog box for the Administrator user appears.

11. Choose all custom access rights except Delete Files (Figure 11.17).

12. Choose OK twice to save your new share.

Managing Existing Shared Folders

To modify the properties of existing shares, return to the Sharing tab of the shared folder's Properties dialog box by right-clicking on the folder and choosing Sharing from the menu (as in Exercises 11.9 and 11.10). From the Sharing tab of a share using Share level security (Figure 11.14), you can change the share name, how it is shared, or the passwords. From the Sharing tab of a User level security share (Figure 11.15), you can change the share name, how it is shared, or which users and groups have rights to the share.

Browsing on a Microsoft Network

The network browsing service is designed to allow clients to access a complete list of available servers, shared folders, and shared printers, without needing to keep their own copy of the list. When a computer browses the network, it downloads a list of available servers and shares from a central computer that maintains the list. As the number of clients increases, Windows (both NT and 95) will increase the number of servers keeping lists. The default number of browse servers is one server for every 32 clients. If Windows 95 is part of a domain, the primary domain controller (PDC) of the domain will be the browse master for the entire domain, and will have helper servers (backup browsers) to give lists to clients. When a browse master or backup browser is turned off, there will be an "election" to pick a new browse master. The order of precedence is as follows:

- Windows NT Server

- Windows NT Workstation

- Windows 95

- Windows for Workgroups

You can "stuff the ballot box" by editing the registry to make one server preferred over another to become browse master. For example, you may have two Windows 95 computers—one is a 486 with 8MB of RAM, and the other is a Pentium 200 with 64MB of RAM. Obviously, the Pentium computer would make the faster browse master.

Microsoft ✓ *Exam* *Objective*

Configure system services. Services include:

- Browser

Browse Master is a property of file and printer sharing for Microsoft Networks, as shown in Figure 11.18. There are three settings for this property:

- **Automatic:** This is the default. It means that the computer can be elected to become a browse master if it is needed.

- **Enabled:** This means that the computer will always be a browse master.

- **Disabled:** This means the computer will never become a browse master.

FIGURE 11.18

Enabling the Browse
Master property

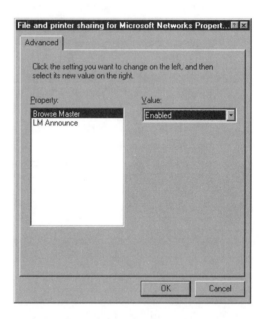

Follow the steps in Exercise 11.11 to make a Windows 95 computer a preferred browse master.

EXERCISE 11.11

Setting Windows 95 to Be a Preferred Browse Master

1. Go to Control Panel ≻ Network.

2. In the Configuration tab (Figure 11.9, earlier in the chapter), highlight File and printer sharing for Microsoft Networks and choose Properties.

> **EXERCISE 11.11 (CONTINUED FROM PREVIOUS PAGE)**
>
> **3.** Highlight Browse Master and choose Enabled (Figure 11.18).
>
> **4.** Choose OK twice to save your changes.
>
> **5.** Reboot Windows 95.

Summary

As you learned in this chapter, connecting a Windows 95 computer to a Windows NT network is fairly straightforward. Installing the Client for Microsoft Networks software allows Windows 95 to connect to Windows NT servers and use their shared resources as if they were its own. A network usually consists of a few servers, with the majority of computers configured as clients.

Before you install the client, you need to install the network card and drivers. Windows 95 can automatically detect and configure Plug-and-Play cards. You can configure the network protocols and client software through the Network Control Panel.

Windows 95 can also be set up to share its local resources in a peer-to-peer network. When a Windows 95 computer shares its resources, it can use either Share level security, the default, which puts passwords on the shared resource, or User level security, which grants rights to existing users and groups from an NT or NetWare server. User level security is tighter than Share level security, but does require an existing NT or NetWare server to link to.

Browsing allows Windows 95 to see the servers and shared resources available on the network. By default, there is one browse server for every 32 clients. When Windows 95 is part of a domain, there is a browse master for the entire domain. You can enable the Browse Master property for a Windows 95 machine (through its File and printer sharing for Microsoft Networks property sheet) to make it always be the browse master.

Review Questions

1. When installing a network card, what items may you need to configure? (Select all that apply.)

   A. Interrupt

   B. I/O port

   C. Memory address

   D. Slot number

2. You can use which program(s) to configure the network card?

   A. Control Panel ➤ Network ➤ Properties of the card

   B. Network Neighborhood ➤ Properties ➤ Properties of the card

   C. Control Panel ➤ Devices ➤ Properties of the card

   D. Control Panel ➤ System ➤ Device Manager ➤ Properties of the card

3. By installing the Client for Microsoft Networks, you allow Windows 95 to understand which language?

   A. NCP

   B. MMP

   C. NTB

   D. SMB

4. If Windows 95 is set up to use IPX/SPX, and it cannot auto-detect a frame type, what frame will it pick?

   A. No frames

   B. All frames

   C. Ethernet_802.2

   D. Ethernet_II

5. Which service allows automatic assignment of TCP/IP addresses?

    A. DHCP

    B. WINS

    C. DNS

    D. DXNP

6. NetBEUI packets can cross a router.

    A. Yes, always.

    B. Only if the router is connected to the Internet

    C. Only if the router is the latest model

    D. No, they can't.

7. You can change your NT password from within Windows 95.

    A. True, but not your screensaver

    B. True, and also your screensaver at the same time

    C. True, and all other passwords (including NetWare)

    D. False

8. Which of the following statements are true? (Select all that apply.)

    A. Windows 95 can be a client to NT while it is acting as an NT server as well.

    B. You can set Read-Only rights using just Share level security.

    C. A stand-alone Windows 95 computer can use User level security.

    D. A stand-alone Windows 95 computer can use Share level security.

9. In order to configure a slow computer to be as fast as possible, how would you configure the browser service?

A. Enabled

B. Tuned

C. Automatic

D. Disabled

10. In order for Sue, Katie, and Linda to see each other's computers in the same screen in Network Neighborhood, how would you configure the workgroups and Network Neighborhood?

A. Set the workgroups to unique names and set the Preferred Workgroups option.

B. Set the workgroups to the same names and set the Preferred Workgroups option.

C. Set the workgroups to unique names and rely on default Network Neighborhood settings.

D. Set the workgroups to the same names and rely on default Network Neighborhood settings.

11. In order to be a client to a Windows NT Server running the TCP/IP compatible protocol, and a client to a NetWare 3.12 Server, which of the following components will need to be installed? (Select all that apply.)

A. Microsoft Client for Microsoft Networks

B. Microsoft Client for NetWare Networks

C. IPX/SPX-compatible Protocol

D. TCP/IP Protocol

12. In order to be a client to a NetWare 4.0 server running in Bindery mode, and to share files to other NetWare clients, which of the following components will need to be installed? (Select all that apply.)

A. Microsoft Client for Microsoft Networks

B. Microsoft Client for NetWare Networks

C. File and printer sharing for Microsoft

D. File and printer sharing for NetWare

13. Which component would you install if you wanted to grant users and groups on a Windows NT domain rights to your shared printer?

A. File and printer sharing for Microsoft Networks—set to User level security

B. File and printer sharing for Microsoft Networks—set to Share level security

C. File and printer sharing for NetWare Networks—set to User level security

D. File and printer sharing for NetWare Networks—set to Share level security

14. You are a member of the Sales domain, with a Windows NT primary domain controller (PDC) called Sales_1, and a backup domain controller (BDC) called Sales_2. You are a member of a group called western_sales. How would you configure your sharing service so you can grant the western_sales group access to memos on your hard drive?

A. Set yourself to Share level security and e-mail the password to your group.

B. Set yourself to User level security, based on Server_1.

C. Set yourself to User level security, based on Server_1 or Server_2.

D. Set yourself to User level security, based on the Sales domain.

CHAPTER

12

Networking with NetWare Servers

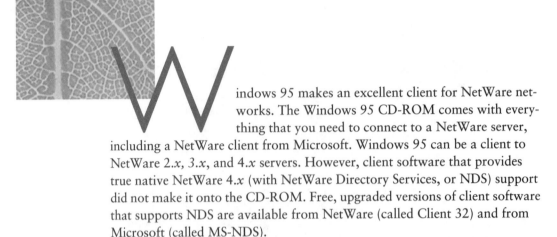

indows 95 makes an excellent client for NetWare networks. The Windows 95 CD-ROM comes with everything that you need to connect to a NetWare server, including a NetWare client from Microsoft. Windows 95 can be a client to NetWare 2.*x*, 3.*x*, and 4.*x* servers. However, client software that provides true native NetWare 4.*x* (with NetWare Directory Services, or NDS) support did not make it onto the CD-ROM. Free, upgraded versions of client software that supports NDS are available from NetWare (called Client 32) and from Microsoft (called MS-NDS).

Windows 95 can also act as a NetWare server, by sharing its files and printers using the NetWare Core Protocol (NCP) standard. As explained in Chapter 9, Windows 95 can only share files and printers as either a NetWare server or as a Microsoft server—not both.

In this chapter, you will learn how to install and configure the client software so that Windows 95 can connect to NetWare servers. You will also learn how to allow a Windows 95 computer to share its resources so that NetWare clients can gain access to your folders and printers. Finally, we will cover the network browsing service, which allows users to see the shared resources on the network.

NetWare Client Installation and Configuration

NetWare servers communicate using a language called NCP (NetWare Core Protocol). By installing the NetWare client software, you enable Windows 95 to communicate with NetWare servers.

The Windows 95 beta had a few bugs that could disrupt a NetWare network. Many NetWare administrators are still wary of Windows 95 for this and other reasons. But once you understand and use Windows 95 in a NetWare network, you may find it to be a superior networking client.

Before you begin client installation, you should check to make sure that you have enough NetWare client licenses for all of your clients. NetWare will not allow more than the licensed number of clients to connect to a server.

If you need to modify user accounts, groups, printers, or security on a Net-Ware server, you will probably need to log in as the Supervisor or as a Supervisor Equivalent (NetWare 3.12 and earlier), or Admin or as someone with Admin rights (NetWare 4.x).

In order for Windows 95 clients to save files on NetWare servers using long filenames (LFNs), you need to install NetWare's OS/2 support for the server volumes. See your NetWare documentation for instructions.

To set up the client software for NetWare on a Windows 95 machine, you need to install and configure the network card and drivers, the client software, and the protocols. These procedures are described in the following sections.

Installing and Configuring the Network Card and Drivers

When installing the network card, you have two basic choices for the drivers you can use:

- ODI real-mode drivers

- NDIS 3.1 protected-mode drivers

If you choose to use NDIS 3.1 protected-mode drivers, you follow the same procedures for installing a network card and drivers as you use for a Microsoft client (see Chapter 11). All of the protected-mode clients mentioned in this chapter can use the NDIS drivers for the network card.

If you choose to use the older ODI drivers, which are necessary for NETX or VLM (real-mode) client software, you load the drivers from the AUTOEXEC .BAT file. One way of doing this is by adding the following commands to your AUTOEXEC.BAT:

LSL	The supporting driver
NE2000	This is the driver for a NE2000-compatible card. Other cards would have a differently named driver.
IPXODI	The protocol driver
VLM or NETX	The client software

Windows 95 reads your AUTOEXEC.BAT file during the boot process, and opens an MS-DOS window to load the drivers. You are then prompted to log in at the MS-DOS screen. After you log in, Windows 95 continues loading.

Configuring the network card to avoid hardware conflicts is covered in Chapter 11 (network card configuration is the same whether you are connecting to NetWare or Microsoft servers). As a general rule, you should always install your actual hardware first, and then use the Add New Hardware Wizard from the Control Panel to install the drivers and support files (see Figures 11.1 and 11.2 in Chapter 11).

Installing and Configuring the Client Software

Once the network card and driver are installed, you will need to install client software. You can choose from four client software packages:

Microsoft ✓ *Exam* *Objective*	**Configure a Windows 95 computer as a client computer in a NetWare network.**

- **Microsoft Client for NetWare Networks:** This is a 32-bit, protected-mode client that can connect to NetWare servers. It is a bindery-emulation client, however, and connects to NetWare 4.*x* servers in bindery mode (it does not support NDS).

- **Microsoft's MS-NDS client:** This is a true, protected-mode NDS client. Unfortunately, it wasn't done in time for the original CD-ROM. MS-NDS comes with the Windows 95 Service Pack 1 or with OSR2. You can also download the client for no additional charge from Microsoft's Web site (www.microsoft.com).

- **Novell's VLM or NETX:** NETX is a real-mode MS-DOS client that was used extensively to connect to NetWare 2.*x* and 3.*x* servers. NETX is a bindery client, and does not provide true NDS support. VLM came out when NetWare 4.*x* did, and it is a real-mode, true NDS client. NETX and VLM are loaded from the AUTOEXEC.BAT file as Windows 95 boots. As mentioned in the previous section, if you're using NETX or VLM, you must use ODI drivers.

- **Novell's Client 32:** This is a protected-mode client that provides true NDS support. Client 32 can be obtained from Novell's Web site (www.novell.com).

Microsoft's clients and Novell's clients are incompatible with each other. First we will explain how to install and configure Microsoft's client, and then how to install and configure Novell's client.

NetWare 2.*x* and 3.*x* servers rely on a bindery to hold all user, group, password, and printer information. The bindery is essentially a flat-file database, and is server specific. NetWare 4.*x* uses NDS (NetWare Directory Services), which holds the users, groups, printers, and other resources in a hierarchical tree. The same NDS tree can link many servers, and is not server specific. Because many applications are not yet NDS-aware, the NDS tree supports bindery emulation, which makes the 4.*x* servers look and function like 3.*x* servers. True NDS support is preferred to bindery emulation, because NDS is more flexible than bindery emulation.

Installing the Microsoft Client for NetWare Networks

You install the Microsoft Client for NetWare Networks by adding a client using the Network Control Panel, as shown in Figure 12.1. Follow the steps in Exercise 12.1 to install this client.

FIGURE 12.1

Installing Microsoft Client for NetWare Networks

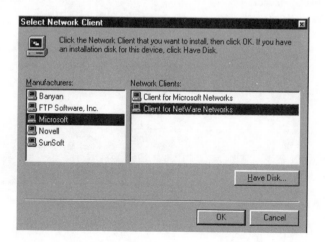

EXERCISE 12.1

Installing Microsoft Client for NetWare Networks

1. Go to Control Panel ➤ Network and choose Add.

2. Highlight Client and choose Add.

3. Highlight Microsoft in the list of Manufacturers.

4. Highlight Client for NetWare Networks in the list of Network Clients (Figure 12.1).

5. Click on OK.

6. Reboot Windows 95.

Installing the MS-NDS Client

You install the MS-NDS client software by adding it as a service using the Network Control Panel, as shown in Figure 12.2. Follow the steps in Exercise 12.2 to install this client.

FIGURE 12.2

Installing the Service for
NetWare Directory
Services (MS-NDS)

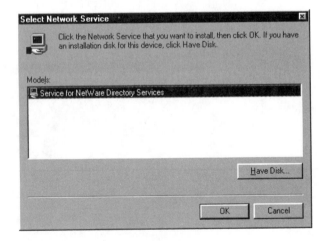

Installing the Service for NetWare Directory Services (MS-NDS)

1. Go to Control Panel ➤ Network and choose Add.

2. Highlight Service and choose Add.

3. Choose Have Disk.

4. Enter the path to the MS-NDS source files or use the Browse button to find the source folder.

5. Choose OK twice. Service for NetWare Directory Services should be highlighted (Figure 12.2). Choose OK again.

6. Choose OK in the Network Control Panel to save your changes. You may need to supply the original Windows 95 CD-ROM if you didn't have the Microsoft Client for NetWare Networks installed.

7. Reboot Windows 95.

Configuring the Protocols

NetWare uses the IPX/SPX protocol to communicate between the servers and clients. There are several parameters that may need to be adjusted for IPX/SPX protocol. The main parameters are frame type and NETBIOS support.

As explained in Chapter 11, different frame types can be run on your network. A frame type can be considered a dialect. Ethernet has four possible frame types or dialects; Token Ring has two possible frame types.

The protocol is called IPX/SPX because the IPX piece is connectionless, while the SPX part is connection-oriented. Connectionless protocols can be compared to first-class mail, while connection-oriented protocols are like registered mail. We send the bulk of our mail first class, even though there is no guarantee of delivery. Only valuable documents are worth sending as registered mail.

If IPX/SPX doesn't seem to work, check your frame type. Automatic is the default setting for the frame type, and may not correctly detect the frame type that you are running. If the Automatic setting fails to find a frame, it will default to the 802.2 frame type.

The procedures for changing the frame type and adding NETBIOS support are explained in Chapter 11 (see Exercises 11.2 and 11.3).

Configuring a Microsoft NetWare Client

There are various options that can be set for the client. You can set the preferred server and enable login script support in the Client for NetWare Networks property sheet, as shown in Figure 12.3.

If you are using the MS-NDS client (Service for NetWare Directory Services), it will also be listed in the Configuration tab of the Network Control Panel, as shown in Figure 12.4. Its property sheet includes settings for the preferred tree and context, as shown in Figure 12.5. In Exercise 12.3, we will configure the MS-NDS client.

FIGURE 12.3

Options for setting the preferred server and enabling login script support

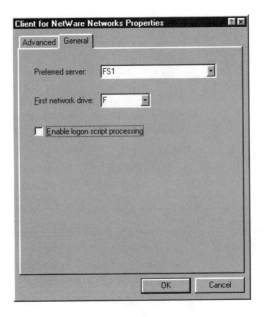

F I G U R E 12.4

Selecting the Service for
NetWare Directory
Services

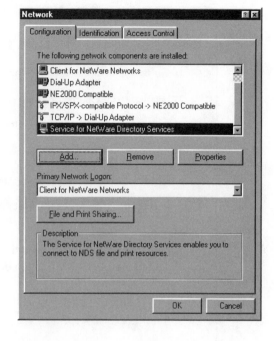

F I G U R E 12.5

Setting the preferred tree
and context

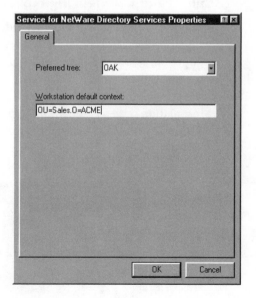

EXERCISE 12.3

Configuring the MS-NDS Client

1. Go to Control Panel ➣ Network.

2. Highlight the Client for NetWare Networks and choose Properties.

3. Enter the preferred server. Use the name **FS1** if you don't have one.

4. Turn off login script processing (Figure 12.3).

5. Choose OK to save your changes.

6. Highlight the Services for NetWare Directory Services and choose Properties (Figure 12.4).

7. Enter your preferred tree and context. Use **OAK** and **OU=Sales.O=ACME** if you don't have them (Figure 12.5).

8. Choose OK twice.

9. Reboot Windows 95 to have your changes take effect.

Installing and Configuring Novell's Client 32

Client 32 is Novell's protected-mode Windows 95 client that has native NDS support. Client 32 comes in two versions: one designed to be installed from floppy disks (it takes seven disks) and one designed to be installed off a network. You will need to download (from Novell's Web site) and decompress the software. Then you can install and configure it. The NetWare Client 32 Installation screen is shown in Figure 12.6. The tabs in the Novell NetWare Client 32 Properties dialog box are shown in Figures 12.7 through 12.10. Follow the steps in Exercise 12.4 to install and configure Novell's Client 32.

FIGURE 12.6

Installing Novell's
Client 32

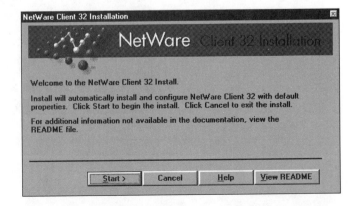

FIGURE 12.7

Entering the preferred
server and tree

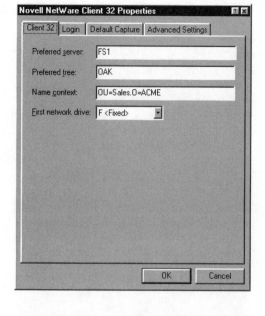

FIGURE 12.8

Configuring login script
support

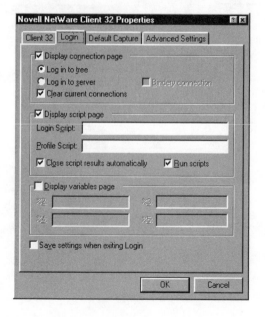

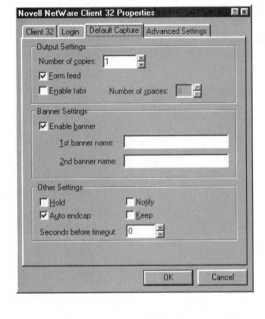

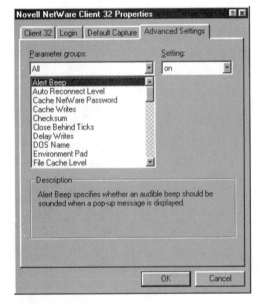

EXERCISE 12.4

Installing and Configuring Novell's Client 32

1. Go to the folder where Client 32 has been decompressed.

2. Start the Setup program.

3. Answer Yes to the licensing question.

4. Choose Start to begin the installation process (Figure 12.6).

5. After the installation (before rebooting) choose the Customize button. This will take you to Network Control Panel.

6. Highlight Novell NetWare Client 32 and choose Properties.

7. If you upgraded from an earlier client, your parameters should be listed on the Client 32 tab. If not, enter your preferred server, tree, context, and first network drive (Figure 12.7).

8. Select the Login tab to change the way the login script is processed (Figure 12.8).

9. Select the Default Capture tab to change the way printer capturing (redirecting output to network printers) is done (Figure 12.9). You may want to turn off banners.

10. Select the Advance Settings tab to change variables associated with the client (Figure 12.10). The default settings will probably be best, unless you have a specific problem you are trying to solve.

11. Choose OK twice to save your changes.

12. Reboot Windows 95 to have the changes take effect.

Sharing Resources on a NetWare Network

Windows 95 has the unique ability to imitate a NetWare server. A NetWare client can log in to and copy files to and from a Windows 95 computer as if it were a real NetWare server.

Microsoft
Exam
Objective

Create, share, and monitor resources. Resources include:

- Remote
- Network printers
- Shared fax modem
- Unimodem/V

Once file and printer sharing for NetWare Networks is installed, you can share files and printers so that NetWare clients can connect to your resources. NetWare servers have no support for Share level security. Thus, if a Windows 95 computer wants to share its resources on a NetWare network, it must be configured for User level access, with the list of users based on an existing NetWare server. When a client connects to the Windows 95 machine and tries to log on to it, Windows 95 doesn't actually authenticate the request—it passes it to the server assigned for the User level security. Setting User level security and creating shares are discussed in Chapter 11 (see Exercises 11.8 and 11.10). You also need to enable SAP (Service Advertising Protocol) support so that non-Windows 95 clients can see the Windows 95 machines.

Novell's Client 32 does not work with Microsoft's file and printer sharing for NetWare. You have to install Microsoft Client for NetWare before you can install File and Print Services for NetWare.

Windows 95 can also function as a NetWare print server, much like the PSERVER.EXE program that came with NetWare 2.*x* and 3.*x*. This allows Windows 95 to pull print jobs from a NetWare print queue and feed those jobs to a local printer. You don't need to be running file and printer sharing for NetWare to use this service; you just need to have NetWare client software installed. Windows 95 also has the ability to edit the printer information on NetWare servers so that the path for printer drivers exists with the printer. After installing Point-and-Print support on a NetWare server, clients will automatically install the print drivers when they attach to a printer. See Chapter 13 for more information about setting up Windows 95 as a NetWare print server and Point-and-Print installation for NetWare machines.

Installing File and Printer Sharing for NetWare Networks

Installing file and printer sharing is a simple matter of adding a network service. You install the service from the Network Control Panel, as shown in Figure 12.11. Follow the steps in Exercise 12.5 to install file and printer sharing for NetWare Networks.

FIGURE 12.11

Installing file and printer sharing for NetWare Networks

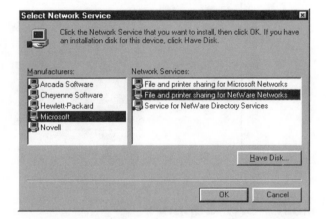

EXERCISE 12.5

Installing File and Printer Sharing for NetWare Networks

1. Go to Control Panel ➢ Network.

2. If you have file and printer sharing for Microsoft Networks installed, highlight it and choose Remove.

3. Choose Add, and then select Service.

4. Choose Microsoft in the Manufacturers list, and File and printer sharing for NetWare Networks in the Network Services list (Figure 12.11).

5. Choose OK to install the service.

6. Choose OK in the Network Control Panel to save your changes.

EXERCISE 12.5 (CONTINUED FROM PREVIOUS PAGE)

7. If User level security is not set, you will see the warning shown below. Choose OK. This takes you to the Access Control tab, where you can enter the name of the NetWare server that will be used to authenticate the users (use **FS1** if you don't have one). Choose OK twice to save your changes.

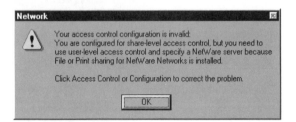

Network

⚠ Your access control configuration is invalid:
You are configured for share-level access control, but you need to use user-level access control and specify a NetWare server because File or Print sharing for NetWare Networks is installed.

Click Access Control or Configuration to correct the problem.

[OK]

8. Reboot Windows 95.

Enabling SAP Support

Every 60 seconds, NetWare servers broadcast a SAP packet, which contains the server name and the shared resources it has. If you want to allow non-Windows 95 clients to see your Windows 95 server, the Windows 95 machine must also generate SAP packets. SAP Advertising is a property of the file and printer sharing service, as shown in Figure 12.12. Follow the steps in Exercise 12.6 to enable SAP support.

EXERCISE 12.6

Enabling SAP Advertising

1. Go to Control Panel ≻ Network.

2. Highlight File and printer sharing for NetWare Networks and choose Properties.

3. Highlight SAP Advertising and select Enabled (Figure 12.12).

4. Choose OK twice to save your changes.

5. Reboot Windows 95.

FIGURE 12.12

Enabling SAP Advertising

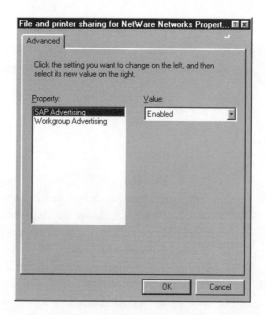

If file and printer sharing for NetWare is installed on all of your Windows 95 computers, and SAP support is enabled, there will be a large amount of background traffic generated by just the SAP broadcasts.

Browsing the NetWare Network

Once you have installed any of the NetWare clients, the Network Neighborhood will also include NetWare servers. Right-click on Network Neighborhood and choose the Who Am I option from the context menu. This brings up a list of all of the servers you are connected to, and who you are connected as.

Double-clicking on any of the NetWare servers will prompt you to log in, if you haven't done so already. Once you have been authenticated, you can use NetWare volumes and printers just like any other NetWare client.

Who Am I is installed only for NetWare support. A number of shareware and freeware programs provide a similar command for Microsoft servers.

Summary

In this chapter, we described how to set up a Windows 95 machine as a NetWare client, and as a machine that can act like a NetWare server. Several NetWare clients are available from Microsoft and Novell. Microsoft's Client for NetWare is a bindery-compatible client, and the MS-NDS client (available from Microsoft's Web site) is a true NDS client. Novell's NETX client is a real-mode bindery client; VLM is a real-mode NDS client. Client 32 (available from Novell's Web site) is a protected-mode NDS client.

Like any other machine on a network, the NetWare client requires a properly configured network card. Once hardware conflicts have been eliminated, the correct protocol and frame type must be selected.

For a Windows 95 machine to act as a NetWare server, it needs the file and printer sharing for NetWare Networks service installed. If Windows 95 is configured as a NetWare server, SAP must be enabled in order for regular NetWare clients to see the Windows 95 computer.

Review Questions

1. NetWare servers communicate using which language?

A. SMB

B. PPP

C. NDS

D. NCP

2. Which NetWare servers can Windows 95 communicate with? (Select all that apply.)

   A. *2.x* (bindery)

   B. *3.x* (bindery)

   C. *4.x* (NDS)

   D. *5.x* (NDS)

3. Which clients are real-mode clients? (Select all that apply.)

   A. NETX

   B. VLM

   C. Microsoft's Client for NetWare

   D. Novell's Client 32

4. Which clients are true NDS clients? (Select all that apply.)

   A. NETX

   B. VLM

   C. Microsoft's Client for NetWare

   D. Novell's Client 32

5. Windows 95 must use which type of security to share files on a NetWare network?

   A. Share level

   B. User level

   C. 'Default' level

   D. Secure level

6. What is the default frame type if the "Automatic" type fails to detect a frame type?

   A. Ethernet_802.2

   B. Ethernet_802.3

   C. Ethernet_II

   D. Ethernet_Snap

7. In order for real mode NetWare clients to see the Windows 95 computer that is sharing its files as a Novell server, which support must be enabled on the Windows 95 machine?

   A. NCP

   B. TUD

   C. SMB

   D. SAP

8. Client 32 allows you to specify whether the _____ will be executed.

   A. anti-virus software

   B. automatic NetWare update

   C. login script

   D. user profile

9. The NetWare client can print a page at the beginning of a print job. This is called a:

   A. Banner

   B. Form Feed

   C. Print Job

   D. Spooling

10. The NetWare client can print a page at the end of a print job. This is called a:

A. Banner

B. Form Feed

C. Print Job

D. Spooling

11. If a NetWare server called FS1 is running the 802.2 frame type, and a NetWare 4.0 server running in Bindery Emulation mode called FS2 is running the 802.3 frame type, and a NetWare 3.12 server called FS3 is running both frame types, what setting(s) should you change on a Windows 95 client to have people log into FS1 by default? (Select all that apply.)

A. Set the frame type to automatic.

B. Set the frame type to 802.2 (single).

C. Set the preferred server to FS1.

D. Set the automatic logon server to FS1.

12. You are using NE2000.EXE as your network card driver. You would like to download the latest drivers for Windows 95. Which drivers should you download?

A. None, NE2000.EXE is the latest driver

B. The NDIS 3.0 version driver

C. The NDIS 3.1 version driver

D. The NDIS 4.0 version driver

13. Which client would be able to connect to a NetWare 4.0 server running in Bindery Emulation mode? (Select all that apply.)

A. Microsoft Client for NetWare

B. Microsoft Client for Microsoft

C. NETX

D. NetWare Client32

14. Which components are necessary to share your files with workers who log into a NetWare 3.12 server?

A. TCP/IP

B. IPX/SPX

C. Microsoft Client for NetWare

D. File and Print Services for NetWare

15. To set up users, groups and printers on a NetWare 4.x server without Bindery Emulation, you need to log in as a(n):

A. Super User

B. Admin

C. Supervisor or Supervisor equivalent

D. Administrator

CHAPTER

13

Printing to Local and Network Printers

indows 95 supports several new printing features:

- **Plug and Play:** If your motherboard is Plug-and-Play compliant, all you need to do to install a printer is plug it in. Windows 95 should recognize the printer and install the appropriate drivers.

- **Drag and drop:** You can place printer shortcuts, to both local and network printers, on your Desktop, and then drag files to be printed onto the printer icon. Your print jobs will be sent to that printer.

- **Extended Capabilities Port (ECP):** ECP allows you to add printer cards to your PC. The additional cards will become ECPs and can be used to attach a printer.

- **Color matching:** Windows 95 uses the Kodak color-matching scheme for device-independent, WYSIWYG color.

- **Point-and-Print setup:** Windows 95 uses a special Point-and-Print setup feature for installing networked printers. All you need to do to install a printer is navigate to the printer or print queue and double-click on its icon. Windows 95 will then begin the printer installation.

- **Microsoft Print Server for NetWare:** Windows 95 can be configured to act as a NetWare print server and despool (remove) print jobs from a NetWare print queue.

- **DLC Support:** Windows 95 supports DLC (Data Link Control). DLC allows Windows 95 to communicate directly with HP JetDirect printers. A JetDirect printer is an HP printer that has an HP JetDirect network card installed in it. The DLC protocol allows the HP JetDirect printer to send status information to Windows 95 and allows Windows 95 to configure the printer and send it print jobs over the network.

- **Working offline:** Windows 95 can print documents to a temporary queue while your computer is not hooked up to any printer. When Windows 95 detects that a printer has been attached, it will print the queued documents.

- **Font loading:** Unlike Windows 3.*x*, Windows 95 will load font files only as it needs them, thus saving valuable memory space.

Printing Architecture

The following sections discuss how Windows 95 applies its modular approach to printing, which involves the universal driver and mini-driver combinations as well as the Windows metafiles. Then you will see where the interchangeable printing components are located in the network architecture.

Print Drivers

Windows 95 uses a set of universal drivers and mini-drivers to handle the complex tasks of rendering and printing. *Mini-drivers* are printer-specific chunks of code that can speak directly with the printer and also speak the common universal driver language.

You can download many of the latest printer drivers from Adobe's Web site (www.adobe.com), or from the Software Downloads pages at www.microsoft.com.

There are currently three types of printers, and therefore three different universal drivers:

- **Regular:** This is used for all black-and-white printers that do not use PostScript. (Some Hewlett-Packard inkjet printers will not use this driver either.) Regular universal drivers use a printer-specific mini-driver.

- **PostScript:** This is used for all black-and-white PostScript printers. PostScript drivers will use PostScript mini-drivers that adhere to the Adobe PPD (PostScript Printer Description) and SPD (Standard Printer Description) formats.

■ **HP Color Inkjet:** This is used for inkjet printers and nearly all color printers. This special case uses a monolithic driver, which means that the mini-driver code that would normally be in the mini-driver is part of the universal driver itself.

These mini-driver/universal driver combinations allow for device independence. In other words, you can have any program send output to any printer, and Windows 95 will be able to print it.

Printer drivers are stored in the \Windows\System directory on your hard drive. Printer registry entries are stored in the HKEY_LOCAL_MACHINE\ System\CurrentControlSet\control\Print folder.

Windows Metafiles

As an administrator, understanding the difference between Windows EMF and RAW files and how the spooling process works is very important, both for troubleshooting printing problems and for finding the best configuration to handle the printing process in your enterprise.

Windows *metafiles* (*.WMF) are files that contain the Windows internal graphics language. Windows 95 supports both the old WMF format and a new Enhanced Metafile format (EMF). These metafiles are basically a collection of internal commands that Windows 95 uses to render graphics to the screen. Metafiles are generally not device-specific, which makes it easy to send them to other computers for printing. When a metafile is converted for output to a specific printer, it becomes a *raw* file. The raw file contains printer-specific codes that tell the printer how to print the images in the file.

Another advantage of using EMF files for printing is that they can be spooled to a hard disk location rather than being printed directly. This means that when a program prints a job, you can start working with the program again as soon as the file has been spooled. You no longer need to wait for the print job to be sent to the printer and for the printer to finish receiving the entire print job. This can return you the control of your system as much as four times more quickly. Spooled print jobs are located in the \Windows\Spool\ Printers directory.

With the exception of PostScript print jobs, all Windows 95 EMF print jobs are spooled by default. PostScript files are always sent directly to the printer.

Printing Components

Because Windows 95 has embraced the OSI network architecture, with its multiple layers and interchangeable components, the network printing architecture was reasonably easy for Microsoft to implement. (For more information about the OSI model, see Chapter 9.)

The following sections describe where Windows 95 has placed printing components within the networking architecture. These components include the Win32/Win16 Print APIs (Application Program Interfaces), the print router, and the Print Provider Interface (PPI).

Figure 13.1 depicts the general network printing architecture. A Windows program makes a request to either send a print job or manage a print queue through the Win32/Win16 Print APIs. That request is sent through the print router, and then on to the PPI.

FIGURE 13.1

Network printing
architecture

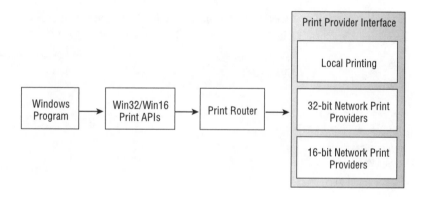

The Win32/Win16 Print APIs

The Win32/Win16 Print APIs are used in conjunction with the print router and the PPI to open, write, and close print jobs and to manage both local and remote print queues. The Print APIs have functionality to support queue management and printing.

The Print Router

The print router is part of the SPOOLSS.DLL and routes printing requests to the appropriate drivers in the PPI. If it is a local print request, the router sends the request to the local print provider. If it is a request for a networked printer or network print queue, the request is sent through the appropriate 16-bit or 32-bit PPI.

The Print Provider Interface (PPI)

The PPI is a modular interface with interchangeable components. This interface allows third-party vendors to seamlessly integrate network print drivers into Windows 95. The PPI drivers allow for various printing methods:

- **Local PPI:** This is part of the SPOOLSS.DLL and sends print requests to the local printer ports and local print queues.

- **Network PPI:** This sends print requests to the network redirectors, which are specific to the type of network installed.

- **WinNet16 PPI:** This print provider is used for backward compatibility with Windows 3.*x* applications.

The following sections provide more details about the Microsoft PPI, the NetWare PPI, and third-party PPI components.

Microsoft Network PPI The Microsoft Network PPI consists of the MSPP32.DLL file, which works with the MSNET32.DLL and the IFSMGR .VXD/IFSHLP.SYS. Figure 13.2 shows how a print request is handled with this interface.

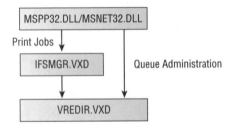

FIGURE 13.2

32-bit Microsoft network client Print Provider Interface

Print requests are sent to the MSPP32/MSNET layer, where they are examined. If the request is for print queue management (view the print queue, delete a job from the queue, and so on), the request is sent directly to the VREDIR.VXD, which passes the job down through the rest of the OSI architecture and over the wire to the other machine. If the request is to submit a print job (open, write, or close), the job is passed to the IFSMGR.VXD. The IFSMGR will then handle the print job in the same way that it handles normal file I/O. The print job will eventually get to the VREDIR.VXD and then onto the wire.

Official Microsoft Objectives for Exam 70-64 : Implementing and Supporting Microsoft® Windows® 95

Exam objectives are subject to change at any time without prior notice and at Microsoft's sole discretion. Please visit Microsoft's Training & Certification Web site (www.microsoft.com/Train_Cert) for the most current exam objectives listing.

OBJECTIVE	PAGE NUMBER
PLANNING	
Develop an appropriate implementation model for specific requirements in a Microsoft environment and a mixed Microsoft and NetWare environment. Considerations include:	6, 362
• Choosing a workgroup configuration or logging on to an existing domain	
Develop a security strategy in a Microsoft environment and a mixed Microsoft and NetWare environment. Strategies include:	438, 452
• System policies	
• User profiles	
• File and printer sharing	
INSTALLATION AND CONFIGURATION	
Install Windows 95. Installation options include:	14
• Automated Windows setup	
• New	
• Upgrade	
• Uninstall	
• Dual-boot combination with Microsoft Windows NT®	
Install and configure the network components of a client computer and server in a Microsoft environment and a mixed Microsoft and NetWare environment.	303, 308, 329, 349
Install and configure network protocols in a Microsoft environment and a mixed Microsoft and NetWare environment. Protocols include:	329, 355, 426
• NetBEUI	
• IPX/SPX-compatible Protocol	
• TCP/IP	
• Microsoft DLC	
• PPTP/VPN	
Install and configure hardware devices in a Microsoft environment and a mixed Microsoft and NetWare environment. Hardware devices include:	417, 500
• Modems	
• Printers	
Configure system services. Services include:	377
• Browser	
Install and configure backup hardware and software. Hardware and software include:	271
• Tape drives	
• The Backup application	
CONFIGURING AND MANAGING RESOURCE ACCESS	
Assign access permissions for shared folders in a Microsoft environment and a mixed Microsoft and NetWare environment. Methods include:	366
• Passwords	
• User permissions	
• Group permissions	

WinNet16 PPI   The WinNet16 PPI is used for backward compatibility with 16-bit programs. The architecture is essentially the same as the 32-bit Microsoft client. Figure 13.2 shows how this interface works. If you compare Figure 13.3 and Figure 13.2, you can see that we have added a WinNet16 .DRV file. This file thunks 32-bit requests into 16-bit requests. The requests are then passed on to the 16-bit Microsoft network client through the 3pNet16.386 virtual device driver.

FIGURE 13.3

16-bit Microsoft network client Print Provider Interface

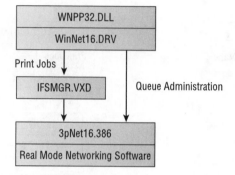

The NetWare PPI   The Novell NetWare PPI consists of the NWPP32.DLL ile, which works with the NWNET32.DLL and the IFSMGR.VXD. Figure 13.4 illustrates how this interface works.

FIGURE 13.4

32-bit NetWare network client Print Provider Interface

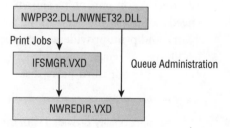

Print requests are handled in exactly the same way as they are handled by the Microsoft PPI. In the figure, you can see how Microsoft components in the architecture are replaced with Novell components.

If you are using a real-mode NetWare client, NETX or VLM (Virtual Loadable Module), your redirector component will be broken down into the pieces shown in Figure 13.5. The NW16.DLL will thunk 32-bit requests into 16-bit requests that the NETX or VLM can understand. These thunked requests will then be transferred by VNETWARE.386 to the NETX or VLM redirector service.

FIGURE 13.5

Real-mode NetWare
client components

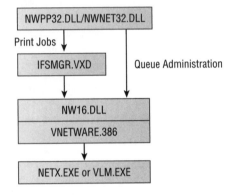

Third-Party Network PPIs   Windows 95 supports multiple additional print providers. A third-party vendor needs only to supply the PPI .DLLs and the redirector component, as shown in Figure 13.6. The third-party developer needs to supply the networking software as well. You can add third-party network and print providers using the Network Control Panel. Simply click on Add, then Service, then Add again. In the next dialog box, click on Have Disk and insert your third-party disk.

The functionality provided with the print queue management depends entirely on the capabilities that the third-party vendor incorporates into its PPI. Options that are not available will be grayed out.

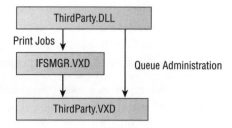

FIGURE 13.6

Third-party network
client Print Provider
Interface

The Printing Process

The following sequence of events takes place when you send a print job from an application to the printer:

1. The printer driver is located. If the driver is on a network printer and you do not have a local copy of the driver, it will be copied from the network print server. If you have a local copy that is older than the driver on the network print server, again the newer driver will be copied to your machine. The printer driver is then loaded into RAM.

2. The application uses the current printer settings from the drivers (fonts, resolution, orientation, and so on) to build a WYSIWYG Enhanced Metafile (EMF).

3. The program creates a description of the output using the GDI (Graphical Device Interface). The GDI will specify everything Windows 95 needs to know about the content and formatting of the image, but it does not tell the printer how to print the document. We are building the EMF (see "Windows Metafiles," earlier in the chapter).

4. If you have EMF spooling turned on, the GDI writes the EMF to the EMF spooler and returns control to the application. If you do not have EMF spooling turned on, the program must wait until the print job has completed before regaining control.

5. The spooler passes the document back through the drivers with a pass through the mini-driver. The mini-driver embeds printer-specific commands into the file and converts it to a raw printer file. The file is then submitted to the print spooler.

6. The spooler passes the document to the print server spooler through the router software. If the client PC and the print server are the same machine, this step is bypassed.

If the router software fails for any reason, you will not receive any error messages regarding the lost print job.

7. When the print server spooler receives the document, it passes it on to the printer monitor, which will write the data to the appropriate printer destination (LPT1, or *servername\printername*, or directly to a network adapter card if it is installed on a printer).

8. The printer prints the document. The monitor will display a message letting the user know that the document is printing.

The printer monitor can use bidirectional communications in nibble mode to let the application know the printer status (e.g., printing, low on toner, jammed) and other kinds of printer-related information.

Figure 13.7 illustrates the steps in the printing process.

FIGURE 13.7

The Windows 95 printing process

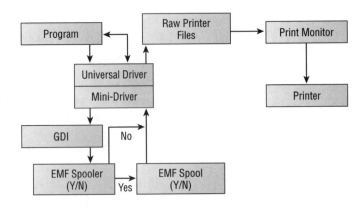

Printer Installation

Microsoft ✓ **Exam Objective**

Install and configure hardware devices. Hardware devices include:

- Modems
- Printers

The procedure you use for installing a printer depends on whether you install a printer locally or across the network. In the following sections, we will discuss how to set up local printers and networked printers, including Point-and-Print setup.

Printer installation and management is handled through the Windows Explorer or the Printers folder, located under Start ➤ Settings ➤ Printers. From the Printers folder, shown in Figure 13.8, you can perform the following tasks:

- Install a printer.

- Share a printer.

- Administer both local and remote printers and print queues.

- Control printer configurations, such as font and orientation.

FIGURE 13.8

The Printers folder allows you to install and administer printers.

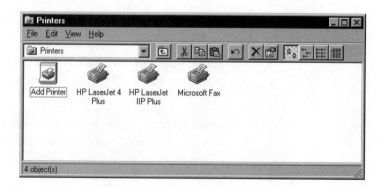

Installing Local Printers

If you have a Plug-and-Play printer, local installation is a snap. Simply attach the printer cables and turn on your printer. When you restart Windows 95, it should recognize the new printer and install the appropriate printer drivers for you.

If you do not have a Plug-and-Play printer, you can easily install a local printer from the Printers folder. The Add Printer Wizard allows you to select the printer manufacturer and model, as shown in Figure 13.9. Follow the steps in Exercise 13.1 to install a local printer through the Printers folder.

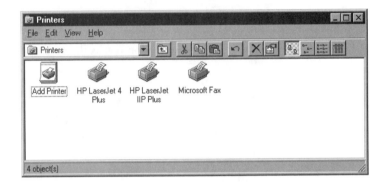

FIGURE 13.9

Selecting a manufacturer and printer model

EXERCISE 13.1

Installing a Local Printer Manually

1. Open the Printers folder by selecting Start ➤ Settings ➤ Printers.

2. Double-click on the Add Printer icon (Figure 13.8) to start the Add Printer Wizard.

3. Click on the Next button to begin the installation process. This brings up a screen asking you whether this is a local printer or a network printer.

4. Choose the Local printer option and then click on Next. Windows 95 builds a driver information database and loads it into memory. The driver information database is a list of manufacturers and their printers, and the drivers needed to support those printers (Figure 13.9).

5. Choose the manufacturer of your printer in the Manufacturers list, and then choose the printer in the Printers list. If you do not see your printer listed, click on the Have Disk button. The wizard will ask you to put the floppy disk that shipped with your printer into the floppy drive. The next screen asks you to select the port where your printer is located.

6. Choose your printer port. In most cases, your printer will be hooked up through a parallel port to LPT1. If you want to configure your ports from here, click on the Configure button. When you have made your selection, click on the Next button to move to the screen that asks for a printer name.

7. Enter a name for this printer. This name can be up to 31 characters in length and is known as the "friendly name." Your friendly name must be unique. If you plan on allowing others access to your printer from across the network, it may be safer to use a UNC name. This means that your friendly name should be 15 or fewer characters. From this screen, you also have the option to make this printer the default printer for your Windows programs. Click on the Next button when you are finished.

8. The last screen of this wizard gives the option to print a test page. This is usually a good idea. The test page will not only show you that the printer is hooked up and running properly, but it will also tell you which printer drivers your printer is using and their version numbers, and print a sample graphic. If you are using a color printer, the Windows logo graphic will be in color. When you are finished, click on the Finish button. Your new printer icon will show up in the Printers folder.

If you don't see your printer in the Add Printer Wizard's list, check the printer manufacturer's documentation to see if there is a compatible driver you can select.

Installing Network Printers Manually

There are two types of installation methods used for network printers. The first method is a manual installation, which follows essentially the same steps outlined in Exercise 13.1. The second method is called Point and Print, which allows you to browse the network for a printer or print queue and then double-click on that printer or queue; the driver files and printer information are then copied directly to your workstation.

An advantage of Point-and-Print installation is that you copy the current printer configurations over to your workstation. With manual installation, you are using fresh, unmodified drivers and configurations. You may need to make changes to these configurations for paper size, fonts, orientation, and so on.

Exercise 13.2 shows the steps for a manual network printer installation.

EXERCISE 13.2

Installing a Network Printer Manually

1. Open the Printers folder by selecting Start ➤ Settings ➤ Printers.

2. Double-click on the Add Printer icon to start the Add Printer Wizard.

3. Click on the Next button to begin the installation process. This brings up a screen asking you whether this is a local printer or a network printer.

4. Choose the Network printer option and then click on Next. The next screen asks you for the network path or queue name.

5. You can type in a UNC name, or you can click on the Browse button to browse the network and locate the printer or queue. You also need to specify whether or not you print from MS-DOS-based programs. If you choose Yes to print from MS-DOS-based programs, you will be presented with a screen that has a Capture Printer Port button. Click on this button to capture the printer port. In the Capture Printer Port dialog box, select the port to capture from the Device list (usually you will choose LPT1), and then click on OK.

6. Click on the Next button to move to the manufacturers and printers screen (Figure 13.9). Select the manufacturer and the appropriate printer from the lists. Click on Next to move to the screen that asks for a printer name.

> **EXERCISE 13.2 (CONTINUED FROM PREVIOUS PAGE)**
>
> **7.** Enter a name for the printer. This name can be up to 31 characters in length and is known as the "friendly name." Your friendly name must be unique. If you plan on allowing others access to your printer from across the network, it might be safer to use a UNC name. This means that your friendly name should be 15 or fewer characters. From this screen, you also have the option to make this printer the default printer for your Windows programs. Click on the Next button when you are finished.
>
> **8.** The last screen of this wizard gives the option to print a test page. This is usually a good idea. The test page shows you that the printer is hooked up and running properly, and will also tell you which printer drivers and versions your printer is using and print a sample graphic. If you are using a color printer, the Windows logo graphic will be in color. When you are finished, click on the Finish button. Your new printer icon will show up in the Printers folder.

If you are manually installing a printer from a Novell NetWare network, you should designate the print queue rather than a printer. This is because printers are not shared under NetWare.

Installing with Point and Print

With Point and Print, you can install driver files for a networked printer in several ways:

- Drag the Point-and-Print printer icon from the networked PC to your Printers folder or Desktop.

- Select the Install option from the context menu of the networked printer.

- Double-click on the networked printer icon and begin the Point-and-Print installation.

You can also print to a networked printer by simply dragging and dropping documents onto the printer icon. If the printer hasn't been installed yet, this will initiate the installation process and then send the print job to the printer.

> For a machine with a printer to support Point and Print, it needs to know the printer name and configuration, which printer driver files are needed, and the location of those files.

Point and Print from a Windows 95 Machine

Point and Print is automatically supported by Windows 95 machines and requires very little setup. All that you need to do to set up Point and Print on a Windows 95 server is to install the printer and then share it.

> The printer drivers needed for a Windows 95 machine to support Point and Print are specified in the MSPRINT.INF, MSPRINT1.INF, MSPRINT2.INF, and PRNTUPD.INF files located in the hidden directory C:\Windows\Inf.

When you share a printer on a Windows 95 machine, Windows 95 will create a special hidden share called PRINTER$. This hidden share is used by other Windows 95 machines to copy the driver and configuration files from the server. The hidden share PRINTER$ has no password. It can be mapped through a network drive connection as *servername*\PASSWORD$.

Point and Print from an NT Machine

The Point-and-Print installation for a Windows 95 client from a Windows NT machine is supported a bit differently than from a Windows 95 to Windows 95 configuration. This is because of the way Windows NT handles printing.

Printer drivers are downloaded to your Windows 95 machine from the NT machine in their original format. This means that you will not inherit the current printer configurations on your Windows 95 machine. You may need to make modifications locally to match the current printer configuration.

To install the network printer, follow the steps outlined in Exercise 13.2. If the .INF file on the NT machine is the same as the .INF file on the Windows 95 machine, you will not be prompted for a printer manufacturer and model, but you will still need to supply a friendly name.

Point and Print from a Windows 95 print server to a Windows NT client is currently not supported.

Point and Print from a NetWare Machine

To use a Point-and-Print setup from a Novell NetWare machine, the NetWare server must be running bindery emulation. A NetWare *bindery* is similar to the Windows 95 and Windows NT registry. The bindery is composed of three parts:

- **Objects:** These are identified by their name and type of object. Objects are things like print queues, users, and file servers. Objects have properties associated with them.

- **Properties:** These are attributes that describe the object. For example, a user object might have properties for username, user password, and user e-mail directory. Properties have values.

- **Values:** These are the actual settings of particular properties. For example, the username property of a user object might have the value Dooless N. Seymore.

Before Point and Print can be used from the NetWare bindery-based server, the bindery needs to be updated with the printer name, driver files, and the driver file locations. To add these entries to the NetWare bindery, follow the steps in Exercise 13.3.

EXERCISE 13.3

Adding Printer Information to a NetWare Bindery

1. Log in to the NetWare server as a Supervisor or equivalent. (You need to have Supervisor privileges to modify a NetWare bindery.)

2. From your Windows 95 machine, navigate to a NetWare print queue and right-click on the queue. This brings up a context menu with a Point and Print Setup menu item.

3. Click on the Point and Print Setup menu item to see a submenu with two options: Set Printer Model and Set Driver Path.

4. Select the Set Printer Model menu item to display the standard printer manufacturer and printer model dialog box. Select your manufacturer and the printer from the lists, and then select OK. This adds an entry to the NetWare bindery.

5. Return to the Point and Print Setup submenu and select the Set Driver Path option. This brings up the Printer Driver Directory dialog box. Add a UNC path (in the format \\server\volume\path, such as \\NW312\ SYS\PUBLIC) where the drivers can be found.

6. Manually copy the printer drivers to this directory on the NetWare server. To figure out which files you need, check for the appropriate drivers listed in the MSPRINT.INF file located in the \Windows\Inf directory.

7. Grant at least Read and File Scan rights to the directory on the NetWare server where you placed the driver files.

After you have added Point-and-Print information to the NetWare bindery, you can install printers simply by navigating to the NetWare print queue and double-clicking on its icon. The driver files and the printer information will be downloaded to your local Windows 95 machine.

Installing Microsoft Print Server for NetWare

Microsoft Print Server for NetWare (MSPSRV.EXE) runs on a Windows 95 machine that has been set up with the Microsoft Client for NetWare Networks (see Chapter 12 for details on how to install and set up this network client). You enable the Microsoft Print Server for NetWare through the Print Server tab of the printer's Properties dialog box, as shown in Figure 13.10.

When you install the Print Server for NetWare, you will be able to despool print jobs from a NetWare print queue and print them on your local printer. The print server basically becomes just another program on the network, submitting print jobs to your local printer. Follow the steps in Exercise 13.4 to enable a print server for NetWare.

FIGURE 13.10

Enabling the Microsoft
Print Server for NetWare

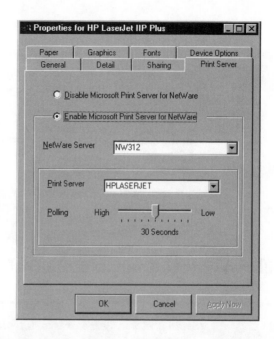

FIGURE 13.10

Enabling the Microsoft
Print Server for NetWare

EXERCISE 13.4

Enabling Microsoft Print Server for NetWare

1. Verify that a print server object has been created and that the print queue object is configured to print on Printer 0–Remote, LPT1:. (For more information about this setup, refer to your Novell NetWare manuals.)

2. In your Printers folder, select your printer and open its property sheet. Select the Print Server tab (Figure 13.10).

3. Select the Enable Microsoft Print Server for NetWare option.

4. Select a server from the NetWare Server list box, which shows all of the available NetWare servers.

5. In the Print Server list box, choose the printer object that you would like. These printer objects are the available printers as defined by the NetWare server that you chose in step 4.

6. Adjust the polling interval for your print queue. Polling checks the print queue for waiting jobs at the interval you specify. To maximize print queue performance, set the polling to 15 seconds. To maximize local printer performance, change this setting to 3 minutes.

Installing the Microsoft Print Server for NetWare does not hinder your ability to print directly to your locally installed printer. You can still administer your local printer in the same way that you have in the past. This includes the ability to share your printer on the network.

Administrative control of the print queue is shared by both the Windows 95 machine and the NetWare server. Your administrative privileges depend on what the NetWare administrator has allowed. If the NetWare administrator has not given you any administrative privileges on the print queue, when you attempt to administer the queue using Windows 95 your administrative options will be grayed out.

Installing HP JetAdmin and the DLC Protocol

<table>
<tr><td>Microsoft
Exam
Objective</td><td>Install and configure network protocols. Protocols include:

• NetBEUI
• IPX/SPX-compatible Protocol
• TCP/IP
• Microsoft DLC
• PPTP/VPN</td></tr>
</table>

Before you can use the HP JetAdmin utilities, you need to install the Microsoft DLC protocol. The DLC protocol can be used for direct communication and connection with mainframe computers that support DLC as well as PC-based peripherals like HP Printers that have an HP JetDirect network card installed. The JetDirect card allows you to connect your printer directly to the network rather than to a printer port on a PC.

To add the protocol do the following:

1. In the Control Panel, start the Network applet.

2. Click the Add button.

3. Double-click Protocol in the Select Network Component Type window.

4. Select Microsoft from the manufacturers list and click Microsoft DLC from the Network Protocols list.

5. Click OK until you are asked to reboot your machine.

6. Reboot the system.

To use an HP Printer with an HP JetDirect card on your network, you must have the following configuration:

- An HP Printer with an HP JetDirect card installed and connected to the network

- Microsoft DLC installed and running on the PC that is to be the Print Server

- A network printer in the Printers folder on the Print Server

Only the Print Server needs to have the DLC protocol installed. All other computers can send print jobs to the Print Server using any available protocol that has been configured.

To use the HP JetAdmin program, you must first install the DLC protocol and then you must install the HP JetAdmin Network Service. To do this, follow the steps outlined above, but rather than selecting a protocol, you will be selecting the Hewlett-Packard HP JetAdmin service. Once you have rebooted, the JetAdmin icon will appear in your Control Panel.

The HP JetAdmin utility allows you to manage your networked HP printers. With the HP JetAdmin utility, you can:

- Create or modify printer configurations and settings.

- Filter and sort printers.

- Add and remove print queues.

- Select drivers to install and assign to a network printer.

- Select the printer operating modes.

- Change a printer's description.

Printer Configuration

You can modify a printer's configuration through its property sheet. To open a printer property sheet, navigate to the Printers folder and right-click on an installed printer. Choose Properties from the context menu. You will see a dialog box similar to the one shown in Figure 13.10. This dialog box has the following tabs (the exact contents of the tabs depend on the specific printer):

- **General tab:** Lists the printer's name and any comments that you would like to add. You can specify a separator page to be printed between print jobs and even send a test page to the printer.

- **Details tab:** Allows you to specify a printer location and the drivers. You can also change the configuration of the printer port and the settings for spooling of print jobs. Additional settings displayed on this tab depend on the type of printer.

- **Paper tab:** Contains settings for paper size, orientation, paper source, and number of copies. This tab may have an Advanced button, which offers advanced options such as duplexing (printing on both sides of the paper).

- **Graphics tab:** Allows you to modify detail or resolution described in dots per inch (dpi). High-quality printers print at a minimum of 600 dpi. This tab may contain options for halftoning (which determines how graphics are rendered and printed), scaling, and mirroring. Color printers might have a setting for color calibration.

- **Fonts tab:** Determines how TrueType fonts are printed. Many PostScript printers print faster when the fonts used are native to the printer. You have three options that will allow you to adjust how these fonts are used (other printers might have different or additional settings located here):

  - The Send TrueType fonts to printer according to the font substitution table option converts specific TrueType fonts into specific PostScript fonts. You can configure this table for optimal speed and print quality. If you make substitutions, you will not necessarily get a WYSIWYG image. Certain fonts that you see on your screen might be substituted when printed.

- The Always use built-in-printer fonts instead of TrueType fonts option makes a best guess at the closest match between the TrueType font and the available built-in font. You might not get a WYSIWYG document, but this will print the fastest, because no font images must be downloaded to the printer.

- The Always use TrueType fonts option guarantees a WYSIWYG image. This will generally be the slowest method of printing.

- **Device Options tab:** Contains settings that involve things like printer memory, installable fonts, and anything else that the manufacturer included.

Printer Administration

Microsoft ✓ *Exam Objective*

Create, share, and monitor resources. Resources include:

- Remote
- Network printers
- Shared fax modem
- Unimodem/V

All printer administration is handled through either the Printers folder or the Explorer. To manage a printer, you need to select it, and then right-click or double-click on the printer to manage the print queue.

Printer administrative options vary depending on the location of the printer (network or local) and the options that the administrator of the printer allows you to have.

For local printers, you can pause and resume print jobs, cancel any print job by deleting it from the list, add separator pages, work offline, or designate the default printer.

Your remote print queue management options are limited by the capabilities of the network operating system that you are using, the components installed, and your level of access to the print queue as specified by the network administrator. The following are the maximum network printer administrative capabilities:

- Pause current job.

- View the queue.

- Resume printing the current job.

- Pause the entire queue.

- Resume the entire queue.

- Delete any or all jobs from the queue.

Troubleshooting Printing Problems

Microsoft
✓ *Exam*
Objective

Diagnose and resolve printing problems.

The following steps can help you troubleshoot printing problems in Windows 95.

1. Check the cable connections between the printer and the computer.

2. Verify that you have the correct printer configuration settings.

3. Verify that you have installed the correct printer driver and it is configured properly.

When dealing with printer driver problems, it may be simplest to just reinstall the printer driver.

4. Verify that enough hard disk space is available to generate your print jobs. Remember that print jobs get spooled to your \Windows\Spool directories.

5. Try printing from other programs in Windows 95. This will let you know whether the printer is causing the problem or if it is the program.

6. Try printing your output to a file and then copying that file to a printer port. This can be done by dragging and dropping the file onto the printer icon, or from an MS-DOS prompt by typing **Copy** *filename* **LPT1.** If this works, your problem is with the spooler or data transmission. If it doesn't work, your problem is with the program or a printer driver.

You can also use the Printing Troubleshooter. This is a simple wizard which will ask you questions about your printer configuration. As you answer the questions (which usually have buttons that specify either Yes or No), more Wizard questions will show up. This will help lead you through the trouble-shooting process. To try this for yourself, select Start ➢ Help. From the Help dialog box, select the Contents tab and double-click on Troubleshooting. From the sub-list that shows up, double-click on If you have problems printing to start the Troubleshooting Wizard.

Summary

In this chapter, we discussed many printing-related issues. We began with the new printing features in Windows 95. Then you learned about the modular approach that Windows 95 takes to the printing architecture within the context of the network structure. The interchangeable components allow third-party developers to concentrate on building their printers, not on the code necessary to make those printers available on a particular network platform.

Next, we provided an overview of the steps in the printing process. Then we got down to the business of installing printers. Local printers can be installed automatically if they are Plug-and-Play devices. Otherwise, you can use the Add Printer Wizard (accessed through the Printers folder) to install a local printer manually. A new Windows 95 feature, Point and Print, supports drag-and-drop printing and installation for network printers. Point-and-Print installations differ for Windows 95, Windows NT, and Novell NetWare servers.

Printer configuration was another area of interest. Properly configuring printers is a relatively simple task, but one that might be beyond the ability of the users you support. We also talked about queue management and administration. We finished the chapter with some real-world troubleshooting techniques that we have found to be the most effective. When you are preparing for the exam, pay close attention to the differences between EMF and RAW files, networking issues, and Microsoft DLC used with the HP JetAdmin program.

Review Questions

1. What are the three different types of printer driver combinations supported in Windows 95?

   A. Standard Universal Driver/mini-driver

   B. HP Driver/HP.dll

   C. PostScript Universal Driver/mini-driver

   D. Monolithic driver used for HP color inkjet printers

2. How can you check the status of a print queue in Windows 95?

   A. Select Start ➤ Run ➤ CheckQueue.

   B. Double-click on the printer icon in the Printers folder.

   C. Go to the Print Queue folder, find your print queue, and click on it.

   D. Both A and C

3. Once you have installed a Point-and-Print printer on your Desktop, how does Windows 95 reference the networked printer?

   A. Using a mapped drive letter (for example: P:)

   B. Using mapped ports (for example: LPT2:)

    C. Using a special printer reference tool (for example: MyPrinter)

    D. Using the UNC name (for example: \\servername\printer)

4. To install a Point-and-Print printer from a Windows 95 machine:

    A. Browse the network until you find the shared printer, and then double-click on its icon.

    B. Browse the Windows 95 CD-ROM and install the printer driver from the CD.

    C. Run PrintSetup from the Printers Folder on the Windows 95 CD-ROM.

    D. Run PrintSetup from the shared folder of the machine on the network that is attached to the printer.

5. When you install a Point-and-Print printer from a Windows 95 server:

    A. The printer configuration is created with the default settings.

    B. The printer configuration will be inherited (copied) to your machine.

    C. You will have to specify that the configuration is to be inherited.

    D. You will have to create the new configuration just like you do for any other installation.

6. When you install a Point-and-Print printer from a Windows NT server:

    A. The printer configuration is created with the default settings.

    B. The printer configuration will be inherited (copied) to your machine.

    C. You will have to specify that the configuration is to be inherited.

    D. You will have to create the new configuration just like you do for any other installation.

7. Novell NetWare machines need to have Point-and-Print information added to their bindery before they can support Point and Print. The information added to the bindery includes which of the following? (Select all that apply.)

A. Printer name

B. Location of printer drivers

C. Printer drivers

D. Location of printer

8. Windows 95 needs what information to support Point and Print? (Select all that apply.)

A. The printer manufacturer's name and printer model

B. The network that you are using

C. The driver names

D. The driver locations

9. What is the maximum number of printers Windows 95 can support?

A. 1

B. 2

C. 6 (LPT1, LPT2, COM1–COM4)

D. There is no predefined maximum.

10. Which of the following should you check if your printer is not printing? (Select all that apply.)

A. The amount of hard disk on the computer

B. The cable connections

C. Whether the printer is on

D. The \Windows\Spools directory to be sure that print jobs are being spooled properly

11. Which of the following are valid methods for supporting a networked printer in Windows 95? (Select all that apply)

A. Using a mapped drive letter (for example: P:)

B. Using mapped ports (for example: LPT2:)

C. Using a special printer reference tool (for example: MyPrinter)

D. Using the UNC name (for example: \\servername\printer)

12. To use the HP JetAdmin utility, which of the following must be true?

A. The printer must have an HP JetDirect card installed.

B. The print server must support the DLC protocol.

C. The PCs sending jobs to the print server must support the DLC protocol.

D. The HP JetAdmin utility needs to be installed on all of the PCs that will be sending print jobs to the HP Printer.

13. Your Windows 95 computer is acting as the print server for a networked printer. Windows 95 has the DLC protocol installed as well as the HP JetAdmin utility. The printer has an HP JetDirect card installed and is connected to the network correctly. What else must you do to your Windows 95 print server to allow others access to that printer? (Select two answers.)

A. You must install the DLC protocol on all computers that will send your print server print jobs.

B. You must create and share a network printer in the Printers folder.

C. You must install the file and printer sharing network services on the print server.

D. You must install file and printer sharing network services on all of the clients.

CHAPTER

14

User Profiles

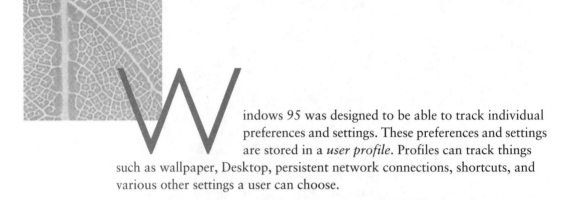

indows 95 was designed to be able to track individual preferences and settings. These preferences and settings are stored in a *user profile*. Profiles can track things such as wallpaper, Desktop, persistent network connections, shortcuts, and various other settings a user can choose.

Microsoft
✓ ***Exam***
Objective

Develop a security strategy. Strategies include:

- System policies
- User profiles
- File and printer sharing

This chapter describes how to enable local user profiles for the local computer and roaming user profiles for networks. It also offers some suggestions for troubleshooting problems with user profiles.

Understanding User Profiles

As you learned in Chapter 6 (about the registry), system settings are held in the SYSTEM.DAT file, and user settings are held in the USER.DAT file. Windows 95 creates user profiles by making a unique USER.DAT file for each user of the system and by making a personal folder for each user as well. This folder contains personal shortcuts, document history, and Start menu settings.

There are two types of user profiles:

- **Local Profiles:** These profiles are stored only on the local computer. If a user logs on to one computer, makes changes to the environment, and then logs on to another computer, the changes from the first computer are not reflected on the second computer.

- **Roaming Profiles:** These profiles are stored on either a NetWare or Microsoft (NT) server. When a user logs on to the server, that user's profile is downloaded to his or her computer. When the user logs off, any changes are then saved back to the copy on the server. When the user logs on to a different computer, the profile (and any changes) are downloaded to the local computer again.

Enabling Local Profiles

User profiles are not enabled by default. Everyone uses the same settings on a computer until profiles are enabled. Once profiles are enabled, everyone on that computer will be asked to log in, so that Windows 95 will know who the user is and can load the appropriate profile.

The user will be prompted the first time he or she logs in and a profile is not found. If the user chooses not to create a profile, the default profile will be used.

Microsoft ✓ *Exam Objective* | **Set up user environments by using user profiles and system policies.**

You can enable user profiles from the User Profiles tab of the Passwords Control Panel, shown in Figure 14.1. The first two options disable or enable profiles:

- **All users of this PC use the same preferences and desktop settings:** This is the default option. Windows 95 uses the same settings for everyone. Choose this option to turn off profiles.

- **Users can customize their preferences and desktop settings. Windows switches to your personal settings whenever you log in:** Choose this option to enable profiles. You need to restart Windows 95 after you select this option to have profiles take effect.

FIGURE 14.1

Enabling user profiles
through the User Profiles
tab of the Passwords
Properties dialog box

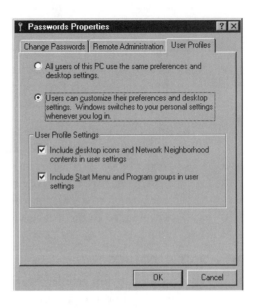

Profiles always contain the USER.DAT file, with unique user registry settings. In addition to those settings, you can choose the following options in the User Profiles tab of the Passwords Control Panel:

- **Include desktop icons and Network Neighborhood contents in user settings:** Choose this setting to create folders called Desktop, Recent, and NetHood under the user profile folder. The Desktop folder contains shortcuts from the common Desktop, and changes the common Desktop to a unique one for each user. The Recent folder keeps track of the documents that the user has recently opened. The NetHood folder contains any network shortcuts. Folders and files stored on the Desktop are not included in profiles; just the shortcuts are included.

- **Include Start Menu and Program groups in user settings:** Choose this setting to create a folder called Start Menu under the user profile folder. This folder is used as the Start menu for the user, instead of the common one found under <Windows Root>\Start Menu. Note that applications installed when saving the Start menu in profiles will be available to only the user who installed the program, because that user is the only one who will have the program group and icon in his or her unique Start menu folder.

In Exercise 14.1, we will enable user profiles, and log in as two different users, with different settings.

In Exercise 14.1, we will make new shortcuts on the Desktop, change the wallpaper and color scheme, and add an item to the Start menu. See Chapter 5 if you need a refresher on performing these tasks.

EXERCISE 14.1

Enabling Local Profiles

1. Go to Control Panel ➢ Passwords.

2. Go to the User Profiles tab.

3. Choose Users can customize their preferences and desktop settings.

4. Choose the Include desktop icons... option.

5. Choose the Include Start Menu... option (Figure 14.1).

6. Choose OK.

7. Restart Windows 95.

8. Log in as yourself. Use a blank password.

9. Answer Yes when prompted if you want to save a profile.

10. Make any two new shortcuts on the Desktop.

11. Change your wallpaper and color scheme.

12. Add an item to the Start menu.

13. Select Shut Down ➢ Close all programs and log on as a different user, as shown below.

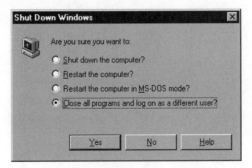

EXERCISE 14.1 (CONTINUED FROM PREVIOUS PAGE)

14. Choose Yes, and then log back in as "Bigfoot."

15. Check to see if your changes are present (they shouldn't be).

16. Log out as Bigfoot and log back in as yourself. Your changes should now be there.

If you want to disable user profiles, return to the User Profiles tab of the Passwords Control Panel and choose All users of this PC use the same preferences and desktop settings, and then restart Windows 95.

Before you enable profiles, user configurations are stored in the USER.DAT file, and in the Desktop, Start Menu, Recent, and NetHood folders located in the root of the Windows installation folder. User settings in the registry are held in the USER.DAT file, which makes up the Hkey_Current_User key.

After you enable profiles, Windows 95 will create a Profiles folder and hold settings for each user in a folder named after that user. A unique copy of USER.DAT will be saved in the user's folder as well. Figure 14.2 shows an example of a user's folder within the Profiles folder.

FIGURE 14.2

Storing the USER.DAT file in the local profile

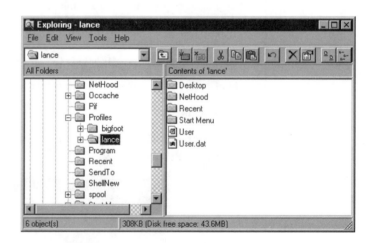

Enabling Roaming Profiles

User profiles are local when they are created, in that they reside on the local hard drive. You can enable roaming profiles by configuring profiles to reside on a server, so the user profile will be available to the user no matter which computer that user logs in from.

Roaming profiles are stored on a central server, and are loaded into the current workstation when a user logs on. You can enable roaming user profiles on Windows NT and NetWare servers.

A user profile can be changed so that it is read-only; that is, the profile can be used by a user, but no changes are allowed. To create a mandatory profile, simply rename the USER.DAT file to USER.MAN. Mandatory profiles work only with roaming user profiles.

Roaming Profiles on an NT Server

Roaming profiles are held in the NT server's home folder. When a user logs in to an NT domain and profiles are enabled, Windows 95 will ask the user if he or she would like to enable profiles. If the user answers no, the default profile will be used for that user. If the user answers yes, Windows 95 will do one of four things:

- If Windows 95 can't find a profile for the user, the default profile is copied into the user's profile.

- If there is a profile both locally and on the server, Windows 95 compares the date and time of the profiles, and loads the most recent one.

- If there is no profile on the server, but there is one locally, the local profile will be used, and then saved to the server when the user logs out.

- If there is a profile on the server but not one locally, Windows 95 copies the profile from the server to the local computer.

Profiles from Windows 95 and Windows NT (all versions) are not compatible. Any changes made to one will not be reflected if the user logs in from the other type of operating system.

Follow the steps in Exercise 14.2 to enable user profiles on an NT server.

EXERCISE 14.2

Enabling Roaming Profiles on an NT Server

1. Enable user profiles through the User Profiles tab of the Passwords Control Panel (see Exercise 14.1).

2. Synchronize the clocks of the client and server. You can put the following command into the logon script to synchronize the workstation clock to the server:

```
Net Time \\Server /set /y
```

Alternatively, you could use a time synchronization program to keep the workstation clock in sync with the server.

3. Make sure you are using a 32-bit client. The Client for Microsoft Networks is a 32-bit client, and works when using roaming profiles.

4. Make the Microsoft client the primary network logon. In the Network Control Panel, the Client for Microsoft Networks needs to be selected for the Primary Network Logon option (see Exercise 11.4 in Chapter 11) for the Windows 95 client.

5. Assign the user a home directory on the NT server. In NT's User Manager, choose Properties ➢ Profile. Choose a drive letter and enter the UNC to the path, as shown in the example below.

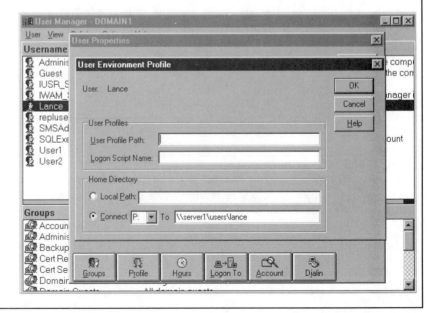

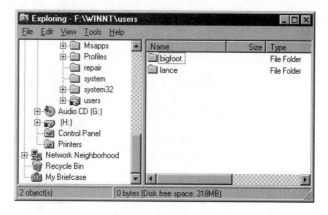

If you are using NTFS security on your volume, and you use User Manager to create the home folders, NT will not only create the home folder but will assign rights only to that user.

After you enable roaming profiles, the user's home directory on the NT server should look something like the example shown in Figure 14.3. If the home directory does not contain the profile, either the home directory hasn't been assigned correctly or profiles haven't been enabled correctly.

F I G U R E   14.3

Roaming profiles stored
on the NT server

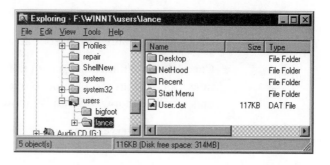

Roaming Profiles on a NetWare Server

If you have NetWare servers as your main servers, you can enable the NetWare servers to store user profiles. On a NetWare server, roaming profiles are stored in the Mail\User_Id directory.

The procedure is essentially the same as the one for enabling roaming profiles on an NT server (Exercise 14.2):

- Enable profiles through the Passwords Control Panel, User Profiles tab (see Exercise 14.1).

- Synchronize the clocks of the client and server.

- Make sure you are using a 32-bit client.

- Make the NetWare client the primary network logon (see Exercise 11.4 in Chapter 11).

- Make sure the user has a directory under the Mail directory that corresponds to his or her ID number.

- Make sure the NetWare server supports long filenames (see Chapter 12).

When Windows 95 looks for a profile from a NetWare server, it compares date and time stamps and loads the most recent one (much as it does on an NT server).

Troubleshooting User Profiles

If user profiles are not working correctly, here are some steps to take to try to find out where the problem lies:

- Check to make sure profiles are enabled on the workstation.

- Check to make sure the appropriate client is picked as the default.

- Check the date/time/time zone of the workstation and server. Incorrect time zone settings are a major source of time synchronization problems under both Windows 95 and Windows NT.

- Check the NT server to ensure home directories have been assigned.

- Check the NetWare server for Mail\User_Id directories.

- Check the directories on the NT server for the folders and files to see if profiles are being saved to the server.

WARNING If a user is logged on to more than one computer, when he or she logs off from the first computer, the profile will be saved to the server. Changes made at this logoff are then lost when the user logs off from the second computer (and the profile is once again saved to the server).

- Any Briefcases that were created prior to enabling profiles will need to be re-created, because the links in the Briefcase are not updated to reflect the profile (See Chapter 18 for more information about the Briefcase utility).

- Programs that do not record their information in the registry (such as 16-bit programs) will probably record their information in the WIN.INI or another INI file.

Summary

Windows 95 stores settings and preferences in a profile. By default, all users on the same computer use the same profile. Windows 95 has the ability to track individual profiles for different users, so preferences and settings can be maintained by multiple users of a computer. You can enable user profiles (they are not enabled by default) through the Passwords Control Panel, User Profiles tab.

Local profiles are stored on the local computer, and they don't follow the user around. Local profiles are held in the <Windows Root>\Profiles folder.

Roaming profiles are stored on a central server, and are loaded into the current workstation a user logs on to. To enable roaming profiles, you must be using a 32-bit client (such as the Client for Microsoft Networks or the Client for NetWare Networks), and that client must be selected as the Windows 95 client's primary network logon. Roaming profiles are held in the home folder of an NT server, or in the Mail\User_Id directory of a NetWare server.

Profiles from Windows 95 and Windows NT are not compatible. You will need to create profiles for each if you log in to both of them.

Review Questions

1. Profiles work by saving a unique copy of which registry file?

    A. REG.DAT

    B. REGISTRY.OUT

    C. SYSTEM.DAT

    D. USER.DAT

2. Roaming profiles (with all options) are enabled. You are logged in at two computers. You add a shortcut to your Desktop and log out from the first computer. You log out of the second computer. You log back in at the first, but your shortcut isn't there. Why?

    A. Your local profile is not enabled.

    B. The profile from the second computer overwrote the profile from the first.

    C. The roaming profile is cached, and isn't available for immediate loading.

    D. Profiles don't track shortcuts.

3. Which of the following is required to enable roaming profiles on an NT server? (Select all that apply.)

    A. Users must have a home folder.

    B. Users must use TCP/IP.

    C. Usernames must be eight or fewer characters.

    D. The Client for Microsoft Networks must be the default logon.

4. Roaming profiles (with all options) are enabled. Profiles are being saved locally, and are present on the server, but are not downloading from the server to all workstations. What could be the cause? (Select all that apply.)

   A. The time on the problematic workstations is ahead of the time of the server.

   B. The problematic workstations are not using the same protocol as the server.

   C. The problematic workstations don't have profiles enabled.

   D. The problematic workstations are Windows NT workstations.

5. You want the local profile to include the Start menu, but not the Desktop. Is that possible? If so, which option do you pick?

   A. Yes—enable profiles normally (with no options picked).

   B. Yes—enable profiles with the Include Desktop Icons... option.

   C. Yes—enable profiles with the Include Start Menu... option.

   D. No—this is not possible.

6. Using a Windows 95 client when Windows 95 is installed in the C:\Windows folder, where are roaming profiles stored on a NetWare 3.12 network?

   A. On the local computer, in the C:\Windows folder

   B. On the local computer, in the C:\Windows\System32 folder

   C. On the NetWare server, in the PUBLIC folder

   D. On the NetWare server, in the \Mail\Userid folder

7. How do you make a mandatory profile?

 A. Create a new group called "Mandatory" and assign the user to the group.

 B. Check the box "Create Mandatory Profile" when initially creating the profile.

 C. Set USER.DAT to read-only.

 D. Rename the profile to USER.MAN.

8. What is required to enable roaming profiles on a NetWare 3.12 server? (Select all that apply.)

 A. The IPX/SPX protocol

 B. Microsoft Client for NetWare

 C. Default Login set to Microsoft Client for NetWare

 D. Profiles enabled on the Windows 95 client

9. When can the same roaming profile be used on Windows NT workstations and Windows 95 clients?

 A. Never—they are incompatible.

 B. If you rename the profile to USER.NT it will also work for Windows NT.

 C. If you place the profile in the NETLOGON share, both operating systems can use it.

 D. Check the box "Create NT Compatible Profile" when initially setting up the profile.

CHAPTER

15

System Policies

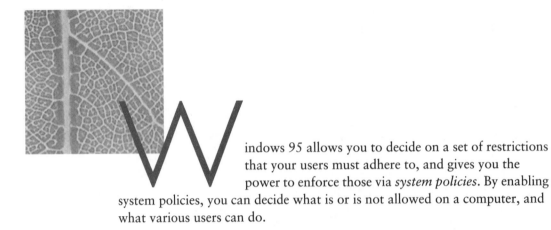

indows 95 allows you to decide on a set of restrictions that your users must adhere to, and gives you the power to enforce those via *system policies*. By enabling system policies, you can decide what is or is not allowed on a computer, and what various users can do.

Microsoft Exam Objective

Develop a security strategy. Strategies include:
- System policies
- User profiles
- File and printer sharing

System policies work by selectively editing the registry when a user logs in. Policies can be based on specific users, groups, and computers, or generic policies can be created that affect all users or computers.

You create policies through the System Policy Editor. In this editor, you load a template, make the desired changes, and then save the template as a policy file. This chapter describes how to install the System Policy Editor and support for group policies; create policies for groups, users, and computers; and use the System Policy Editor to edit the registry directly.

Microsoft is emphasizing its new Zero Administration Workstation, which will heavily rely on implementing system policies in order to prevent users from changing their configurations (thus requiring administration).

Understanding Policies and Templates

System policies are no more than an automated way to enforce certain restrictions on certain users or computers. System policies work by selectively editing the registry when a user logs in. You can set policies that not only restrict the user when he or she logs in, but that also restrict the user from making changes during his or her session by not allowing the Registry Editor to be run.

There are two types of files used in creating system policies:

- **Template (.ADM) files:** ASCII files that are filled in and modified

- **Policy (.POL) files:** The files that template files are saved as, which are read by Windows 95

Template files can be thought of as source code (which can be changed and added to), and the policy files can be looked at as compiled code (which is loaded and executed on a computer). When the policies are read and applied by Windows 95, they edit the registry to enforce one or more restrictions. Figure 15.1 shows how the two types of files are used, and Figure 15.2 illustrates how Windows 95 processes policy files.

FIGURE 15.1

Templates, policies, and the registry

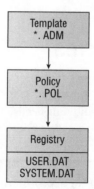

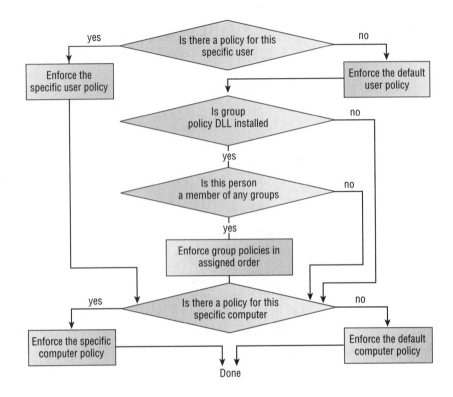

Creating Policies

The process for creating policies involves loading a template, modifying it to suit your needs, and saving it so Windows 95 can find it. This process can be broken down into the following steps:

Microsoft **Set up user environments by using user profiles and system policies.**
✓ ***Exam***
Objective

User profiles must be enabled (through the User Profiles tab of the Passwords Control Panel) before system policies can be used. For more information about profiles, see Chapter 14.

- Enable user profiles.

- Decide on the appropriate policies for your company.

- Decide if policies will be based on group membership.

- Install the System Policy Editor and support for group policies (if you decided to base policies on group membership).

- Load or create the appropriate template.

- Create policies for groups (if you decided to take this approach).

- Configure the order in which groups will take effect.

- Create default settings for users via the Default User.

- Create default settings for computers via the Default Computer.

 The Default User and Default Computer are part of a default template, called ADMIN.ADM, supplied by Microsoft. This template is discussed below.

- Create exceptions for users via unique user settings.

- Create exceptions for computers via unique computer settings.

- Save the policy as Config.pol where Windows 95 will find it.

Deciding How to Use Policies

Policies are flexible enough to be able to do almost anything that you want, with respect to enforcing restrictions that may be required for your network. Some companies have even formed committees to look at the ADMIN.ADM template (a default template that contains many common registry settings) and decide which restrictions should be enforced. If your network requires restrictions that are not present in the ADMIN.ADM template, you can edit the template or create a new one.

Policies can be based on group membership. Groups can come from either an NT server or a NetWare server. Support for group policies is not installed by default; you must install this support for every computer that is expected to load group policies.

Installing the System Policy Editor and Group Policy Support

Policies are created using the System Policy Editor. This program is not installed by default; you must first install it from the Windows 95 distribution CD-ROM before you can create or edit policies. If you plan to use group policies, you must also install group policy support on the computer that creates the policy. The System Policy Editor is located in the Admin\Apptools\Poledit folder of the CD-ROM, as shown in Figure 15.3.

FIGURE 15.3

Locating the System
Policy Editor

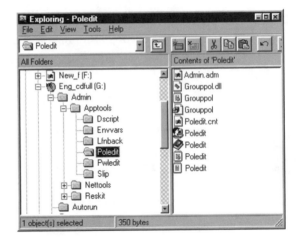

You can install group policies at the same time that you install the System Policy Editor. For those computers that will be using group policies but will not be running the System Policy Editor, you still need to install group policy support. You can verify that group policy support is installed by searching for the file called Grouppol.dll.

Follow the steps in Exercise 15.1 to install the System Policy Editor and/or group policies.

EXERCISE 15.1

Installing the System Policy Editor and Group Policies

1. Go to Control Panel ➤ Add/Remove Programs.

2. Select the Windows Setup tab.

3. Choose Have Disk.

4. Type the path to the folder (**Admin\Apptools\Poledit**), or use the Browse button to point to the Poledit folder. If you use the Browse button, both the grouppol.inf file and Poledit.inf file appear in the Open dialog box, as shown below. Windows 95 lets you select only the grouppol.inf file (because it is the first INF file in the list). Choose OK after indicating the folder to open.

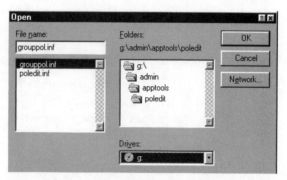

5. In the next dialog box, shown below, choose which components you wish to install: Group policies and/or System Policy Editor. Then click on Install.

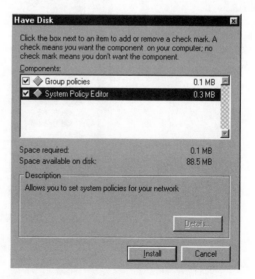

6. If you installed the System Policy Editor, verify that it is installed correctly by selecting Start ➣ Programs ➣ Accessories ➣ System Tools. There should be an icon for the System Policy Editor.

Loading the ADMIN Template

Microsoft supplies a default template called ADMIN.ADM, which contains many popular registry settings. This file is located in the (hidden) INF folder located in the Windows installation folder after the System Policy Editor is installed. There are two major sections to the template: the Default Computer (which pertains to the Hkey_Local_Machine registry key) and the Default User (which pertains to the Hkey_Users registry key). You can view the Default Computer and Default User entries in the System Policy Editor by double-clicking on their icons in the System Policy Editor window. These parts of the template are described in the following sections.

Default Computer Settings

The Default Computer part of the ADMIN.ADM template includes Network and System entries. You can see this by opening the ADMIN template using the System Policy Editor, as shown in Figure 15.4. Through the System entry, you can enable profiles and set paths for things such as a Start menu, Desktop, and other items.

FIGURE 15.4

The Default Computer
Properties window

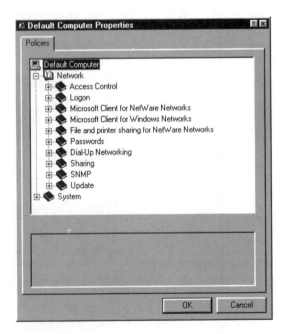

The Network entry is divided into the following elements:

- **Access Control:** Allows you to assign User level security, and enter the server to base security on

- **Logon:** Allows you to make a logon banner, and require a valid logon before Windows 95 will let the user into the system (selecting Cancel, to bypass the network logon and still be able to use the local computer, will not work)

- **Microsoft Client for NetWare Networks:** Allows you to set the preferred server and other various options for a NetWare client machine

- **Microsoft Client for Windows Networks:** Allows you to assign the workgroup name, or enter the NT domain the user will log on to

- **File and printer sharing for NetWare Networks:** Allows you to set whether or not SAP (Service Advertising Protocol) will be sent out

- **Passwords:** Allows you to set a minimum length for the Windows password, disable password caching, and set other password options

- **Dial-Up Networking:** Allows you to disable the dial-in client

- **Sharing:** Allows you to disable file and/or printer sharing

- **SNMP:** Allows you to set where the SNMP (Simple Network Management Protocol) error codes will go

- **Update:** Allows you to set the path for future system policy updates

Default User Settings

The Default User part of the ADMIN.ADM template is shown in Figure 15.5. It has the following entries:

- **Control Panel:** Each one of these entries allows you to restrict various tabs of the Control Panel applet's dialog box—Display, Network, Passwords, Printers, and System.

- **Desktop:** This entry allows you to set various items dealing with the Desktop, including the wallpaper and color scheme.

- **Network:** Through the Sharing subentry, you can restrict the user from changing any of the current shares or creating new shares.

- **Shell:** Through the Custom Folders subentry, you can set various parts of Windows 95 (such as the Start menu or Desktop) to reside on places other than the local hard drive. Through the Restrictions subentry, you can shut down most of the functionality of Windows 95; for example, you could disable the Run command or hide the drives in My Computer and Network Neighborhood.

- **System:** Through the Restrictions subentry, you can disable MS-DOS mode, disable the Registry Editor, and create a list of approved programs so that Windows 95 will run only those programs.

FIGURE 15.5

The Default User
Properties window

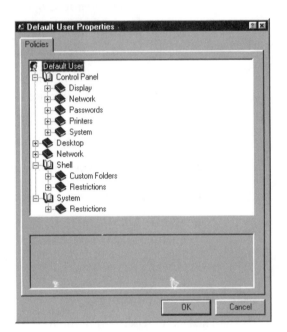

Setting Policy Restrictions

Along with the ADMIN template that is loaded with the System Policy Editor, you can find other templates and policies in the Windows 95 Resource Kit or on Microsoft's Web site (www.microsoft.com).

After you've loaded a template, you can set various restrictions by filling out the template. You generally have three choices:

- A gray setting is the default. No change is made by the policy—the restrictions are left as they were.

- A checked setting means that the policy is enforced—the restrictions are put in place.

- A blank, or white, setting means that the policy is reset—the restrictions are removed.

When you leave a policy gray (which is the default), Windows 95 doesn't change whatever is currently recorded in the registry. Although leaving boxes gray is faster (because nothing is being changed), Windows 95 will not reset a restriction to an earlier version. For example, if you had a restriction set (checked) for a low-security person, that restriction is in place on the computer until someone who has the restriction reset (set to white) logs in.

Creating Policies for Groups

You can create policies for either NetWare or NT groups by adding a group and assigning policies to it. You can also change the order in which Windows 95 implements groups so that users who belong to more than one group can receive the rights of the groups in the order you choose.

Windows 95 does not support group policies by default. Group policy support must be installed on the computer that creates group policies, and on every computer that will implement policies based on groups.

After you have installed group policy support for all the computers that will be using group policies (see Exercise 15.1), you can create and modify group policies. In Exercise 15.2, we will create a policy for a group so that its members cannot see the virtual memory settings. You do this by restricting the System Control Panel, as shown in Figure 15.6.

In Exercises 15.2 and 15.3, we will be building policies for the Sales and Management groups. You can change those names to match the groups on your network.

EXERCISE 15.2

Creating a Group Policy

1. Start the System Policy Editor by selecting Start ➤ Programs ➤ Accessories ➤ System Tools ➤ System Policy Editor.

2. Create a new policy by choosing File ➤ New File.

3. Create a new group policy by choosing Edit ➤ Add Group.

4. Type **Sales** for the group. If User level security is installed (see Chapter 11), you can browse for the group name.

5. Choose OK. Your policy should appear in the System Policy Editor window, as shown below.

6. Highlight the Sales group and select Edit ➤ Properties, or double-click on the Sales group.

7. Choose Control Panel ➤ System ➤ Restrictions, check Restrict System Control Panel, and check the Hide Virtual Memory button box (Figure 15.6).

8. Save the policy as **Group.pol** and close the editor.

If a policy exists for a specific user, group policies are not applied for that user.

FIGURE 15.6

Hiding the virtual
memory settings

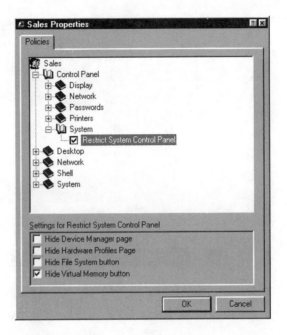

Setting Group Priority

When you use group policies, the policies for groups that come later will override those for groups that come earlier. For example, suppose that Phil is a member of both the Sales and Management groups. The Sales group is restricted from sharing folders; the Management group has no such restriction. If the Sales group is processed first (Phil is a member, so he loses the right) and then the Management group is processed (Phil is a member so he gains the right), Phil will end up being able to share his folders. If the Sales group is processed last, the restrictions of the Sales group will take precedence, and Phil won't be able to share his folders. To make sure that the desired group policy is applied, you can specify group priority, as shown in Figure 15.7.

In Exercise 15.3, we will resolve the conflicts in the example by giving the Management group priority.

FIGURE 15.7

Specifying group priorities

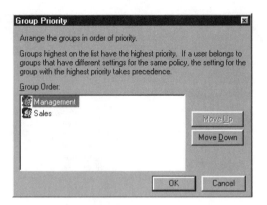

EXERCISE 15.3

Specifying Group Order

1. Start the System Policy Editor and load the policy Group.pol (created in Exercise 15.2).

2. Create a new group policy for the Management group by choosing Edit ➤ Add Group and specifying the Management group.

3. To set the order of the groups, select Options ➤ Group Priority.

4. Make the Management group have priority over the Sales group by highlighting Management group and choosing Move Up until Management is on top (Figure 15.7).

5. Save the policy as Group.pol and close the editor.

Creating Policies for Users

Policies set for the Default User apply to everyone except those who have a specific user policy. In Exercise 15.4, we will make a policy that sets a default wallpaper for users. You can do this through the Desktop settings for Default User properties, as shown in Figure 15.8.

FIGURE 15.8

Setting the default
wallpaper

FIGURE 15.8

Setting the default wallpaper

EXERCISE 15.4

Creating a Default User Policy

1. Start the System Policy Editor and load the policy Group.pol (created in Exercises 15.2 and 15.3).

2. Select Default User ➢ Desktop and check the Wallpaper box.

3. Choose the Bubbles.bmp for the wallpaper and select Tile Wallpaper (Figure 15.8).

4. Choose OK to save the setting.

5. Save the policy as Group.pol and close the editor.

All exceptions to the Default User policies must be specified by adding a policy for each specific user or group you want excepted.

Adding Specific Users

By creating entries for specific users, you can override both the Default User settings and any group policies that would have been enforced for that user. In Exercise 15.5, we will create a policy for a user called Phil, and log in as that user to test the policy.

EXERCISE 15.5

Creating a Specific User Policy

1. Start the System Policy Editor and load the policy Group.pol (created in previous exercises).

2. Create a user policy for Phil by choosing Edit ➤ New User, and entering **Phil** for the username, as shown below.

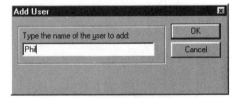

3. Open the policy for Phil, and select Desktop. There should be a check in the Wallpaper box, and Bubbles.bmp should be selected.

4. Change the wallpaper by selecting Straw Mat.bmp (instead of Bubbles.bmp).

5. Choose OK to save your changes.

6. Save the policy as Config.pol in the Windows 95 folder and close the editor.

Creating Policies for Computers

Policies can be set for all computers using the Default Computer specifications. Specific exceptions can be made by creating a separate computer entry for each excepted computer. Computer policies are based on the computer name.

In Exercise 15.6, we will make a policy that disables the password caching for computers. You can do this through the Network ➢ Password settings for the Default Computer properties, as shown in Figure 15.9.

FIGURE 15.9

Disabling password
caching

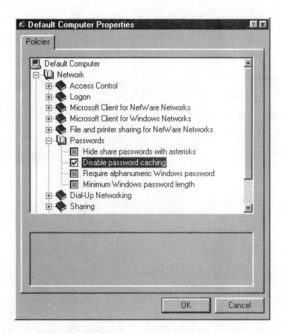

EXERCISE 15.6

Creating a Default Computer Policy

1. Start the System Policy Editor and load the policy Group.pol (created in previous exercises).

2. Select Default Computer ➢ Network ➢ Passwords.

3. Check the Disable password caching box (Figure 15.9).

4. Choose OK to save the setting.

5. Save the policy as **Group.pol** and close the editor.

Adding Specific Computers

By creating entries for specific computers, you can override the Default Computer settings. In Exercise 15.7, we will create a policy that will set the access control to an NT domain for a specific computer called Win95Server. You can do this through the Network ➤ Access Control settings for the Default Computer properties, as shown in Figure 15.10.

FIGURE 15.10

Setting user level access via a policy

EXERCISE 15.7

Creating a Specific Computer Policy

1. Start the System Policy Editor and load the policy Config.pol (created in Exercise 15.5).

2. Create a new computer account by selecting Edit ➤ Add Computer.

EXERCISE 15.7 (CONTINUED FROM PREVIOUS PAGE)

3. Enter **Win95Server** as the computer name, as shown below. (Notice the Browse button, which allows you to browse the Network Neighborhood to find a computer name.)

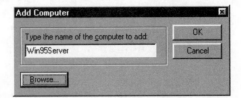

4. Open the Win95Server computer and select Network ➤ Access Control.

5. Check the User-level Access Control box, type **NT Domain** for the Authenticator name, and choose Windows NT Domain for the type (Figure 15.10).

6. Choose OK to save your changes.

7. Save the policy as **Config.pol** in the Windows 95 folder and close the editor.

Entries for the computer are based on the computer name, and thus will not work if the computer name changes.

Saving Policies

After making the appropriate changes in the System Policy Editor, you can save the policy and put it in the appropriate location.

Windows 95 looks for the file Config.pol in one of two places:

- \\NT Server\NETLOGON share

- NetWare Server:SYS/PUBLIC directory

If the Client for Microsoft Networks is the primary logon, Windows 95 will look in the NETLOGON share of the PDC (primary domain controller) of the domain. The NETLOGON share is usually the <NT Root>\System32\ Repl\Import\Scripts folder, which is also where logon scripts are stored by default. Windows 95 loads policies only from the PDC by default, which could cause a bottleneck in a large environment. To avoid such a bottleneck, you can enable load balancing, which forces Windows 95 to look on other domain controller servers than the PDC for the policy file. For this to work, all of the controllers in the domain must have a current copy of the profile.

You can use replication to automatically synchronize policy files. See *MCSE: NT Server 4 Study Guide* and *MCSE: Windows NT in the Enterprise* (published by Sybex) for more information.

If the Client for NetWare Networks is chosen as the primary network logon, Windows 95 will look for the policy file in the PUBLIC directory of the preferred NetWare server.

Windows 95 can also be directed to load a policy by specifying the path and filename of the policy. This is called Manual Update mode, and the procedure is explained in the next section.

Although the documentation (including the Windows 95 Resource Kit) states that policies are loaded automatically on a stand-alone workstation, this is incorrect—you need to enable Manual Update mode. Microsoft's PSS article Q147381 corrects the error.

Specifying a Policy Path

You can specify a path to a local computer through the Network ➤ Update settings for the Local Computer properties, as shown in Figure 15.11. In Exercise 15.8, we will set up Windows 95 to use policies on a stand-alone computer, and test the policy file we have built so far.

Windows NT 4.0 also uses system policies. The default filename that NT uses is NTCONFIG.POL. NT 4.0 policies are incompatible with Windows 95 policies. If you have both types of workstations, you will need to make two sets of policies.

Specifying the policy file

EXERCISE 15.8

Setting the Policy Path Manually

1. Start the System Policy Editor.

2. Select File ➢ Open Registry. This will open the local registry for editing, instead of making changes to a policy file.

3. Select Local Computer ➢ Network ➢ Update.

4. Check the Remote Update box, change the type to Manual, and add the path, including the policy name, to your policy file (Figure 15.11).

5. Choose OK to save your changes.

6. Exit the System Policy Editor. When you are asked if you want to save your registry changes, answer Yes.

7. Restart Windows 95.

8. Log in as Phil. You should see the straw mat wallpaper.

9. Log in as anyone else. You should see the bubbles wallpaper.

Creating Templates

Microsoft has supplied other templates and policies for use with the System Policy Editor. These can be found on the Windows 95 Resource Kit CD-ROM, and on Microsoft's Web site (www.microsoft.com). The great thing about templates is that they are written in ASCII, so they can be edited.

WARNING Be careful when you create or edit templates. Because templates are used to create the system policies that edit the registry, any mistake in the original template could have severe repercussions in the registry.

Looking at a piece of the registry and at a portion of a template written to modify it will help you to understand how templates are created. Figure 15.11 (in the previous section) shows the System Policy Editor opened to the Local Computer ➤Network ➤ Update ➤ Remote Update page. Now take a look at the actual template in Figure 15.12, and you will see how it was constructed.

FIGURE 15.12

The update options and path inside the template

```
Admin.adm - Notepad
File  Edit  Search  Help

    CATEGORY !!Update
            POLICY !!RemoteUpdate
            KEYNAME System\CurrentControlSet\Control\Update
            ACTIONLISTOFF
                    VALUENAME "UpdateMode" VALUE NUMERIC 0
            END ACTIONLISTOFF

                    PART !!UpdateMode DROPDOWNLIST REQUIRED
                    VALUENAME "UpdateMode"
                    ITEMLIST
                            NAME !!UM_Automatic VALUE NUMERIC 1
                            NAME !!UM_Manual        VALUE NUMERIC 2
                    END ITEMLIST
                    END PART

                    PART !!UM_Manual_Path EDITTEXT
                    VALUENAME "NetworkPath"
                    END PART
```

Examining the registry reveals the final piece of the puzzle. In the registry, you can see the actual subkey that will be modified if the policy is enforced, as shown in Figure 15.13. You know that this is under Hkey_Local_Machine because you are looking at the local computer (not the local user), and it will take effect under Hkey_Local_Machine\System\CurrentControlSet\Control\Update.

FIGURE 15.13

The registry update
options and path

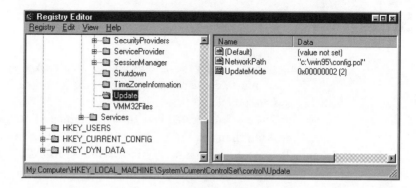

For more details about creating and editing templates, and a list of all the keywords used in templates, refer to the Windows 95 Resource Kit.

Editing the Registry Directly Using the System Policy Editor

The System Policy Editor has an additional function besides creating policies: It can open the registry and make direct edits to the registry database. We used this function in Exercise 15.8, when we modified the local registry to find the policy file on the local hard drive instead of on a network drive.

Using the System Policy Editor to make changes to the registry is a safe and fast way to edit the registry, because the only values that can be set are those that the template allows to be set. The pieces of the registry that can be edited are directly related to the template that is being used. (See Chapter 6 for more information about editing the registry.)

If remote administration is also enabled (see Chapter 16), the System Policy Editor can also open and make changes to remote registries.

Summary

Windows 95 allows you to decide on a set of restrictions that your users must adhere to, and gives you the power to enforce those restrictions via system policies.

Policies are created by loading a template into the System Policy Editor, making changes, and saving it as a policy file. You must install the System Policy Editor from the Windows 95 CD-ROM before you can create or edit policies. You must also enable user profiles (discussed in Chapter 14) in order for system policies to take effect.

Templates are ASCII files that correspond to subkeys and values in the registry. Microsoft supplies the default ADMIN template, which is a powerful vehicle for enforcing policies that your company may have in place concerning how Windows 95 will operate on the network. The ADMIN template contains Default Computer and Default User sections. Windows 95 looks for policy files in either the NETLOGON share of the NT server acting as the PDC or in the PUBLIC directory of a NetWare server. You can also specify where the policy file will be held, and set up load balancing across the NT servers.

Along with creating and editing policies, the System Policy Editor can also open and edit the local and remote registries directly.

Review Questions

1. The System Policy Editor is installed by which method?

    A. It is installed by default.

    B. It is installed when you do a "Custom" installation.

    C. It is installed automatically when you log onto a Windows NT server with Administrator rights.

    D. You have to install it manually.

2. Policies can be used to enforce restrictions based on which of the following? (Select all that apply.)

    A. Users

    B. Groups

    C. Time of Logon

    D. Computers

3. Policy templates end with which extension?

    A. TEM

    B. FIL

    C. ADM

    D. POL

4. Policies end with which extension?

    A. POL

    B. ADM

    C. DLL

    D. SEC

5. Group policies are not working. What step(s) should you check? (Select all that apply.)

    A. Group policy support must be installed on every computer that will load policies based on groups.

    B. Users may not be assigned to the correct groups.

    C. The policy file should be named GroupPolicy.pol.

    D. The policy file should be named Config.pol.

6. Phil is a member of both the Management and Sales groups. You want the Management group to take precedence over the Sales group. How would you set this up?

   A. Make the Sales group higher in the list.

   B. Make the Management group higher in the list.

   C. You can't control it—it goes alphabetically.

   D. Set Phil's primary group to the Management group.

7. Sally and Phil share a computer. Sally will have a restriction in place, but Phil shouldn't. How should you set Phil's checkbox for that restriction?

   A. Leave it gray (default).

   B. Put a check in it.

   C. Uncheck it (make it white).

   D. Leave Phil's checkbox alone; set Sally's checkbox to gray.

8. Windows 95 looks for the policy file in which NT share by default?

   A. The NETLOGON share of all domain controllers

   B. The NETLOGON share of the primary domain controller

   C. The USERS share of all domain controllers

   D. The USERS share of the primary domain controller

9. The System Policy Editor is found in which folder on the original Windows CD-ROM?

   A. Admin\Apptools\Poledit

   B. Admin\Poledit

   C. Admin\Tools\Policies\Editor

   D. Admin\Apptools\Policy\Poledit

10. Templates can be stored as which type of file(s)? (Select all that apply.)

    A. ASCII text files

    B. Compressed binary files

    C. Word (.doc) files

    D. Policy Editor (.pol) files

11. You want to enable system policies on a NetWare network. You have 3.12 servers and 4.*x* servers running in Bindery Emulation. Where do you need to put the system policy file so that your clients will find it?

    A. In the PUBLIC folders of the 3.12 servers, and the POLICY folders of the 4.*x* servers

    B. In the PUBLIC folders of all of the NetWare servers

    C. In the POLICY folders of all of the NetWare servers

    D. In the POLICY folders of the 3.12 servers, and the PUBLIC folders of the 4.*x* servers

12. You have a group created for your temporary employees called temp_users. You don't want them to be able to share their folders or printers. How would you set your policy file?

    A. Create a policy file that selects "Disable file sharing" and "Disable printer sharing" and assign it to the temp_users group.

    B. Create a policy file that selects "Disable file sharing" and "Disable printer sharing" and name it temp_users.pol.

    C. Edit your existing policy file. Create a new group policy for the temp_users group, and select the "Disable file sharing" and "Disable printer sharing" options.

    D. Edit your existing policy file. Create user policies for all of the temporary employees and select the "Disable file sharing" and "Disable printer sharing" options.

13. You need to save your policy file on a NetWare server. What do you name it so that your Windows 95 clients can find it by default?

A. Config.pol

B. NWConfig.pol

C. NTConfig.pol

D. 95Config.pol

14. You have 10,000 clients (both Windows NT and Windows 95) in one large Windows NT domain. You have a large PDC in the central office, with a BDC in each of your 30 regional offices. Users complain that logging in from the Windows 95 clients takes twice as long as logging in from the Windows NT clients. What steps do you need to take in order to speed up the login process? (Select all that apply.)

A. Make sure the policy file is on all the BDCs.

B. Enable Manual Updates, and specify load balancing on the Windows 95 clients.

C. Copy the policy file to the local hard drives of all of the Windows 95 clients.

D. Set the policy file to only test for user configurations.

CHAPTER

16

Remote Administration

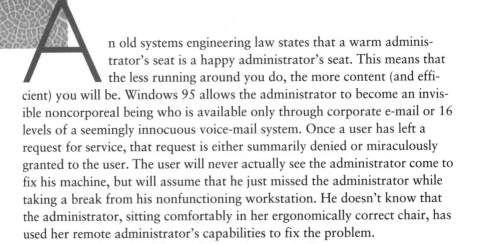

An old systems engineering law states that a warm administrator's seat is a happy administrator's seat. This means that the less running around you do, the more content (and efficient) you will be. Windows 95 allows the administrator to become an invisible noncorporeal being who is available only through corporate e-mail or 16 levels of a seemingly innocuous voice-mail system. Once a user has left a request for service, that request is either summarily denied or miraculously granted to the user. The user will never actually see the administrator come to fix his machine, but will assume that he just missed the administrator while taking a break from his nonfunctioning workstation. He doesn't know that the administrator, sitting comfortably in her ergonomically correct chair, has used her remote administrator's capabilities to fix the problem.

Microsoft ✓ *Exam Objective*

Create, share, and monitor resources. Resources include:

- Remote
- Network printers
- Shared fax modem
- Unimodem/V

There are several tools that you can use for remote administration of Windows 95 computers on your network. These include the Net Watcher, System Monitor, Administer, and Remote Registry Editor utilities. Before these tools can be used, the networked Windows 95 machines must be configured to accept RPCs (remote procedure calls) from the administrator's machine. Your administrative capabilities are also affected by the security level (Share or User) that has been configured on both the remote PC and the administrating PC.

In this chapter, we begin with a look at how remote administration is accomplished, then at how it is related to security levels. Next, you will learn how to enable remote administration and use each of the remote administration utilities.

Remote Administration Architecture

Remote administration makes use of RPCs. Every Windows 95 machine that has been configured to participate in remote administration has a set of DLLs (dynamic-link libraries) installed.

The administrator's machine will send an RPC to the client PC and run a particular procedure within the remote PC's local DLL files. The DLL file will run that procedure on that remote machine. This is analogous to you calling up a friend across town and having him turn on a television. He is doing the work at his house, but you are telling him what to do.

Remote Administration and Security

Your level of access to remote workstations is affected by the security level that has been configured on both the remote PC and the administrating PC. These security levels are described in detail in Chapter 11. Here is a brief review:

- **Share level security** is normally used in small peer-to-peer networks. Users assign passwords to shared folders and printers. Other users have access to those shared resources as long as they know the password.

- **User level security** is used in larger enterprise networking environments. The Windows 95 machine assigns sharing to resources based on a user account. The user accounts are stored on a validation server (such as a Windows NT or a NetWare server).

Share level security is the default. You can enable User level security through the Access Control tab of the Network Control Panel (see Chapter 11 for more information).

We'll explain how the security level in use affects what you can do with the Windows 95 remote administration tools in the discussion of those tools, later in this chapter.

Enabling Remote Administration

You enable remote administration through the Remote Administration tab of the Passwords Properties dialog box, shown in Figure 16.1. (If you don't see the Remote Administration tab, your computer might be using a system policy that does not allow this tab; see Chapter 15 for information about system policies.) Follow the steps in Exercise 16.1 to enable remote administration on your Windows 95 machine.

FIGURE 16.1

The Remote Administration tab of the Passwords Properties dialog box

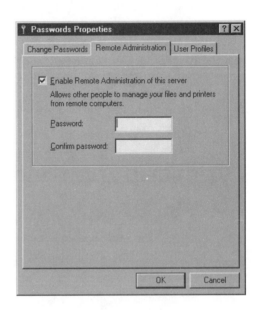

EXERCISE 16.1

Enabling Remote Administration

1. Go to Control Panel ➢ Passwords.

2. Choose the Remote Administration tab.

3. Click on the Enable Remote Administration of this server checkbox.

EXERCISE 16.1 (CONTINUED FROM PREVIOUS PAGE)

4. If this PC is using Share level security, set a password and then confirm the password. If the PC is using User level security, select the users and groups who have permission to administer this PC.

5. Click on OK when you are finished.

The other tabs in the Passwords Properties dialog box (Passwords Control Panel) are covered in earlier chapters. Chapter 11 includes information about using the options on the Change Passwords tab to change your Windows and other passwords. Chapter 14 describes how to use the User Profiles tab to set up user profiles.

When you make someone an administrator, you have given them full administration privileges, including the ability to add and remove other administrators.

Remote Administration Tools

Four Windows 95 tools are useful for remote administration:

- **Net Watcher:** Allows you to administer shared resources on a remote workstation. This includes the ability to view who is accessing those shared resources.

- **System Monitor:** Allows you to view performance statistics of a remote workstation

- **Administer:** Allows you to access a special hidden share called C$. C$ is the root directory of a remote workstation

- **Remote Registry Editor:** Allows you to edit and modify a remote workstation's registry

Because the System Monitor and the Remote Registry Editor need access to a workstation's registry database, they can be used only when User level security has been enabled on both the remote workstation and the administrating computer. They also require Remote Registry Services to be installed.

Microsoft ✓ *Exam* *Objective*

Monitor system performance. Tools include:

• Net Watcher

• System Monitor

The Net Watcher, System Monitor, and Administer tools are accessed from the Tools tab of the Properties dialog box for the Windows 95-based computer that you want to remotely administer, as shown in Figure 16.2. You can access the Remote Registry Editor from the Registry Editor program (Regedit).

FIGURE 16.2

The Tools tab of a remote machine's Properties dialog box

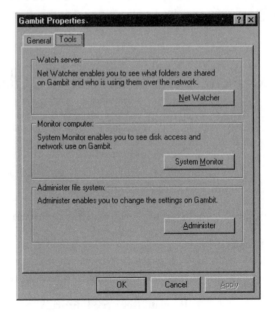

Table 16.1 summarizes the requirements for running the remote administration utilities. The following sections describe the use of each of these tools in more detail.

Please study Table 16.1 carefully, as some of the exam questions pertain to both client and administrating computer configurations.

TABLE 16.1	TOOL	REMOTE WORKSTATION			ADMINISTERING WORKSTATION	
Requirements for the Remote Administration Tools		User/ Share	File & Printer Sharing Enabled	Remote Registry Services	User/ Share	Remote Registry Services
	Net Watcher	Share	Yes	N/A	Either	N/A
		User	Yes	N/A	User	N/A
	Administer	Share	Yes	N/A	Either	N/A
		User	Yes	N/A	User	N/A
	Remote System Monitor	User	Yes	Yes	User	Yes
	Remote Registry Editor	User	Yes	Yes	User	Yes

The Net Watcher

The Net Watcher is an interactive tool for creating, controlling, and monitoring remote shared resources. Net Watcher can be run on remote computers using either Share or User level security. If the remote PC is using User level security, the administrating PC must also be using User level security.

As an administrator, you can create, add, and delete shares, change resource properties, and monitor who is connected to which resource. Figure 16.3 shows an example of a Net Watcher screen.

FIGURE 16.3

The Net Watcher tool allows you to manage shares.

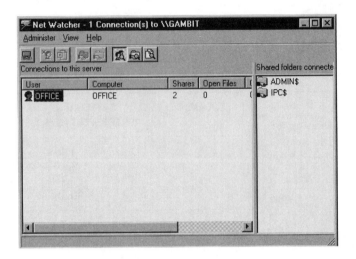

Follow the steps in Exercise 16.2 to use the Net Watcher tool. Of course, the remote workstation must be sharing resources, folders, and/or printers for this tool to be useful. If it is not sharing resources, nothing will show up in the Net Watcher window.

EXERCISE 16.2

Using the Net Watcher Utility

1. Double-click on the Network Neighborhood icon on your Desktop.

2. Navigate to a Windows 95-based computer involved in remote administration and right-click on its icon.

3. From the context menu, choose Properties to open the Properties dialog box for that PC.

4. Choose the Tools tab (Figure 16.2).

5. Click on the Net Watcher button. The Net Watcher application starts and shows you the status of shared resources on the remote PC (Figure 16.3).

When you use the Net Watcher, two special shares are created:

- Admin$ gives administrators access to the \Windows folder on the remote PC.

- IPC$ is an interprocess channel between the two computers. This is a buffer area for RPCs to move between the workstations.

If you disconnect a user from a shared resource, the user will reconnect to the resource immediately. To prevent this, if you are using Share level security, you need to change the password on the resource. If you are using User level security, you need to remove the user from the users list. This is also true when you are closing a file. The user will still have access to the shared folder, but will be momentarily disconnected from the file. The user will immediately reconnect to the file unless you do something to prevent it.

WARNING

If you are using Share level security and you change a password on a shared resource, everyone who is currently using that resource will be thrown out. They will need to supply the new password in order to reconnect.

The Remote System Monitor

The Remote System Monitor tool can be used to monitor performance statistics on the remote workstation. The System Monitor uses values stored in the Hkey_Dyn_Data key in the registry to get its information. To access the registry on a remote computer, both the remote workstation and the administrating workstation must be using User level security.

Installing Remote Registry Services

Since the Remote System Monitor must pull information from the registry, you must install Remote Registry Services on both workstations to allow remote administrators to see the registry. Installing Remote Registry Services is also necessary for using the Remote Registry Editor. Figure 16.4 shows the screens involved in this procedure.

Follow the steps in Exercise 16.3 to add Remote Registry Services.

FIGURE 16.4

Installing Remote Registry Services

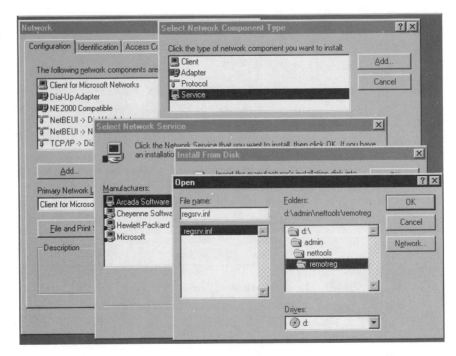

EXERCISE 16.3

Installing Remote Registry Services

1. Go to Control Panel ➢ Network.

2. From the Configuration tab, click on the Add button.

3. Select Service, then Add, then Have Disk.

4. Insert the Windows 95 CD-ROM, and go to the \admin\nettools\ remotereg folder (Figure 16.4).

5. Click on OK in the dialog boxes. You are told that you must reboot your system before these changes will take effect.

6. Click on OK and let the system reboot.

Do not install Remote Registry Services unless you need it. Workstations with this installed take a slight performance hit in the memory, disk space, and CPU areas.

Running the Remote System Monitor

With Remote Registry Services installed, and both the remote workstation and the administrating workstation using User level security, you can run the System Monitor. Figure 16.5 shows an example of the CPU utilization statistic on a remote workstation.

FIGURE 16.5

The System Monitor can be used to view performance statistics on a remote workstation.

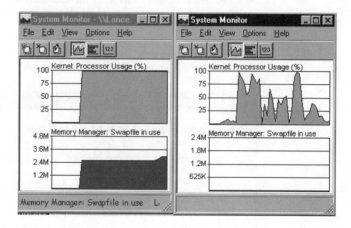

Follow the steps in Exercise 16.4 to use the monitor.

EXERCISE 16.4

Running System Monitor on a Remote Workstation

1. Double-click on the Network Neighborhood icon on your Desktop.

2. Navigate to a Windows 95-based computer involved in remote administration and right-click on its icon.

3. From the context menu, choose Properties to open the Properties dialog box for that PC.

4. Choose the Tools tab (Figure 16.2).

5. Click on the System Monitor button. The System Monitor starts and shows performance statistics for the other workstation (Figure 16.5).

6. To look at different statistics, select Edit ➤ Add Item, choose a category, and click on OK.

The Administer Utility

The Administer utility gives an administrator access to the hard disks on the remote workstation. From the local computer, you can administer the file system as if you were sitting at the remote workstation. The Administer tool can be used with both User and Share level security. Follow the steps in Exercise 16.5 to use Administer.

EXERCISE 16.5

Using the Administer Utility

1. Double-click on the Network Neighborhood icon on your Desktop.

2. Navigate to a Windows 95-based computer involved in remote administration and right-click on its icon.

3. From the context menu, choose Properties to open the Properties dialog box for that PC.

4. Choose the Tools tab (Figure 16.2).

5. Click on the Administer button. The Administer utility starts and allows you to look at the remote workstation's C:\ drive. You can share resources and delete, create, and modify files as if you were sitting at that remote workstation.

The Remote Registry Editor

The Remote Registry Editor allows you to edit the registry database on networked computers. To use the Remote Registry Editor, both computers must be using User level security and you must have Remote Registry Services installed as a network component (see Exercise 16.3).

You access the Remote Registry Editor from the Registry Editor by choosing to connect the registry of the computer you want to administer. Follow the steps in Exercise 16.6 to run the editor.

EXERCISE 16.6

Using the Remote Registry Editor

1. Select Start ➢ Run.

2. In the Run program dialog box, type **REGEDIT** to start the Registry Editor.

3. Select Registry ➢ Connect Network Registry to open the Connect Network Registry dialog box.

4. Type in the name of the computer you want to remotely administer, or click on the Browse button to browse the network and find the machine you are looking for.

5. Click on the OK button and close the dialog box. You can view and edit the registry on the remote machine.

For more information about the registry and using the Registry Editor (Regedit) see Chapter 6.

Summary

Using the remote administration utilities included with Windows 95 allows systems engineers and network administrators to accomplish more work with less running around. While not as robust as the utilities available in Windows NT or Novell's NetWare, they are powerful nonetheless.

Remote administration takes place through the use of RPCs (remote procedure calls). These procedures are implemented as *.DLL files and allow you to track system performance statistics, manage and monitor shared resources, manipulate the file structures, and edit the registry on remote workstations without ever leaving your chair.

Different levels of remote administration are available depending on the security level (Share or User) and installed components (like Remote Registry Services) of both the administering workstation and the remote workstation. The four remote administration tools are the Net Watcher, System Monitor, Administer, and Remote Registry Editor. The Remote Registry Editor is accessed from the Registry Editor (Regedit). The other tools are available from the Tools tab of the remote machine's property sheet (accessed from the Network Neighborhood).

Review Questions

1. Remote administration is accomplished through the use of which mechanism?

   A. Named pipes

   B. RPCs

   C. IPX/SPX

   D. TCP/IP

2. Which utility do you use to administer the file structure on a remote computer?

   A. Net Watcher

   B. Remote System Monitor

   C. Administer

   D. Remote Registry Editor

3. Which utility do you use to view which resources are shared and who is using them?

   A. Net Watcher

   B. Remote System Monitor

   C. Administer

   D. Remote Registry Editor

4. Which utility do you use to view performance statistics on a remote workstation?

   A. Net Watcher

   B. Remote System Monitor

   C. Administer

   D. Remote Registry Editor

5. To modify the registry database on a remote workstation, you need to install which additional network service?

   A. Net Watcher Services

   B. Remote Registry Services

   C. Client Services for Remote Administration

   D. Novell NetWare Client32 for Windows 95

6. Which of the following utilities require User level security on both the remote workstation and the administering workstation? (Select all that apply.)

   A. Net Watcher

   B. Remote System Monitor

   C. Administer

   D. Remote Registry Editor

7. To remotely administer a client PC, you must first enable remote administration. Where is this accomplished from?

A. Network property sheets

B. Add/Remove Programs in Control Panel

C. Passwords in Control Panel

D. Remote Administration in Control Panel

8. Your Windows 95 computer is currently configured to use User level security. You want to use the Remote Net Watcher utility to monitor shares on another Windows 95 computer. Which of the following must be true?

A. The client computer must be configured to use User level security and must also have Remote Registry Services installed.

B. The client computer must be configured to use either Share or User level security and must also have Remote Registry Services installed.

C. The client computer must be configured to use User level security and must also have file and print sharing installed.

D. The client computer must be configured to use either Share or User level security and must also have file and print sharing installed.

9. Which of the following statements are true concerning using the Remote Net Watcher utility? (Select all that apply.)

A. If the administering computer is using Share level security, then the client computer can be configured with either Share level security or User level security.

B. If the administering computer is using Share level security, then the client computer must be configured with Share level security.

C. If the administering computer is using User level security, then the client computer can be configured with either Share level security or User level security.

D. If the administering computer is using User level security, then the client computer must be configured to use User level security.

10. Which of the following statements are true concerning using the Remote System Monitor Utility? (Select all that apply.)

    A. Both the administering computer and the client PC must be configured to use User level security.

    B. The administering computer must be configured to use User level security, but the client computer can use either Share level security or User level security.

    C. Both the administering computer and the client computer must have Remote Registry Services installed.

    D. Only the client computer must have Remote Registry Services installed.

11. Your Windows 95 computer is currently configured to use User level security. You want to use the Administer utility to monitor another Windows 95 computer. Which of the following must be true?

    A. The client computer must be configured to use User level security and must also have Remote Registry Services installed.

    B. The client computer must be configured to use either Share or User level security and must also have Remote Registry Services installed.

    C. The client computer must be configured to use User level security and must also have file and printer sharing installed.

    D. The client computer must be configured to use either Share or User level security and must also have file and printer sharing installed.

12. Which of the following statements are true concerning using the Remote Net Watcher utility? (Select all that apply.)

    A. If the administering computer is using Share level security, then the client computer can be configured with either Share or User level security.

    B. If the administering computer is using Share level security, then the client computer must be configured with Share level security.

C. If the administering computer is using User level security, then the client computer can be configured with either Share or User level security.

D. If the administering computer is using User level security, then the client computer must be configured to use User level security.

13. Which of the following statements are true concerning using the Remote Registry Editor Utility? (Select all that apply.)

A. Both the administering computer and the client PC must be configured to use User level security.

B. The administering computer must be configured to use User level security, but the client computer can use either Share or User level security.

C. Both the administering computer and the client computer must have Remote Registry Services installed.

D. Only the client computer must have Remote Registry Services installed.

CHAPTER

17

Communications

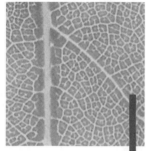

I n the expanding world of high-speed communications—the World Wide Web, the Internet, and corporate intranets and extranets— understanding how Windows 95 handles telephony becomes a necessity. Modems provide a single asynchronous data stream for sending and receiving information across a telephone line. Since modems are considered virtual devices by the Windows 95 operating system, they have their own unique architecture and installation features.

In this chapter, we will discuss the communications architecture of Windows 95 and how it impacts your computer system. We will also talk about modems, their installation, configuration, and diagnostics. We will end our chapter with a discussion of the Telephony Application Programming Interface (TAPI), including special dialing properties that can be set for location-specific information as well as handling calling cards. Dial-Up Networking, another communications feature of Windows 95, is covered in Chapter 18.

Communications Architecture

C ommunications resources are devices that provide a single, asynchronous data stream. An *asynchronous data stream* is one in which packets of information are passed one packet at a time in a continuous stream (as opposed to a synchronous data stream, in which several packets are sent in a synchronized discrete burst). These resources can be physical, like your modem, or logical, like a fax service on your computer that uses the modem for transmittal and reception of faxes.

Microsoft
Exam
Objective

Create, share, and monitor resources. Resources include:

- Remote
- Network printers
- Shared fax modem
- Unimodem/V

The communications architecture in Windows 95 is set up as a series of layers with several interchangeable components, as illustrated in Figure 17.1. The Unimodem driver (UNIMODEM.VXD), virtual communications driver (VCOMM), and the mini-drivers or port drivers make up the core of the communications architecture.

FIGURE 17.1

The communications architecture

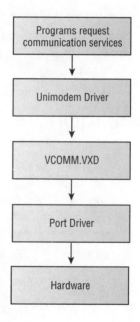

VCOMM manages all access to your communications resources. This architecture allows third-party 32-bit software to be independent of the type of communications hardware that exists in your system. Third-party software vendors just need to enable their software to make use of the Unimodem driver in order to have access to your modem, fax, and any other communications hardware in your system. The Unimodem driver contains general information that is used for any type of communications. Mini-drivers are device-specific drivers that can translate between the Unimodem and the hardware itself.

The 16-bit programs still make use of the old COMM.DRV program, which acts like the 32-bit Unimodem driver. All communications requests are funneled to VCOMM, which then passes those requests on to the appropriate port driver, which in turn talks directly with the hardware. This makes it easy for third-party hardware vendors to create new hardware. The new hardware merely needs to come with a mini-driver that can communicate with the VCOMM driver and the communications hardware.

Because the communications architecture is virtualized, you no longer have a software-based limit on the number of COM and LPT ports on your system.

Modem Installation

If you have a Plug-and-Play-compliant computer and a Plug-and-Play-compliant modem, Windows 95 should auto-detect the modem when your system is booted. Windows 95 will then install the appropriate drivers.

Microsoft ✓ *Exam* *Objective*

Install and configure hardware devices. Hardware devices include:

- Modems
- Printers

Modem is short for modulate/demodulate. Modems work by converting binary electrical signals into acoustic signals for transmission over telephone lines (called *modulation*), and then converting these acoustic signals back into binary form at the receiving end (*demodulation*).

If you don't have a Plug-and-Play system, you can easily install a modem (or, actually, install a modem mini-driver) through the Modems Control Panel, shown in Figure 17.2. When you click on the Add button, the Install New Modem Wizard takes you through a series of steps for installing the modem, as shown in Figures 17.3 through 17.5.

FIGURE 17.2

The Modems Properties
dialog box

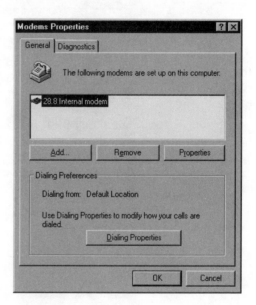

Follow the steps in Exercise 17.1 to install a modem on your system.

You can also start the modem installation process from the Add New Hardware Wizard in the Control Panel, which will search your system for any new hardware and then present you with installation options for the modem that it found. See Chapter 5 for more information about the Add New Hardware Wizard.

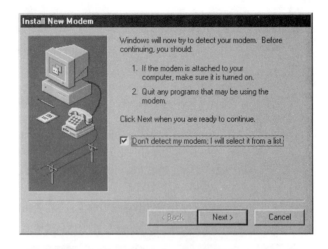

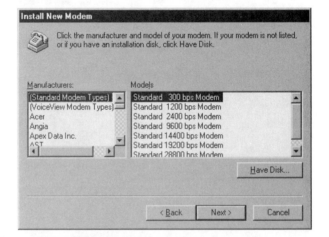

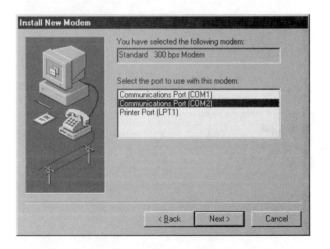

EXERCISE 17.1

Installing a Modem

1. Open the Control Panel and double-click on the Modems icon.

2. Click on the Add button in the Modems Properties dialog box (Figure 17.2) to start the Install New Modem Wizard.

3. To install the modem automatically, leave the Don't detect my modem... checkbox unchecked, click on Next, and the wizard will auto-detect and install the modem. For the auto-detection to work, your modem must be installed and turned on. To step through the wizard, choose the Don't detect my modem... option (Figure 17.3) and click on Next. The next screen presents a list of manufacturers and their corresponding models (Figure 17.4).

4. Choose the manufacturer of your modem in the Manufacturers list, and then choose the model in the Models list. If you do not see your modem listed, click on the Have Disk button. The wizard will ask you to insert the floppy disk that shipped with your modem. After you've selected the manufacturer and model, click on the Next button to move to the next screen, which asks you to select the port where your modem is installed (Figure 17.5).

5. Choose your modem port. Generally, your modem will be on either COM1 or COM2.

Note that if your mouse is installed on COM1, your modem must be installed on either COM2 or COM4. If your mouse is installed on COM2, your modem must be installed on either COM1 or COM3. This is because COM2 and COM4 share the same IRQ. Likewise, COM1 and COM3 also share the same IRQ. If you choose the wrong port, you will need to edit the port properties from the modem's property sheet. Depending on what type of modem you have, you may need to make changes to switches on the modem itself.

6. When you have selected your communications port, click on Next to finish the installation. The wizard will install the appropriate mini-drivers for that particular modem, and then return you to the Modems Properties dialog box. From there, you can configure the modem and perform diagnostics.

Modem Configuration

You can make changes to your modem's default settings through its property sheet. You can change things like the speaker volume and connection settings.

To begin, go to the Modems Control Panel (double-click on the Modems icon in the Control Panel), select the modem that you want to configure, and then click on the Properties button. The modem's Properties dialog box has two tabs: General and Connection. The following sections describe the options available for most modems.

Adjusting General Modem Settings

The General tab of the modem's Properties dialog box, shown in Figure 17.6, allows you to modify the general features that are part of all modems.

FIGURE 17.6

The General tab on the modem's Properties dialog box

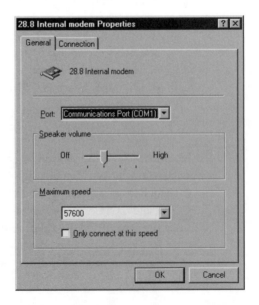

This tab includes the following settings:

■ **Port:** Allows you to change to a different communications port.

- **Speaker volume:** Allows you to change the setting for the speaker volume. Normally, you will hear your modem dialing out, which sounds like a normal telephone call. Once the other modem answers, there will be a "handshake" period in which the modems try to synchronize themselves and let each other know at what speed they want to communicate. This will sound like a high-pitched whine that may change in tone several times. Once the modems have synchronized, you will be connected, and the speakers will shut themselves off.

- **Maximum speed:** Allows you to specify the maximum speed at which your modems will communicate. In the past, some manufacturers' modems were not compatible with other manufacturers' modems at high speeds. To avoid this problem, you could connect at a slower speed. If you have purchased a new modem since mid-1994, you should not have this problem. Set your maximum speed to the speed that is greater than or equal to your modem's speed. For example, if you have a 28,800 bps modem, you should choose 28,800 or 38,400.

Modifying Connection Settings

The Connection tab of the modem's Properties dialog box, shown in Figure 17.7, allows you to modify your connection and call preferences.

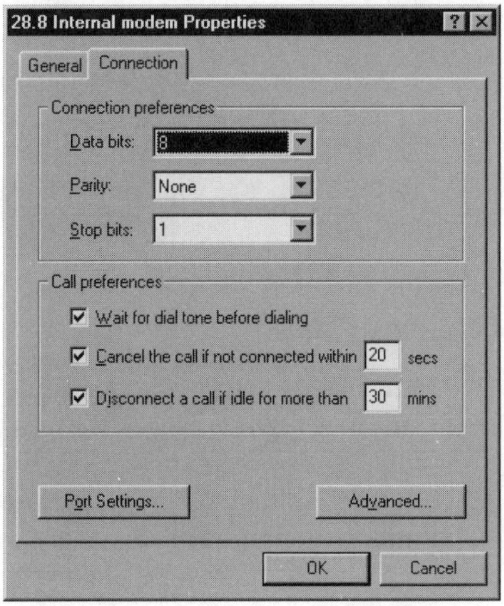

FIGURE 17.7

The Connection tab on the modem's Properties dialog box

Connection Preferences

The Connection preferences options allow you to modify how the packets of data are configured and sent across the telephone line:

- **Data bits:** The data bits are normally either 7 or 8; 8 has become the default setting for most modems (in the past, 7 data bits were the norm). This setting means that 7 or 8 bits of packet information will be sent across the wire at a time.

- **Parity:** In the past, parity was used to make sure that the information sent across the wire was received properly. For instance, if you sent 7 bits across the wire, the other side would expect to receive 7 bits. None is the default setting. Occasionally, if you are using 7 data bits, this setting might need to be Even.

- **Stop bits:** The stop bits are normally always set to 1. Occasionally, you might encounter an older network that uses 2. The stop bits are used to identify the end of a packet. (In the past, modems could speak in only one direction at time—Modem A would send a burst of information and a stop bit and then wait for an acknowledgment from Modem B.)

Call Preferences

The Call preferences options allow you to determine how your modem will behave. You can set the modem to wait for a dial tone before dialing, cancel the call if it's not connected within the specified number of seconds, and disconnect if the connection is idle for more than the specified number of seconds.

These settings are especially useful for dealing with unattended modem activity. For example, you might like to use a batch file that will run at midnight, connect to your network using Dial-Up Networking, and download some information (see Chapter 18 for more information about Dial-Up Networking).

Port Settings

Clicking on the Port Settings button in the Connection tab brings up the Advanced Port Settings dialog box, shown in Figure 17.8. These settings allow you to decide how your FIFO (First In-First Out) buffers are used. These buffers are temporary storage areas for transmitting and receiving packet information through your modems. You should set them to their maximum levels for the best throughput of information.

FIGURE 17.8

The Advanced Port
Settings dialog box

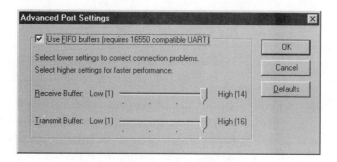

There are two types of FIFO buffers: the 16550 UART (Universal Asynchronous Receiver/Transmitter), which is standard on all 486 and later computers, and the 8250 UART. The 8250 is a much older standard, which allows a maximum rate of only 9600 bps.

16550 UARTs provide larger and faster buffers than their 8250 counterparts. UART chips are found in many different places in your system. They can be located on modem hardware, parallel port boards, hard disk controllers, and other locations where communications are taking place.

Advanced Connection Settings

Clicking on the Advanced button in the Connection tab brings up the Advanced Connection Settings dialog box, shown in Figure 17.9.

FIGURE 17.9

The Advanced
Connection Settings
dialog box

These settings allow you to modify what type of error control and flow control you use, as well as set a modulation type and enter extra settings:

- **Use error control:** Allows you to specify whether or not you use error control and compression. Windows 95 can support v42.bis compression and MNP/5 error correction.

- **Use flow control:** Allows you to specify whether or not the modem or the software handles flow control between the modem and your computer. The default is for the hardware to do this. (XON/XOFF may not work with certain programs.)

- **Modulation type:** Must be the same on both modems in order for them to communicate. If you are having trouble communicating with an older modem, try using the Non-standard setting.

- **Extra settings:** Allows you to enter special modem initialization strings that older modems require in order to connect and communicate. These are strings like "AT&FE=S0." They tell the modem exactly how to behave.

- **Record a log file:** Allows you to record a modem log file called MODEMLOG.TXT, which will be placed in your \Windows folder. You can use this file to monitor the modem and for troubleshooting.

Modem Diagnostics

To find out which drivers are installed for which modems and to test your modems, use the Diagnostics tab of the Modems Properties dialog box, shown in Figure 17.10. This dialog box shows all of the currently installed serial ports and what is attached to them.

Clicking on the Driver button pops up a dialog box that will tell you what driver that particular port is using.

If you have selected a port with a device installed on it and you click on the More Info button, you will see information about that port. Windows 95 will send a standard set of AT commands to the port and then display your modem's

FIGURE 17.10

The Diagnostics tab of
the Modems Properties
dialog box

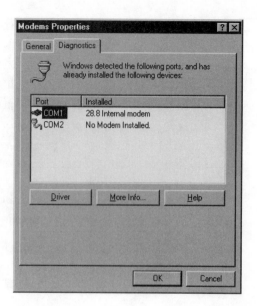

response, as shown in Figure 17.11. You can compare the responses with the
documentation supplied with your modem to make sure that everything is
working properly. The More Info dialog box also shows which IRQ channel
(interrupt) that port is using, its base address expressed as a hexadecimal
value, and the type of UART it is using. You may also see information about
the highest speed available on that port. If you choose a port that does not
have a device attached to it and select More Info, you will get to the same
dialog box, but it will not display any of the AT commands.

The standard set of AT commands run from ATI through AT17. AT+FCLASS=?
will display a list of fax modem classes supported by this modem.

Clicking on the Help button brings up troubleshooting information to walk
you through some diagnostics.

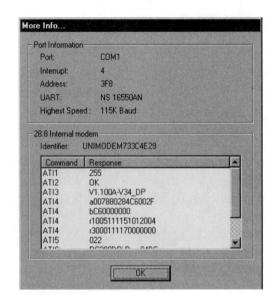

F I G U R E   17.11

The More Info...
dialog box

TAPI Settings

TAPI (Telephony Application Programming Interface) is a standard
way for programs to interact with the telephony functionality in Windows 95.
TAPI works much like the Unimodem driver discussed earlier.

All programs that want to use telephony can do so through a standard set
of calls to the TAPI interface. This makes it easier for third-party developers
to create programs that are modem- and fax-ready. All the programmers must
do is invoke the TAPI functionality to achieve a standard interface that the
user is already familiar with. If this were not the case, every program a developer created would need to have its own dialing properties, location settings,
and access to the modem hardware.

Viewing TAPI Settings

You can view the TAPI settings through the Modems Control Panel. In the
General tab, click on the Dialing Properties button to see the Dialing Properties dialog box, shown in Figure 17.12.

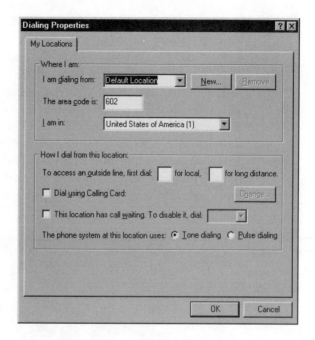

FIGURE 17.12

The Dialing Properties
dialog box

Modifying Dialing Settings

The location settings in the Dialing Properties dialog box allow Windows 95
to analyze different telephone numbers and then decide how to dial them.
For example, if your area code is 602 and you decide to send a fax from
Microsoft Word, Word will fire up the fax service. The fax service will eventually ask you to type in a fax number. When you type in that number—
(602) 555-4567, for example—TAPI will compare the 602 entries and will
recognize that the number is a local call rather than a long-distance call.

You can add many different locations in the Where I am section. This is
especially useful if you travel a lot and are in different area codes or even different countries.

The To access an outside line boxes are useful for dialing through PBX-type
systems, which require dialing a number to get an outside line. For example, you
may need to dial a 9 and wait a second or two to get an outside line. If you place
a comma in the telephone numbers, or in the Outside line box, this tells the
computer to pause for 1 second before it continues dialing. If you placed "9,,"
in the "first dial :" box, this would dial the number 9, pause two seconds, and
then proceed to dial the rest of the number.

If you choose Dial using Calling Card, your system will use your calling card to dial out. To set up a calling card, click on the Dial using Calling Card option, and then click on the Change button. You will see the Change Calling Card dialog box, shown in Figure 17.13. Choose your calling card from the list box. If you do not see your calling card in the list, choose New and add a new calling card. The Dialing Rules dialog box will be displayed, as shown in Figure 17.14. The text boxes can be filled with information from another calling card by choosing the Copy From button. Each box uses special letters and $ signs to denote different things. For instance, the *G* might signify "Wait for the dial tone before dialing." A *T* might signify "Wait until you hear the bong before proceeding."

FIGURE 17.13

The Change Calling Card dialog box

FIGURE 17.14

The Dialing Rules dialog box

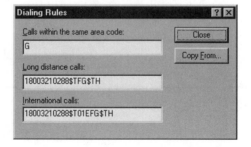

For more information about calling card codes, contact your calling card company.

If you have call waiting, you can disable it by selecting the This location has call waiting... option in the Dialing Properties dialog box. The standard is *70, which will disable call waiting for the duration of this call. Once you hang up, call waiting will automatically re-enable itself. If for some reason it does not, pick up your telephone and dial *71.

Summary

The modem architecture in Windows 95 has been designed to allow for device independence. This is accomplished through the use of VCOMM, which has all telephony activity routed through it and then onto the mini-drivers and the hardware. The Unimodem driver allows developers to create hardware that is program-independent and software that is modem-independent.

Installing and configuring modems are fairly straightforward processes, with few areas for getting into trouble. You can use the modem diagnostics in conjunction with your modem documentation to troubleshoot your modem. The installation, configuration, and diagnostics options are available through the Modems Control Panel.

TAPI is a piece of software that operates in a fashion similar to VCOMM. It can be used to route software calls to a standard telephony interface. The telephony interface most commonly used is the Dialing Properties dialog box, accessed through the Modems Control Panel. From this dialog box, you can set up location-specific information, such as area codes and numbers used to dial an outside line.

Review Questions

1. What is the central component in the communications architecture?

   A. UNIMODEM.VXD

   B. VCOMM

   C. TAPI

   D. Mini-drivers

2. What is the main device driver used to handle modem operations that is provided with Windows 95?

   A. UNIMODEM.VXD

   B. VCOMM

   C. TAPI

   D. Mini-drivers

3. What is the software written by the manufacturers that provides device-specific information used by each modem?

   A. UNIMODEM.VXD

   B. VCOMM

   C. TAPI

   D. Mini-drivers

4. What is the Windows 95 software that provides a method for programs to interact with telephony functionality in a standard, user-friendly format?

   A. UNIMODEM.VXD

   B. VCOMM

   C. TAPI

   D. Mini-drivers

CHAPTER

18

Mobile Computing

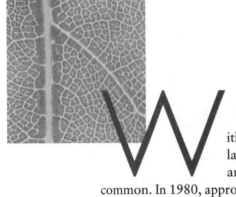

With faster modems and the increasing popularity of laptop computers, doing work from a hotel room or any other off-site location has become more and more common. In 1980, approximately 100,000 people telecommuted in the United States; in 1995, an estimated 12 million telecommuted. If we extrapolate these numbers, 1998 should have approximately 30 million telecommuters.

Windows 95 allows you to remotely connect to your computer at the office and have the machine sitting in front of you share resources as if you were on the network. The modems at both computers act as the network cable. You can download e-mail, get those Microsoft Excel files that you forgot at the office, play a networked computer game like Hearts or Diablo, or anything else that you would normally do on the network.

In this chapter, we will discuss two Windows 95 methods for connecting to a remote host: Dial-Up Networking using a modem and Direct Cable Connection using a null-modem cable attached to serial or parallel ports.

As a footnote to this chapter, we will discuss file synchronization using the Briefcase utility included with Windows 95. The Briefcase allows you to keep the same set of files synchronized between two separate computers. All types of networking support the Briefcase utility, including Dial-Up Networking and Direct Cable Connection.

Dial-Up Networking

Dial-Up Networking allows you to have access to all available resources on a network from a remote location like your home. The remote location essentially becomes a node on the network utilizing a "slow link." Modem connections to a network are considered slow links because they generally run between 14,400 to 28,800 bps on an analog modem and up to

128,800 bps on a digital modem using ISDN (Integrated Services Digital Network) connections or even 2.5 megabits (roughly 2.5 million bps) on a cable modem. A standard 10 megabit network cable in your office can run between 4.2 million to 10 million bps, or 65 to 200 times faster than a standard modem connection.

Dial-Up Networking Features

Dial-Up Networking encompasses many features found only in Windows 95 and Windows NT, including the following:

- **Compatibility:** As a dial-up server, Windows 95 can support Microsoft Windows NT, LAN Manager, Windows for Workgroups, LAN Manager for Unix, IBM LAN servers, and Shiva LAN Rover. When running as a dial-up client, Windows 95 can connect to systems supporting Microsoft RAS, Novell NRN, or SLIP or servers running PPP. (See the discussion of line protocols, under "Dial-Up Networking Architecture," for definitions of these protocols.)

- **LAN topology independent:** As a dial-up server, Windows 95 supports Ethernet, Token Ring, FDDI, and ArcNet.

- **Advanced security:** Dial-Up Networking allows the use of encrypted passwords to prevent their capture and use over public-switched telephone lines.

- **Advanced modem support:** Dial-Up Networking supports all modems that work with the Windows 95 Unimodem driver system. This includes support for flow control and both software and hardware compression. (See Chapter 17 for information about modem setup in Windows 95.)

- **Slow links:** Dial-Up Networking exposes the slow link API to indicate to programs that they are running over a slow link. This is useful because programs will wait for a predetermined amount of time to receive data across the network. Since networks are so much faster than modems, most programs would issue a timeout error while waiting for the information to come across a slow link. Because programs know that they are using a slow link, the timeout waiting period is much longer.

- **Dial-up server:** Windows 95 with the Microsoft Plus! package installed can be used as a dial-up server. As a dial-up server, Windows 95 can support one connection.

If you install the RAS (Remote Access Service) on a Windows NT Server machine, it can support up to 255 simultaneous connections.

Dial-Up Networking Architecture

Like the other parts of Windows 95, the Dial-Up Networking architecture is based on a networking model that uses multiple layers and interchangeable components. The layers for Dial-Up Networking include the Network Interface, Network Protocol, and Line Protocol layers. Each layer communicates with the layer above it and the layer below it, as illustrated in Figure 18.1.

FIGURE 18.1

Dial-Up Networking architecture

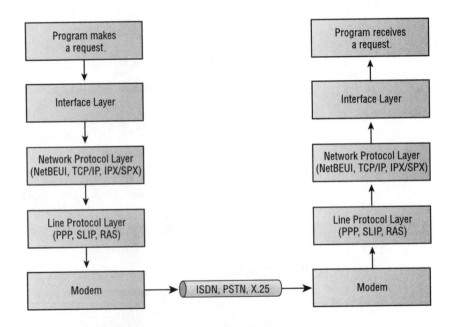

In the following sections, we will take a look at the different layers and their architecture, the different types of networks Dial-Up Networking can connect through, and an example of how the various parts of the architecture interact.

The Network Interface Layer

A *network interface* (also known as a *LAN adapter driver* or *network driver*) is the software that lets your network card talk to the network protocol. Dial-Up Networking supports the following network interfaces:

- **NETBIOS (Network Basic Input Output System):** Establishes sessions in which computers talk with each other. Computers will acknowledge receipt of messages from other computers in a two-way communication scheme. (See Chapter 11 for more information about NETBIOS support.)

- **Mailslots:** One-way communications, which do not establish sessions. Using mailslots is like writing a note on a paper airplane and then throwing it to someone else. You don't know whether or not the other person received the message.

- **Named pipes:** Another way to establish one-to-one connections with another computer

- **RPCs (remote procedure calls):** Send messages to another computer telling it what to do. For example, you might tell another computer to start a particular program. For RPCs to work, the computer receiving the RPCs must be configured to receive them and make use of the calls. (See Chapter 16 for more information about RPCs.)

- **LAN Manager APIs:** Calls to an API, which then executes those calls. These are similar to RPCs, but do not use the RPC interface.

- **TCP/IP tools:** A set of protocols and interfaces for session-based communications. (See Chapter 10 for more information about TCP/IP.)

- **WinSockets:** A library of support procedures for TCP/IP

The Network Protocol Layer

As explained in Chapter 9, *network protocols* are like languages (English, German, French, and so on) which allow two computers to communicate with each other across the network. Dial-Up Networking is protocol independent and supports the same standard protocols as other networking features in Windows 95: NetBEUI, IPX/SPX, and TCP/IP. (See Chapters 9 through 12 for more information about these protocols.)

The Line Protocol Layer

Line protocols are used to encapsulate data into a format suitable for transmittal over telephone lines or null-modem cables. Dial-Up Networking supports the following line protocols:

- **Windows NT RAS (Remote Access Service):** An older protocol developed for Windows NT 3.1. It has been carried forward and is still available under NT 4.0. RAS uses asynchronous NetBEUI. This protocol is slower and less compact than SLIP and PPP, but it has the added advantage of being well tested and runs with few errors and even fewer opportunities for improper configuration.

- **SLIP (Serial Line Internet Protocol):** A subset of the tools and utilities included with TCP/IP. SLIP should be used in a networking environment that requires machines to have their own unique IP addresses. SLIP is not installed automatically with Windows 95, as it is an older protocol that has been replaced with the more reliable PPP protocol. To add SLIP, use the Add/Remove Programs Control Panel. The files are located on your Windows 95 CD-ROM in the \Admin\Apptools\Slip folder.

If you installed Windows 95 using floppy disks, the Slip folder is not available. The \Admin folder does not ship with the floppy disk version.

- **PPP (Point-to-Point Protocol):** A standard low-speed protocol that originated from TCP/IP. It has become the most widely used protocol because it is very flexible. Dial-Up Networking is compliant with the industry-standard PPP communications protocol. SLIP requires a preassigned IP address, whereas PPP can use a DHCP server and "lease" an IP address for a short period of time. (See Chapter 10 for more information about IP addresses and DHCP.)

- **PPTP/VPN:** A new standard Point-to-Point Tunneling Protocol/Virtual Private Network. This new protocol allows a user to dial up an Internet service provider (ISP) and then use the PPTP to tunnel into the network at their office using the VPN protocol for secure communications. The PPTP/VPN must be installed on the office equipment. On the dial-up client side, however, PPTP/VPN can be installed on the client or on the ISP's computer. As long as one of these machines supports the protocol, you can log on and take advantage of your new secure connection. In the past, the only way to get this type of security was to use an expensive private telephone line. You can now use the Internet as an inexpensive alternative.

- **NRN NetWare Connect:** A proprietary connection protocol that allows a Windows 95 machine to directly connect with a NetWare Connect server. Novell's IPX/SPX network protocol must be used for this type of connection.

WARNING

NetWare Connect clients cannot connect to a Windows 95 dial-up server.

Wide-Area Network Support

Dial-Up Networking can make use of the modem and TAPI (Telephony Applications Programming Interface) components to work over different types of wide-area networks (WANs):

- **Public-Switched Telephone Networks (PSTNs):** The regular telephone lines that you use every day to make phone calls. The modem in your computer can use these same telephone lines to transmit and receive data.

- **X.25:** A special packet-switching network. An X.25 packet is delivered to another X.25 node on a worldwide X.25 network. That node then forwards the packet to the next node, and so on until the packet finally reaches a packet assembler/disassembler (PAD) at the other machine. The PAD takes the place of your standard modem.

- **Integrated Services Digital Network (ISDN):** A standard for digital telephony. ISDN offers faster communications than you can get with a standard analog telephone line. ISDN speeds range from 64,000 to 128,800 bps. ISDN requires a special digital modem and an ISDN telephone line to your home and office.

How Dial-Up Networking Works

Let's go through an example of what happens when you use Dial-Up Networking. After dinner, you decide to do some work on a Microsoft Word document. You fire up the computer and then use Dial-Up Networking to log in to your computer at the office. You start up Microsoft Word on the client (your home PC), and then open a document located on the host (your computer at the office). When you open that document, Word is making a request for service at the top layer in the Dial-Up Networking architecture (Figure 18.1).

The Network Interface layer will then format your request into a packet that the Network Protocol layer can understand. Essentially, you have a core piece of data that will get successive layers added around it. This process is called *encapsulation*. The packet is then passed to the Network Protocol layer, which will encapsulate your packet with the appropriate network protocol (like NetBEUI or TCP/IP). In a normal networked environment, your packet would then be sent across the wire to the appropriate server. Since you are using a dial-up interface, your network packet is passed on to the Line Protocol layer. This layer encapsulates the packet into a format that can be transmitted across the telephone lines (such as SLIP or PPP).

After the packet has been encapsulated for transmittal, it is sent through your modem to the telephone lines, where it travels through an ISDN, a PSTN, or an X.25 telephone service. Once the other modem receives the packet of information, it is passed up through the layers, where each layer of encapsulation is removed at the appropriate level. After all of the layers are removed, the host machine can then act upon the request, which was "give me this file."

You can use Dial-Up Networking over a telephone line or through a null-modem interface, using a serial cable or parallel cable linked between the two computers.

Dial-Up Networking Installation and Configuration

The requirements for Dial-Up Networking include one or more compatible modems. You also need 2MB of free hard disk space to install the client, server, and administrative utilities. There are four parts to the installation process:

- Install Dial-Up Networking.

- Install and configure your modem.

- Create a client connection to a server.

- Create a dial-up server.

Microsoft
✓ **Exam**
Objective

Configure a client computer to use Dial-Up Networking for remote access.

You install Dial-Up Networking using the Internet Connection Wizard or through the Add/Remove Programs Control Panel, as described in Chapter 10. The procedures for installing and configuring a modem are covered in Chapter 17. The following sections describe how to create dial-up connections and a dial-up server.

Creating Dial-Up Connections

Creating a connection places a connection object in your Dial-Up Networking folder. The connection object is analogous to an index card. It tells Windows 95 where to go to connect to the host computer and can provide details like a user ID and password to the host system that it is attempting to log on to.

Setting up a connection involves specifying the computer you are dialing, the type of modem you are using, and the telephone number to dial. The New Connection Wizard steps you through the procedure, as shown in Figures 18.2 and 18.3.

FIGURE 18.2

Specifying the computer name and modem

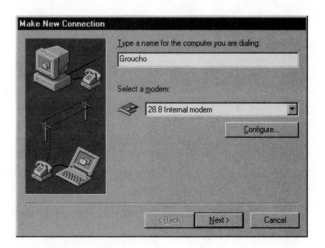

FIGURE 18.3

Entering the telephone
number information

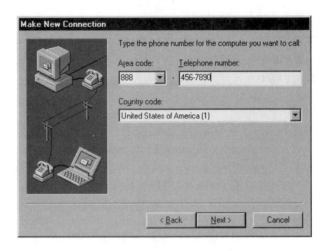

Exercise 18.1 will take you through the steps for creating a dial-up connection.

In Exercise 18.1, we use a sample computer name and telephone number.
Substitute your own information if you want to set up an actual connection.

EXERCISE 18.1

Creating a Dial-Up Connection

1. Select Start ➤ Programs ➤ Accessories ➤ Dial-Up Networking to
   open the Dial-Up Networking folder.

2. Double-click on the Make New Connection icon to start the New
   Connection Wizard.

3. If you see the "Welcome to Dial-Up Networking" screen, click on the
   Next button. (Your version of Windows 95 might bypass this screen.)
   This takes you to the first Make New Connection dialog box.

4. In the Type a name for the computer you are dialing box, enter a
   name for this connection: **Groucho** (Figure 18.2).

EXERCISE 18.1 (CONTINUED FROM PREVIOUS PAGE)

5. Select your modem. If you haven't installed your modem yet, see Chapter 17. (The Configure button allows you to make configuration changes to your currently selected modem.) Then click on Next to move to the screen requesting the telephone number that you want to call.

6. Type in the area code **888** and the telephone number **456-7890** (Figure 18.3). Then click on Next to go to the confirmation screen.

7. If everything looks correct on the final screen, click on the Finish button. Your Dial-Up Networking folder now has a new icon in it called Groucho.

Dial-Up Networking will treat your modem as a network card. This will require the PPP protocol to be installed. If you have not already installed PPP, don't worry—the wizard will automatically install it for you.

Creating a Dial-Up Server

If you have installed the Microsoft Plus! package, you will be able to use Windows 95 as a dial-up server (see Chapter 8 for details on installing and using the Plus! software). When used as a dial-up server, Windows 95 allows a single connection to its resources. Windows 95 supports other Windows 95 machines, LAN Manager, Windows for Workgroups 3.11, Windows NT, and any PPP-based remote client.

To set up a dial-up server, you need to enable caller access, as shown in Figure 18.4. You can also choose the server type and set password encryption and software compression options, as shown in Figure 18.5.

Follow the steps in Exercise 18.2 to turn your Windows 95 machine into a dial-up server.

FIGURE 18.4

The Dial-Up Server
dialog box

FIGURE 18.5

Selecting the server type

EXERCISE 18.2

Setting Up a Dial-Up Server

1. From the Dial-Up Networking folder, select Connections ➢ Dial-Up Server to bring up the Dial-Up Server dialog box (Figure 18.4).

2. To make your Windows 95 machine a dial-up server, click on the Allow caller access option.

3. If you want to create a password that a client must use to access your dial-up server, click on the Change Password button.

4. Click on the Server Type button to bring up the Server Types dialog box (Figure 18.5). Choose a server type from the drop-down list, and click on the Enable software compression and/or Require encrypted password checkboxes if you want to use these options. Then choose OK.

5. In the Dial-Up Server dialog box, click on Apply or OK to complete the setup. Your Windows 95 machine is now ready to accept calls from clients.

Making a Connection

When you select your connection icon in the Dial-Up Networking folder, Windows 95 presents the Connect To dialog box, shown in Figure 18.6. The Dial Properties button in this dialog box will take you to the Dialing Properties dialog box, which is discussed in Chapter 17 (in the section about TAPI).

FIGURE 18.6

The Connect To dialog box

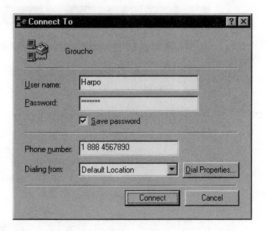

While you are connected, you can see what type of server you have connected to and which protocols you are currently using. In the example shown in Figure 18.7, the connection is to a Windows for Workgroups and Windows NT server using the NetBEUI protocol.

FIGURE 18.7

Viewing connection details

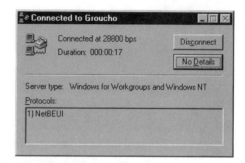

Once you have connected, you can use the resources on the dial-up server just as if you were working at the office. You can go to your Network Neighborhood and see the server there. If you have mapped drive letters to network resources, these should now be accessible through Windows Explorer or My Computer.

Follow the steps in Exercise 18.3 to make a connection and view connection details. (In order to complete this exercise, you need a dial-up server to connect to.)

EXERCISE 18.3

Connecting to a Dial-Up Server

1. Double-click on the Groucho icon in your Dial-Up Networking folder (created in Exercise 18.1).

2. Type in a username and password that the dial-up server will recognize (Figure 18.6). Make sure that the telephone number is correct.

3. Click on the Connect button. Your computer dials the telephone number and attempts to connect to the server, displaying the message shown below.

EXERCISE 18.3 (CONTINUED FROM PREVIOUS PAGE)

4. Once you have connected to the server, it will verify your username and password. The Connected To box, shown below, indicates the speed of your connection and the duration of time that you've been connected.

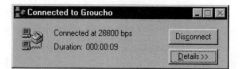

5. Click on Details to see the type of server you are connected to and which protocols you are currently using (Figure 18.7).

6. To disconnect and end your dial-up session, click on the Disconnect button.

If you do not have a dial-up session currently running and you try to access one of your mapped drive letters, the computer will try to connect to the network via the dial-up connection, by starting the Dial-Up Networking program on your PC. This is called a *ghosted connection*, or an *implicit connection*. The ghosted connection is not really established until you log in and connect, but a ghost of the connection will be in your folder in the form of a mapped drive icon.

Direct Cable Connections

A direct cable connection uses a null-modem cable that connects to both machines through their serial or parallel ports. You also need to install software to manage this type of connection. You can use the Direct Cable Connection software included with Windows 95 (DIRECTCC.EXE) or a third-party piece of software like LapLink.

Serial cables have only 9 pins and are somewhat slower than parallel cables, which have 25 pins. The parallel cable looks like a printer cable.

Setting up a direct cable connection involves specifying whether your computer is the host or a guest, choosing a port, and setting a password (if desired). The *host* computer is the one that has the resources that the other computer wants to access. A *guest* computer accesses the resources on the host computer. The Direct Cable Connection Wizard steps you through the procedure, as shown in Figures 18.8, 18.9, and 18.10.

F I G U R E   18.8

Specifying whether your computer is a host or a guest

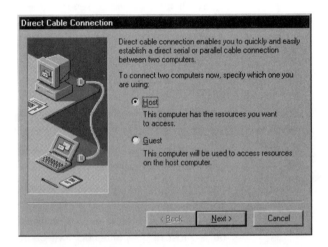

F I G U R E   18.9

Selecting a port

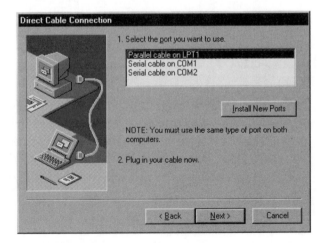

FIGURE 18.10

Setting a password

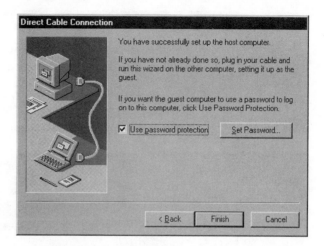

Exercise 18.4 will take you through the steps for running the wizard to set up a direct cable connection.

EXERCISE 18.4

Creating a Direct Cable Connection

1. To connect the two workstations, attach the null-modem cable to both machines.

2. On the machine that is going to be the host, select Start ➢ Programs ➢ Accessories ➢ Direct Cable Connection to start the Direct Cable Connection Wizard (Figure 18.8).

3. Choose the Host option, and then click on Next. The next screen asks you to choose which ports your cables are attached to (Figure 18.9).

4. Select the port on which you have installed your cable. (The parallel port on LPT1 is where your printer cable would normally be installed. One of the serial ports is usually used by your mouse.) Click on Next after you've specified the port. The next screen allows you to set a password (Figure 18.10).

EXERCISE 18.4 (CONTINUED FROM PREVIOUS PAGE)

5. To set passwords, click on the Use password protection checkbox, and then click on the Set Password button.

6. To close the password screen and begin "listening" for a guest computer, click on the Finish button. The host displays the message below while waiting for a guest computer to log in.

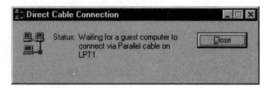

7. On the guest computer, repeat steps 2 through 6, except choose the Guest option in step 3. When you are finished, a connection will be established. The guest machine will see all of the shared folders and resources available on the host.

Security for Mobile Computing

Anytime you open up your computer system to the outside world, you take a chance that someone will try to break in and destroy information. When setting up your computers for dial-up access, you should consider implementing the following security strategies to prevent unauthorized access to your systems:

- Use User level security on the server side. This forces the server to check both the user ID and the password before allowing access. (See Chapter 11 for more information about User level security.)

- Use system policies in conjunction with dial-up access. Windows 95 system policies can implement different levels of access to the computer resources based upon the login. (See Chapter 15 for more information about system policies.)

- Use encrypted passwords. This keeps outsiders from getting your password as it is passed along the telephone networks.

- Use firewalls for large servers that allow Internet access. A firewall is a set of multiple layers of security strategies to keep outsiders out of your system.

- You might want to encrypt sensitive documents that you will be sending over the Internet. There is encryption software available from a variety of sources, including the Internet.

- Use PPTP/VPN to ensure a secure session with your server. Remember that the server must have PPTP configured and either the client or ISP must have PPTP configured. To make use of a Virtual Private Network, simply create a dial-up connection just as you normally would. If the ISP supports PPTP, then you don't have to do anything else. If the PPTP support is on your client PC, then you need to create a phone book entry with the TCP/IP address of the server computer to which you are trying to connect. When you create your dial-up connection, specify the phone book entry and the phone number for the ISP. That's all there is to it.

Data-Transfer Performance

There are steps that you can take to improve your data-transfer performance. Here are just a couple of things you might try:

- Use compression. Windows 95 supports both hardware and software compression. This setting is available from the Modems Control Panel. (See Chapter 17 for more information about modem configuration.)

- Use the System Monitor to check your performance. Look at the bytes read per second and bytes written per second under the Microsoft Client. (See Chapter 21 for more information about using the System Monitor.)

File Synchronization Using Briefcase

Briefcase is a utility that can keep track of changes in a set of files that exist on a host machine and a client machine. It is particularly handy if you are working on a laptop when you are away from your office (or home computer). Figure 18.11 shows the Welcome to the Windows Briefcase screen, which explains the Briefcase's functions.

FIGURE 18.11

An introduction to the
Briefcase

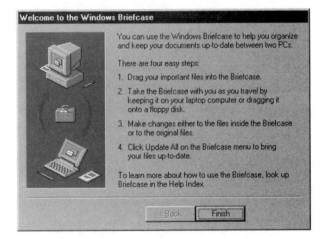

For example, you might keep a master version of a manuscript on your home PC and a synchronized copy in your Briefcase on a laptop computer. When you are out of town, you can use your laptop to add to your manuscript. When you want to back something up, or retrieve some extra information, you can use Dial-Up Networking and then update the information between the two computers using the Briefcase utility, as shown in Figure 18.12. Only the files that have changed will be moved.

The Briefcase can be used to synchronize (update the modified files in) entire network directories.

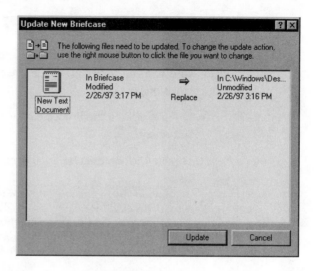

In Exercise 18.5, we will create a new Briefcase object and then use it to
synchronize some files.

EXERCISE 18.5

Using the Briefcase Utility

1. Right-click on your Desktop and choose New ≻ Briefcase. This creates a new Briefcase object on your Desktop.

2. Double-click on the new object to activate it.

3. When you are finished reading the Welcome screen (Figure 18.11),
click on Finish. You are now ready to start using your Briefcase.

4. Close the Briefcase window.

5. Right-click on your Desktop and create a new text document.

6. Open the text document and type some text in there: **10 Million
Lemmings Can't Be Wrong!!!**

7. Save and close the text document.

8. Drag-and-drop the document on your Briefcase. This makes a "sync"
copy of the file in your Briefcase.

9. Let's pretend that we are going to go out of town. We copy the Briefcase to a floppy disk. (Don't do this; we are only simulating this situation.)

10. Double-click on the Briefcase object. Inside you will see your text document.

11. Double-click on the text document. You should see what you wrote before.

12. Let's make some changes. Add another line of text to the document: **If at first you don't succeed, then skydiving isn't for you!!!**

13. Save and close the text document.

14. Now we are back at the office. We put our floppy disk in the drive, Explore to it, and right-click on the Briefcase icon. Choose the Update All option. This compares the date and time stamps of the files in the Briefcase with the files on the PC (Figure 18.12).

15. We see that the document in the Briefcase is fresher than the copy on our Desktop. If we click on the Update button, the file on the Desktop will be replaced by the fresher document in our Briefcase. If you don't want to overwrite the document, you can right-click on the Replace arrow and then choose a different option, as shown below.

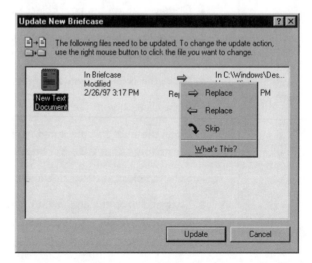

If for some reason the file in your briefcase becomes orphaned (there is no synchronized copy on the Desktop), you have the option of creating a new synchronized copy or deleting the orphaned file. This will work in both directions—either from the Briefcase to the Desktop or the Desktop to the Briefcase.

The Briefcase uses the SYNCENG.DLL and LINKINFO.DLL files in your \Windows\System directory to track your files. It also uses two special hidden files, which are stored in the Briefcase object itself. They are a database file that keeps track of date and time stamps as well as file locations, and a DESKTOP.INI file that contains OLE registration information. You shouldn't delete these files.

OLE registration information tells your computer things like: *.DOC files should be opened with Microsoft Word.

Summary

Mobile computing allows you to connect a client computer to a host computer without the aid of a network cable. In this chapter, you learned about the Windows 95 support for mobile computing, including the Dial-Up Networking, Direct Cable Connection, and Briefcase features.

Windows 95 has many new features that are part of the Dial-Up Networking interface, including compatibility with many existing networks and protocols, security in the form of encryption and system policies, the PPTP/VPN protocol, and advanced modem support for today's latest and greatest. The Dial-Up Networking architecture comprises several layers that support network interfaces, network protocols (including NetBEUI, IPX/SPX, and TCP/IP), and line protocols (like PPP and SLIP). To use Dial-Up Networking, you need to set up both the dial-up client and server components.

The Direct Cable Connection feature allows you to connect two computers using a null-modem cable. You need to set up this feature on both machines, and specify whether the machine is the host computer (the one that has the resources that the other computer wants to access) or the guest computer (the one that accesses the resources on the host computer).

The Briefcase is a Windows 95 utility that can keep track of changes in a set of files that exist on a host machine and a client machine. It is useful for file synchronization (updating modified files).

Review Questions

1. What three network protocols are supported by Dial-Up Networking?

   A. NetBEUI

   B. PPP

   C. IPX/SPX

   D. TCP/IP

2. What can you do to increase security when using mobile computing? (Select all that apply.)

   A. On the host computer, use User level security.

   B. Use password encryption.

   C. Encrypt your data files when transferring them.

   D. Use a system policy.

3. A Windows 95 dial-up server can support all of the following except:

   A. Windows 95 client

   B. PPP-based client

   C. Windows NT client

   D. Macintosh client using AppleTalk

4. Which protocol is the most flexible and is the default used by Windows 95?

A. SLIP

B. PPP

C. NRN NetWare Connect

D. NT RAS

5. The Briefcase can synchronize files using all of the following except:

A. Modem

B. Win95Synch

C. Floppy disk

D. Null-modem cable

6. What is networking that does not take place over a standard network cable, but rather across the telephone lines, sometimes called?

A. Slow link

B. Hyperlink

C. Direct cable connection

D. Indirect cable connection

7. What three wide-area telephone networks does Windows 95 support with Dial-Up Networking?

A. WANs

B. PSTN

C. X.25

D. ISDN

8. To ensure a secure connection between a client and a server across the Internet, you can use PPTP. Which of the following must be true to use PPTP? (Select all that apply.)

   A. The server must be configured with PPTP.

   B. The client must be configured with PPTP.

   C. The ISP must be configured with PPTP.

   D. Either the client or the ISP needs to have PPTP installed.

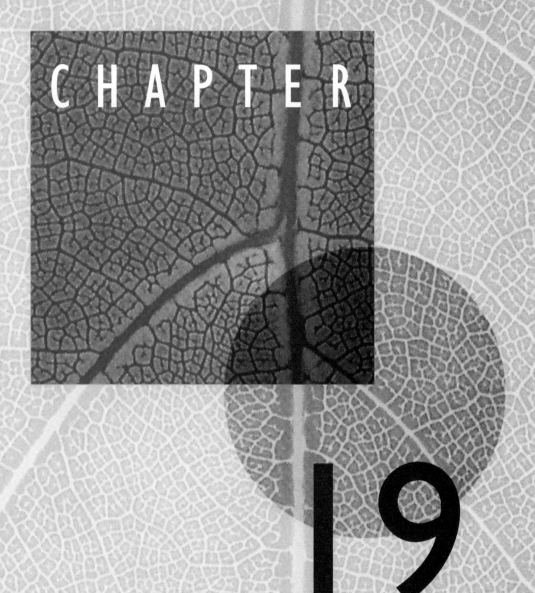

CHAPTER

19

The Microsoft Exchange Client

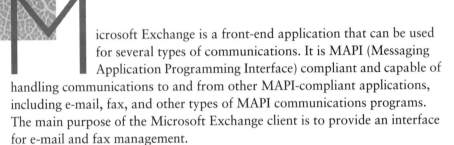

icrosoft Exchange is a front-end application that can be used for several types of communications. It is MAPI (Messaging Application Programming Interface) compliant and capable of handling communications to and from other MAPI-compliant applications, including e-mail, fax, and other types of MAPI communications programs. The main purpose of the Microsoft Exchange client is to provide an interface for e-mail and fax management.

In this chapter, we will look at how MAPI works. Then we will describe how to set up and use the Exchange client, beginning by installing a peer-to-peer post office, followed by installing and configuring the client. Finally, we will describe how to install fax software, Microsoft Fax, for Windows 95.

The Exchange client will not be included in Windows 98, as Outlook Express is replacing it. Office 97 includes the Outlook client, which is the default client for Exchange Server 5.5.

An Overview of MAPI

MAPI is a messaging application standard developed by Microsoft to allow for interaction between an application and various message service providers. In this way, an application like the Exchange client is not dependent on a particular underlying service, as long as that service has a MAPI service provider available. For example, the Microsoft Exchange client can be the mail reader for its own workgroup post office, but it can also be used to participate in a Microsoft Mail system. It doesn't matter which system is used, as long as it has a MAPI service provider that allows the Exchange client to send and receive commands that both sides understand.

The MAPI service provider for the underlying system is installed locally and can be thought of as a local gateway to that system. Figure 19.1 illustrates how applications, MAPI, and Windows 95 work together.

FIGURE 19.1

Applications, MAPI, and
Windows 95

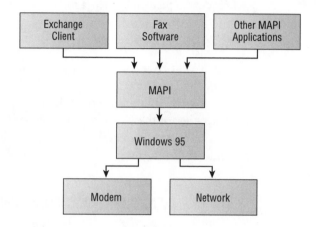

Creating and Administering Post Offices

The Microsoft Exchange client that comes with Windows 95 is a peer-to-peer type messaging system. In other words, end users can configure and use it without an administrator setting up anything on the server. The only requirement is the existence of a centrally located "post office" for storage of messages. This storage can be either on a volunteering user's hard drive or on a network server. Such a setup provides a relatively quick and easy way to allow messaging between users in a workgroup; however, it can be inefficient for large numbers of users.

Windows 95 comes with an e-mail post office that is designed for peer-to-peer networks. It is a workgroup edition of Microsoft Mail Server; it does not allow mail to be exchanged with other post offices or access to any mail gateways (such as the Internet). The post office works well in small environments, but was not designed for large companies.

Since Windows 95 was released, Microsoft has released Exchange Server for Windows NT. This is an enterprise messaging product that has a much broader scope than Exchange for Windows 95.

Creating a Workgroup Post Office

The Microsoft Exchange client can use either an existing Microsoft Mail post office or the built-in Windows 95 (or Windows NT) workgroup post office. The Microsoft Mail service provider that is included with the Exchange client can use either of these connections. Before installing the Exchange client, it may be necessary to create a post office. You can set up a new post office through the Workgroup Postoffice Admin utility, as shown in Figure 19.2.

FIGURE 19.2

Creating a new workgroup post office

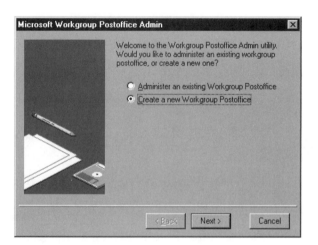

Exercise 19.1 will take you through the steps for creating a local peer-to-peer post office using Windows 95.

EXERCISE 19.1

Creating a Peer-to-Peer Post Office

1. Go to Control Panel ➤ Microsoft Mail Postoffice.

EXERCISE 19.1 (CONTINUED FROM PREVIOUS PAGE)

2. Click on the radio button to Create a new Workgroup Postoffice (Figure 19.2) and click on Next.

3. Enter the location for the new post office. This can be on the local computer or a computer on the network. The computer where the post office is installed must be left on at all times when users may need to access the post office.

4. In the Administrator Account Details dialog box, shown below, enter the information for the account that will be responsible for administering the post office. Then click on OK.

5. Click on OK to finish creating the post office.

Administering a Workgroup Post Office

The user who created the post office is automatically made the post office administrator. This user will be responsible for creating new accounts, deleting accounts, and changing accounts in the post office. You can manage an existing post office through the Postoffice Manager dialog box, shown in Figure 19.3.

Follow the steps in Exercise 19.2 to access the Postoffice Manager dialog box.

FIGURE 19.3

Administering a
workgroup post office

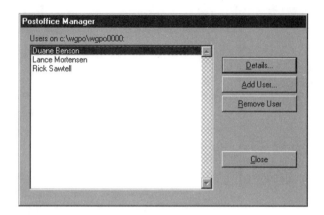

EXERCISE 19.2

Administering an Existing Post Office

1. Go to Control Panel ➢ Microsoft Mail Postoffice.

2. Click on the radio button for Administer an existing Workgroup Postoffice, then click on Next.

3. Enter the path to the existing post office.

4. Enter the password for the administrator. This is the password that was entered in the Administrator Account Details dialog box when the post office was created (see Exercise 19.1).

5. In the Postoffice Manager dialog box (Figure 19.3), click on the Add User button to add a user. To remove a user, select that user in the list box, and then click on Remove User. To change an existing user's account (the user's password, for example), select the user in the list box and then click on the Details button.

Setting Up the Exchange Client

Like many of the Windows 95 components, Microsoft Exchange can be installed during the setup of Windows 95 itself. If you select to include

Microsoft Mail or Microsoft Fax in the installation, you are prompted to configure those services as part of the setup process. OSR2*x* includes Internet Explorer, which also includes the Internet Mail client, if you choose to install it. If you add Microsoft Mail software to your system after installation, the first time you start Exchange, the Inbox Setup Wizard will take you through the setup, as shown in Figures 19.4, 19.5, and 19.6.

FIGURE 19.4

Starting the Inbox
Setup Wizard

FIGURE 19.5

Selecting Exchange
information services

FIGURE 19.6

Specifying you post
office location

Follow the steps in Exercise 19.3 to add the Exchange client to Windows 95.

EXERCISE 19.3

Setting Up the Exchange Client

1. To add the Microsoft Mail software, go to Control Panel ➢ Add/
   Remove Programs. Choose the Windows Setup tab, select Microsoft
   Exchange, and then choose Microsoft Mail Services.

2. Start Microsoft Exchange for the first time, and the Inbox Setup Wizard should appear (Figure 19.4).

3. If you've never used Exchange on this system, click on No. Then click
   on Next.

The next screen displays the services you can use with Exchange, such as
Microsoft Mail, Microsoft Fax, and the Microsoft Network (Figure 19.5). By
default, whatever is displayed here is selected. Setup will automatically configure these services (recommended for most users) unless you click on
the Manually configure information services button.

4. Click on Next. The next screen asks for your post office location.

5. Enter the path to your post office or click on the Browse button and
   select its location (Figure 19.6). Then click on Next.

6. The wizard finishes and prompts you to shut down and restart the
   computer for the changes to take effect. Click on OK.

For Exchange setup, you need to know the location of the post office. If you don't have a post office, you will need to create one before installing the Exchange client. See Exercise 19.1 for the procedure.

Adding Services to the Exchange Client

After you install the Exchange client, you may want to have it recognize new services as they become available to your system. You can add new services through the Mail and Fax Control Panel, or within the Exchange client by selecting Tools ➣ Options. Figure 19.7 shows the Services tab of the Options dialog box.

FIGURE 19.7

Services available for the Exchange client

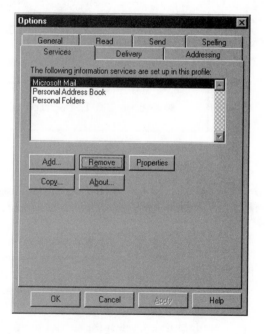

Exercise 19.4 will take you through the steps for adding a new service (Internet Mail) to the Exchange client.

EXERCISE 19.4

Adding Internet Mail to the Exchange Client

1. Go to Control Panel ➤ Mail and Fax application. You should see a list of services already installed.

2. Make sure you are on the Services tab (Figure 19.7) and click on Add. You should see a list of services, similar to the list shown below.

3. Choose the Internet Mail service.

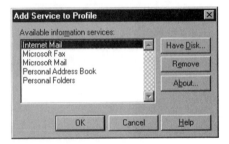

4. Enter your name, e-mail name, and mail server name (use made-up names if you don't actually have Internet Mail).

5. Choose OK. The wizard installs the Internet Mail service.

Each of the services has an associated wizard that runs when you select to add it. This makes it easy to supply the necessary setup information.

The services that you select in the Add Service to Profile dialog box determine which specific DLLs are enabled when the Exchange client is started. For example, there may be many DLLs in the Windows\System directory that are for Exchange services, but they remain unused until you explicitly add the services to the Exchange client. To find out which DLLs are loaded with a particular service, select the service in the Services tab (Figure 19.7) and click on the About button.

To remove a service, return to the Services tab that lists the installed services (Figure 19.7), highlight the service, and click on Remove. Windows 95 will ask you to confirm the deletion before removing the service.

Using the Exchange Client

The Microsoft Exchange client has many features designed to make it useful. Here we will cover the basic features of the client interface, including the Personal Address Book, Personal Folder, and message profiles. Note that there are additional Exchange tools available on Microsoft's web site.

The Exchange client opens by default with the single-pane view. This allows either folders or messages to be displayed. In double-pane view, folders and messages can be displayed alongside each other, as shown in Figure 19.8. This view also allows you to drag and drop messages into folders. To switch to double-pane view, either click on the Show/Hide Folder List toolbar button or select View ➤ Folders.

FIGURE 19.8

The Exchange client in double-pane view

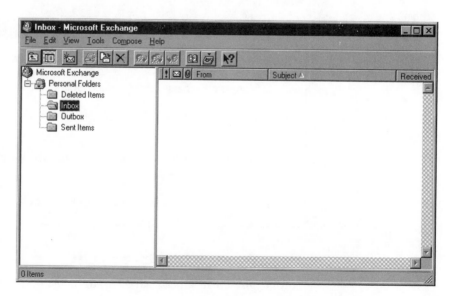

When you first open the Exchange client, it automatically downloads mail from all of the available services. If there are multiple services configured, it may take several minutes to retrieve mail from all of them.

Later in a session, you can choose to check for new mail from individual services. Select Tools ➤ Deliver Now Using, and then select the service you want to check from the submenu. If there is only one service, the Tools menu option will simply be named Deliver Now. Also, through the property sheets of each service, you can set intervals for downloading mail automatically.

The Personal Address Book

The Personal Address Book is a file created for each user that contains the user's customized list of addresses. This list may contain mail or fax recipients. Address Book files have a .PAB extension.

Customizing the Address List

You can customize the address list by making manual entries or by adding names and addresses from other lists, such as the main post office list or the Microsoft Network (MSN) list. In Exercise 19.5, we will add names from another address list.

EXERCISE 19.5

Adding Names to the Personal Address Book

1. From the Exchange client, select Tools ➤ Address Book.

2. In the Show Names drop-down list box, click on a different address book.

3. In that address list, click on a name that you want to add to the Personal Address Book.

4. Select File ➤ Add To Personal Address Book.

Creating a Personal Distribution List

You can also create a personal distribution list for Exchange. Follow the steps in Exercise 19.6 to create a distribution list.

EXERCISE 19.6

Creating a Personal Distribution List

1. From the Exchange client, select Tools ➤ Address Book.

2. Select File ➤ New Entry.

3. In the New Entry dialog box, double-click on Personal Distribution List.

4. Type in a name for your list.

5. Click on the Add/Remove Members button.

6. Select the names you want to include in your personal list, and then click on Members to add them to your list.

7. When you are finished, click on OK.

8. Click on OK again to add the new list to the Personal Address Book.

Using Multiple Address Lists

Another Address Book option is to use multiple address lists (one for work and one for the road, for example). You can control which address list will be checked first for entries that were added manually. Select Tools ➤ Options and click on the Addressing tab. To choose the search order of the address books, click on an address book in the box headed When sending mail, check names using these Address Lists in the following order. Then click on the up or down arrow to put the lists in the desired order.

Personal Folder Files

A Personal Folder file is a local file with a .PST extension for storing e-mail, faxes, and other information. This is the file used for storing sent and received messages in each user's universal Inbox and Outbox. Notice in the Exchange client that the hierarchy for the available folders begins with Personal Folders. Although Windows 95 includes one Personal Folder file for storing all your messages, multiple Personal Folders can be used for such things as storing archived mail. You can create a new Personal Folder and set up encryption and a password, as shown in Figure 19.9.

Exercise 19.7 will take you through the step for adding another Personal Folder.

FIGURE 19.9

Creating a Microsoft
Personal Folder

EXERCISE 19.7

Adding a Personal Folder File

1. From the Exchange client, select Tools ➤ Options.

2. Choose the Services tab and click on Add.

3. Select Personal Folders from the dialog box and click on OK.

4. In the Create/Open Personal Folder dialog box, enter a filename for the new folder and click on Open.

5. In the Create Microsoft Personal Folders dialog box, enter a name for the new folder (Figure 19.9). This is the name that will appear within the Inbox.

6. Choose the level of encryption and a password if desired.

7. Click on OK to create the new folder.

The encryption and password features are designed to enhance the privacy of your Personal Folders. However, if the password is lost or forgotten, the folder and its contents will be inaccessible.

Message Profiles

The Microsoft Exchange client maintains one or more separate message profiles for each user. The message profiles contain a list of the available services installed for use with the Exchange client. This determines what kinds of messages the client can send and receive. The initial profile, called MS Exchange Settings, is created when a user runs the Inbox Setup Wizard for the first time. Later, other profiles can be added for different service configurations.

With multiple profiles, you can accommodate different environments, such as those encountered when traveling. If a user has multiple services available, a profile will securely store the associated passwords so that the user can log on once and be connected to all available services. This also allows for multiple users sharing the same computer to send and receive mail, and each retain an individual set of preferences. If multiple users are sharing a computer, a user can select the profile he or she wants to use as the default when starting Windows 95, or the user can have Windows 95 prompt for a profile to use. Figure 19.10 shows these settings on the General tab of the Exchange Options dialog box.

FIGURE 19.10

Setting Microsoft
Exchange to prompt
for a profile

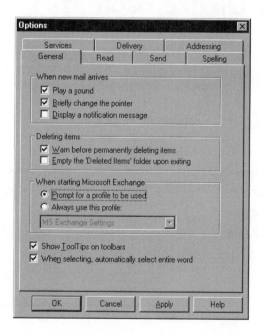

Exercise 19.8 will take you through the steps for creating a new profile and then configuring Exchange to prompt for which profile to use.

EXERCISE 19.8

Creating and Configuring Message Profiles

1. Go to Control Panel ➢ Mail and Fax.

2. Choose Show Profiles.

3. In the Microsoft Exchange Profiles dialog box, click on Add. This starts the Inbox Setup Wizard, which takes you through the steps to create the new profile (see Exercise 19.3).

4. From the Exchange client, select Tools ➢ Options.

5. In the General tab, click on Prompt for a profile to be used. Now you will be able to choose a profile each time the Exchange client is started.

Setting Up Microsoft Fax

Besides e-mail, the Microsoft Exchange client can handle sending and receiving faxes. All messages, whether they are e-mail or faxes, will appear in the Inbox. With Microsoft Fax, users can exchange rendered faxes and binary files. As with other Windows 95 services, however, to get this functionality, you must make sure that the necessary components (both hardware and software) have been installed and correctly configured.

Microsoft ✓ *Exam Objective*

Create, share, and monitor resources. Resources include:

- Remote
- Network printers
- Shared fax modem
- Unimodem/V

Installing and Configuring Microsoft Fax

The easiest way to install Microsoft Fax is to select it during Windows 95 setup. However, it can be installed later by using the Add/Remove Programs Control Panel.

Once Microsoft Fax has been installed, it still needs to be added as a service to the Exchange client to make it available for use. You configure the fax user information through the User tab of the Microsoft Fax Properties dialog box, as shown in Figure 19.11.

FIGURE 19.11

Entering Microsoft Fax user information

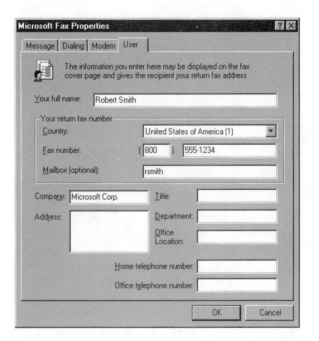

Exercise 19.9 will take you through the steps for installing Microsoft Fax and then adding the fax service to the Exchange client.

If you have not installed a modem yet, or want to use a different modem, go to Control Panel ➢ Modems and choose Add. This will start the Install New Modem Wizard. The new modem can be a locally installed modem or a shared modem on a network computer. See Chapter 17 for details on modem setup.

EXERCISE 19.9

Installing and Configuring Microsoft Fax

1. Go to Control Panel ➤ Add/Remove Programs.

2. Click on the Windows Setup tab.

3. In the Components box, click on the checkbox for Microsoft Fax (Microsoft Exchange will also be installed if it hasn't been yet). Then click on OK.

4. Go to Control Panel ➤ Mail and Fax and click on Add. (Or, from the Exchange client, select Tools ➤ Options, and on the Services tab, click on Add.)

5. In the Add Services to Profile dialog box, select Microsoft Fax and click on OK.

6. In the dialog box that asks if you want to enter your fax information now, shown below, click on Yes.

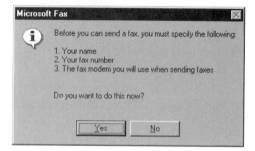

7. In the User tab, enter the appropriate information for Microsoft Fax configuration (Figure 19.11). Then click on OK.

The user information entered appears automatically on the cover page of your faxes sent from Microsoft Fax. You can change these properties from the Microsoft Exchange client by selecting Tools ➤ Microsoft Fax Tools and Options.

Sharing a Fax Modem

Users in the same workgroup can also share a fax modem on a computer. You set this up through the Modem tab of the Microsoft Fax Properties dialog box, as shown in Figure 19.12. Follow the steps in Exercise 19.10 to share a fax modem.

FIGURE 19.12

Sharing a fax modem for network fax service

EXERCISE 19.10

Sharing a Fax Modem

1. Go to Control Panel ≻ Mail and Fax.

2. Highlight Microsoft Fax and choose Properties.

3. In the Modem tab, click on the checkbox labeled Let other people on the network use my modem to send faxes (Figure 19.12).

4. In the Share name field, Microsoft Fax displays the name of the shared folder C:\Netfax, which is shared as Fax by default. If you want to change the name, click on the Properties button. In the shared directory's property sheet, change the name of the shared directory in the Share name box.

EXERCISE 19.10 (CONTINUED FROM PREVIOUS PAGE)

5. You can also set security options from the directory's property sheet. If you have User level security enabled, you can define which users will have access to the network fax service, as well as what their access rights are. If you have Share level security enabled, define whether a password is required to connect to the network fax service, and then give the password to users in the Windows 95 workgroup.

6. Click on OK in each dialog box when you are finished.

Sending a Fax

To send a fax, simply type your message and choose Microsoft Fax from the list of possible printers, as shown in Figure 19.13. This brings up the Compose New Fax dialog box, shown in Figure 19.14. Enter the fax recipient and number, and, optionally, a message. Clicking on the Next button brings up the Send Options for this Message dialog box, shown in Figure 19.15. Here you can set other options, including sending a cover page and specifying when the fax will be sent.

FIGURE 19.13

Choosing Microsoft Fax to send a fax

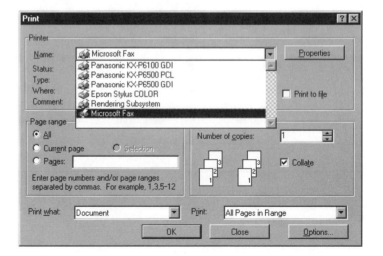

FIGURE 19.14

Entering a fax recipient's
name and number

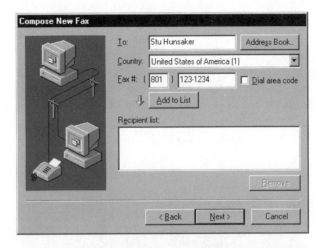

FIGURE 19.15

Choosing fax options

Summary

The Microsoft Exchange client is a MAPI-compliant, front-end application. It can be used to access any mail system that is also MAPI compliant by means of a MAPI service provider. It has a universal Inbox that can be used to read and manage e-mail and faxes.

MAPI is a messaging application standard developed by Microsoft to allow for interaction between an application and various message service providers. Windows 95 includes an e-mail post office, as well as client and fax software. Functionality is added to the Exchange client by adding and configuring MAPI services. In this chapter, we gave examples of adding the Internet Mail service and installing Microsoft Fax. We also took a look at some of the features of Exchange, including the Personal Address Book, Personal Folder, and message profiles.

Review Questions

1. What is MAPI?

    A. A set of common commands that allows programs to communicate with mail systems and other MAPI-compliant programs

    B. A component in Global Positioning Systems

    C. Microsoft Application Programming Instructions

    D. A standard for 3D graphics

2. What is a MAPI service provider?

    A. A method for connecting to the Internet

    B. An add-on component sold separately

    C. A component similar to a personal gateway that provides access to specified MAPI-compliant services

    D. A Microsoft Authorized Programming company

3. What must you do to access a new MAPI service?

    A. Belong to the group with rights to the service.

    B. Install the core MAPI services, which gives you access to all other MAPI services.

    C. Install a new service provider for each MAPI service.

    D. Do nothing, because by default you have access to all MAPI services.

4. Which of the following statements are true? (Select all that apply.)

    A. Post offices created with Windows 95 can easily communicate with each other.

    B. Windows Messaging is an add-on product that ships with the Microsoft Plus! pack.

    C. You can check services individually for new messages.

    D. You can connect to both Microsoft Mail and Windows 95 post offices using the default mail client.

5. How can you control the order in which address books will be searched for manual entries?

    A. Drag the icon for the address book to be searched first to the top of the Inbox.

    B. Type the order of the available address books in the message with the Subject: Address list order.

    C. In the Exchange client, select Tools ➤ Options ➤ Addressing tab, and set the order of the address books in the When sending mail... box.

    D. It's handled automatically; you can't configure it.

6. How can you secure your Personal Folder files?

    A. Store them only on a floppy disk.

    B. Put a password on them.

    C. You can't—everyone who can get to your computer can get to your personal folders.

    D. Save your folders with the name of Encrypted—this will automatically encrypt them.

7. What is the purpose of message profiles?

   A. To identify incoming message types

   B. To determine what service providers will be available in different environments

   C. To store message preferences

   D. For security use (encryption) only

8. What program would you use to create a new Windows 95 post office?

   A. Exchange Server running on Windows NT

   B. Windows Explorer

   C. PostOffice.exe

   D. The Microsoft Exchange client

9. Who can administer a post office?

   A. Any workgroup member with access to the post office share

   B. Only those workgroup members who are made members of the Admins group

   C. The user who created the post office

   D. Any user whose password is admin

10. How can you make a fax modem available to all of your users?

   A. You can't using Windows 95.

   B. Install an external modem with an automatic switch box, and cable all the users who want access to the box.

   C. Copy the files to be faxed to the computer with the modem, and then have that person do the faxing.

   D. Install the fax modem and then share it across the network.

11. How can you send a fax?

    A. Drag and drop a document onto a shortcut to your fax.

    B. Go to Accessories ➤ Compose New Fax.

    C. Print a document to the Fax printer driver.

    D. Use the Exchange client to send e-mail to a fax recipient.

20

Windows 95 and the Internet

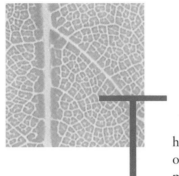

his chapter provides an overview of how Windows 95 can interoperate with the Internet. We will start with some general information about the Internet, including how to make Internet connections and the extension of Internet technology to intranets and extranets. Then we will describe the Internet-related features of Windows 95, with some details on using Internet Explorer and the Personal Web Server.

About the Internet

The Internet is defined as a matrix of networks that connects computers around the world. Since it began, the Internet has continued to grow rapidly. In the first months of 1995, access was available to approximately 180 countries, and there were around 30 million users. It is expected that about 100 million computers will be connected via the Internet by the twenty-first century, and even more via smaller intranets. The Internet now supports global information exchanges among individuals and organizations, as well as hardware innovations.

The development of the global World Wide Web has made the Internet accessible to everyone. The Web has generated many new and innovative businesses, which in turn have produced billions of dollars in new business and created many new jobs.

The Internet uses the TCP/IP protocol, which is required in order to connect to the Internet. The most popular types of servers on the Internet are World Wide Web (WWW) servers, which use the HTTP (Hypertext Transfer Protocol) type of packet, and FTP servers, which are servers that clients can copy files from. The HTTP language allows browsers, such as Internet Explorer (IE) or Netscape Navigator and Communicator, to interpret formatting commands in order to present data in a friendly, easy-to-read format.

The Web was developed by a University of Illinois student named Michael Andreesen. Michael and others began building the Web and a Web browser called Mosaic. When Michael graduated, he added functionality to his browser and created Netscape Navigator, one of the most popular Web browsers on the market.

Look at the Internet as if it were your local telephone system connecting all of your friends and family together. It allows all of you to simultaneously talk and exchange information and video pictures (with the appropriate hardware) globally. And to think that it was not so long ago that we marveled at the idea of Dick Tracy communicating with other people on a watch that could not only send voice, but could also send pictures!

With the use of the Internet, you now have the ability to communicate with virtually anyone, anytime, anywhere, all over the world. When you visit Microsoft's Web site (www.microsoft.com), for example, you are instantly transported into the center of what is happening at Microsoft. Whether your interests are the latest beta versions of your favorite software or the latest technical information about Windows NT and what's planned for the future, you will quickly realize you are in the right place.

You can keep up with business information, stock quotes, and even book your travel reservations—all from your personal computer over the Internet. Need to know what your bank balance is? Many banking institutions allow you to access your bank account and make transactions via the Internet.

The list of what you can do on the Internet is huge and continues to grow. Suffice it to say that as a systems engineer or administrator, you need to know about connecting to the Internet and other Internet-related functions.

Connecting to the Internet

Now that the price of hardware has dropped drastically, almost one out of every two homes in the United States has access to some kind of computer system—a laptop from work or a home system ranging from an older 386 to the new Pentium II machine. The only thing left to do is download the software (which is usually available free from the software giants such as Microsoft), find yourself an ISP (Internet service provider), and get online.

People usually connect to the Internet through an ISP, or through one of the major online services such as America Online, MSN (Microsoft Network), CompuServe, or Prodigy. There are advantages to either choice—an ISP may have faster Internet connections, but the online services are usually easier to use and may have more native content.

The nice thing about our free enterprise system is that anyone can start up and own a business; ISPs are no different. There are probably many to choose from in your area. Before you decide which one to use, you should do some investigation to find one that is reliable and meets your needs. For example, you should ask the following questions:

- How long has the ISP been in business?

- How many users does the ISP have per line and how many total lines?

- Does the ISP have a definite plan for expansion?

WARNING With the ever-growing popularity of the Internet, most ISPs tend to add more users than their hardware will handle. You might find yourself spending all your time getting busy tones and not being able to get to your e-mail.

Intranets and Extranets

With Internet technology abounding, companies can put into place their own internal, independent Internet, which is called an *intranet*. An intranet is a network of computers within the confines of an individual company, and it is meant to be private. This is in contrast to the Internet, which is designed to be public. The layout for an intranet is much the same as that of the Internet, but it may be applied on a much smaller scale. One advantage of an intranet is that it can be local as well as global, depending on the size of the individual company.

For years, companies have been trying to set up intercompany communications to share interdepartmental information, ranging from news about the company ball team to the latest financial statistics. Many different systems, some ingenious, have been put into place to facilitate this need to move large amounts of information throughout thousands of computers. The problem was that it required many different programs to make this happen. Some people run MS-DOS-based programs, some run Mac-based programs, and many run Windows-based software.

The great thing about an intranet is that you can use a Web browser, such as Internet Explorer, to cruise the internal network (the intranet) as well as the outside network (the Internet). Intranets can be designed so that workstations running any type of operating system can see the data exactly the same way. Macintosh, MS-DOS, Windows 3.*x*, Windows 95, Windows NT, and even Unix workstations can get to the company data.

As the popularity of the Internet has spread since early 1995, so has the popularity of intranets. One of the most important issues facing many companies is the problem of administration and management of their internal networks. By using the intranet philosophy, that job can be made much simpler. Network administrators do not need to spend all of their time helping users reset the Desktops and find their lost applications. They can have more time to do their necessary day-to-day tasks.

Extranets are the next generation in intranets. They are intranets that are shared among partner companies. Extranets promise increased communication and information flow among companies that work together. Just like intranets, extranets are designed to be private and for company (rather than personal) use.

Windows 95 Internet-Related Capabilities

You will find that Windows 95 has been designed with the Internet in mind. It allows even the most nontechnical people to fire up their computer and, within minutes, start cruising the Web.

Microsoft ✓ *Exam* *Objective*	**Configure a Windows 95 computer to access the Internet.**

Windows 95 includes, or has available as a free download, the following Internet-related pieces:

- TCP/IP support, including a DHCP client

- Dial-Up Networking

- Internet Explorer

- Internet Mail Client

- Internet News Reader

- Internet Meeting Software

- Personal Web Server

The communications features in Windows 95 are discussed in detail earlier in this book. See Chapter 10 for information about TCP/IP and DHCP. Chapters 17 through 19 cover other related topics, including modems, Dial-Up Networking, and Microsoft Exchange's e-mail facilities.

Windows 95 can not only be a client on the Internet by using Internet Explorer (or any other browser software), it can also be a server by installing Personal Web Server (PWS). PWS is available as a free download from Microsoft. The latest version of Windows 95 (OSR2*x*) even comes with Internet Explorer (IE) and PWS built into it.

Connecting to the Internet becomes a simple matter of adding the Dial-Up Networking component and creating a connection to your local ISP if you are using a modem, or using IE to directly connect to the Internet from work.

Internet Explorer

From the moment that you click on the Internet Explorer icon on your Desktop, its ease of operation is quite evident. IE is designed with the user in mind.

At the time this book was written, Internet Explorer 4.02 was the current version on the market. Many people still use the 3.02 version of Internet Explorer, however. Microsoft has announced Windows 95 OSR2.5, which will contain IE 4.02, among other things.

IE makes even the novice surfer feel right at home, with its built-in Help screens and its ability to remember all the Web sites you have visited. It allows you to create a "hot list" of all your favorite sites so that, the next time you log on, with a click on the Favorites button you can pick up right where you left off in your last session.

Installing Internet Explorer 4.0x

You may have to install IE 4.0 either to upgrade an existing version of IE or as part of a new installation of Windows 95.

If you install the latest version of Internet Explorer 4.*x*, you will be prompted to install either the standard or full installation of IE 4.*x* (Figure 20.1). The standard version includes the Web browser, Outlook Express, and various other multimedia enhancements, while the full version adds NetMeeting, FrontPage Express, NetShow, Web Publishing Wizard, and Microsoft Chat 2.0.

FIGURE 20.1

Choosing the Full installation of IE 4.0

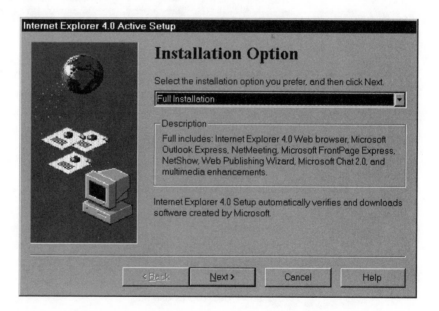

The next major decision you will have to make during the installation is whether you want Active Desktop installed (Figure 20.2).

FIGURE 20.2

Choosing to install Active
Desktop

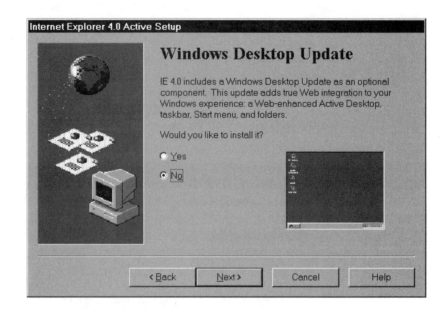

By installing the active desktop you dramatically change the way you work
with your computer—instead of the Explorer, you basically use IE to view and
manage your local hard drives as well as Internet resources. If you are very
comfortable with the current interface, I suggest you say no to the active desktop.
If you love the look of the Internet, have a powerful computer with lots of
spare CPU cycles and RAM, and wish that everything on your computer was
more consistent, go ahead and try the active desktop.

Installing the active desktop can consume up to 16MB more RAM than the
plain, default desktop. If your computer seems slow running Windows 95,
installing the active desktop will probably make it slower. Also, the active
desktop is most useful when you have a constant connection to the Internet.
Home computers that use a dial-up connection to the Internet may not find
the active desktop as useful.

The first time you run IE 4.x, it prompts you for connection setup options
via the Internet Connection Wizard (Figure 20.3). It can also be run manually
at a later time if you wish to set up a new connection, such as when you
switch ISPs. If you already have an Internet account set up, or if you are connecting to the Internet at work, you should probably choose I already have an
Internet account set up on this computer and do not want to change it.

FIGURE 20.3

Connection Setup
Options

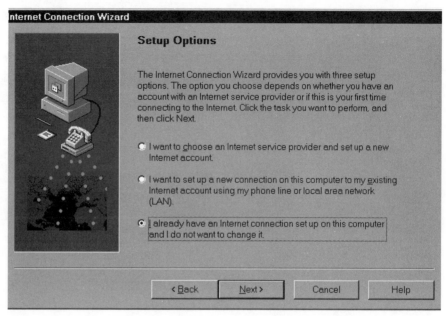

FIGURE 20.3

Connection Setup
Options

Internet Explorer will go to a startup page which will prompt for your time zone and zip code, after which you will go to a personalizable start page.

As you can see in Figure 20.4, IE has all the familiar pull-down menus that you are used to seeing in Microsoft products. It allows you to quickly access links and information that you can customize to fit your needs in the business, education, and just-plain-fun categories.

You can usually refer to WWW servers by their "friendly" name instead of their TCP/IP address because the domain name service (DNS) is resolving the name into the address. DNS works like a directory listing for phone numbers. A symptom of a misconfigured DNS is when you are unable to connect to sites using the friendly name, but can still connect using the actual TCP/IP address.

IE and E-mail

IE makes sending and receiving e-mail simple. It is not necessary to go through all the Microsoft Mail or Exchange settings within Windows 95. You just need to fill in a few simple pieces of information and Outlook Express can then send and receive e-mail. Note that Windows Messaging will be replaced after Windows 95—Outlook Express will become the primary mail client in later versions. Figure 20.5 shows the Internet Mail screen.

FIGURE 20.4

Internet Explorer 4.*x*
main screen

FIGURE 20.5

E-mail using IE 4.*x* and
Outlook Express

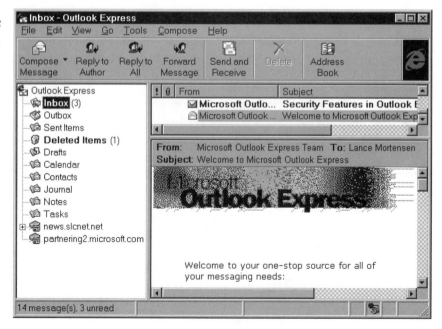

When you click on the Mail button, your Internet e-mail shows up. Through the Tools ➤ Options menu, you can select the exact setup you need. You can also choose whether to send your message immediately or save a batch of messages to send the next time you log on to your mail connection service.

Ratings and IE

A big concern of most parents is what their children will find while surfing on the Internet. IE has a built-in security feature that virtually eliminates this worry. When properly set up, IE will not allow users to venture into any area that they should not be in.

To enable the ratings system, click on the View menu and choose Internet Options. Then go to the Content tab, shown in Figure 20.6.

FIGURE 20.6

The Content tab of the Internet Explorer Internet Options dialog box

Click on the Enable Ratings button, and enter a password. Then click on the Settings button to set the scale of different items that can be viewed, such as Language, Nudity, Sex, or Violence, as shown in Figure 20.7.

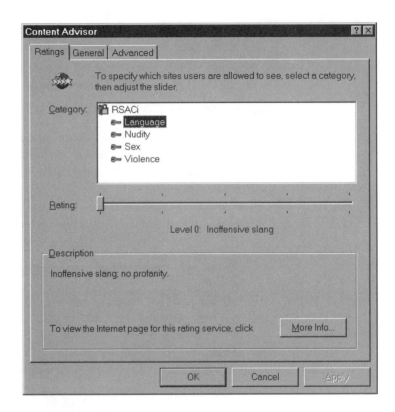

The General tab lets you specify whether IE will display pages that are not rated, and if the password can be entered to bypass the ratings system. This tab is shown in Figure 20.8.

Personal Web Server for Windows 95

If you are considering putting your own Web page on the World Wide Web, using Personal Web Server (PWS) is an alternative to paying someone to create your page for you. With a copy of PWS and Microsoft FrontPage or Microsoft Publisher, you can create your own professional-looking Web page documents.

FIGURE 20.8

The General tab of the
Internet Explorer Content
Advisor dialog box

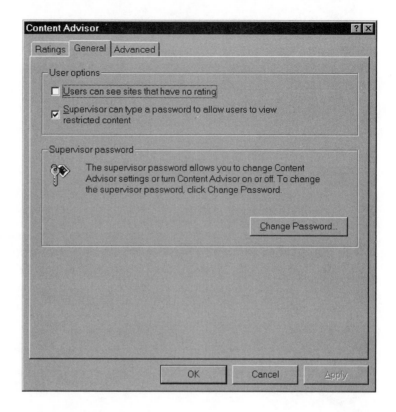

FIGURE 20.8

The General tab of the
Internet Explorer Content
Advisor dialog box

Installing PWS

Installing PWS into Windows 95 is quick and simple.

PWS version 4.0 has been released, and can be downloaded for no charge
from www.microsoft.com. PWS 4.0 also comes as part of the Windows NT
4.0 Option Pack CD-ROM.

Just run the PWS10a install file (or the setup program from other versions of
PWS). If you have OSR2, you can also install PWS as a service. If you install
Microsoft FrontPage, PWS will be installed automatically as one of the add-on
items. Whichever way you install it, with PWS your Windows 95 machine has
now been turned into a fully operational Web server.

Although Windows 95 can operate as an HTTP server, it was not designed for heavy-use, mission-critical production environments. For a heavy-use informational HTTP server, you should use Windows NT server, coupled with Internet Information Server (IIS). For a mission-critical electronic commerce HTTP server, Site Server for Windows NT should be used. Note that IIS is available for no additional charge, while Site Server is an add-on product for Windows NT, and thus costs extra. Details about IIS and Site Server can be found in *MCSE: IIS Study Guide* by Sybex.

Configuring PWS

You configure PWS by clicking on the PWS icon that is added to your Control Panel (for older versions of PWS) or by going to Start ➢ Programs ➢ Microsoft Personal Web Server ➢ Personal Web Manager (for version 4.0). This brings up the Personal Web Server Properties dialog box (for older versions) or the Personal Web Manager (for 4.0). Either program allows you to start, configure, and stop the HTTP service.

Please refer to *MCSE: IIS Study Guide* from Sybex Press for more information on installing, configuring, and administering HTTP servers.

Creating a Web Page

Perhaps the idea of creating a Web site that may be seen by millions of people makes you nervous. The plain and simple truth is that this should not be the case any longer. With Microsoft products, even a person with only basic word-processing skills can create professional-looking Web pages. You don't need to take an HTML programming course.

If you have Office 97, you basically have all you need. Word 97 allows you to create a document and insert all kinds of clip art, which can be supplied from its built-in clip art gallery. After you have finished, you simply save the document in the HTML format, and it is ready to go to your Web site.

The newest version of Excel is designed in the same way as all the new Office 97 products. Do you need to publish a spreadsheet on your Web site? Create it in Excel, save it as an HTML document, and you are ready to publish on your Web site.

All of the Office 97 products, even PowerPoint, will let you save and publish HTML documents. However, if you are still using the Office 95 product line, don't despair—there is an add-on for Word 7.0 that you can download from the Microsoft Web site. This add-on gives Word 7 the ability to edit and save HTML documents.

As mentioned earlier, Microsoft FrontPage and Microsoft Publisher are products that make it simple to create Web pages. Both are driven by built-in wizards that give you a multitude of choices for Web page design. You can instantly transform your screen into a Web page that compares to those created by even the most advanced HTML expert. With FrontPage Editor, you can open Web pages that were previously created by anyone, edit them, and add background sounds, pictures, videos, and even hyperlinks—just by a click of your mouse.

If you are into Web page development and are running your own Web site, Microsoft has come up with a great add-on for IE that lets you edit your Web pages. If you have a copy of Microsoft FrontPage, it automatically adds Edit to the menu bar. Simply go to your Web site and click on Edit. You can make live changes to your Web site and then save those changes without stopping to run additional software to download the changes to your site.

Summary

The Internet is a public network that offers information, entertainment, and commercial activities to anyone connected to the Internet.

The Internet consists of World Wide Web servers and clients running a browser. These communicate using the HTTP language, which piggybacks on the TCP/IP protocol.

Intranets are for internal company use only, while an extranet is designed for use by partner companies to exchange data.

Windows 95 can be both an HTTP server (when Personal Web Server is installed) and a client (when a browser such as Internet Explorer is used).

The latest version of both the PWS and IE are 4.0x, and can be downloaded for free from Microsoft's Web site (www.microsoft.com). Internet Explorer 4.x also includes an option to install Active Desktop, which makes your desktop, and all the resources on your computer, appear as Internet-type resources. If you install Active Desktop, Internet Explorer replaces My Computer and Explorer as the way you look at resources.

IIS (Internet Information Server) and Site Server are high-level HTTP server products, designed for mission-critical servers using Windows NT.

E-mail, newsgroup, and netmeeting client software is also freely available from Microsoft.

Publishing your own Web pages is relatively simple with today's software, as Office 97 and FrontPage 9.0*x* have been designed to help you easily save your work in HTML format, the format of the Internet.

Review Questions

1. What protocol is required in order to use Internet Explorer?

   A. TCP/IP

   B. IPX/SPX

   C. NetBEUI

   D. DLC

2. Can Windows 95 run Internet browsers?

   A. Yes, but only Microsoft's Internet Explorer.

   B. Yes, but only if you have the latest version of Internet Explorer.

   C. Yes, it can run any Internet browser written for Windows 95.

   D. No.

3. What is Active Desktop?

   A. It turns your computer into a Personal Web Server.

   B. It converts your desktop into an ActiveX object.

   C. It converts your desktop into HTTP objects, which means that IE is then used to manage local as well as Internet resources.

   D. It changes the Explorer to more of a file-manager type interface.

4. What is the language that WWW servers and browsers communicate in?

A. DLC

B. TCP/IP

C. FTP

D. HTTP

5. Which HTTP server would be the best fit for a small doctor's office intranet server?

A. Personal Web Server on Windows 95

B. IIS on Windows NT Server

C. Peer Web Services on Windows NT Workstation

D. Site Server on Windows NT Server

6. Which HTTP server should be used for a large, informational HTTP server?

A. Personal Web Server

B. IIS on Windows NT Server

C. Peer Web Services on Windows NT Workstation

D. Site Server on Windows NT Server

7. Which HTTP server should be used for a mission-critical electronic commerce server?

A. Personal Web Server

B. IIS on Windows NT Server

C. Peer Web Services on Windows NT Workstation

D. Site Server on Windows NT Server

8. If you are accessing the Internet using a dial-up connection, which protocol(s) is required? (Select all that apply.)

   A. NetBEUI

   B. IPX/SPX

   C. TCP/IP

   D. DLC

9. To access the Internet as a client you need to run which type of software?

   A. An HTTP Server

   B. An HTTP browser

   C. Explorer will work fine.

   D. My Computer will work fine.

10. To connect to an HTTP server running on a NetWare 3.12 server you will need which protocol(s)? (Select all that apply.)

   A. NetBEUI

   B. IPX/SPX

   C. TCP/IP

   D. DLC

11. If you can connect to a Unix HTTP server by address, but not by name, which software program is probably at fault?

   A. WINS

   B. DNS

   C. DHCP

   D. NETBIOS

12. Which type of computers can be HTTP servers? (Select all that apply.)

   A. Windows 95

   B. Windows NT

   C. NetWare

   D. Unix

13. If you can connect to an Internet server and can copy files, but cannot view any Web pages on that server, which type of Internet server did you connect to?

   A. DHCP

   B. DNS

   C. FTP

   D. HTTP

CHAPTER

21

Troubleshooting Windows 95

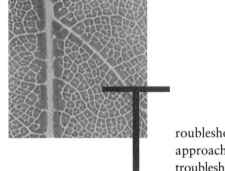

roubleshooting any problem is best done using a multifaceted approach. Most of this chapter focuses on a general approach to troubleshooting, including initial diagnosis of the problem, troubleshooting resources, and Windows 95 troubleshooting tools. It also offers suggestions for monitoring the system, auditing Windows 95, optimizing Windows 95 memory usage, and optimizing the swapfile. Finally, we will review some techniques for troubleshooting applications, printing, and a few other areas. For more details on troubleshooting particular situations, see the chapter in which the individual topic is covered. Of course, you should also check your online Help programs and documentation for specific troubleshooting steps.

Initial Diagnosis

There are several basic steps you can follow in troubleshooting Windows 95 problems:

- **Diagnose specific symptoms and factors:** Start by analyzing the symptoms to determine a strategy for finding a resolution. Here are some things you might consider:

  - Has the current configuration ever worked? If so, what changes have been made to the configuration?

  - Is it reproducible?

  - Is it specific to a certain system or application?

  - Does the problem occur when you boot in Safe mode?

  - Is there specific hardware involved?

  - Are any real-mode drivers or TSR (terminate-and-stay-resident) programs involved?

- **Find out if it is a common issue:** Has the problem been documented in any Help or any .TXT files? These types of files may note many common issues along with their solutions. Some good places to start are any README.TXT, README.1ST, and SETUP.TXT files. Other technical resources, some of which will be discussed later, can also provide information about common issues and resolutions.

- **Isolate error conditions:** Try to determine the specifics of a problem. Have you added anything to the CONFIG.SYS or AUTOEXEC.BAT file? If so, remove your changes and see if the issue continues. Have you loaded any new drivers? If so, replace them with the original drivers and retest. The more specific you can get in determining any changes made since the system worked the last time, the sooner you can solve the problem.

- **Consult technical support resources:** Use Help files and documentation whenever available. There are also many online areas available for seeking technical solutions. These include Internet newsgroups, World Wide Web pages, chat rooms, and BBS (bulletin board system) services.

Resources for Troubleshooting

Microsoft offers some very good resources to help you troubleshoot and fix problems that you may encounter with Windows 95. The following sections describe three of these resources: TechNet, Microsoft's Web site, and the Windows 95 Resource Kit.

Microsoft TechNet

Microsoft TechNet is a comprehensive worldwide information service designed for those who support or educate users, administer networks or databases, create automated solutions, and recommend or evaluate information-technology solutions.

For an annual TechNet subscription fee, subscribers receive two CDs per month containing Microsoft Knowledge Base, Resource Kits, up-to-date drivers, and other information. To subscribe in the United States and Canada, using your credit card, call (800) 344-2121, weekdays between 6:30 A.M. and

5:30 P.M. Pacific Standard Time. For international orders, call (303) 684-0914 (in the United States) for contacts in your area.

Microsoft's Web Site

Microsoft's Web page (www.microsoft.com) has many valuable resources, most of which are available for just the cost of your Internet connection. The Web pages are full of news articles, product releases, device drivers, and other valuable tools and information. The main Web page looks similar to Figure 21.1.

FIGURE 21.1

Microsoft's Web page

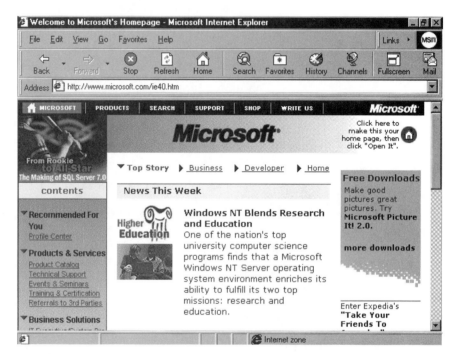

You can also find free software, demos, upgrades, and device drivers in the download section of Microsoft's Web site. You can get there from Microsoft's main Web page by clicking on the Free Downloads target area, or you can enter **www.microsoft.com/msdownload** in your Web browser's URL pane as shown in Figure 21.2. Figure 21.2 shows an example of the Free Downloads page. As its name suggests, all of the software on this page is free. You can download software from many different categories. These can then be used to update old drivers or programs, or to replace software that may have become corrupted, when diskettes are not available.

FIGURE 21.2

Downloading new
software from the
Web site

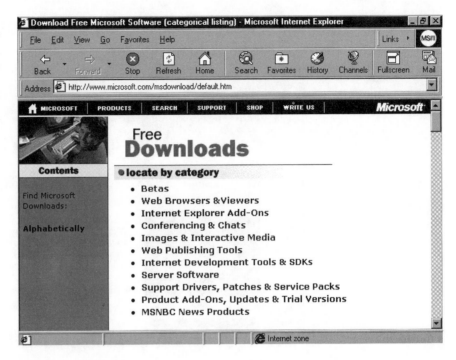

Another subpage contains links for contacting Microsoft Technical Support, as shown in Figure 21.3. You can reach this page by choosing the Support link at the top of the main page. From here, you have several options for contacting Microsoft to get answers to your questions or suggestions for solving problems.

There are many other options available from the Microsoft Web page. It is a fine resource to become acquainted with. The best way to do this is to actually visit the site and explore it yourself.

The Windows 95 Resource Kit

The *Windows 95 Resource Kit* (Microsoft Press) is written for administrators and MIS professionals, and provides the information required for rolling out, supporting, and understanding Windows 95. The Resource Kit is a technical resource that supplements the documentation included with the Windows 95 product.

FIGURE 21.3

The Microsoft Technical
Support page

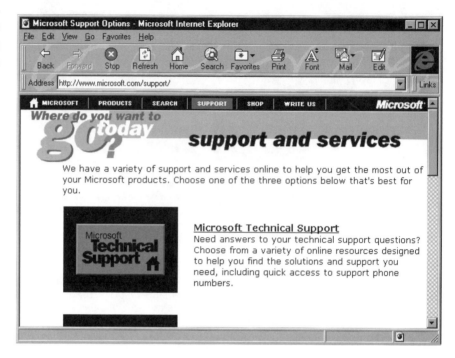

The Resource Kit covers the details of planning and implementing Windows 95. The process is broken down into main sections, each with several subsections:

1. Deployment Planning Guide

2. Installation

3. Networking

4. System Management

5. System Configuration

6. Communications

7. Windows 95 Reference

8. Appendices

The Resource Kit is available at all major bookstores. It is an excellent resource to keep around for reference and research. An online edition can be found on the Windows 95 CD-ROM in the Admin\Reskit folder, or downloaded from Microsoft's Web site.

Windows 95 Tools for Troubleshooting

Several troubleshooting utilities come with Windows 95. The following sections describe the main tools that are helpful in tracking down and solving problems: Microsoft Diagnostics, the Device Manager, Control Panel applets, and the System Configuration Editor.

Microsoft ✓ *Exam Objective*

Diagnose and resolve hardware device and device driver problems. Tools include:

- MSD
- Add/Remove Hardware Wizard

There are many different software tools available for troubleshooting. Many of these are shareware or freeware and are available from a variety of sources. For example, you can download a wide variety of troubleshooting tools from the Internet. For example, try www.winfiles.com.

Microsoft Diagnostics

Microsoft Diagnostics (MSD) is a hardware diagnostics program that runs from a command prompt. MSD doesn't come with Windows 95—you will only find it on computers that have been upgraded from MS-DOS. Normally, you would troubleshoot a suspected hardware problem by going into the Windows 95 Device Manager (described in the next section). But what if you have a hardware situation that prevents you from going into Windows 95? By running MSD.EXE, you can examine many different aspects of the system. Figure 21.4 shows MSD's main screen.

FIGURE 21.4

The MSD main screen

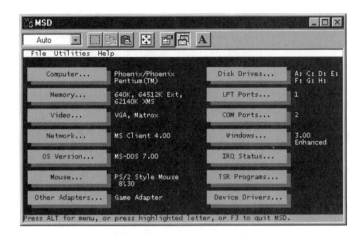

For best results MSD should be run from a command prompt, although it will also work from a DOS window.

MSD Buttons

Each button on the MSD screen gives you further information about the hardware in your system and how it is functioning:

- **Computer:** Shows basic system information, such as manufacturer, BIOS data, and bus type

- **Memory:** Displays a map of the upper memory area. This can be useful if you want to reconfigure upper memory blocks using EMM386.

- **Video:** Shows the manufacturer of your video card, as well as the current video mode

- **Network:** Displays information about your network configuration

- **OS Version:** Displays the version of the current operating system

- **Mouse:** Shows the type of mouse, IRQ used, real-mode driver version, and other settings

- **Other Adapters:** Shows the status of any installed game cards, SCSI cards, or other specialty cards

- **Disk Drives:** Shows which drive letters you currently have mapped, along with the size of and the space available on each drive

- **LPT Ports:** Shows the I/O address and status of all parallel ports attached to the system

- **COM Ports:** Shows the I/O address and status of all serial ports attached to the system

- **Windows:** Lists the Windows version loaded on the system, what mode it is in, where it is located, and any drivers that are running

- **IRQ Status:** Displays a list of IRQs and which devices, if any, are using them

- **TSR Programs:** Lists the name and memory address of any installed real-mode TSRs

- **Device Drivers:** Lists the names of any installed real-mode device drivers

MSD Menus

The File menu offers some different options:

- **Find File:** Allows you to search for a specific file by entering the filename

- **Print Report:** Sends a printout of the MSD information to the printer

- **Listed Files:** Choosing one of these files displays a text version of the file that can be read but not edited

You can exit MSD by choosing File ➤ Exit or by pressing F3.

The Utilities menu also has several useful commands:

- **Memory Block Display:** Displays a memory map that shows where each resident program is residing in RAM

- **Memory Browser:** Lets you look at different areas of the memory map, such as ROM BIOS or Video ROM BIOS

- **Insert Command:** Displays common commands that can be added to the CONFIG.SYS and AUTOEXEC.BAT files

- **Test Printer:** Sends a test page to your printer

- **Black & White:** Toggles the screen display between black and white and color. The F5 key will do this as well.

The Help menu simply gives you the About information for MSD.

The Device Manager

The Device Manager provides a graphical representation of devices connected to the system. From here, you can check the properties of different devices to determine whether they are functioning properly. You can also discover what may be wrong with devices that are not working as they should. To access the Device Manager, right-click on the My Computer icon on the Desktop or go to the System Control Panel.

When you start up the Device Manager on a system with no hardware problems and select the View Devices by Type button, it looks something like the dialog box shown in Figure 21.5. All the main hardware devices are listed, each on a single line.

FIGURE 21.5

The Device Manager

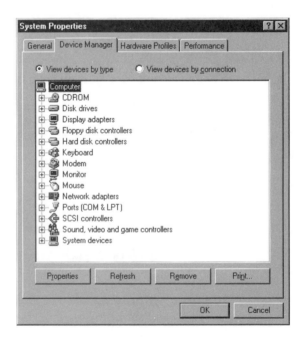

To look at specific devices listed under each main category, click on the plus sign (+) to the left of the heading. Each main category heading now lists the individual devices below it. By double-clicking on any specific device, or highlighting it and pressing the Enter key, you can see the properties for that device. Figure 21.6 shows an example of the property sheet for a Sound Blaster device.

FIGURE 21.6

Properties of a device

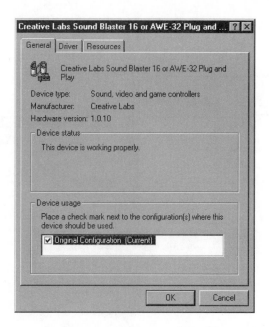

You can obtain the following information from a device's property sheet:

- Device type

- Manufacturer

- Hardware version

- Supporting drivers installed

- Whether or not the installed drivers are functioning properly

- Resources used by the device, including any conflicts that might be present

Clicking on the View devices by connection button on the main Device Manager screen (Figure 21.5) changes the view to show items listed under what they are connected to. For example, your CD-ROM will be listed under your sound card if it is using the sound card for its connection.

When you boot your system in Safe mode (press F5 after the "Starting Windows 95" message, or press F8 and choose Safe Mode from the Startup menu), you may see devices listed more than once, as in the example shown in Figure 21.7. This is a fairly common occurrence, but can cause problems. For this reason, when you are working in Device Manager after a Safe mode boot, you should always check for multiple instances of any device, and remove any that you find. Even if this is not the cause of the current problem, it may save you further trouble.

FIGURE 21.7

Devices listed twice by
Device Manager after a
Safe mode boot

 Safe mode is a way of booting Windows 95 without the registry, CONFIG .SYS, AUTOEXEC.BAT, and any protected-mode drivers. In this mode, you can work with system files, Device Manager, or anything else you suspect might be causing problems. See Chapter 3 for more information about Safe mode and other startup options.

Other Control Panel Tools

As in previous versions of Windows, you can configure components of the system using the Control Panel. The Windows 95 version, however, is much more powerful than the one in previous versions.

The System Control Panel's Device Manager was explained in the previous section. Here are some explanations of other Control Panel applets that can be useful for problem solving:

- **Add New Hardware:** Used to add new hardware to the system. This option is not available during a Safe mode boot. (See Chapter 5 for details.)

- **Add/Remove Programs:** Used to add or remove software from the system and create a Startup disk. Only 32-bit applications will be registered in the remove section. (See Chapter 6 for information about creating a Startup disk and Appendix B for information about adding and removing software.)

- **Display:** Used to change the display settings, including resolution and number of colors displayed. This can also be accessed by right-clicking on an empty area of the Desktop. (See Chapter 5 for details.)

- **Modems:** Used to add or remove modems and perform modem diagnostics. (See Chapter 17 for details.)

The System Configuration Editor

The System Configuration Editor (SYSEDIT.COM) allows you to edit multiple Windows and system files without needing to open and close each one separately. This is the same as in previous versions of Windows, except with a Windows 95 look, as shown in Figure 21.8.

In the System Configuration Editor, you can easily add or remove lines from files to assist in the troubleshooting process.

Monitoring Windows 95

In order to troubleshoot your system effectively, you need to know what its "normal" operation is. By monitoring your system on a regular basis, you can see how the system is working when things are going smoothly and spot possible problem areas before they become critical conditions.

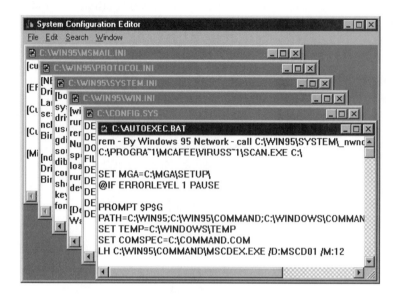

FIGURE 21.8

The System
Configuration Editor
displays multiple files.

Windows 95 provides a powerful tool that you can use to monitor the system: the System Monitor. If you are using Windows 95 as a server, you can monitor its operations with the Net Watcher tool.

The System Monitor

As you learned in Chapter 4, the System Monitor is a tool for tracking memory and other system resources for usage and possible problems. The following sections examine different ways to use the System Monitor's options in the file system, IPX/SPX compatible protocol, Kernel, Memory Manager, Microsoft Client for NetWare Networks, and Microsoft Client for Microsoft Networks categories. The System Monitor options vary depending on what you have installed on the system, so you may not see all of the options described here.

File System

Choose Edit ➤ Add Item ➤ File System to access options for viewing items associated with the file system and how it is being used.

Microsoft ✓ ***Exam*** ***Objective*** | **Diagnose and resolve file system problems.**

You can monitor the following items:

- **Bytes read/second:** The number of bytes read from the file system each second

- **Bytes written/second:** The number of bytes written by the file system each second

- **Dirty data:** The number of bytes waiting to be written to the disk. Dirty data is stored in cache blocks, so the number reported might be larger than the actual number of bytes waiting.

- **Reads/second:** The number of read operations delivered to the file system each second

- **Writes/second:** The number of write operations delivered to the file system each second

IPX/SPX Compatible Protocol

If you are using the IPX/SPX compatible protocol, choose Edit ➢ Add Item ➢ IPX/SPX Compatible Protocol to view details of IPX/SPX activities. You can monitor the following items:

- **IPX packets lost/second:** The number of IPX packets received by the computer from an IPX network that were ignored

- **IPX packets received/second:** The number of packets received by the computer from an IPX network each second

- **IPX packets sent/second:** The number of packets sent by the computer to an IPX network each second

- **Open sockets:** The number of free sockets

- **Routing Table entries:** The number of IPX internetworking routes known

- **SAP Table entries:** The number of service advertisements known

- **SPX packets received/second:** The number of packets received by the computer from an SPX network each second

- **SPX packets sent/second:** The number of packets sent by the computer to an SPX network each second

Kernel

Choose Edit ➤ Add Item ➤ Kernel to view details of Kernel activities. You can monitor the following items:

- **Processor Usage:** The approximate percentage of time that the processor is busy. Monitoring this setting will increase processor usage slightly.

- **Threads:** The current number of threads present in the system

- **Virtual Machines:** The current number of virtual machines present in the system

Memory Manager

Choose Edit ➤ Add Item ➤ Memory Manager to view memory details. Here are the memory-related items you can monitor:

- **Allocated memory:** The total number of bytes allocated to applications and system processes. This is the sum of the Other memory and Swapfile memory settings.

- **Discards:** The number of pages discarded from memory per second. These pages are discarded rather than swapped because their data already exists on the hard drive and the data hasn't changed.

- **Disk cache size:** The current size of the disk cache in bytes

- **Free memory:** The total amount of free physical RAM in bytes. This number is not related to Allocated memory. If this value is zero, memory can still be allocated, depending on the free disk space available on the drive that contains the swapfile.

- **Instance faults:** The number of instance faults per second

- **Locked memory:** The amount of memory, in bytes, that is locked by the system, or an application, and cannot be swapped out

- **Maximum disk cache size:** The largest possible disk cache size, in bytes

- **Minimum disk cache size:** The smallest possible disk cache size, in bytes

- **Other memory:** The amount of allocated memory, in bytes, that cannot be stored in the swapfile. This includes code from Win32 DLLs and executable files, memory-mapped files, memory that cannot be paged, and disk cache pages.

- **Page faults:** The number of page faults per second

- **Page-ins:** The number of pages swapped from the page file to physical RAM per second

- **Page-outs:** The number of pages swapped from physical RAM to the page file per second

- **Swapfile defective:** The number of defective bytes in the swapfile. These are caused by bad sectors on the hard drive.

- **Swapfile in use:** The number of bytes currently being used by the swapfile

- **Swapfile size:** The current size of the swapfile, in bytes

- **Swappable memory:** The number of bytes allocated from the swapfile. This includes locked pages.

Microsoft Client for NetWare Networks

If the machine has the Microsoft Client for NetWare Networks installed, choose Edit ➤ Add Item ➤ Microsoft Client for NetWare Networks to view details about the NetWare network connection. You can monitor the following items:

- **BURST packets dropped:** The number of burst packets from this computer lost in transit

- **Burst receive gap time:** Interpacket gap for incoming traffic, in microseconds

- **Burst send gap time:** Interpacket gap for outgoing traffic, in microseconds

- **Bytes in cache:** The amount of data, in bytes, that is currently cached by the redirector

- **Bytes read/second:** Bytes read from the redirector per second

- **Bytes written/second:** Bytes written to the redirector per second

- **Dirty bytes in cache:** The amount of dirty data, in bytes, that is currently cached by the redirector and is waiting to be written

- **NCP packets dropped:** The number of regular NCP packets lost in transit

- **Requests pending:** The number of requests that are waiting to be processed by the server

Microsoft Network Client

If the machine has the Microsoft Client for Microsoft Networks installed, choose Edit ➤ Add Item ➤ Microsoft Network Client to view details about the Microsoft network connection. You can monitor the following items:

- **Bytes read/second:** The number of bytes read from the redirector each second

- **Bytes written/second:** The number of bytes written to the redirector each second

- **Number of nets:** The number of networks currently running

- **Open files:** The number of open files on the network

- **Resources:** The number of resources used

- **Sessions:** The number of sessions running

- **Transactions/second:** The number of SMB transactions managed by the redirector each second

Microsoft Network Server

If the machine has file and printer sharing installed for a Microsoft or NetWare network, choose Edit ➤ Add Item ➤ Microsoft Network Server to view details about the sharing connection. You can monitor the following items:

- **Buffers:** The number of buffers used by the server

- **Bytes read/second:** The total number of bytes read from a disk each second

- **Bytes written/second:** The total number of bytes written to a disk each second

- **Bytes/second:** The total number of bytes read from and written to a disk each second

- **Memory:** The total amount of memory used by the server

- **Server threads:** The current number of threads used by the server

Microsoft Network Monitor Performance Data

If the machine is a Microsoft server on a network, choose Edit ➢ Add Item ➢ Microsoft Network Monitor Performance Data to view details about its performance. You can monitor the following items:

- **Mediatype broadcasts/sec:** Broadcast frames transmitted over the network adapter each second

- **Mediatype bytes/sec:** Total number of bytes transmitted over the network adapter each second

- **Mediatype frames/sec:** The total number of frames transmitted over the network adapter each second

- **Mediatype multicasts/sec:** The total number of multicast frames transmitted over the network adapter each second

The System Monitor can also be used over a network to monitor remote systems, if proper access privileges are present, as explained in Chapter 16. You can run multiple instances side by side to compare the performance of different computers.

To use the Remote System Monitor, the Microsoft Remote Registry Service must be installed and enabled. See Chapter 16 for details.

The Net Watcher

As you learned in Chapter 16, the Windows 95 Net Watcher tool allows you to create, control, and monitor remote shared resources. It can be useful for managing peer sharing in Windows 95.

Microsoft Exam Objective

Diagnose and resolve resource access problems.

Net Watcher has easy-to-use icons that give you several options:

- Add a shared resource or stop sharing a resource, on a local or remote system

- Show all shared resources, connected users, and open files

- Close any files that users have open

- Disconnect a user

- Change the properties of a remote shared folder, including its share name and the access rights to the folder

- For shared folder(s) on any remote system, find out which users are connected to the shared resource, how long they've been connected, and which files they have open

File and printer sharing services must be installed and enabled to use Net Watcher. See Chapter 16 for details.

Auditing Windows 95 with Log Files

Windows 95 has the ability to log certain items to ASCII text files. These files can be extremely useful in tracking down elusive problems. The available log files are described in the following sections.

Detailed information about interpreting the Windows 95 log files, including individual line-by-line breakdowns, is available in the Windows 95 Resource Kit.

The Boot Log

BOOTLOG.TXT is a text file that is automatically created during the first boot sequence following a successful setup. After that, Windows 95 creates this file when you choose the Logged option from the Startup menu (press F8 after the "Starting Windows 95" message to see this menu).

This log records all devices and drivers loaded by the system. You can use this information to diagnose driver load failures, by determining whether or not the driver was found and if there were driver initialization failures. For more information, see Chapter 3.

The Hardware-Detection Logs

DETLOG.TXT is a text file that contains a record of whether or not specific hardware devices were detected and identifies the parameters for each specific device. When you run the Windows 95 Setup program, a hardware-detection procedure is performed on the system. This hardware detection also takes place when you run the Add New Hardware Wizard. During this detection, DETLOG.TXT is created as each piece of hardware is successfully detected.

The Windows 95 file that keeps track of any hardware-detection failures is DETCRASH.LOG. This is not an ASCII file and can be read only by Windows. If a piece of hardware crashes the detection process, a failure code is added to the file. The next time that the hardware detection is run, the file is checked, and the hardware that caused the failure is ignored. This process is continued until all hardware is either successfully detected and properly installed or ignored and bypassed. Once a completely successful detection is completed, the DETCRASH.LOG file is deleted.

By using a text editor, you can view DETLOG.TXT and determine which hardware was not successfully detected, and you can attempt to manually correct the problem. For more information, see Chapter 2.

The Setup Log

When you run the Windows 95 Setup program, the SETUPLOG.TXT file is created to document all successes and failures during the setup process. Similar to the procedure used during hardware detection, Windows finds where the process was interrupted, skips the step, and attempts to continue.

By using a text editor, you can review this text file to determine what errors occurred if Setup fails prior to hardware detection. See Chapter 2 for more details.

The Network Log

NETLOG.TXT is a text file similar to SETUPLOG.TXT and DETLOG.TXT. This log documents successes and failures during network component detection and installation. Like the other text file logs, NETLOG.TXT can be viewed with any text editor. Check this file if errors occur in your network setup procedures.

Optimizing Windows 95 Memory Usage

Sometimes the problems with Windows 95 aren't so much fatal errors as they are slow performance, which could be caused by inefficient use of memory. Here are some ways that you can optimize memory usage:

- **Have only necessary programs open:** Each program you have open uses some physical RAM. By increasing the number of applications that you have open, you force Windows 95 to use paging more frequently and hinder system performance.

- **Minimize network services:** Network clients and protocols use memory even when you are not logged in to the network. By only loading the client you are currently using, and only loading necessary protocols, system performance can be improved.

- **Make wise use of system resources:** System resource heaps exist in memory. By keeping resources to a minimum, you can increase memory performance. Here are some tips for reducing the amount of system resources in use:

  - Close unnecessary applications.

  - Close unnecessary files within an application.

  - Run DOS applications at full screen rather than in a window.

  - Turn off unused application objects, such as toolbars, rulers, and status bars.

  - If you need multiple applications open, minimize them while they are not in use.

  - Turn off appearance features, such as themes or wallpaper.

- **Enable caching:** The system cache plays a very important part in system performance. Check your system BIOS to ensure that caching is properly enabled. Depending on the BIOS on your system, the cache may be called L1 cache, internal cache (built into the processor), external cache (on the motherboard), or system memory cache.

- **Empty the clipboard:** Whenever you cut or copy text or an object, it is placed in the clipboard for retrieval at a later time. When large items are left in the clipboard, they use up resources. Empty the clipboard by copying something small to overwrite the large item, or open the Clipboard Viewer and delete the contents. (The Clipboard Viewer is an accessory that you can add to Windows 95; see Appendix B.)

- **Reboot the system:** Although Windows 95 tries to free up system resources as it can, not all applications will let go of resources, even after they have been closed. These resources should be automatically released back to Windows, but this doesn't always happen. By rebooting the system, these resources can be reclaimed by the system.

- **Add more memory:** The easiest way to increase the available memory in a system is to add more memory. Windows 95 will take advantage of any and all memory installed in the system. Consult your computer manufacturer for information about the correct type of memory for your system.

Optimizing the Swapfile

Windows 95 creates a special file on the hard drive called a *virtual-memory swapfile* or *paging file*. This file uses the space on the hard drive as virtual RAM. Some of the program code and other information is kept in physical RAM, while other information is swapped in virtual memory. When the information is needed, it is pulled back into RAM and information no longer being used is transferred to the swapfile. The only noticeable indication that this process is taking place is that the hard drive light is flashing. This allows the system to run more applications than would normally be allowed by the RAM.

In Windows 3.*x*, the swapfile could be temporary or permanent, but it required contiguous (nonfragmented) space on the hard drive. In Windows 95, the swapfile is dynamic. This means that it can shrink or grow as needed by the current applications. Fragmentation of the swapfile is no longer an issue.

You can change the virtual memory settings from the Performance tab of the System Control Panel. Clicking on the Virtual Memory button brings up the Virtual Memory dialog box. As explained in Chapter 4, it's best to let Windows manage the swapfile settings for you, but you can make changes if necessary. There are some things to keep in mind when making changes to the swapfile settings:

- **Use the hard disk with the most free space:** The more space available on the drive, the better the swapfile will perform. This will allow the file to grow as required by the current applications. Putting the swapfile on a drive with limited space can cause swapfile problems and lead to other abnormalities.

- **Use the drive with the fastest access:** In addition to space, you want the swapfile to be on a drive with fast access time. This allows the system to page-swap information from RAM to virtual memory and back in less time, so that your system performs faster and better.

- **Use the System Monitor to track the swapfile size:** As explained earlier in this chapter, one of the items you can view in the System Monitor is the size of the Swapfile (choose Edit ➤ Add Item ➤ Memory Manager). When this approaches the size of the amount of the free space on the drive, you will probably want to free up some space on the drive to allow the swapfile complete flexibility (room to grow).

- **Defragment the drive containing the swapfile:** Keep the drive with the swapfile defragmented to allow the swapfile to be as contiguous as possible. Although Windows 95 does not require a contiguous block on the drive, having an area available helps optimize performance.

- **Do not use a compressed drive:** Putting the swapfile on a compressed drive forces the information being swapped in and out to be compressed and uncompressed, slowing system performance.

- **Do not use a network drive:** As with a compressed drive, on a network drive the information being swapped must travel a greater distance, over hardware with a slower throughput, which hinders system performance.

WARNING Do **not** disable virtual memory. Doing this will result in drastic adverse effects on Windows 95 performance. If you are running out of disk space, moving or deleting files is a much better course of action.

Troubleshooting Applications

Application problems may occur during or after installation, or while you are using the application. The following sections describe some techniques for troubleshooting various application problems.

The Task Manager

In previous versions of MS-DOS, the Ctrl+Alt+Del keyboard combination would reboot the system in the event of a lockup or program crash. In earlier versions of Windows, pressing these keys would give you the opportunity to close the application that had stopped responding if you were in that application when it crashed; otherwise, your only option was to reboot, just like with DOS.

In Windows 95, Ctrl+Alt+Del brings up the Task Manager. Windows 3.*x* also had the Task Manager, which you could use to switch between applications or close applications, but only if the system was not locked up. Now you can get to it even in the event of a lockup. The Task Manager will look something like Figure 21.9 on a typical system.

The Task Manager shows which applications are open on the system and which, if any, have stopped responding. In the event that an application has stopped responding, it will have the words "Not Responding" in brackets just to the right of the application name.

One option is simply to close the application that has stopped responding. You can also try closing another application, even though it has not stopped responding, in an attempt to bring back the application that has stopped. This capability can be very helpful when you have several applications open with unsaved information. By closing unnecessary applications, or those that don't require saving, you can often avoid losing information that would have been lost in earlier operating systems.

FIGURE 21.9

The Windows 95
Task Manager

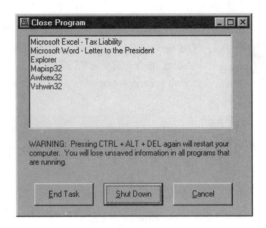

The Task Manager can be useful at any point during installation or normal operation of an application or Windows 95 itself.

Reboot or Reinstall

If problems persist, such as lockups or crashes, they can often be corrected by simply rebooting the system. This allows memory components to rearrange, applications to reload, and resources to refresh. If this does not correct the problem, it is probably either the application or Windows 95 itself. You may need to reinstall the application or Windows 95.

Some problems with an application's installation may not become apparent until the application is used regularly. By reinstalling the application, any errors that occurred can be corrected. This procedure can also be used with Windows 95 itself if a common situation occurs in several different applications.

Troubleshooting Printing

One of the most frustrating problems is a printer that just won't print. Windows 95 has some built-in features that can help you with printer problems, and there are others options you can try as well. Here, we cover some of the most common problems and the Windows 95 Print Troubleshooter tool. See Chapter 13 for more details about Windows 95 printing.

Diagnose and resolve printing problems.

Printer Installation Problems

Here are some tips for troubleshooting problems with installing printers:

- **No printers are listed in the Printer box:** If nothing appears in the dialog box when you are trying to install a printer, you should verify that the printer INF file exists. The PRTUPD.INF is the built-in list of printer manufacturers and models. You may also need an updated INF file from your printer's manufacturer.

- **Setup cannot find the printer driver files:** The Add Printer Wizard will try to pull the required driver files from the Windows 95 default installation drive and directory if they are not found from an updated file. If these files cannot be found, you will be prompted to enter a path to their location. You can either enter the path to the required files or use the Browse button to search for them.

- **Copy errors occur during printer installation:** If an error occurs while the system is trying to copy files during the installation process, a dialog box is displayed with the expected source and destination paths and file-names that were being copied when the error occurred. Verify the proper location of the files and retry the installation.

Printing Problems

There are several things you can try to resolve problems with printing. The following sections provide suggestions for troubleshooting some of the most common problems.

The Printer Will Not Print

If the printer simply won't print, here are some ways to discover what the problem is:

- Check to see that the printer is turned on, it is online, and all cables are connected correctly.

- Check to see that the printer has paper and is not jammed.

- Try turning the printer off, waiting a few seconds, and turning it back on. This will clear the printer memory buffer.

- Try printing to a file and copying the file to the printer port (local printers only).

- Try printing directly to a port without spooling. If this works, you may have run out of disk space on the drive that handles print spooling.

- Delete the printer and reinstall it in the Printers folder.

Printing Is Delayed or Slow

Here are some techniques for troubleshooting delayed or slow printing problems:

- Check to see that spooling is enabled and is spooling to EMF files.

- Restart in Safe mode and try printing.

- Make sure you have plenty of room on the drive for spooling.

- Run Disk Defragmenter to create contiguous space on the drive for spooling.

- Check for available space on the disk for temporary files.

- Check for low system resources.

- Delete and reinstall the printer driver in the Printers folder.

- Make sure that TrueType fonts are being sent as outlines and not as bitmaps (check the Fonts tab of the printer's property sheet).

Print Jobs Are Garbled or Missing Data

When your print jobs are not printing correctly, you can try the following solutions:

- Restart in Safe mode and try printing.

- There may not be enough printer memory. Try using a lower resolution or increasing memory.

- Try spooling in RAW format rather than EMF format.

- If available, try printing with a PostScript driver. If this corrects the problem, you probably have a corrupted UNIDRV.DLL. This file can be extracted from WIN95_09.CAB or from the Windows 95 CD-ROM.

- If PostScript fails, there is either a problem with the application or the GDI. Try printing from another application.

- Try printing one job at a time to avoid jobs conflicting.

Only Partial Pages Are Printed

When only part of the page is being printed, try the following techniques:

- There may not be enough printer memory. Try printing at a lower resolution or adding more memory.

- If it is a graphic, try printing it from a different document or application.

- Make sure that the font used is valid and correctly installed.

- Check the printable region of the printer by printing a test page.

- Try printing from a different document or application with the same font.

- Try printing from the same document or application with a different font.

- Enable Print TrueType as Graphics (an option on the Fonts tab of the printer's property sheet).

- Simplify the page by reducing the number of graphics or fonts.

The Print Troubleshooter

Windows 95 has a tool built in for dealing with printer trouble, called the Print Troubleshooter. You access it by selecting Start ➤ Help. When the Help dialog box appears, open the Troubleshooting book, and choose If You Have Trouble Printing. This brings up the Print Troubleshooter, as shown in Figure 21.10. You will be guided through a series of questions, each answer leading to another set of questions, that will narrow down the problem and help you find a solution.

FIGURE 21.10

The Print Troubleshooter
in Windows Help

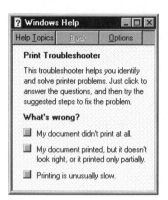

There is also an Enhanced Print Troubleshooter (EPTS) available on the Windows 95 CD-ROM. It is located in the Other\Misc\Epts folder. This is a very in-depth printer help guide. You should consult the online documentation on the Windows 95 CD-ROM before using EPTS.

Other Troubleshooting Tips

The following are some other areas in which you may experience problems:

- **The boot process:** If the system hangs during booting, try using either the Safe mode or Step-by-Step Confirmation option from the Startup menu. This will help you to determine whether device drivers, hardware, or conflicts are causing the problem. The Windows 95 Startup disk can also be useful in troubleshooting a problem with the boot process. Try running FDISK /MBR at a command prompt from your Windows 95 Startup disk if you suspect you have a boot virus. See Chapter 3 for details about the Startup menu options, the Startup (emergency boot) disk, and other techniques for troubleshooting booting problems.

- **The file system:** The Performance tab of the System Control Panel has several options for configuring the file system which can be helpful in troubleshooting problems. You can also access these options by right-clicking on the My Computer icon on the Desktop. See Chapter 8 for details about these options and other techniques for troubleshooting disk-related problems.

- **Dial-up networking:** The Help system has a guide for troubleshooting network problems, similar to the Print Troubleshooter. Select Start ➢ Help ➢ Troubleshooting ➢ If you have trouble using Dial-Up Networking to start this online aid, which walks you through a series of questions to narrow down, and solve, different situations. See Chapters 17 and 18 for more information about troubleshooting modems and other problems related to dial-up connections.

Summary

As a systems engineer or administrator, it is essential that you know how to troubleshoot Windows 95 effectively. This chapter explained the general approach to troubleshooting and offered suggestions for solving common problems.

We began with the basics of diagnosing the problem, finding troubleshooting resources, and using the Windows 95 troubleshooting tools. Next, we covered ways to avoid system problems, including monitoring the system, auditing Windows 95, optimizing Windows 95 memory usage, and optimizing the swapfile. Then we talked about troubleshooting problems with applications, printing, the boot process, the file system, and dial-up networking. You can find more information about troubleshooting specific problems in this book's previous chapters.

Review Questions

1. What is the first step in troubleshooting?

   A. Isolate error conditions.

   B. Find out if it is a common issue.

   C. Diagnose specific symptoms.

   D. Consult technical support resources.

2. What is the quickest form of electronic help in Windows 95?

   A. The Internet

   B. Online Help files

   C. BBS services

   D. 1-900 help lines

3. Which application can be helpful if you can't get into Windows?

   A. Device Manager

   B. Control Panel

   C. MSD

   D. TechNet

4. Which files are bypassed during a Safe mode boot?

   A. CONFIG.SYS, AUTOEXEC.BAT, and the Startup group

   B. The registry and the Startup group

   C. The registry, SYSTEM.INI, and WIN.INI

   D. CONFIG.SYS, AUTOEXEC.BAT, and the registry

5. Which application allows you to monitor a variety of system resources?

   A. Net Watcher

   B. FreeCell

   C. System Monitor

   D. Remote Registry Service

6. Which application allows you to monitor a variety of network information?

   A. Net Watcher

   B. FreeCell

   C. System Monitor

   D. Remote Registry Service

7. Which log file tracks items during the boot process?

   A. BOOTLOG.TXT

   B. DETCRASH.LOG

   C. NETLOG.TXT

   D. SETUPLOG.TXT

8. Which ASCII log files are created during Windows 95 setup?

   A. BOOTLOG.TXT

   B. DETLOG.TXT

   C. SETUPLOG.TXT

   D. All of the above

9. Which of the following describes the swapfile in Windows 95?

   A. Permanent

   B. Dynamic

   C. Fixed in size

   D. None of the above

10. Which hard drive attribute(s) directly affect swapfile performance?

  A. Access time

  B. Free space

  C. Manufacturer

  D. A and B

11. Which of the following will have the most adverse effect on system performance?

  A. Ten or more applications running

  B. Disabling the swapfile

  C. Having a dual-boot configuration

  D. Installing more than two printers

12. What will pressing Ctrl+Alt+Del do?

  A. Reboot the system

  B. Automatically close the current application

  C. Bring up the online Help system

  D. Start the Task Manager

13. What does the Task Manager allow you to shut down?

  A. Windows 95

  B. An application that has stopped responding

  C. Any running application

  D. All of the above

14. What Windows 95 application will walk you through common printer issues?

   A. Print Troubleshooter

   B. Add New Hardware Wizard

   C. Control Panel

   D. None of the above

APPENDIX

A

Answers to Review Questions

Chapter 1

1. Your company is upgrading its computers. The choice is between Windows 95 and Windows NT. You want to support user profiles, the registry, and 32-bit applications, but you have many DOS applications that access the video card directly. Which operating system should you choose, and why?

   A. Windows 95

   B. Windows NT

   C. Both A and B would work fine.

   D. Neither A nor B would work.

   Answer: A

2. How many CPUs can Windows 95 support?

   A. 1

   B. 2

   C. 4

   D. Unlimited

   Answer: A

3. Which of the following support Plug and Play? (Select all that apply.)

   A. MS-DOS

   B. Windows 95

   C. Windows NT Workstation

   D. Windows NT Server

   Answer: B

4. Which of the following support multithreaded, multitasking applications? (Select all that apply.)

   A. MS-DOS

   B. Windows 95

   C. Windows NT Workstation

   D. Windows NT Server

   Answer: B, C, D

5. What is the revised version of Windows 95 called?

   A. Windows 96

   B. Windows 95-a

   C. OSR1

   D. OSR2

Answer: D

6. Which network model has no dedicated server?

   A. Stand-alone

   B. Networked

   C. Workgroup

   D. Member of an NT Domain

Answer: C

7. In which model can Windows 95 be both a client and a server? (Select all that apply.)

   A. Stand-alone

   B. Networked

   C. Workgroup

   D. Member of an NT Domain

Answer: C, D

8. Which model would be appropriate for the home user with one computer?

   A. Stand-alone

   B. Networked

   C. Workgroup

   D. Member of an NT Domain

Answer: A

9. Which model would be most appropriate for a large company?

   A. Stand-alone

   B. Networked

   C. Workgroup

   D. Member of an NT Domain

Answer: D

Chapter 2

1. The real-mode portion of the setup process does all of the following except:

   A. Runs ScanDisk

   B. Runs Defrag

   C. Finds a current installation of Windows

   D. Checks the CPU, hard disk space, and MS-DOS version

   Answer: B

2. The protected-mode portion of the setup process does all of the following except:

   A. Detects hardware

   B. Modifies boot records

   C. Runs run-once procedures, including migration of Windows 3.*x* program groups

   D. Removes TSR programs from the CONFIG.SYS and AUTOEXEC.BAT files

   Answer: D

3. Which of the following can be used to install Windows 95? (Select all that apply.)

   A. Floppy disks

   B. Network server

   C. Shared installation on a network server

   D. CD-ROM

   Answer: A, B, C, D

4. To dual-boot with Windows 3.*x*, you must do which of the following? (Select all that apply.)

   A. Run the DUALBOOT.EXE program.

   B. Install Windows 95 to a directory other than the current Windows directory.

   C. Create a bootable floppy disk for Windows 3.*x*.

   D. Set the BootMulti=1 property in the MSDOS.SYS file.

   Answer: B, D

5. What are the minimum hardware requirements for Windows 95? (Select all that apply.)

A. 386DX processor or later

B. 12MB of RAM

C. 50 to 55MB free hard disk space

D. VGA card

Answer: A, C, D

6. What is the minimum version of MS-DOS needed for an installation of Windows 95?

A. MS-DOS 6.22

B. MS-DOS 5.0

C. MS-DOS 4.1

D. MS-DOS 3.2

Answer: D

7. As an administrator, which of the following should you do before installation of Windows 95? (Select all that apply.)

A. Uncompress your hard drive.

B. Run ScanDisk and Defrag.

C. Remove TSRs from your CONFIG.SYS and AUTOEXEC.BAT files.

D. Make a backup of user files and boot files.

Answer: B, C, D

8. What can the Windows 95 Startup disk be useful for?

A. Booting to the Windows 95 command prompt for maintenance and troubleshooting

B. It is necessary to have the Startup disk to run any version of Windows 95.

C. It is necessary to have the Startup disk to run a dual-boot version of Windows 95.

D. Creating new disk partitions, because Windows 95 cannot read NTFS partitions

Answer: A

9. To uninstall Windows 95, you need to run the UNINSTAL.EXE file on the Windows 95 Startup disk. What does this program do?

    A. Deletes the current Windows 95 directory and reverts to your old Windows 3.*x* system

    B. Analyzes your current Windows 95 settings and reverts to your old system by making changes to specific files

    C. Loads a new version of Windows 3.*x* on top of Windows 95

    D. You cannot uninstall Windows 95.

Answer: B

10. The Windows 95 boot manager supports dual-booting with which of the following? (Select all that apply.)

    A. Windows NT

    B. Windows 3.*x* with MS DOS 5.0 or later

    C. OS/2

    D. MS-DOS 3.2

Answer: A, B

11. To enable dual-booting on Windows 95, you must do which of the following?

    A. Set DualBoot=1 in the CONFIG.SYS file.

    B. Set BootMulti=1 in the CONFIG.SYS file.

    C. Set DualBoot=1 in the MSDOS.SYS file.

    D. Set BootMulti=1 in the MSDOS.SYS file.

Answer: B

12. You can create batch setup scripts using which of the following programs? (Select all that apply.)

    A. NewBatch.EXE

    B. BATCH.EXE

    C. NetSetup.EXE

    D. INFINST.EXE

Answer: B, C, D

13. The NetSetup program has what additional feature that BATCH.EXE does not have?

A. You can install an administrative version of Windows 95 for server-based distribution.

B. You can specify network clients.

C. You can specify custom setup options.

D. You can specify a default Windows setup location.

Answer: A

14. During the setup process, what three files does Windows 95 use?

A. DETLOG.TXT

B. SETUPLOG.TXT

C. BOOTLOG.INI

D. DETCRASH.LOG

Answer: A, B, D

15. Which file contains everything that occurred during the Windows 95 setup procedures, including any crashes and reboots?

A. BOOTLOG.TXT

B. INSTALL.LOG

C. SETUPLOG.TXT

D. DETLOG.TXT

Answer: C

16. Which file contains all of the successfully detected hardware devices and their associated parameters?

A. BOOTLOG.TXT

B. INSTALL.LOG

C. SETUPLOG.TXT

D. DETLOG.TXT

Answer: D

Chapter 3

1. What is the first step in the Windows 95 boot process?

   A. BIOS bootstrap phase

   B. Master boot record and boot sector phase

   C. Real-mode boot phase

   D. Protected-mode boot phase

   Answer: A

2. During what step of the boot process is VMM32.VXD loaded?

   A. BIOS bootstrap phase

   B. Master boot record and boot sector phase

   C. Real-mode boot phase

   D. Protected-mode boot phase

   Answer: D

3. What are the two ways Windows 95 allows you to configure the boot process?

   A. The Startup menu

   B. Editing BOOT.INI

   C. Editing IO.SYS

   D. Editing MSDOS.SYS

   Answer: A, D

4. What Startup menu option should you choose to see which real-mode driver(s) might be giving you trouble?

   A. Previous version of DOS

   B. Safe mode with network support

   C. Safe mode

   D. Step-by-step confirmation

   Answer: D

5. What Startup menu option should you choose to see which protected-mode driver(s) might be giving you trouble?

   A. Logged (to create BOOTLOG.TXT)

   B. Step-by-step confirmation

C. Command prompt only

D. Previous version of DOS

Answer: A

6. What drivers are loaded during a plain Safe mode boot? (Select all that apply.)

A. Mouse driver

B. Keyboard driver

C. Standard VGA device driver

D. Network drivers

Answer: A, B, C

7. What additional files might you want to put on an emergency boot (Startup) disk? (Select all that apply.)

A. SYSTEM.DAT

B. CONFIG.SYS

C. AUTOEXEC.BAT

D. CD-ROM drivers

Answer: A, B, C, D

8. How can you find out which switches are available with WIN.COM?

A. Win /?

B. Win /help

C. Win /switches

D. Help /Win

Answer: A

9. What key or key combination do you press to get the Windows 95 Startup menu?

A. F4

B. F6

C. F8

D. Shift+F4

Answer: C

10. Which MSDOS.SYS parameter will force the "Starting Windows 95" line to display for 4 seconds?

   A. BootDelay=4000

   B. BootDelay=4

   C. None; the default is 4 seconds.

   D. None; you cannot change this option.

   Answer: B

11. You can provide tighter security on a Windows 95 client by setting which one of the following parameters?

   A. BootMulti=0

   B. BootMulti=1

   C. BootKeys=1

   D. BootKeys=0

   Answer: D

Chapter 4

1. If you open up three MS-DOS-based programs, three 16-bit Windows programs, and two 32-bit Windows programs, how many virtual machines are running?

   A. 8

   B. 3

   C. 4

   D. 2

   Answer: C

2. Which of the following is not a core component of the Windows 95 operating system?

   A. Kernel

   B. OSCore

   C. GDI

   D. User

   Answer: B

3. You are experiencing disk thrashing. How could you fix this problem? (Select all that apply.)

   A. Add more RAM to your system.

   B. Take your hard disk in for repairs.

   C. Run fewer programs simultaneously.

   D. Move the operating system components to another drive.

   Answer: A, C

4. What area of virtual address space is reserved for the core operating system components?

   A. 0 to 1MB

   B. 1MB to 2GB

   C. 2GB to 3GB

   D. 3GB to 4GB

   Answer: D

5. What is the benefit of using a device driver?

   A. It allows for device independence.

   B. It moves a device from one location to another.

   C. It prevents programs from communicating with hardware.

   D. Device drivers aren't available for Windows 95.

   Answer: A

6. Virtual device drivers are combined at setup time into a single file called:

   A. VirtDev.VXD

   B. VXD.VXD

   C. VMM32.VXD

   D. Device drivers are not combined.

   Answer: C

7. Which one of the following statements is true regarding real-mode and protected-mode drivers?

    A. Real-mode drivers are better than protected-mode drivers because real-mode drivers are always loaded in memory.

    B. Protected-mode drivers are better than real-mode drivers because they can be loaded and unloaded from memory as needed.

    C. Real-mode drivers are better than protected-mode drivers because they can be loaded and unloaded from memory as needed.

    D. Protected-mode drivers are better than real-mode drivers because they are always loaded in memory.

Answer: B

8. When does a page fault occur?

    A. When data was found in RAM

    B. When data was found in the swapfile

    C. When pages were corrupted

    D. When memory was lost

Answer: B

9. Which of the following is not done by the secondary scheduler?

    A. Boosting priority levels of all threads periodically

    B. Lowering priority levels of compute-bound threads

    C. Raising priority levels of threads from the active window

    D. Lowering priority levels of threads from the active window

Answer: D

10. Which of the following is true about the primary and secondary schedulers? (Select all that apply.)

    A. The primary scheduler looks at all processing threads and gives time slices to the thread with the highest priority.

    B. The primary scheduler looks at all threads and can adjust the priority of each processing thread.

    C. The secondary scheduler looks at all threads and can adjust the priority of each processing thread.

    D. The secondary scheduler looks at all processing threads and gives time slices to the thread with the highest priority.

Answer: A, C

11. What happens in a cooperative multitasking environment?

   A. Multiple executing threads are given CPU time slices by a scheduling mechanism.

   B. A single thread is shared by all running programs.

   C. Every program receives its own threads.

   D. Threads are given priorities based on how many programs are using them.

   Answer: B

12. Which of the following statements is true regarding multitasking?

   A. Preemptive multitasking means that a scheduler is deciding which threads among many get CPU time slices.

   B. Cooperative multitasking means that a scheduler is deciding which threads among many get CPU time slices.

   C. Windows 3.*x* takes advantage of a scheduler to create a preemptive multitasking environment.

   D. Windows 95 takes advantage of a scheduler to create a cooperative multitasking environment.

   Answer: A

13. The relationship between processes and threads can best be described by which of the following statements?

   A. Threads own multiple processes.

   B. A single process can own multiple threads.

   C. Threads have no relationship to a process.

   D. Threads own a single process.

   Answer: B

14. Which of the following is true of threading in Windows 95? (Select all that apply.)

   A. 16-bit programs each have their own thread.

   B. 32-bit programs each have their own thread.

   C. 16-bit programs can have multiple threads.

   D. 32-bit programs can have multiple threads.

   Answer: B, D

Chapter 5

1. What are the new names for directories and files?

    A. Directories and documents

    B. Directories and folders

    C. Folders and files

    D. Folders and documents

    Answer: D

2. What is the name of the new program that lets you see folders and files?

    A. Windows Explorer

    B. File Manager Plus

    C. Browser

    D. Folder Manager

    Answer: A

3. What feature prevents novice users from changing document associations?

    A. Locking Explorer to Read-Only Mode

    B. Locking the taskbar

    C. Hiding file extensions

    D. Hiding long filenames

    Answer: C

4. The Taskbar can be moved to which side of the Desktop? (Select all that apply.)

    A. Top

    B. Right

    C. Left

    D. Bottom

    Answer: A, B, C, D

5. What is the name of the main working area in Windows 95?

    A. The screen

    B. The Temp folder

C. The Windows folder

D. The Desktop

Answer: D

6. What is the new focus for managing your work in Windows 95?

   A. Documents

   B. Applications

   C. Date of files

   D. Name of user

   Answer: A

7. What new feature of Windows 95 allows you to undelete files?

   A. The Trash Can

   B. The Undo command

   C. The Undelete utility

   D. The Recycle Bin

   Answer: D

8. Which mouse button is used in Windows 95?

   A. The left mouse button

   B. The right mouse button

   C. Both mouse buttons

   D. Neither mouse button—keyboard commands are the main way of doing things.

   Answer: C

9. How many characters can a long filename have in Windows 95?

   A. 8.3

   B. 254

   C. 255

   D. 512

   Answer: C

10. Which of the following long filenames are valid? (Select all that apply.)

    A. This is a valid filename

    B. This.is.a.valid.filename

    C. This_is_a_valid_filename

    D. Thisisavalidfilename

    Answer: A, B, C, D

11. How does Windows 95 ensure backward compatibility with earlier versions of MS-DOS and applications?

    A. Windows 95 autogenerates a valid 8.3 filename.

    B. Windows 95 operates in "MS-DOS 6.22 compatibility mode."

    C. The previous version of MS-DOS is run side-by-side with Windows 95.

    D. Windows 95 does nothing special to ensure compatibility.

    Answer: A

12. If using the correct video driver, Windows 95 helps protect you from fatal configuration errors by which of the following?

    A. By not allowing you to choose a display property your video adapter does not support

    B. By handling all video card configurations for you

    C. By automatically updating video drivers when you connect to the Internet

    D. By automatically testing your video card when the screen saver is running

    Answer: A

13. What is the default setting of the graphics hardware acceleration feature?

    A. Basic

    B. None

    C. Full

    D. Most

    Answer: C

14. If starting the system in Safe mode solves your display problem, what may have caused the problem?

A. Bit block transfers were being prevented from performing on the display card.

B. Mouse pointer settings were incorrect.

C. The display driver is incorrect.

D. Choices A and C

Answer: C

15. Unexpected errors in applications can be due to which of the following? (Select all that apply.)

A. Memory problems

B. Display problems

C. Bad coding in the application

D. Hard drive problems

Answer: A, B, C, D

16. In order to troubleshoot your graphics card, the setting for hardware acceleration should be set to:

A. Basic

B. None

C. Full

D. Most

Answer: B

17. In order to see all possible choices for video card drivers, you should pick which option when choosing a new driver?

A. Show Compatible Devices

B. Have Disk

C. Show All Devices

D. Show All Device Choices

Answer: C

Chapter 6

1. What is the name of the registry key that holds user settings?

   A. Hkey_Local_Machine

   B. Hkey_Users

   C. Hkey_Dyn_Data

   D. Hkey_Current_Config

   Answer: B

2. What is the name of the registry key that holds Plug-and-Play settings?

   A. Hkey_Local_Machine

   B. Hkey_Users

   C. Hkey_Dyn_Data

   D. Hkey_Current_Config

   Answer: C

3. What is the name of the registry key that holds generic hardware information?

   A. Hkey_Local_Machine

   B. Hkey_Users

   C. Hkey_Dyn_Data

   D. Hkey_Current_Config

   Answer: A

4. What is the name of the registry key that holds hardware profile information?

   A. Hkey_Local_Machine

   B. Hkey_Users

   C. Hkey_Dyn_Data

   D. Hkey_Current_Config

   Answer: D

5. What is the name of the registry file that holds system settings?

   A. USER.INI

   B. USER.DAT

C. SYSTEM.DAT

D. SYSTEM.INI

Answer: C

6. What is the name of the registry file that holds user settings?

A. USER.INI

B. USER.DAT

C. SYSTEM.DAT

D. SYSTEM.INI

Answer: B

7. What are the two types of data that a registry value can hold?

A. Binary

B. Time/Date

C. Character

D. Integer

Answer: A

8. What is the name of the registry editor for Windows 95?

A. REGEDT32.EXE

B. REGISTRY EDITOR.EXE

C. REGEDIT.EXE

D. REGISTRY.EXE

Answer: C

9. What is the name of the backup registry file that is automatically created and contains user-specific information?

A. USER.DA0

B. USER.BAK

C. SYSTEM.BAK

D. SYSTEM.DA0

Answer: A

10. What is the name of the backup registry file that is automatically created and contains system information?

    A. USER.DA0

    B. USER.BAK

    C. SYSTEM.BAK

    D. SYSTEM.DA0

    Answer: D

11. Which of the following methods allow you to back up the registry? (Select all that apply.)

    A. Regedit /e

    B. Regedit ➤ Registry ➤ Export Registry File

    C. The Configuration Backup (CFGBACK) utility

    D. Copying your SYSTEM.DAT and USER.DAT files to a disk

    Answer: A, B, C, D

12. Which of the following methods allow you to restore the registry? (Select all that apply.)

    A. Regedit /c

    B. Regedit ➤ Registry ➤ Import Registry File

    C. The Configuration Backup (CFGBACK) utility

    D. Overwriting your SYSTEM.DAT and USER.DAT files with previous versions

    Answer: A, B, C, D

Chapter 7

1. Which of the following are virtual machines used in Windows 95? (Select all that apply.)

    A. System VM

    B. Core VM

    C. W95 VM

    D. MS-DOS VM

    Answer: A, D

For the next three questions, please use the following scenario: You have three 16-bit applications, a 32-bit application, and two MS-DOS-based applications running.

2. If one of the 16-bit applications is hung, how many programs altogether will be hung, including the hung application?

   A. 1

   B. 2

   C. 3

   D. 5

Answer: C

3. If one of the 32-bit applications has hung, how many programs altogether will be hung, including the hung application?

   A. 1

   B. 2

   C. 3

   D. 5

Answer: A

4. If an MS-DOS application has a GPF, how many programs will be affected, including the crashed MS-DOS application?

   A. 1

   B. 2

   C. 3

   D. 5

Answer: A

5. You want to run a batch file to log on to a network server before your MS-DOS application runs. What is the easiest method to accomplish this?

   A. Build a shortcut to the batch file and to the MS-DOS program; double-click on the batch shortcut first, and then run the MS-DOS program.

   B. Go to a command prompt and run the batch file before running the MS-DOS program.

C. Add the batch file to the Batch File parameter in the property sheet for the MS-DOS program.

D. You don't need to run the batch file because Windows 95 will automatically detect that the MS-DOS program needs access to the server and will log you in.

Answer: C

6. Your MS-DOS program is named FOO.EXE. You create a PIF file for your MS-DOS program. What is the name of the PIF file?

A. MS-DOS.PIF

B. PIF.EXE

C. DEFAULT.PIF

D. FOO.PIF

Answer: D

7. In the Working parameter of an MS-DOS property sheet, you specify C:\TEMP. What will be placed in the C:\TEMP directory, if anything?

A. Output files used by your MS-DOS program

B. The files used by Windows 95 to track program performance

C. The .INI files used by all the Windows programs running at the same time your MS-DOS program is running

D. There will never be anything stored here.

Answer: A

8. You are editing a document in Microsoft Word. You highlight a line of text and press Ctrl+C to copy it to the clipboard, when suddenly your MS-DOS application starts up. What could cause this?

A. You have the OLE functionality of Microsoft Word linked to your MS-DOS program.

B. You have chosen Ctrl+C as a shortcut for your MS-DOS-based application.

C. Ctrl+C always starts up the last used MS-DOS program.

D. This is a glitch in the computer system and should never happen.

Answer: B

9. When you are in your MS-DOS program, you want to be able to press Alt+Tab to switch to another running application. How could you enable this feature?

  A. In the Misc tab of the MS-DOS property sheet, click on the Alt+Tab checkbox.

  B. You don't have to do anything—this functionality always exists for MS-DOS applications.

  C. This is not an available feature and can't be implemented.

  D. You must edit the registry in order to do this.

Answer: A

Chapter 8

1. What is the name of the program that can fix minor errors on your hard drive?

  A. Format

  B. Fdisk

  C. ScanDisk

  D. Vcache

Answer: C

2. What is it called when files get scattered over a hard drive?

  A. Compression

  B. Corruption

  C. Clustering

  D. Fragmentation

Answer: D

3. What is the name of the new 32-bit caching piece of Windows 95?

  A. Format

  B. Fdisk

  C. ScanDisk

  D. Vcache

Answer: D

4. Windows 95 includes a native anti-virus program.

    A. Yes, but only on the CD-ROM version of Windows 95.

    B. Yes, but you have to pay for it before you can install it.

    C. Yes, but it only comes with OSR2.

    D. No.

Answer: D

5. Windows 95's Backup program is backward-compatible with older DOS versions of backup and restore.

    A. True

    B. False

Answer: B

6. Creating smaller partitions may be a more efficient way of formatting your hard drive.

    A. Yes, because files take up less room on your disk.

    B. Yes, because the hard drive works faster.

    C. Yes, because the hard drive spins less often, saving wear and tear.

    D. No, there is no difference.

Answer: A

7. The long filename "This is a company memo about the party for.1998.doc" would have which 8.3 name created for it?

    A. This is .doc

    B. Thisis~1.199

    C. Thisis~1.doc

    D. Thisisal.doc

Answer: C

8. Disabling the write-behind cache is done with which program?

    A. Control Panel ➤ System

    B. Control Panel ➤ Devices

    C. Control Panel ➤ Drives

    D. My Computer ➤ Properties of the Drive

Answer: A

9. You can restore deleted files in Windows 95 due to which program?

    A. Vcache

    B. Recycle Bin

    C. Trash Can

    D. Undelete

    Answer: B

10. Which program can be used to schedule tasks such as ScanDisk and Disk Defragmenter in Windows 95?

    A. My Computer ≻ Properties

    B. Shortcuts

    C. System Agent

    D. The AT command

    Answer: C

11. You purchase a 6GB drive, but can only create 2GB partitions on it. Why?

    A. Your motherboard needs a BIOS upgrade.

    B. You installed Windows 95 as an upgrade to MS-DOS 5.0.

    C. You are running the original version of Windows 95.

    D. You haven't set the master/slave settings on the hard drive correctly.

    Answer: C

12. You use the `format c: /s` switch to recover from a virus. What will happen to your data on the C: drive?

    A. The data will be fine.

    B. The data will be completely gone.

    C. Your data will be OK but you will have to reinstall Windows 95.

    D. Windows 95 will be OK but your data will be gone.

    Answer: B

13. How can you configure the Backup program so that you won't have to change tapes as often? (Select all that apply.)

A. Buy the new QIC-250 type tapes.

B. Use compression.

C. Back up to a network drive.

D. Back up only data files.

Answer: B, C, D

14. Which advanced option would you choose for DEFRAG.EXE in order to gain the most speed from your computer?

A. Full defragmentation

B. Consolidate free space only

C. Optimize defragmentation

D. Defragment files only

Answer: A

15. Which advanced option would you choose if you were only worried about increasing the speed of your current applications?

A. Full defragmentation

B. Consolidate free space only

C. Optimize defragmentation

D. Defragment files only

Answer: D

16. A user calls and says they can't create any folders on their C:\ even though they still have over 500MB free. What could be the cause?

A. They have too many long file and folder names already on C:\.

B. They are using a 16-bit program to create the folder.

C. They need to defragment their hard drive, then it will work.

D. They need to create folder names that are 8.3 or fewer characters on the C:\.

Answer: A

Chapter 9

1. Which Microsoft layer talks to the network card?

A. Device Driver Interface

B. Physical Driver Interface

C. Transport Driver Interface

D. Session Driver Interface

Answer: A

2. Which is *not* a protocol that Windows 95 supports?

A. IPX/SPX

B. Frame0

C. NetBEUI

D. TCP/IP

Answer: B

3. Which NDIS specification was designed for Windows 95?

A. NDIS 2.0

B. NDIS 2.1

C. NDIS 3.0

D. NDIS 3.1

Answer: D

4. Does Windows 95 support autoreconnect for both Windows NT and NetWare environments?

A. Yes, for both environments.

B. No, only for the Windows NT environment.

C. No, only for the NetWare environment.

D. No, for neither environment.

Answer: A

5. What does UNC stand for?

A. Universal Network Convention

B. Universal Naming Convention

C. Universal NETBIOS Convention

D. Universal NetWare Convention

Answer: B

6. Microsoft servers communicate natively with which language?

A. NCP

B. MMP

C. BTT

D. SMB

Answer: D

7. Can Windows 95 be both a Microsoft and a NetWare client simultaneously?

A. Yes, it can be both.

B. No, it can only function as a Microsoft client.

C. No, it can only function as a NetWare client.

D. No, it can do both, but not simultaneously.

Answer: A

8. Can Windows 95 be both a Microsoft and NetWare server simultaneously?

A. Yes, it can be both.

B. No, it can function only as a Microsoft server.

C. No, it can function only as a NetWare server.

D. No, it can function as one or the other, but not both simultaneously.

Answer: D

9. Which type of name must be unique? (Select all that apply.)

A. Computer names

B. User names

C. Workgroup names

D. Domain names

Answer: A, D

10. Which protocols can cross routers (under normal conditions)? (Select all that apply.)

  A. TCP/IP

  B. NetBEUI

  C. IPX/SPX

  D. AppleTalk

  Answer: A, C, D

11. Which new feature of Windows 95 lets you see network resources?

  A. My Computer

  B. Network Resources

  C. Network Servers

  D. Network Neighborhood

  Answer: D

12. If Sue, Katie, and Linda are in the same workgroup, how would they see each other's computers?

  A. Network Neighborhood ➤ Entire Network

  B. Network Neighborhood (all computers in their workgroup are visible by default)

  C. Network Neighborhood ➤ Scan for Workgroup Computers

  D. Network Neighborhood ➤ Find Computers in My Workgroup

  Answer: B

13. What pieces of software would be required to connect to Windows NT as a client, share your printers to other Microsoft clients, and connect to a NetWare 3.12 computer? (Select all that apply.)

  A. Microsoft Client for NetWare

  B. Microsoft Client for Microsoft

  C. File and printer sharing for Microsoft

  D. File and printer sharing for NetWare

  Answer: A, B, C

Chapter 10

1. What was the first operating system to include TCP/IP?

   A. BSD Unix

   B. Macintosh System 1.0

   C. IBM DOS

   D. Amiga DOS

   Answer: A

2. Which type of document contains the standards for TCP/IP?

   A. DOCs (Documentation Files)

   B. RFCs (Requests for Comments)

   C. IPREQs (TCP/IP Requests)

   D. TCP/IP Specifications

   Answer: B

3. How many bits long is an IP address?

   A. 8 bits

   B. 16 bits

   C. 32 bits

   D. 64 bits

   Answer: C

4. What is the largest class of IP address?

   A. Class A

   B. Class B

   C. Class C

   D. Class D

   Answer: A

5. 127.118.175.211 is a valid IP address.

   A. True, this is always a valid address.

   B. True, but only if you are not connected to the Internet.

C. False, there are too many digits.

D. False, the 127 range is reserved.

Answer: D

6. What are the three main components of an IP address?

A. Address itself

B. Subnet mask

C. DHCP server

D. Default gateway

Answer: A, B, D

7. With a subnet mask of 255.255.255.0, are the two addresses 106.108.10.50 and 106.108.11.51 located on the same subnet?

A. Yes.

B. No, the subnet makes them different networks.

C. No, the address of 106 is reserved for Internet addresses only.

D. No, the address of 106.108 is for loopback purposes.

Answer: B

8. With a subnet mask of 255.255.0.0, are the two addresses 106.108.10.50 and 106.108.11.51 located on the same subnet?

A. Yes.

B. No, the subnet makes them different networks.

C. No, the address of 106 is reserved for Internet addresses only.

D. No, the address of 106.108 is for loopback purposes.

Answer: A

9. What subnet mask would give you at least 15 subnets for the net ID of 160.108.0.0?

A. 255.255.248.0

B. 255.255.255.0

C. 255.255.240.0

D. 255.255.0.0

Answer: A

10. With the subnet mask from question 9 (above), what is the first subnet net ID?

    A. 160.108.1.0

    B. 160.108.255.0

    C. 160.108.8.0

    D. 160.108.16.0

    Answer: C

11. How can you find out what IP address has been assigned to you by DHCP in Windows 95?

    A. Use the WinIPCfg utility.

    B. Use the PING utility.

    C. Use the TCPIP utility.

    D. Use the IPCONFIG utility.

    Answer: A

12. Which two software components in Windows 95 are necessary to allow you to use your Web browser on the Internet from a LAN?

    A. DHCP

    B. Windows Sockets

    C. TCP/IP protocol

    D. Router

    Answer: B, C

13. If you can see computers on your LAN, but cannot access the Internet, which networking configuration would you probably suspect is bad?

    A. DNS

    B. TCP/IP Address

    C. Subnet Mask

    D. Default Gateway

    Answer: D

14. Which software component helps prevent duplicate TCP/IP addresses?

A. DHCP

B. WINS

C. DNS

D. HTTP

Answer: A

15. Windows 95 can function as which type of server using software from Microsoft? (Select all that apply.)

A. DHCP

B. WINS

C. DNS

D. HTTP

Answer: D

16. Refer to Figure 10.1. For the computer with the address of 131.107.8.31, what would you enter as the default gateway?

A. 131.107.8.31

B. 131.107.8.1

C. 131.107.16.1

D. 131.107.8.33

Answer: B

Chapter 11

1. When installing a network card, what items may you need to configure? (Select all that apply.)

A. Interrupt

B. I/O port

C. Memory address

D. Slot number

Answer: A, B, C

2. You can use which program(s) to configure the network card?

A. Control Panel ➤ Network ➤ Properties of the card

B. Network Neighborhood ➤ Properties ➤ Properties of the card

C. Control Panel ➤ Devices ➤ Properties of the card

D. Control Panel ➤ System ➤ Device Manager ➤ Properties of the card

Answer: A, B, D

3. By installing the Client for Microsoft Networks, you allow Windows 95 to understand which language?

A. NCP

B. MMP

C. NTB

D. SMB

Answer: D

4. If Windows 95 is set up to use IPX/SPX, and it cannot auto-detect a frame type, what frame will it pick?

A. No frames

B. All frames

C. Ethernet_802.2

D. Ethernet_II

Answer: C

5. Which service allows automatic assignment of TCP/IP addresses?

A. DHCP

B. WINS

C. DNS

D. DXNP

Answer: A

6. NetBEUI packets can cross a router.

A. Yes, always.

B. Only if the router is connected to the Internet

C. Only if the router is the latest model

D. No, they can't.

Answer: D

7. You can change your NT password from within Windows 95.

A. True, but not your screensaver

B. True, and also your screensaver at the same time

C. True, and all other passwords (including NetWare)

D. False

Answer: B

8. Which of the following statements are true? (Select all that apply.)

A. Windows 95 can be a client to NT while it is acting as an NT server as well.

B. You can set Read-Only rights using just Share level security.

C. A stand-alone Windows 95 computer can use User level security.

D. A stand-alone Windows 95 computer can use Share level security.

Answer: A, B, D

9. In order to configure a slow computer to be as fast as possible, how would you configure the browser service?

A. Enabled

B. Tuned

C. Automatic

D. Disabled

Answer: D

10. In order for Sue, Katie, and Linda to see each other's computers in the same screen in Network Neighborhood, how would you configure the workgroups and Network Neighborhood?

A. Set the workgroups to unique names and set the Preferred Workgroups option.

B. Set the workgroups to the same names and set the Preferred Workgroups option.

C. Set the workgroups to unique names and rely on default Network Neighborhood settings.

D. Set the workgroups to the same names and rely on default Network Neighborhood settings.

Answer: D

11. In order to be a client to a Windows NT Server running the TCP/IP compatible protocol, and a client to a NetWare 3.12 Server, which of the following components will need to be installed? (Select all that apply.)

    A. Microsoft Client for Microsoft Networks

    B. Microsoft Client for NetWare Networks

    C. IPX/SPX Compatible Protocol

    D. TCP/IP Protocol

    Answer: A, B, C, D

12. In order to be a client to a NetWare 4.0 server running in Bindery mode, and to share files to other NetWare clients, which of the following components will need to be installed? (Select all that apply.)

    A. Microsoft Client for Microsoft Networks

    B. Microsoft Client for NetWare Networks

    C. File and printer sharing for Microsoft

    D. File and printer sharing for NetWare

    Answer: B, D

13. Which component would you install if you wanted to grant users and groups on a Windows NT domain rights to your shared printer?

    A. File and printer sharing for Microsoft Networks—set to User level security

    B. File and printer sharing for Microsoft Networks—set to Share level security

    C. File and printer sharing for NetWare Networks—set to User level security

    D. File and printer sharing for NetWare Networks—set to Share level security

    Answer: A

14. You are a member of the Sales domain, with a Windows NT primary domain controller (PDC) called Sales_1, and a backup domain controller (BDC) called Sales_2. You are a member of a group called western_sales. How would you configure your sharing service so you can grant the western_sales group access to memos on your hard drive?

    A. Set yourself to Share level security and e-mail the password to your group.

    B. Set yourself to User level security, based on Sales_1.

    C. Set yourself to User level security, based on Sales_1 or Sales_2.

    D. Set yourself to User level security, based on the Sales domain.

    Answer: D

Chapter 12

1. NetWare servers communicate using which language?

A. SMB

B. PPP

C. NDS

D. NCP

Answer: D

2. Which NetWare servers can Windows 95 communicate with? (Select all that apply.)

A. 2.*x* (bindery)

B. 3.*x* (bindery)

C. 4.*x* (NDS)

D. 5.*x* (NDS)

Answer: A, B, C

3. Which clients are real-mode clients? (Select all that apply.)

A. NETX

B. VLM

C. Microsoft's Client for NetWare

D. Novell's Client 32

Answer: A, B

4. Which clients are true NDS clients? (Select all that apply.)

A. NETX

B. VLM

C. Microsoft's Client for NetWare

D. Novell's Client 32

Answer: B, D

5. Windows 95 must use which type of security to share files on a NetWare network?

A. Share level

B. User level

C. 'Default' level

D. Secure level

Answer: B

6. What is the default frame type if the "Automatic" type fails to detect a frame type?

A. Ethernet_802.2

B. Ethernet_802.3

C. Ethernet_II

D. Ethernet_Snap

Answer: A

7. In order for real mode NetWare clients to see the Windows 95 computer that is sharing its files as a Novell server, which support must be enabled on the Windows 95 machine?

A. NCP

B. TUD

C. SMB

D. SAP

Answer: D

8. Client 32 allows you to specify if the _____ will be executed.

A. anti-virus software

B. automatic NetWare update

C. login script

D. user profile

Answer: C

9. The NetWare client can print a page at the beginning of a print job. This is called a:

A. Banner

B. Form Feed

C. Print Job

D. Spooling

Answer: A

10. The NetWare client can print a page at the end of a print job. This is called a:

   A. Banner

   B. Form Feed

   C. Print Job

   D. Spooling

   Answer: B

11. If a NetWare server called FS1 is running the 802.2 frame type, and a NetWare 4.0 server running in Bindery Emulation mode called FS2 is running the 802.3 frame type, and a NetWare 3.12 server called FS3 is running both frame types, what setting(s) should you change on a Windows 95 client to have people log into FS1 by default? (Select all that apply.)

   A. Set the frame type to automatic.

   B. Set the frame type to 802.2 (single).

   C. Set the preferred server to FS1.

   D. Set the automatic logon server to FS1.

   Answer: B, C

12. You are using NE2000.EXE as your network card driver. You would like to download the latest drivers for Windows 95. Which drivers should you download?

   A. None, NE2000.EXE is the latest driver

   B. The NDIS 3.0 version driver

   C. The NDIS 3.1 version driver

   D. The NDIS 4.0 version driver

   Answer: C

13. Which client would be able to connect to a NetWare 4.0 server running in Bindery Emulation mode? (Select all that apply.)

    A. Microsoft Client for NetWare

    B. Microsoft Client for Microsoft

    C. NETX

    D. NetWare Client32

    Answer: A, C, D

14. Which components are necessary to share your files with workers who log into a NetWare 3.12 server?

    A. TCP/IP

    B. IPX/SPX

    C. Microsoft Client for NetWare

    D. File and Print Services for NetWare

    Answer: B, C, D

15. To set up users, groups and printers on a NetWare 4.*x* server without Bindery Emulation, you need to log in as a(n):

    A. Super User

    B. Admin

    C. Supervisor or Supervisor equivalent

    D. Administrator

    Answer: B

Chapter 13

1. What are the three different types of printer driver combinations supported in Windows 95?

    A. Standard Universal Driver/mini-driver

    B. HP Driver/HP.dll

    C. PostScript Universal Driver/mini-driver

    D. Monolithic driver used for HP color inkjet printers

    Answer: A, C, D

2. How can you check the status of a print queue in Windows 95?

A. Select Start ➢ Run ➢ CheckQueue.

B. Double-click on the printer icon in the Printers folder.

C. Go to the Print Queue folder, find your print queue, and click on it.

D. Both A and C

Answer: B

3. Once you have installed a Point-and-Print printer on your Desktop, how does Windows 95 reference the networked printer?

A. Using a mapped drive letter (for example: P:)

B. Using mapped ports (for example: LPT2:)

C. Using a special printer reference tool (for example: MyPrinter)

D. Using the UNC name (for example: \\servername\printer)

Answer: D

4. To install a Point-and-Print printer from a Windows 95 machine:

A. Browse the network until you find the shared printer, and then double-click on its icon.

B. Browse the Windows 95 CD-ROM and install the printer driver from the CD.

C. Run PrintSetup from the Printers Folder on the Windows 95 CD-ROM.

D. Run PrintSetup from the shared folder of the machine on the network that is attached to the printer.

Answer: A

5. When you install a Point-and-Print printer from a Windows 95 server:

A. The printer configuration is created with the default settings.

B. The printer configuration will be inherited (copied) to your machine.

C. You will have to specify that the configuration is to be inherited.

D. You will have to create the new configuration just like you do for any other installation.

Answer: B

6. When you install a Point-and-Print printer from a Windows NT server:

A. The printer configuration is created with the default settings.

B. The printer configuration will be inherited (copied) to your machine.

C. You will have to specify that the configuration is to be inherited

D. You will have to create the new configuration just like you do for any other installation.

Answer: A

7. Novell NetWare machines need to have Point-and-Print information added to their bindery before they can support Point and Print. The information added to the bindery includes which of the following? (Select all that apply.)

A. Printer name

B. Location of printer drivers

C. Printer drivers

D. Location of printer

Answer: A, B, C

8. Windows 95 needs what information to support Point and Print? (Select all that apply.)

A. The printer manufacturer's name and printer model

B. The network that you are using

C. The driver names

D. The driver locations

Answer: A, C, D

9. What is the maximum number of printers Windows 95 can support?

A. 1

B. 2

C. 6 (LPT1, LPT2, COM1–COM4)

D. There is no predefined maximum

Answer: D

10. Which of the following should you check if your printer is not printing? (Select all that apply.)

   A. The amount of hard disk space on the computer

   B. The cable connections

   C. Whether the printer is on

   D. The \Windows\Spools directory to be sure that print jobs are being spooled properly

   Answer: A, B, C, D

11. Which of the following are valid methods for supporting a networked printer in Windows 95? (Select all that apply.)

   A. Using a mapped drive letter (for example: P:)

   B. Using mapped ports (for example: LPT2:)

   C. Using a special printer reference tool (for example: MyPrinter)

   D. Using the UNC name (for example: \\servername\printer)

   Answer: A, B, D

12. To use the HP JetAdmin utility, which of the following must be true? (Select all that apply.)

   A. The printer must have an HP JetDirect card installed.

   B. The print server must support the DLC protocol.

   C. The PCs sending jobs to the print server must support the DLC protocol.

   D. The HP JetAdmin utility needs to be installed on all of the PCs that will be sending print jobs to the HP Printer.

   Answer: A, B

13. Your Windows 95 computer is acting as the print server for a networked printer. Windows 95 has the DLC protocol installed as well as the HP JetAdmin utility. The printer has an HP JetDirect card installed and is connected to the network correctly. What else must you do to your Windows 95 print server to allow others access to that printer? (Select two answers.)

   A. You must install the DLC protocol on all computers that will send print jobs to your print server.

   B. You must create and share a network printer in the Printers folder.

   C. You must install the file and printer sharing network services on the print server.

   D. You must install file and printer sharing network services on all of the clients.

   Answer: B, C

Chapter 14

1. Profiles work by saving a unique copy of which registry file?

A. REG.DAT

B. REGISTRY.OUT

C. SYSTEM.DAT

D. USER.DAT

Answer: D

2. Roaming profiles (with all options) are enabled. You are logged in at two computers. You add a shortcut to your Desktop and log out from the first computer. You log out of the second computer. You log back in at the first, but your shortcut isn't there. Why?

A. Your local profile is not enabled.

B. The profile from the second computer overwrote the profile from the first.

C. The roaming profile is cached, and isn't available for immediate loading.

D. Profiles don't track shortcuts.

Answer: B

3. Which of the following is required to enable roaming profiles on an NT server? (Select all that apply.)

A. Users must have a home folder.

B. Users must use TCP/IP.

C. Usernames must be eight or fewer characters.

D. The Client for Microsoft Networks must be the default logon.

Answer: A, D

4. Roaming profiles (with all options) are enabled. Profiles are being saved locally, and are present on the server, but are not downloading from the server to all workstations. What could be the cause? (Select all that apply.)

A. The time on the problematic workstations is ahead of the time of the server.

B. The problematic workstations are not using the same protocol as the server.

C. The problematic workstations don't have profiles enabled.

D. The problematic workstations are Windows NT workstations.

Answer: A, B, C, D

5. You want the local profile to include the Start menu, but not the Desktop. Is that possible? If so, which option do you pick?

   A. Yes—enable profiles normally (with no options picked).

   B. Yes—enable profiles with the Include Desktop Icons... option.

   C. Yes—enable profiles with the Include Start Menu... option.

   D. No—this is not possible.

   Answer: C

6. Using a Windows 95 client when Windows 95 is installed in the C:\Windows folder, where are roaming profiles stored on a NetWare 3.12 network?

   A. On the local computer, in the C:\Windows folder

   B. On the local computer, in the C:\Windows\System32 folder

   C. On the NetWare server, in the PUBLIC folder

   D. On the NetWare server, in the \Mail\Userid folder

   Answer: D

7. How do you make a mandatory profile?

   A. Create a new group called "Mandatory" and assign the user to the group.

   B. Check the box "Create Mandatory Profile" when initially creating the profile.

   C. Set USER.DAT to read-only.

   D. Rename the profile to USER.MAN.

   Answer: D

8. What is required to enable roaming profiles on a NetWare 3.12 server? (Select all that apply.)

   A. The IPX/SPX protocol

   B. Microsoft Client for NetWare

   C. Default Login set to Microsoft Client for NetWare

   D. Profiles enabled on the Windows 95 client

   Answer: A, B, C, D

9. When can the same roaming profile be used on Windows NT workstations and Windows 95 clients?

   A. Never—they are incompatible.

   B. If you rename the profile to USER.NT it will also work for Windows NT.

   C. If you place the profile in the NETLOGON share, both operating systems can use it.

   D. If you check the box "Create NT Compatible Profile" when initially setting up the profile.

   Answer: A

Chapter 15

1. The System Policy Editor is installed by which method?

   A. It is installed by default.

   B. It is installed when you do a "Custom" installation.

   C. It is installed automatically when you log onto a Windows NT server with Administrator rights.

   D. You have to install it manually.

   Answer: D

2. Policies can be used to enforce restrictions based on which of the following? (Select all that apply.)

   A. Users

   B. Groups

   C. Time of Logon

   D. Computers

   Answer: A, B, D

3. Policy templates end with which extension?

   A. .TEM

   B. .FIL

   C. .ADM

   D. .POL

   Answer: C

4. Policies end with which extension?

   A. .POL

   B. .ADM

   C. .DLL

   D. .SEC

   Answer: A

5. Group policies are not working. What step(s) should you check? (Select all that apply.)

   A. Group policy support must be installed on every computer that will load policies based on groups.

   B. Users may not be assigned to the correct groups.

   C. The policy file should be named GroupPolicy.pol.

   D. The policy file should be named Config.pol.

   Answer: A, B, D

6. Phil is a member of both the Management and Sales groups. You want the Management group to take precedence over the Sales group. How would you set this up?

   A. Make the Sales group higher in the list.

   B. Make the Management group higher in the list.

   C. You can't control it—it goes alphabetically.

   D. Set Phil's primary group to the Management group.

   Answer: B

7. Sally and Phil share a computer. Sally will have a restriction in place, but Phil shouldn't. How should you set Phil's checkbox for that restriction?

   A. Leave it gray (default).

   B. Put a check in it.

   C. Uncheck it (make it white).

   D. Leave Phil's checkbox alone; set Sally's checkbox to gray.

   Answer: C

8. Windows 95 looks in which NT share by default?

    A. The NETLOGON share of all domain controllers

    B. The NETLOGON share of the primary domain controller

    C. The USERS share of all domain controllers

    D. The USERS share of the primary domain controller

    Answer: B

9. The System Policy Editor is found in which folder on the original Windows CD-ROM?

    A. Admin\Apptools\Poledit

    B. Admin\Poledit

    C. Admin\Tools\Policies\Editor

    D. Admin\Apptools\Policy\Poledit

    Answer: A

10. Templates can be stored as which type of file(s)? (Select all that apply.)

    A. ASCII text files

    B. Compressed binary files

    C. Word (.doc) files

    D. Policy Editor (.pol) files

    Answer: A

11. You want to enable system policies on a NetWare network. You have 3.12 servers and 4.*x* servers running in Bindery Emulation. Where do you need to put the system policy file so that your clients will find it?

    A. In the PUBLIC folders of the 3.12 servers, and the POLICY folders of the 4.*x* servers

    B. In the PUBLIC folders of all of the NetWare servers

    C. In the POLICY folders of all of the NetWare servers

    D. In the POLICY folders of the 3.12 servers, and the PUBLIC folders of the 4.*x* servers

    Answer: B

12. You have a group created for your temporary employees called temp_users. You don't want them to be able to share their folders or printers. How would you set your policy file?

A. Create a policy file that selects "Disable file sharing" and "Disable printer sharing" and assign it to the temp_users group.

B. Create a policy file that selects "Disable file sharing" and "Disable printer sharing" and name it temp_users.pol.

C. Edit your existing policy file. Create a new group policy for the temp_users group, and select the "Disable file sharing" and "Disable printer sharing" options.

D. Edit your existing policy file. Create user policies for all of the temporary employees and select the "Disable file sharing" and "Disable printer sharing" options.

Answer: C

13. You need to save your policy file on a NetWare server. What do you name it so that your Windows 95 clients can find it by default?

A. Config.pol

B. NWConfig.pol

C. NTConfig.pol

D. 95Config.pol

Answer: A

14. You have 10,000 clients (both Windows NT and Windows 95) in one large Windows NT domain. You have a large PDC in the central office, with a BDC in each of your 30 regional offices. Users complain that logging in from the Windows 95 clients takes twice as long as logging in from the Windows NT clients. What steps do you need to take in order to speed up the login process? (Select all that apply.)

A. Make sure the policy file is on all the BDCs.

B. Enable Manual Updates, and specify load balancing on the Windows 95 clients.

C. Copy the policy file to the local hard drives of all of the Windows 95 clients.

D. Set the policy file to only test for user configurations.

Answer: A, B

Chapter 16

1. Remote administration is accomplished through the use of which mechanism?

   A. Named pipes

   B. RPCs

   C. IPX/SPX

   D. TCP/IP

   Answer: B

2. Which utility do you use to administer the file structure on a remote computer?

   A. Net Watcher

   B. Remote System Monitor

   C. Administer

   D. Remote Registry Editor

   Answer: C

3. Which utility do you use to view which resources are shared and who is using them?

   A. Net Watcher

   B. Remote System Monitor

   C. Administer

   D. Remote Registry Editor

   Answer: A

4. Which utility do you use to view performance statistics on a remote workstation?

   A. Net Watcher

   B. Remote System Monitor

   C. Administer

   D. Remote Registry Editor

   Answer: B

5. To modify the registry database on a remote workstation, you need to install which additional network service?

   A. Net Watcher Services

   B. Remote Registry Services

C. Client Services for Remote Administration

D. Novell NetWare Client32 for Windows 95

Answer: B

6. Which of the following utilities require User level security on both the remote workstation and the administering workstation? (Select all that apply.)

A. Net Watcher

B. Remote System Monitor

C. Administer

D. Remote Registry Editor

Answer: B, D

7. To remotely administer a client PC, you must first enable remote administration. Where is this accomplished from?

A. Network property sheets

B. Add/Remove Programs in Control Panel

C. Passwords in Control Panel

D. Remote Administration in Control Panel

Answer: C

8. Your Windows 95 computer is currently configured to use User level security. You want to use the Remote Net Watcher utility to monitor shares on another Windows 95 computer. Which of the following must be true?

A. The client computer must be configured to use User level security and must also have Remote Registry Services installed.

B. The client computer must be configured to use either Share or User level security and must also have Remote Registry Services installed.

C. The client computer must be configured to use User level security and must also have file and printer sharing installed.

D. The client computer must be configured to use either Share or User level security and must also have file and printer sharing installed.

Answer: C

9. Your Windows 95 computer is currently configured to use User level security. You want to use the Administer utility to monitor another Windows 95 computer. Which of the following must be true?

   A. The client computer must be configured to use User level security and must also have Remote Registry Services installed.

   B. The client computer must be configured to use either Share or User level security and must also have Remote Registry Services installed.

   C. The client computer must be configured to use User level security and must also have file and printer sharing installed.

   D. The client computer must be configured to use either Share or User level security and must also have file and printer sharing installed.

   Answer: C

10. Which of the following statements are true concerning using the Remote Net Watcher utility? (Select all that apply.)

   A. If the administering computer is using Share level security, then the client computer can be configured with either Share or User level security.

   B. If the administering computer is using Share level security, then the client computer must be configured with Share level security.

   C. If the administering computer is using User level security, then the client computer can be configured with either Share or User level security.

   D. If the administering computer is using User level security, then the client computer must be configured to use User level security.

   Answer: A, D

11. Which of the following statements are true concerning using the Administer utility? (Select all that apply.)

   A. If the administering computer is using Share level security, then the client computer can be configured with either Share or User level security.

   B. If the administering computer is using Share level security, then the client computer must be configured with Share level security.

   C. If the administering computer is using User level security, then the client computer can be configured with either Share or User level security.

   D. If the administering computer is using User level security, then the client computer must be configured to use User level security.

   Answer: A, D

12. Which of the following statements are true concerning using the Remote System Monitor Utility? (Select all that apply.)

A. Both the administering computer and the client PC must be configured to use User level security.

B. The administering computer must be configured to use User level security, but the client computer can use either Share or User level security.

C. Both the administering computer and the client computer must have Remote Registry Services installed.

D. Only the client computer must have Remote Registry Services installed.

Answer: A, C

13. Which of the following statements are true concerning using the Remote Registry Editor Utility? (Select all that apply.)

A. Both the administering computer and the client PC must be configured to use User level security.

B. The administering computer must be configured to use User level security, but the client computer can use either Share or User level security.

C. Both the administering computer and the client computer must have Remote Registry Services installed.

D. Only the client computer must have Remote Registry Services installed.

Answer: A, C

Chapter 17

1. What is the central component in the communications architecture?

A. UNIMODEM.VXD

B. VCOMM

C. TAPI

D. Mini-drivers

Answer: B

2. What is the main device driver used to handle modem operations that is provided with Windows 95?

A. UNIMODEM.VXD

B. VCOMM

C. TAPI

D. Mini-drivers

Answer: A

3. What is the software written by the manufacturers that provides device-specific information used by each modem?

A. UNIMODEM.VXD

B. VCOMM

C. TAPI

D. Mini-drivers

Answer: D

4. What is the Windows 95 software that provides a method for programs to interact with telephony functionality in a standard, user-friendly format?

A. UNIMODEM.VXD

B. VCOMM

C. TAPI

D. Mini-drivers

Answer: C

Chapter 18

1. What three network protocols are supported by Dial-Up Networking?

A. NetBEUI

B. PPP

C. IPX/SPX

D. TCP/IP

Answer: A, C, D

2. What can you do to increase security when using mobile computing? (Select all that apply.)

   A. On the host computer, use User level security.

   B. Use password encryption.

   C. Encrypt your data files when transferring them.

   D. Use a system policy.

   Answer: A, B, C, D

3. A Windows 95 dial-up server can support all of the following except:

   A. Windows 95 client

   B. PPP-based client

   C. Windows NT client

   D. Macintosh client using AppleTalk

   Answer: D

4. Which protocol is the most flexible and is the default used by Windows 95?

   A. SLIP

   B. PPP

   C. NRN NetWare Connect

   D. NT RAS

   Answer: B

5. The Briefcase can synchronize files using all of the following except:

   A. Modem

   B. Win95Synch

   C. Floppy disk

   D. Null-modem cable

   Answer: B

6. What is networking that does not take place over a standard network cable, but rather across the telephone lines, sometimes called?

   A. Slow link

   B. Hyperlink

   C. Direct cable connection

   D. Indirect cable connection

   Answer: A

7. What three wide-area telephone networks does Windows 95 support with Dial-Up Networking?

   A. WANs

   B. PSTN

   C. X.25

   D. ISDN

   Answer: B, C, D

8. To ensure a secure connection between a client and a server across the Internet, you can use PPTP. Which of the following must be true to use PPTP? (Select all that apply.)

   A. The server must be configured with PPTP.

   B. The client must be configured with PPTP.

   C. The ISP must be configured with PPTP.

   D. Either the client or the ISP needs to have PPTP installed.

   Answer: A, D

Chapter 19

1. What is MAPI?

   A. A set of common commands that allows programs to communicate with mail systems and other MAPI-compliant programs

   B. A component in Global Positioning Systems

   C. Microsoft Application Programming Instructions

   D. A standard for 3D graphics

   Answer: A

2. What is a MAPI service provider?

   A. A method for connecting to the Internet

   B. An add-on component sold separately

   C. A component similar to a personal gateway that provides access to specified MAPI-compliant services

   D. A Microsoft Authorized Programming company

Answer: C

3. What must you do to access a new MAPI service?

   A. Belong to the group with rights to the service.

   B. Install the core MAPI services, which gives you access to all other MAPI services.

   C. Install a new service provider for each MAPI service.

   D. Do nothing, because by default you have access to all MAPI services.

Answer: C

4. Which of the following statements are true? (Select all that apply.)

   A. Post offices created with Windows 95 can easily communicate with each other.

   B. Windows Messaging is an add-on product that ships with the Microsoft Plus! pack.

   C. You can check services individually for new messages.

   D. You can connect to both Microsoft Mail and Windows 95 post offices using the default mail client.

Answer: C, D

5. How can you control the order in which address books will be searched for manual entries?

   A. Drag the icon for the address book to be searched first to the top of the Inbox.

   B. Type the order of the available address books in the message with the Subject: Address list order.

   C. In the Exchange client, select Tools ➢ Options ➢ Addressing tab, and set the order of the address books in the When Sending Mail... box.

   D. It's handled automatically; you can't configure it.

Answer: C

6. How can you secure your Personal Folder files?

  A. Store them only on a floppy disk.

  B. Put a password on them.

  C. You can't—everyone who can get to your computer can get to your personal folders.

  D. Save your folders with the name of Encrypted—this will automatically encrypt them.

Answer: B

7. What is the purpose of message profiles?

  A. To identify incoming message types

  B. To determine what service providers will be available in different environments

  C. To store message preferences

  D. For security use (encryption) only

Answer: B

8. What program would you use to create a new Windows 95 post office?

  A. Exchange Server running on Windows NT

  B. Windows Explorer

  C. PostOffice.exe

  D. The Microsoft Exchange client

Answer: D

9. Who can administer a post office?

  A. Any workgroup member with access to the post office share

  B. Only those workgroup members who are made members of the Admins group

  C. The user who created the post office

  D. Any user whose password is admin

Answer: C

10. How can you make a fax modem available to all of your users?

   A. You can't using Windows 95.

   B. Install an external modem with an automatic switch box, and cable all the users who want access to the box.

   C. Copy the files to be faxed to the computer with the modem, and then have that person do the faxing.

   D. Install the fax modem and then share it across the network.

   Answer: D

11. How can you send a fax?

   A. Drag and drop a document onto a shortcut to your fax.

   B. Go to Accessories ➤ Compose New Fax.

   C. Print a document to the Fax printer driver.

   D. Use the Exchange client to send e-mail to a fax recipient.

   Answer: A, B, C, D

Chapter 20

1. What protocol is required in order to use Internet Explorer?

   A. TCP/IP

   B. IPX/SPX

   C. NetBEUI

   D. DLC

   Answer: A

2. Can Windows 95 run Internet browsers?

   A. Yes, but only Microsoft's Internet Explorer.

   B. Yes, but only if you have the latest version of Internet Explorer.

   C. Yes, it can run any Internet browser written for Windows 95.

   D. No.

   Answer: C

3. What is Active Desktop?

   A. It turns your computer into a Personal Web Server.

   B. It converts your desktop into an ActiveX object.

   C. It converts your desktop into HTTP objects, which means that IE is then used to manage local as well as Internet resources.

   D. It changes the Explorer to more of a file-manager type interface.

   Answer: C

4. What is the language that WWW servers and browsers communicate in?

   A. DLC

   B. TCP/IP

   C. FTP

   D. HTTP

   Answer: D

5. Which HTTP server would be the best fit for a small doctor's office intranet server?

   A. Personal Web Server on Windows 95

   B. IIS on Windows NT Server

   C. Peer Web Services on Windows NT Workstation

   D. Site Server on Windows NT Server

   Answer: A

6. Which HTTP server should be used for a large, informational HTTP server?

   A. Personal Web Server

   B. IIS on Windows NT Server

   C. Peer Web Services on Windows NT Workstation

   D. Site Server on Windows NT Server

   Answer: B

7. Which HTTP server should be used for a mission-critical electronic commerce server?

   A. Personal Web Server

   B. IIS on Windows NT Server

C. Peer Web Services on Windows NT Workstation

D. Site Server on Windows NT Server

Answer: D

8. If you are accessing the Internet using a dial-up connection, which protocol(s) is required? (Select all that apply.)

A. NetBEUI

B. IPX/SPX

C. TCP/IP

D. DLC

Answer: C

9. To access the Internet as a client, you need to run which type of software?

A. An HTTP Server

B. An HTTP browser

C. Explorer will work fine.

D. My Computer will work fine.

Answer: B

10. To connect to an HTTP server running on a NetWare 3.12 server, you will need which protocol(s)? (Select all that apply.)

A. NetBEUI

B. IPX/SPX

C. TCP/IP

D. DLC

Answer: C

11. If you can connect to a Unix HTTP server by address, but not by name, which software program is probably at fault?

A. WINS

B. DNS

C. DHCP

D. NETBIOS

Answer: B

12. Which type of computers can be HTTP servers? (Select all that apply.)

   A. Windows 95

   B. Windows NT

   C. NetWare

   D. Unix

   Answer: A, B, C, D

13. If you can connect to an Internet server and can copy files, but cannot view any Web pages on that server, which type of Internet server did you connect to?.

   A. DHCP

   B. DNS

   C. FTP

   D. HTTP

   Answer: C

Chapter 21

1. What is the first step in troubleshooting?

   A. Isolate error conditions.

   B. Find out if it is a common issue.

   C. Diagnose specific symptoms.

   D. Consult technical support resources.

   Answer: C

2. What is the quickest form of electronic help in Windows 95?

   A. The Internet

   B. Online Help files

   C. BBS services

   D. 1-900 help lines

   Answer: B

3. Which application can be helpful if you can't get into Windows?

   A. Device Manager

   B. Control Panel

C. MSD

D. TechNet

Answer: C

4. Which files are bypassed during a Safe mode boot?

   A. CONFIG.SYS, AUTOEXEC.BAT, and the Startup group

   B. The registry and the Startup group

   C. The registry, SYSTEM.INI, and WIN.INI

   D. CONFIG.SYS, AUTOEXEC.BAT, and the registry

   Answer: D

5. Which application allows you to monitor a variety of system resources?

   A. Net Watcher

   B. FreeCell

   C. System Monitor

   D. Remote Registry Service

   Answer: C

6. Which application allows you to monitor a variety of network information?

   A. Net Watcher

   B. FreeCell

   C. System Monitor

   D. Remote Registry Service

   Answer: A

7. Which log file tracks items during the boot process?

   A. BOOTLOG.TXT

   B. DETCRASH.LOG

   C. NETLOG.TXT

   D. SETUPLOG.TXT

   Answer: A

8. Which ASCII log files are created during Windows 95 setup?

   A. BOOTLOG.TXT

   B. DETLOG.TXT

   C. SETUPLOG.TXT

   D. All of the above

   Answer: D

9. Which of the following describes the swapfile in Windows 95?

   A. Permanent

   B. Dynamic

   C. Fixed in size

   D. None of the above

   Answer: B

10. Which hard drive attribute(s) directly affect swapfile performance?

    A. Access time

    B. Free space

    C. Manufacturer

    D. A and B

    Answer: A

11. Which of the following will have the most adverse effect on system performance?

    A. Ten or more applications running

    B. Disabling the swapfile

    C. Having a dual-boot configuration

    D. Installing more than two printers

    Answer: B

12. What will pressing Ctrl+Alt+Del do?

    A. Reboot the system

    B. Automatically close the current application

    C. Bring up the online Help system

    D. Start the Task Manager

    Answer: D

13. What does the Task Manager allow you to shut down?

   A. Windows 95

   B. An application that has stopped responding

   C. Any running application

   D. All of the above

   Answer: D

14. What Windows 95 application will walk you through common printer issues?

   A. Print Troubleshooter

   B. Add New Hardware Wizard

   C. Control Panel

   D. None of the above

   Answer: A

APPENDIX

B

Adding and Removing
Windows 95 Components

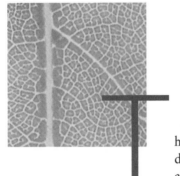

hroughout this book, we assume that when you installed Windows 95, you chose a Custom setup and then selected to install all the options (as we recommend in Chapter 2, Exercise 2.1). If you did not do this, or if you have a version of Windows 95 that was installed off of floppies rather than the CD-ROM version, you will need to add components to your system to follow the exercises in this book. For example, we demonstrate the use of the System Monitor, Registry Editor, and Backup programs, which are essential tools for systems engineers and administrators. You may also wish to add other optional components, such as the Clipboard Viewer, Quick View, and HyperTerminal.

This appendix explains how to add components after Windows 95 is installed on your system, as well as how to remove components and other software that you do not need.

Adding and Removing Components

You add and remove components through the Add/Remove Programs applet in the Windows 95 Control Panel. To open the Control Panel, select Start ➤ Settings ➤ Control Panel. From the Control Panel, double-click on the Add/Remove Programs icon. Then select the Windows Setup tab, which is shown in Figure B.1.

In most cases, you will need to put the Windows 95 CD back into the CD-ROM drive to install additional components. If you installed from a network share, make sure that you have access to that share before you try to install new components.

FIGURE B.1

The Windows Setup tab
of the Add/Remove
Programs Control Panel

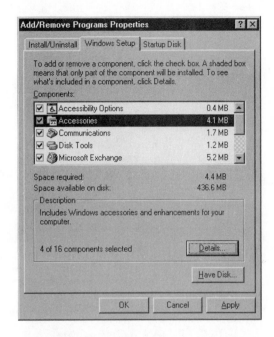

Component Categories

There are several categories of optional Windows 95 components that can be
installed. When you select an item, the dialog box will show the hard drive
space required for that item. To expand a category to see its contents, highlight it and click on the Details button. The categories and their individual
items are listed below.

Accessibility Options

The Accessibility Options category includes software for special needs. For
example, there is an option that provides easier operation of a computer with
only one hand.

Accessories

Accessories is the main category of components. It includes the following items:

- **Calculator:** A Desktop calculator

- **Character Map:** Allows you to insert symbols into documents

- **Clipboard Viewer:** Allows you to see the clipboard contents

- **Desktop Wallpaper:** Additional wallpaper files

- **Document Templates:** Additional templates

- **Games:** Includes FreeCell, MineSweeper, and Hearts

- **Mouse Pointers:** More mouse pointers

- **Net Watcher:** The Net Watcher program (see Chapter 16)

- **Online User's Guide:** A more detailed Help file

- **Paint:** A paint program

- **Quick View:** Allows you to view documents without the original application that made the document

- **Screen Savers:** More screen savers

- **System Monitor:** Allows you to monitor Windows 95 (see Chapters 4, 16, and 21)

- **System Resource Meter:** Allows you to see resource usage (see Chapter 7)

- **Windows 95 Tour:** An online introduction

- **WordPad:** A simple word processor

When you click on Accessories, note that only 4 of 16 components have been selected, as indicated to the left of the Details button in the Description section of the dialog box. To see which accessories have been installed, click on the Details button. This brings up the Accessories dialog box, as shown in Figure B.2.

FIGURE B.2

Click on the Details button of the Windows Setup tab to see which components are installed.

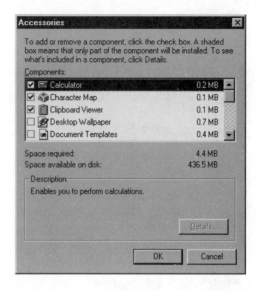

Communications

The Communications category includes the following components:

- **Dial-Up Networking:** Allows you to dial out to a server (see Chapter 18)
- **Direct Cable Connection:** Allows a direct cable connection (see Chapter 18)
- **HyperTerminal:** A modem dialer and terminal program
- **Phone Dialer:** A telephone dialer program

Disk Tools

The Disk Tools category includes Backup. This program allows you to back up and restore files on your hard drive (see Chapter 8).

Microsoft Exchange

The Microsoft Exchange category includes two components:

- **Microsoft Exchange:** Allows peer-to-peer e-mail (see Chapter 19)
- **Microsoft Mail Services:** Allows connection to Microsoft Mail

Microsoft Fax

The Microsoft Fax category includes two components:

- **Microsoft Fax Services:** Allows you to send faxes (see Chapter 19)
- **Microsoft Fax Viewer:** Allows you to view faxes

Multilanguage Support

The Multilanguage Support category includes support for the following languages:

- Central European
- Greek
- Cyrillic

Multimedia Support

The Multimedia Support category includes the following components:

- **CD-ROM Player:** Allows music CDs to be played (see Appendix D)
- **Volume Control:** Allows the volume to be adjusted
- **Various sound schemes:** Different sound samples

The Microsoft Network

The Microsoft Network category includes support for MSN, Microsoft's Internet service. See Chapter 20 for more information about Windows 95 and Internet connections.

Choosing Items

To add an item, click on the checkbox next to the accessory to put a checkmark in the box. To remove an installed component, click on its checkbox to deselect it (remove the checkmark).

When you are finished, click on the OK button to save your changes and leave the Details dialog box. Click on the OK button again to finish. New components will now be installed from the Windows 95 installation source.

Some software that you want to add will not be listed (SNMP, Remote Registry Service, etc.). In this case you have to use the Have Disk button to tell Windows 95 where to install the program from. You will have to specify a path (usually off of the CD-ROM or a floppy) in order to correctly install the program.

Uninstalling Other Software

When 32-bit applications install, they are supposed to register themselves with Windows 95 and the "Uninstall Shield" so they can be uninstalled easily. If the programs are registered, they will appear in the Install/Uninstall tab of the Add/Remove Programs Control Panel.

To uninstall a program, go to the Install/Uninstall tab and highlight the program, then click on the Add/Remove button. You should be prompted one last time before Windows 95 actually removes the program. If it uninstalls correctly, not only will the folders and files be gone from your hard drive, but its settings will be removed from the registry and it will no longer be listed on your Start menu.

APPENDIX

C

Plug and Play

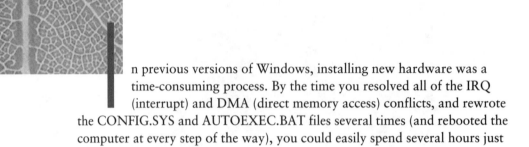

I n previous versions of Windows, installing new hardware was a time-consuming process. By the time you resolved all of the IRQ (interrupt) and DMA (direct memory access) conflicts, and rewrote the CONFIG.SYS and AUTOEXEC.BAT files several times (and rebooted the computer at every step of the way), you could easily spend several hours just installing a sound card.

Plug-and-Play Hardware

W indows 95 uses a technology called *Plug and Play* that makes the whole process a lot easier and less time-consuming. This technology allows you to install Plug-and-Play hardware into your system without needing to reconfigure the hardware or the computer system. When you add a new Plug-and-Play device, Windows 95 will automatically detect and configure the device. The catch is that the new hardware must conform to the Plug-and-Play specification.

Plug and Play is an industry standard design philosophy as well as a set of computer architecture specifications. A Plug-and-Play system can handle changes to the system's configuration without user intervention.

Plug and Play has been implemented in the Apple Macintosh family of computers for years. As long as the hardware you purchase is on Apple's hardware compatibility list and has drivers written for the Macintosh operating system, the configuration can be done automatically. Windows 95 also requires compatible hardware and drivers. However, because it is designed to be compatible with as many resources as possible and runs on the Intel $x86$-based microchips, Windows 95 tends to have more drivers and hardware components to choose from than the Macintosh system.

Here we will review the support required for Plug-and-Play systems, and then look at the Plug-and-Play process within Windows 95. Finally, we will provide some suggestions for avoiding Plug-and-Play problems and describe how to reconfigure devices with the Device Manager if necessary.

Requirements for Plug and Play

In a true Plug-and-Play system, you can add a new PC Card (formerly known as PCMCIA) to your computer, and the system will automatically recognize the card, dynamically load the appropriate drivers, and continue running without a restart of the workstation. You can take a Plug-and-Play laptop computer with an infrared printer port into a room with an infrared printer, and have your system automatically recognize the printer and load the printer drivers. This is all possible with a Windows 95 system, as long as it has the supporting Plug-and-Play hardware.

In a complete Plug-and-Play system, the BIOS, the operating system, and the hardware itself must all work together. The support required from each of these components is described in the following sections.

BIOS Support

The BIOS needs to support the following items:

- **System board device configuration:** During the boot process, the BIOS needs to configure system board devices.

- **Configuration information:** The BIOS needs to maintain the configuration information before relaying it to the operating system.

- **Notification:** The BIOS needs to notify the operating system of changes that occur after the operating system is running.

Operating System Support

The operating system needs to support the following items:

- **BIOS information processing:** The operating system needs to be able to receive and maintain the BIOS information. This includes the ability to handle notification events.

- **Device drivers:** The operating system needs to be able to load and unload the appropriate device drivers as needed.

- **Backward compatibility:** The operating system needs to be able to configure and use legacy components (devices and drivers that are not Plug and Play).

Hardware Support

The hardware needs to support the following items:

- **Self-identification and specification:** Devices must be able to identify themselves and specify their resource needs as well as their capabilities.

- **Dynamic configuration changes:** A Plug-and-Play device can be added to the system at any time, whether or not the system is running. Although it is not suggested that you add hardware while the system is running, you may need to reconfigure hardware while the computer is on.

An example of hardware that may need configuration changes while it is running is a laptop computer that docks at a workstation. The docking bay generally has a different monitor, keyboard, mouse, network card, and modem than those configured on the laptop itself.

There are three types of docking for laptops:

- *Hot docking* occurs when a laptop is placed into the docking bay while the system is up and running.

- *Warm docking* occurs when a laptop is placed into *sleep mode* or *suspend mode* while docking occurs.

- *Cold docking* occurs when you must shut down the laptop before placing it in the docking bay.

Windows 95 supports all three types of laptop docking. The type you choose depends on what the laptop hardware supports.

The Plug-and-Play Process in Windows 95

Windows 95 has many components that work together to implement the operating system portion of the Plug-and-Play standard. First we will discuss the individual components, and then we will see how they work together to configure devices.

Plug-and-Play Components

The Windows 95 components that work together to enable the Plug-and-Play process include bus enumerators, the registry database, a configuration manager, and a resource arbitrator. Let's take a look at what each of these components does.

The Registry Database

During the setup process, every device and bus in your system is identified. (A *bus* is simply a piece of hardware in your system that you can attach devices to.) The information is read from Hkey_Local_Machine and the devices themselves. The device and bus requirements are then stored in the registry database under Hkey_Dyn_Data. The device requirements are things like the IRQs that it can use, base I/O addresses, and memory. Every time your computer starts up, the registry database is read by the bus enumerators to gather this information for configuration of your system.

Bus Enumerators

The bus enumerators are device drivers for every bus in your system. Most computers have a motherboard/BIOS bus and an ISA or a PCI bus for configuring system components, a keyboard controller (bus), and a display controller (bus). There are other buses as well; for example, you might have a SCSI (Small Computer Serial Interface, pronounced "scuzzy") controller and a PC Card bus.

The bus enumerators give each bus a unique identification code. This is called *enumerating*, hence bus enumerators. In addition to assigning the ID code, a bus enumerator needs to gather the device configuration information from the registry (if available) as well as from the devices themselves. Bus enumerators must also assign resources to the buses and their devices.

The Configuration Manager

The configuration manager is responsible for coordinating the flow of information during the process of device configuration. It tells the other components when to take actions.

The Resource Arbitrator

The resource arbitrator gets the information from the bus enumerators and then assigns resources to each device. The resources that it can configure are IRQs, DMA channels, base I/O ports, and memory. Since there are limited numbers of these resources, and certain devices can use only certain IRQs and base I/O ports, the job of the resource arbitrator can be a bit tricky. Let's walk through an example of how it works.

Our example is illustrated in Figure C.1. This system has the following IRQ requirements:

- A modem that can use IRQ 3, 5, or 7

- A printer that must use IRQ 7

- A sound card that requires IRQ 5 or 7

- A legacy network card that requires IRQ 9

The resource arbitrator assigns legacy cards first because they are generally not configurable and don't allow for a range of values to be used. It then looks at the remaining devices and tries to apply a value to each. It will continue plugging in values until all of the resources have been configured. In our example, the legacy network card is assigned IRQ 9, the printer gets IRQ 7, the sound card gets IRQ 5, and the modem ends up with IRQ 3.

FIGURE C.1

The resource arbitrator assigns resources to devices.

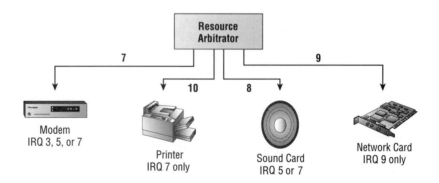

If for some reason your device was not configured properly, or not configured at all, you can manually modify these settings using the Device Manager. We will look at an example of using the Device Manager a little later in this chapter.

The Steps in the Plug-and-Play Process

The Plug-and-Play process in Windows 95 begins by placing all of the devices in configuration mode. They are not running yet, but are awaiting their resource assignments. Each card is identified and its resource requirements are gathered. The resources are then allocated and the cards are activated.

Let's take a closer look at what each component is doing in this process:

1. The configuration manager tells the bus enumerators to place all devices into configuration mode.

2. The bus enumerators gather the device information from the registry and/or the devices themselves.

3. The configuration manager passes that information on to the resource arbitrator.

4. The resource arbitrator makes the assignments and then passes the information back to the bus enumerators.

5. The bus enumerators give each device its resource assignments.

6. Finally, the system is ready to start, and the configuration manager gives the go-ahead.

7. The bus enumerators activate all cards with their new settings.

If a new device is detected while the system is running, the configuration manager will again begin the process of collecting the device information and arbitrating the necessary resources.

Troubleshooting Plug-and-Play Problems

Occasionally Plug and Play may not recognize your devices properly. To minimize these types of errors, you can do the following:

- Be sure that the *.INF files have all of the settings needed for your devices.

- Avoid IRQ and port address conflicts as much as possible. Many legacy cards have jumpers or switches on them to change their base I/O port and IRQ settings.

- Place your legacy cards closest to the power supply in your system. The POST (Power On Self Test) will look at each card in your system beginning with the cards closest to the power supply.

If Plug and Play still cannot configure the device correctly, you can use the Device Manager to reconfigure it. You access the Device Manager from the System Control Panel, as shown in Figure C.2. From there, you can go to the property sheet for the specific device. Figure C.3 shows an example of the Resources tab of a property sheet for a network card. In the example, the network card is set up to use IRQ 5 and has an I/O range of 300 to 31F in hexadecimal. If this does not suit your system, or if the Conflicting Device List box at the bottom of the dialog box shows that a conflict exists, you need to make changes. You can select a resource type from the Resource Settings box and change its settings. Figure C.4 shows the dialog box that allows you to modify the I/O range for the network card. Follow the steps in Exercise C.1 to reconfigure a network card. The procedure for configuring other devices with the Device Manager is similar.

FIGURE C.2

You can use the Device Manager to manually configure devices.

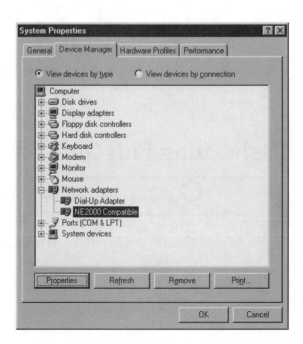

It is usually a good idea to reboot your system after reconfiguring a device, even if Windows 95 didn't tell you it was necessary. When you reboot, the new information is added to the registry database. If you don't reboot after making changes, and for some reason your system locks up and cannot be shut down normally, you will lose the configuration changes you made.

FIGURE C.3

The resources tab of a network card's property sheet

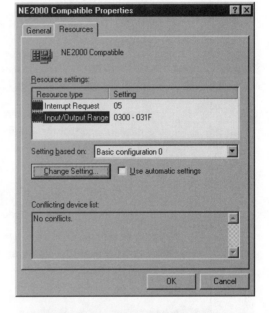

FIGURE C.4

Editing the I/O range of a network card

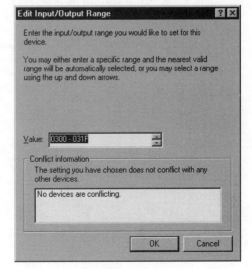

Configuring a Network Card with Device Manager

1. Go to Control Panel ➤ System.

2. Click on the Device Manager tab.

3. Find your network card, highlight it, and then click on the Properties button (Figure C.2).

4. Click on the Resources tab in the network card's property sheet (Figure C.3).

5. To alter the IRQ setting, highlight Interrupt Request in the Resource type list and click on the Change Setting button.

6. Use the up and down arrows to change the IRQ value. As you change the value, notice that the Conflict information box at the bottom of the screen indicates whether or not any devices are conflicting with the selected setting. Click on OK to return to the Resources tab.

7. To change the I/O range, highlight Input/Output Range in the Resource type list and click on the Change Setting button.

8. In the Edit Input/Output Range dialog box (Figure C.4), use the up and down arrows to alter the setting in the Value box. Again, as you change the value, the Conflict information box shows whether or not there are any conflicts.

9. When you are finished, click on OK until you are back at the Control Panel.

10. Depending on the changes you have made, your system may require a reboot.

APPENDIX

D

Multimedia

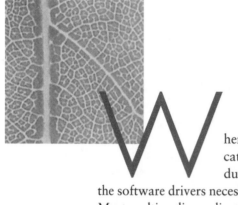

When Windows 95 was first released, multimedia applications were few and far between. This was partially due to the expense of creating hardware and acquiring the software drivers necessary to run the application on a variety of machines. Most multimedia applications were expensive. Many of the best less expensive multimedia applications were video games developed by freelance programmers and hackers. These games tended to push the leading edge in both hardware and CPU performance as well as video and sound technology. A good well-rounded, action-style 3D game is still a great way of testing your equipment. There are not many other applications out there that will test your CPU, video drivers, memory, and sound system like a fast-paced video game.

Windows 95 addressed the software and hardware difficulties by creating a host of "universal" drivers to handle the interface between Windows 95 and the hardware drivers themselves. Developers can simply write drivers specific to their equipment that also speak the universal Windows 95 driver language. These universal drivers include Audio, MIDI, Video, and CD Music. With all of these new drivers, we have a lot more to look forward to in the multimedia environment.

In this chapter, we will take a look at the new multimedia features in Windows 95 and the multimedia architecture. Then we'll cover your options for configuring multimedia features and devices. Finally, we'll go on a hunt for a Windows 95 Easter Egg.

One of the most common places you will find multimedia is on the World Wide Web. The Web is a fully interactive multimedia extravaganza, and is accessible through a multimedia-enabled Web browser like Microsoft's Internet Explorer 3.x or later, or Netscape's Navigator or Communicator.

New Multimedia Features in Windows 95

Windows 95 has many new multimedia features, including the following:

- Compression services for audio, video, and imaging feature an open interface for ease of software development.

- Video for Windows Runtime makes it possible to run digital video on any Windows 95 machine. The programming is easier, too, because the video becomes just another data type that a programmer can use.

- Enhanced MIDI (Musical Instrument Digital Interface) provides support for up to 16 channels and multiple instruments.

- The Sound Recorder allows you to record your own sounds through a microphone, MIDI interface, or even off of a CD.

- The CD Player allows you to play music from a CD.

Multimedia Architecture

As with other features in Windows 95, the multimedia architecture is organized in layers. The architecture is illustrated in Figure D.1.

Multimedia applications send data and commands to the Media Control Interface (MCI). The MCI then passes the binary data and commands on to the MMSYSTEM.DLL for routing to the appropriate drivers. The MMSYSTEM .DLL is the main driver for all multimedia functionality.

If audio data is not compressed, it goes directly to the audio driver and then on to the audio hardware. If it is compressed, it is sent through the Audio Compression Manager (ACM), which sends it to the appropriate decompression codec (coder/decoder), and then on to the audio hardware.

Video data is handled in a similar fashion, with one exception: There is a DCI (Microsoft/Intel Display Control Interface) which allows for high-speed direct access to the frame buffers. Using this interface provides smoother scrolling of images and faster loading.

FIGURE D.I

The Multimedia
architecture

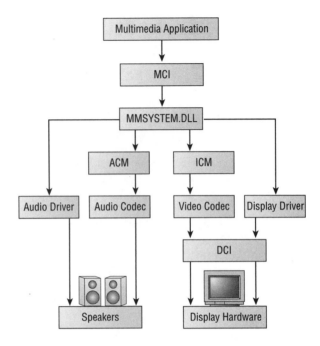

Configuring Multimedia Features

From the Multimedia Control Panel, you can configure the following:

- Audio playback and recording

- Real-time video playback

- MIDI component settings

- CD-ROM drive and playback volume

- Individual multimedia devices

The following sections discuss these features in more detail.

Configuring Audio Settings

The Audio tab of the Multimedia Properties dialog box, shown in Figure D.2, allows you to configure settings for audio playback and recording of *.WAV files (called *wave audio*).

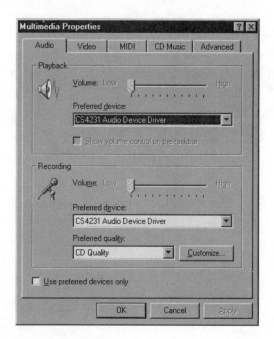

The Playback section includes settings for adjusting the volume and choosing the preferred playback device driver. If you have more than one device driver for wave audio, you can select it here.

The Recording section has a volume setting and a recording device driver selection box. The quality is divided into four different levels. It also has a Preferred quality option. Each quality level has a different sound quality and corresponding file size, as follows:

- **TrueSpeech:** Highly compressed for voice recording only. Nonspeech sounds do not record well, if at all.

- **Telephone:** One of the lowest settings. The quality is what you might expect over a regular telephone. The upside is that the files generated are generally very small.

- **Radio:** This intermediate setting is a nice compromise. It is better than the telephone, not as good as full stereo CD, but takes up a moderate amount of disk space.

- **CD:** The highest quality stereo sound. It also has the largest associated file sizes.

For best recordings, leave the recording Volume slider at about halfway between Low and High (approximately 50 percent). This will cut out static and white noise.

Configuring Video Settings

The Video tab of the Multimedia Properties dialog box, shown in Figure D.3, allows you to configure how your real-time videos will be played. You can choose to show them full screen, which will make the images fit your monitor, or you can display them in a window. Video for Windows real-time files are also known as AVI files and have an .AVI extension. The Windows 95 CD has several AVI files in the \FunStuff folder. Just double-click on one of the files to watch it run.

FIGURE D.3

The Video tab of the Multimedia Properties dialog box

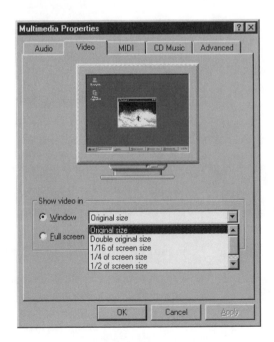

If you choose to display your video in a window, Windows 95 will automatically profile the images and determine what size windows to use for sharpest display and best speed. If you want to override these changes, select from the Video tab's list of options, which include choices such as Original Size, Double Original Size, 1/16 of Screen Size, 1/4 of Screen Size, and so on.

The more colors and depth in the images, the slower they will display. You can modify your monitor's resolution and color palette settings through the Settings tab of the Display Control Panel. See Chapter 5 for details.

Configuring MIDI Components

The MIDI tab of the Multimedia Properties dialog box, shown in Figure D.4, is where you can make changes to your MIDI components. MIDI is a serial interface standard that allows you to connect musical instruments to the computer. Windows 95 MIDI can support up to 16 different channels and assign them to one or more instruments.

FIGURE D.4

The MIDI tab of the Multimedia Properties dialog box

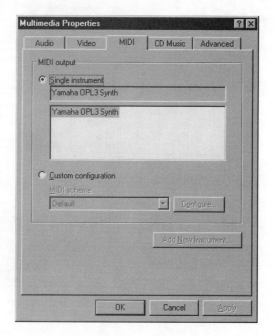

To view the channels and their associated MIDI instruments, double-click on the instrument listed in the Single instrument box.

Windows 95 includes several MIDI samples. Also, most 16-, 32-, and 64-bit sound cards come with MIDI interface software. The quality of playback depends entirely on the quality of the sound card.

Configuring and Playing CD-ROM Music

You can set the CD-ROM drive and the playback volume from the CD Music tab of the Multimedia Properties dialog box, shown in Figure D.5.

When you insert an audio CD into the player, the CD Player will launch automatically, as shown in Figure D.6. From here you can start, stop, fast forward, rewind, and skip tracks, as well as set continuous play mode or a random playback.

FIGURE D.5

The CD Music tab of the Multimedia Properties dialog box

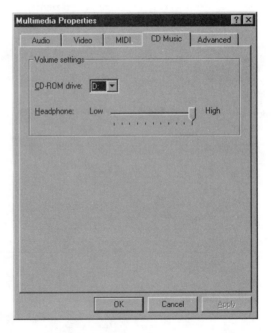

Another nice feature of the CD Player program is that it allows you to create a database of music. As you add new CDs to your system, you can tell the computer who the artist is, what tracks are playing, and even specify a track order, skipping songs you don't like and listening to the ones you do like in your preferred order. You can also name each track. The next time that CD is placed in your PC, you'll be able to edit that list again. Figure D.7 shows the Disc Settings dialog box for the CD Player.

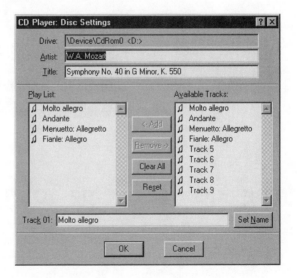

Configuring Multimedia Devices

The Advanced tab of the Multimedia Properties dialog box, shown in Figure D.8, allows you to configure individual multimedia devices that are attached to your PC. You can enable and disable devices. To alter the configuration of a device, select it and click on the Properties button.

FIGURE D.8

The Advanced tab of the Multimedia Properties dialog box

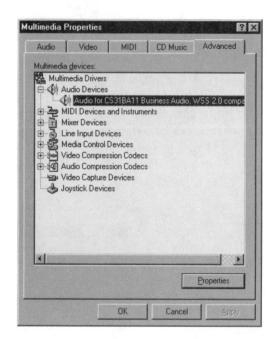

Assigning and Recording Sounds

Through the Sounds Control Panel, shown in Figure D.9, you can assign, or "tag," sounds to system events. For example, you can have a special sound play when Windows 95 starts up.

If you have the Microsoft Plus! package, you can install themes. These themes will automatically tag a whole group of sounds. For example, the Jungle theme will allow your computer to make jungle noises, like birds chirping and frogs croaking, when you perform different actions on your PC.

In addition to tagging sounds, themes also modify screen savers and usually create animated cursors. When the system is busy, you no longer have to look at an hourglass—you might see the R2-D2 android from the movie *Star Wars* walking along.

FIGURE D.9

The Sounds Properties
dialog box

There are many Web sites out there where you can download new and exciting themes. One of our favorite places for themes is www.winfiles.com.

The Sound Recorder, shown in Figure D.10, allows you to record your own sounds. It works much like a regular tape recorder. The sounds are recorded in the quality that you chose from the Audio tab of the Multimedia Properties dialog box (described earlier in the chapter). To use this program, click on the button with the red circle on it. You are now recording. Click on the button with the black box to stop recording. You have just created a .WAV file.

FIGURE D.10

The Sound Recorder can
be used to record your
own custom sounds.

Easter Eggs

Windows 95 and many applications have Easter Eggs in them. An Easter Egg is a mini-application that is normally undocumented. By going through a series of oftentimes odd instructions and procedures, you get to see a small animation, sound scheme, or both. These animations are usually a list of application programmers and contributors.

There are Easter Eggs for Windows 95, most of the Microsoft Office applications, and many third-party applications. Follow the steps in Exercise D.1 to find the Windows 95 Easter Egg. They will take you to the Easter Egg in Figure D.11. The Clouds.mid sequence will also be playing, so if you have speakers configured on your system, turn them on.

FIGURE D.11

The Windows 95
Easter Egg

WARNING

Be sure to follow each step in Exercise D.I very carefully—one mistake, and you must start over.

EXERCISE D.I

Finding the Windows 95 Easter Egg

1. In a clear area on your Desktop, right-click and choose New from the context menu. From the next pop-up menu, choose Folder. You now have a new folder sitting on your Desktop with the cursor waiting for you to change the name. We will be changing the name of this new folder three times.

Note that this Easter Egg is case-sensitive. This means that when you see a capital letter, you must type a capital letter.

2. Begin by typing the following:
   and now, the moment you've all been waiting for

3. Once you have typed in that line, press the Enter key once. This forces Windows 95 to accept the new folder name.

4. Single-click (with your left mouse button) on the name portion of your new folder. This selects the text for editing.

5. Press the Backspace key once. This deletes the current folder name and leaves the insertion point at the beginning of the folder.

6. Now type in the following:
   we proudly present for your viewing pleasure

7. Once you have typed in that line, press the Enter key to make this the new folder name.

8. Single-click on the name of the new folder.

9. Press the Backspace key once to delete the folder name again.

10. With the insertion point at the beginning of the folder, type the following:
    The Microsoft Windows 95 Product Team!

EXERCISE D.1 (CONTINUED FROM PREVIOUS PAGE)

Note the capital letters and the exclamation point at the end of the filename.

11. Press the Enter key.

12. Double-click on the folder (with your left mouse button). If you did everything correctly, your Easter Egg should now be running and look like Figure D.11.

You can find additional Easter Egg instructions for many applications on the Web. Go to your favorite search engine (such as Yahoo or AltaVista) and search for "Easter Eggs."

The DirectX API

Microsoft has written a multimedia API set called DirectX, which developers can use to easily incorporate graphics, sound, and video into their applications. The only problem is that DirectX wasn't ready in time for the initial release of Windows 95, so it must be installed over the old drivers. Some older applications may not work correctly with the DirectX support installed, because they were written to the old specifications. In most cases, these problems are related to incompatibilities with the display driver part of DirectX.

OSR2 and Windows NT 4.0 come with support for DirectX 2.0 built in. DirectX 5.0 (the latest version) is usually installed with the latest games, or can be downloaded for no additional charge from www.microsoft.com. DirectX 6.0 is scheduled to be released in July 1998.

Windows 95 also uses DirectX drivers to establish a common multimedia API set, which may be incompatible with older applications or display adapters. If you are experiencing problems with DirectX drivers, check with your display driver manufacturer.

APPENDIX

E

Glossary

A

accounts Containers for *security* identifiers, *passwords, permissions, group* associations, and *preferences* for each user of a system. User accounts need to be created on a *NetWare* or Windows NT *server* before a Windows 95 machine can log in as a *client*.

adapter Any hardware device that allows communications to occur through physically dissimilar systems. This term usually refers to peripheral cards permanently mounted inside computers that provide an interface from the computer's *bus* to another media, such as a hard disk or a network.

Administer Utility A Windows 95 utility that gives an administrator access to the hard disks on a remote workstation.

API See *Application Programming Interface.*

Application layer The layer of the *OSI model* that interfaces with User mode *programs* called applications by providing high-level network services based on lower-level *Network layers*. Network *file systems* like *named pipes* are an example of Application layer software.

Application Programming Interface (API) An application to allow transparent access to *operating system* or networking functions.

asynchronous data stream In communications, the method of passing *packets* of information one packet at a time in a continuous stream. Communications *resources* that provide this can be physical, like a modem, or logical, like a fax service on a computer that uses the modem for transmittal and reception of faxes.

auto-detect The Windows 95 ability to automatically detect and install *drivers* for newer hardware.

B

backup browser A computer on a Microsoft network that maintains a list of computers and services available on the network. The *master browser* supplies this list. The backup browser distributes the *browsing* service load to a *workgroup* or *domain*.

Basic Input/Output System   See *BIOS*.

bindery   A *NetWare* 2.*x* and 3.*x* structure that contains user *accounts* and *permissions*. NetWare 4.*x* replaces the bindery with *NetWare Directory Services* (NDS).

BIOS (Basic Input/Output System)   A set of routines in firmware that provides the most basic software interface *drivers* for hardware attached to the computer. The BIOS contains the bootstrap routine.

boot   The process of loading a computer's *operating system*. Booting usually occurs in multiple phases, each successively more complex, until the entire operating system and all its services are running. Also called "bootstrap." The computer's *BIOS* must contain the first level of booting.

bridge   A device that connects two networks of the same data link *protocol* by forwarding those *packets* destined for computers on the other side of the bridge. See also *router, Data Link layer*.

Briefcase   A Windows 95 utility that can be used to synchronize files on two computers.

browser   A computer on a Microsoft network that maintains a list of computers and services available on the network. See also *Web browser*.

browsing   The process of requesting the list of computers and services on a network from a *browser*.

bus   The type of *adapter* that the motherboard uses to connect any peripheral devices. Different buses include *ISA, EISA*, and *PCI*.

C

caching   A speed-*optimization* technique that keeps a copy of the most recently used data in a fast, high-cost, low-capacity storage device rather than in the device upon which the actual data resides. Caching assumes that recently used data is likely to be used again. Fetching data from the cache is faster than fetching data from the slower, larger storage device. Most caching algorithms also copy next-most-likely-to-be-used data and perform write caching to further increase speed gains. See also *write-back caching, write-through caching*.

client   A computer on a network that subscribes to the services provided by a *server*.

client/server   A network architecture that dedicates certain computers called *servers* to act as service providers to computers called *clients*, which users operate to perform work. Servers can be dedicated to providing one or more network services, such as file storage, shared printing, communications, *e-mail* service, and Web response. See also *share, peer.*

client/server application   An application that splits large applications into two components: computer-intensive *processes* that run on an application *server* and user interfaces that run on *clients*. Client/server applications communicate over the network through *interprocess communications mechanisms.*

components   Interchangeable elements of a complex software or hardware system. Windows 95 components can be added to an installed system through the Add/Remove Programs applet in the Windows 95 *Control Panel.*

compression   A space-*optimization* scheme that reduces the size (length) of a data set. Compression reduces redundancy in the data by creating symbols smaller than the data they represent and an index that defines the value of the symbols for each compressed set of data.

computer name   A 1- to 15-character *NETBIOS* name used to uniquely identify a computer on the network.

Control Panel   A Windows 95 software utility that controls the functions (*properties*) of specific *operating system* services through property sheets. The *registry* contains the Control Panel settings on a system and/or per user basis. The main Control Panel applets in Windows 95 include Add New Hardware, Add/Remove Programs, Date/Time, Display, Fonts, Internet, Mail and Fax, Modems, Mouse, Multimedia, Network, Passwords, Printers, and System. Some applications add other applets to the Control Panel.

cooperative multitasking   A *multitasking* scheme in which each *process* must voluntarily return time to a central *scheduling* route. If any single process fails to return to the central scheduler, the computer will lock up. Both the Windows and Macintosh *operating systems* use this scheme.

D

Data Link layer   In the *OSI model*, the layer that provides the digital interconnection of network devices and the software that directly operates these devices, such as network interface *adapters.*

database   A related set of data organized by type and purpose. The term also can include the application software that manipulates the data. The Windows 95 *registry* is a database.

Desktop   The Windows 95 GUI (*Graphical User Interface*). Windows 95 *boots* directly to the Desktop, which includes the *Taskbar*. Documents, *folders*, and *shortcuts* to printers can be stored directly on the Desktop.

DHCP (Dynamic Host Configuration Protocol)   A method of automatically assigning *IP addresses* to *client* computers on a network.

Dial-Up Connections   *Data Link layer* digital connections made via modems over regular telephone lines. Refers to temporary digital connections, as opposed to leased telephone lines, which provide permanent connections.

Dial-Up Networking   A Windows 95 feature that allows the system to use a modem to connect to a network using telephone lines. The modem acts like a slow network card.

Direct Cable Connection   A Windows 95 feature that allows the connection of two Windows 95 machines (a *host* and a guest) directly through a null-modem cable. With Direct Cable Connection, files can be copied back and forth between the machines.

DLL   See *dynamic-link library*.

DNS   See *Domain Name Service*.

domain   In Microsoft networks, an arrangement of *client* and *server* computers, referenced by a specific name, that share a single *security permissions database*. On the *Internet*, a domain is a named collection of *hosts* and subdomains, registered with a unique name by the *InterNIC* (the agency responsible for assigning *IP addresses*).

domain name   The textual identifier of a specific Internet *host*. Domain names are in the form server.organization.type (for example, www.microsoft .com) and are resolved to Internet addresses by *domain name servers*.

domain name server   An Internet *host* dedicated to the function of translating fully qualified *domain names* into *IP addresses*.

Domain Name Service (DNS)   The *TCP/IP* network service that translates textual Internet network addresses into numerical Internet network addresses.

driver   A *program* that provides a software interface to a hardware device.

dual-booting   The process of *booting* to another *operating system* while Windows 95 is installed. The other operating system can be a previous version of MS-DOS or Windows, or Windows NT.

Dynamic Data Exchange (DDE)   A method of *interprocess communications* within the Microsoft Windows *operating systems*. When two or more applications that support DDE are running at the same time, they can exchange data and commands.

Dynamic Host Configuration Protocol   See *DHCP*.

dynamic-link library (DLL)   A library of modular functions that can be used by many *programs* simultaneously. The three main components of the Windows 95 *operating system* are implemented as DLLs: the *Kernel* (KERNEL32.DLL and KERNEL.DLL), User (USER32.DLL and USER.DLL), and *GDI* (GDI32.DLL and GDI.DLL). There are hundreds of functions stored within DLLs.

E

Easter Egg   A mini-application built into many applications, usually to display information about the developers. Easter Eggs are usually not documented and are revealed by going through a series of oftentimes odd procedures.

EISA (Extended Industry Standard Architecture)   An architecture that provides 32-bit *bus* access. EISA is compatible with 8-bit and 16-bit *ISA*.

electronic mail (e-mail)   A type of *client/server application* that provides a routed, stored-message service between any two user e-mail accounts. E-mail accounts are not the same as user accounts, but a one-to-one relationship usually exists between them. Because all modern computers can attach to the Internet, users can send e-mail over the Internet to any location that has telephone or wireless digital service. Windows 95 includes an e-mail *post office* and *client*.

emergency repair disk   A floppy diskette that contains critical *registry* information about a Windows 95 installation, also called a *Startup disk*. With an emergency repair disk, a Windows 95 installation can be salvaged using the restore option when re-installing from CD-ROM. This disk can be created during Windows 95 setup, or later through the Add/Remove Programs applet of the *Control Panel*.

encryption   The process of obscuring information by modifying it according to a mathematical function known only to the intended recipient. Encryption secures information being transmitted over nonsecure or untrusted media.

environment variables   Variables, such as the search path, that contain information available to *programs* and batch files about the current *operating system* environment.

Ethernet   The most popular *Data Link layer* standard for local-area networking. Ethernet implements the carrier sense multiple access with collision detection (CSMA/CD) method of arbitrating multiple computer access to the same network. This standard supports the use of Ethernet over any type of media including wireless broadcast. Standard Ethernet operates at 10Mbps (megabits per second). Fast Ethernet operates at 100Mbps.

Exchange   See *Microsoft Exchange.*

Explorer   See *Windows Explorer.*

Extended Industry Standard Architecture   See *EISA.*

extranet   A secured wide-area network between two or more companies that uses the Internet for *packet* transfer.

F

FAT32   A FAT *(file allocation table)* format that overcomes some of the limitations of the original FAT, but loses backward compatibility. The *OSR2* version of Windows 95 is the only operating system that supports FAT32.

File Allocation Table (FAT)   The *file system* used by MS-DOS and available to other *operating systems* such as Windows (all variations), OS/2, and Macintosh. FAT has become something of a mass-storage compatibility standard because of its simplicity and wide availability. FAT has few fault-tolerance features and can become corrupted through normal use over time.

file and printer sharing   A Windows 95 feature that allows Windows 95 to act as a *server.* When file and printer sharing is installed, other computers can connect to the machine and copy files or print to a printer.

file attributes   Bits that show the status of a file (such as archived, hidden, read-only) and are stored along with the name and location of a file in a directory entry. *Operating systems* use file attributes to help in implementing such services as sharing, *compression*, and *security*.

file system   A software component that manages the storage of files on a mass-storage device by providing services that can create, read, write, and delete files. File systems impose an ordered *database* of files, called *volumes*, on the mass-storage device. Volumes use hierarchies of directories to organize files.

File Transfer Protocol   See *FTP*.

folder   A directory in Windows 95.

frame type   The main parameter of the *IPX/SPX protocol*. Different frame types can be run on networks. For example, *Ethernet* has four possible frame types; *Token Ring* has two possible frame types.

FTP (File Transfer Protocol)   A simple Internet *protocol* that transfers complete files from an FTP *server* to a *client* running the FTP client. FTP provides a simple method of transferring files between computers, but cannot perform *browsing* functions. You must know the *URL* or the *IP address* of the FTP server to which you wish to attach.

G

gateway   A computer that serves as a *router*, a format translator, or a *security* filter for an entire network.

GDI   See *Graphical Device Interface*.

General Protection Fault (GPF)   A general protection fault occurs when a *program* violates the integrity of the system. This often happens when a program tries to access memory that is not part of its memory address space. A GPF is a defense mechanism employed by the *operating system*.

Graphical Device Interface (GDI)   The *programming interface* and graphical services provided to *Win32* for programs to interact with graphical devices such as the screen and printer.

Graphical User Interface (GUI)   A computer *shell program* that represents mass-storage devices, directories, and files as graphical objects on a screen. A cursor driven by a pointing device such as a mouse manipulates the objects.

group   A *security* entity to which users can be assigned membership for the purpose of applying the broad set of group *permissions* to the user. By managing permissions for groups and assigning users to groups, rather than assigning permissions to users, security administrators can keep coherent control of very large security environments.

GUI   See *Graphical User Interface.*

H

hardware detection   The Windows 95 ability to automatically find new hardware. An element of *Plug and Play.*

hardware profiles   Used to manage portable computers that have different configurations. For example, laptops may have two different hardware profiles (configurations), one for docked and one for undocked.

home directory   A directory that stores user's personal files and *programs.*

home page   The default page returned by an *HTTP server* when a *URL* containing no specific document is requested.

host   An Internet *server.* Hosts are constantly connected to the Internet.

HTML (Hypertext Markup Language)   A textual data format that identifies sections of a document as headers, lists, hypertext links, and so on. HTML is the data format used on the *World Wide Web* for the publication of *Web pages.* See also *HTTP.*

HTTP (Hypertext Transfer Protocol)   An Internet *protocol* that transfers *HTML* documents over the Internet and responds to context changes that happen when a user clicks on a hypertext link. See also *World Wide Web.*

hyperlink   A link in text or graphics files that has a Web address embedded within it. By clicking on the link, users can jump to another Web address. A hyperlink is usually a different color than the rest of the *Web page.*

Hypertext Markup Language   See *HTML.*

Hypertext Transfer Protocol   See *HTTP.*

I

IDE (Integrated Drive Electronics)   A simple mass-storage device inter-connection *bus* that can handle no more than two attached devices. IDE devices are similar to but less expensive than *SCSI* devices.

Industry Standard Architecture   See *ISA*.

Integrated Services Digital Network   See *ISDN*.

Internet   A voluntarily interconnected global network of computers based upon the *TCP/IP protocol* suite. TCP/IP was originally developed by the U.S. Department of Defense's Advanced Research Projects Agency to facilitate the interconnection of military networks and was provided free to universities. The obvious utility of worldwide digital network connectivity and the avail-ability of free complex networking software developed at universities doing military research attracted other universities, research institutions, private organizations, businesses, and finally the individual home user. The Internet is now available to all current commercial computing platforms.

Internet Explorer   See *Microsoft Internet Explorer*.

Internet Protocol   See *IP*.

Internet service provider (ISP)   A company that provides *Dial-Up Con-nections* to the Internet.

Internetwork Packet Exchange (IPX)   See *IPX*.

InterNIC   The agency that is responsible for assigning *IP addresses*.

interprocess communications (IPC)   A generic term describing any manner of *client/server* communication *protocol*, specifically those operating in the *Session*, *Presentation*, and *Application layers* of the *OSI model*. IPC mecha-nisms provide a method for the client and server to trade information. See also *named pipe, remote procedure calls, NETBIOS*.

interrupt request (IRQ)   A hardware signal from a peripheral device to the *microprocessor* indicating that it has I/O (input/output) traffic to send. If the microprocessor is not running a more important service, it will interrupt its current activity and handle the interrupt request. IBM PCs have 16 levels of interrupt request lines. Each device must have a unique interrupt request line.

intranet   A privately owned network based on the *TCP/IP protocol* suite.

IP (Internet Protocol)   The *Network layer protocol* upon which the Internet is based. IP provides a simple, connectionless *packet* exchange. Other protocols such as *UDP* or *TCP* use IP to perform their connection-oriented or guaranteed delivery services. See also *TCP/IP*.

IP address   A four-byte number that uniquely identifies a computer on an *IP* internetwork. *InterNIC* assigns the first bytes of Internet IP addresses and administers them in hierarchies. Huge organizations like the government or top-level *ISPs* have class A addresses, large organizations and most ISPs have class B addresses, and small companies have class C addresses. In a class A address, InterNIC assigns the first byte, and the owning organization assigns the remaining three bytes. In a class B address, InterNIC or the higher-level ISP assigns the first two bytes, and the organization assigns the remaining two bytes. In a class C address, InterNIC or the higher-level ISP assigns the first three bytes, and the organization assigns the remaining byte. Organizations not attached to the Internet are free to assign IP addresses as they please.

IPC   See *interprocess communications*.

IPX (Internetwork Packet Exchange)   The network *protocol* developed by Novell for its *NetWare* products. IPX is a routable, connection-oriented protocol similar to *IP* but much easier to manage and with lower communication overhead. The term IPX can also refer to the family of protocols that includes the SPX (Synchronous Packet Exchange) *Transport layer* protocol.

IRQ   See *interrupt request*.

ISA (Industry Standard Architecture)   The design standard for 16-bit Intel compatible motherboards and peripheral *buses*. The 32/64-bit *PCI* bus standard is replacing the ISA standard. *Adapters* and interface cards must conform to the bus standard(s) used by the motherboard in order to be used with a computer.

ISDN (Integrated Services Digital Network)   A direct, digital dial-up *PSTN* (Public-Switched Telephone Network) *Data Link layer* connection that operates at 64KB per channel over regular twisted-pair cable between a subscriber site and a PSTN central office. Up to 24 channels can be multiplexed over two twisted pairs.

ISP   See *Internet service provider*.

K

kernel   The core process of a *preemptive operating system*, consisting of a *multitasking* scheduler and the basic services that provide *security*. Depending on the operating system, other services such as *virtual memory* drivers may be built into the kernel. The kernel is responsible for managing the *scheduling* of *threads* and *processes*.

L

LAN Manager   The Microsoft brand of a network product jointly developed by IBM and Microsoft that provided an early *client/server* environment. LAN Manager/Server was eclipsed by *NetWare*, but was the genesis of many important *protocols* and IPC mechanisms used today, such as *NETBIOS, named pipes,* and *NetBEUI.* Portions of this product exist today in OS/2 Warp Server. See also *interprocess communications.*

LFN   See *long filenames.*

local user profile   A *user profile* that is stored only on the local computer. If a user logs on to one computer, makes changes to the environment, and then logs on to another computer, the changes from the first computer are not reflected on the second computer.

logging   The process of recording information about activities and errors in the *operating system.*

logon   The process of being authenticated by a Windows NT *server.*

logon script   Command files that automate the logon process by performing utility functions such as attaching to additional *server resources* or automatically running different *programs* based upon the user *account* that logged in. Logon scripts can be run by both *NetWare* and Windows NT servers.

long filename (LFN)   A filename longer than the eight characters plus three-character extension allowed by MS-DOS. In Windows 95 (and NT), filenames can contain up to 255 characters.

M

MAC layer   See *Media Access Control (MAC) layer.*

mandatory user profile A *user profile* that is created by an administrator and saved with a special extension (.MAN) so that the user cannot modify the profile in any way. Mandatory user profiles can be assigned to a single user or a *group* of users.

MAPI See *Messaging Application Programming Interface.*

master boot record (MBR) Contains the pointer to the machine's *boot* files. After the *BIOS* bootstrap, the system loads the MBR and the *partition* table of the bootable drive, and executes the MBR.

master browser The computer on a network that maintains a list of computers and services available on the network and distributes the list to other *browsers*. The master browser may also promote potential browsers to browsers. See also *backup browser.*

MBR See *master boot record.*

Media Access Control (MAC) layer Another name for the *Data Link layer* of the *OSI model.* It consists of the *driver* for the *network interface card.* This layer helps watch for errors in the transmission and conversion of signals.

Messaging Application Programming Interface (MAPI) A messaging application standard developed by Microsoft to allow for interaction between an application and various message service providers.

metafile In Windows, a file with a .WMF extension that contains a collection of internal commands that Windows 95 uses to render graphics to the screen.

microprocessor An integrated semiconductor circuit designed to automatically perform lists of logical and arithmetic operations. Modern microprocessors independently manage memory pools and support multiple instruction lists called *threads*. Microprocessors are also capable of responding to *interrupt requests* from peripherals and include onboard support for complex floating-point arithmetic. Microprocessors must have instructions when they are first powered on. These instructions are contained in nonvolatile firmware called a *BIOS.*

Microsoft Client for Microsoft Networks Software that allows Windows 95 to be a *client* on a Microsoft network.

Microsoft Client for NetWare Networks Software that allows Windows 95 to be a *client* on a *NetWare* network.

Microsoft Exchange Microsoft's messaging application. Exchange implements Microsoft's *Messaging Application Programming Interface* (MAPI) as well as other messaging *protocols* (such as POP, *SNMP*, and faxing) to provide a flexible message composition and reception service.

Microsoft Fax Software that allows a fax modem to send and/or receive faxes.

Microsoft Internet Explorer A *World Wide Web browser* produced by Microsoft and included with later versions of Windows 95 (the OSR2 version) and Windows NT 4.0.

MIDI (Musical Instrument Digital Interface) A serial interface standard that allows you to connect musical instruments to the computer.

mini-driver A driver from a manufacturer that, combined with Microsoft's *universal driver*, provides full functionality.

module A software component of a modular *operating system* that provides a certain defined service. Modules can be installed or removed depending upon the service requirements of the software running on the computer. Modules allow operating systems and applications to be customized to fit the needs of the user.

multiprocessing Using two or more *processors* simultaneously to perform a computing task. Depending on the *operating system*, processing may be done asymmetrically, wherein certain processors are assigned certain *threads* independent of the load they create, or symmetrically, wherein threads are dynamically assigned to processors according to an equitable *scheduling* scheme. The term usually describes a multiprocessing capacity built into the computer at a hardware level in that the computer itself supports more than one processor. However, multiprocessing can also be applied to network computing applications achieved through *interprocess communications* mechanisms. *Client/ server applications* are, in fact, examples of multiprocessing.

multitasking   The capacity of an *operating system* to rapidly switch among *threads* of execution. Multitasking allows *processor* time to be divided among threads as if each thread ran on its own slower processor. Multi-tasking operating systems allow two or more applications to run at the same time and can provide a greater degree of service to applications than single-tasking operating systems like MS-DOS. See also *multiprocessing, multithreaded*.

multithreaded   Refers to *programs* that have more than one chain of execu-tion, thus relying on the services of a *multitasking* or *multiprocessing operating system* to operate. Multiple chains of execution allow programs to simultaneously perform more than one task. In multitasking computers, multithreading is merely a convenience used to make programs run smoother and free the program from the burden of switching between tasks itself. On multiprocessing computers, multithreading allows the compute burden of the program to be spread across many *processors*. Programs that are not multithreaded cannot take advantage of multiple processors in a computer.

Musical Instrument Digital Interface   See *MIDI*.

N

named pipe   An *interprocess communications* mechanism that is imple-mented as a *file system* service, allowing *programs* to be modified to run on it without using a proprietary *Application Programming Interface*. Named pipes were developed to support more robust *client/server* communications than those allowed by the simpler *NETBIOS*.

NCP   See *NetWare Core Protocol*.

NDIS   See *Network Driver Interface Specification*.

NDS   See *NetWare Directory Services*.

Net Watcher   A built-in Windows 95 interactive tool for creating, control-ling, and monitoring remote shared *resources*.

NetBEUI (NETBIOS Extended User Interface)   A simple *Network layer* transport developed to support *NETBIOS* installations. NetBEUI is not routable, and so it is not appropriate for larger networks. NetBEUI is the fastest *transport protocol* available for Windows 95, although its use is limited.

NETBIOS (Network Basic Input/Output System) A *client/server inter-process communications* service developed by IBM in the early 1980s. NETBIOS presents a relatively primitive mechanism for communication in *client/server applications*, but its widespread acceptance and availability across most *operating systems* make it a logical choice for simple network applications. Many of the network interprocess communications mechanisms in Windows 95 are implemented over NETBIOS.

NETBIOS Extended User Interface See *NetBEUI.*

NETBIOS over TCP/IP (NetBT) A network service that implements *NETBIOS* over the *TCP/IP protocol* stack.

NetDDE See *Network Dynamic Data Exchange.*

NetSetup A Windows 95 *program* used for creating setup scripts that will perform the Windows 95 installation automatically, as well as specifying a setup *server*. NetSetup uses the *System Policy Editor* interface.

NetWare A popular *network operating system* developed by Novell in the early 1980s. NetWare is a cooperative, *multitasking*, highly optimized, dedicated-*server* network operating system that has *client* support for most major operating systems. Recent versions of NetWare include graphical client tools for management from client stations.

NetWare Core Protocol (NCP) The language *NetWare servers* use to communicate. A Windows 95 machine with the *Microsoft Client for NetWare Networks* software installed can communicate with NetWare servers.

NetWare Directory Services (NDS) In *NetWare*, a distributed hierarchy of network services such as *servers*, shared *volumes*, and printers. NetWare implements NDS as a directory structure with elaborate *security* and administration mechanisms.

Network Basic Input/Output System See *NETBIOS.*

Network Driver Interface Specification (NDIS) A Microsoft specification to which network *adapter drivers* must conform in order to work with Microsoft *network operating systems*. NDIS provides a many-to-many binding between network adapter drivers and *transport protocols*.

Network Dynamic Data Exchange (NetDDE)   An *interprocess communications* mechanism developed by Microsoft to support the distribution of *DDE* applications over a network.

Network Interface Card (NIC)   A *Physical layer adapter* device that allows a computer to connect to and communicate over a local-area network. See also *Ethernet, Token Ring*.

Network layer   The layer of the *OSI model* that creates a communication path between two computers via routed *packets*. *Transport protocols* implement both the *Network* layer and the *Transport layer* of the OSI model. *IP* is a Network layer service.

network operating system   A computer *operating system* specifically designed to optimize a computer's ability to respond to service requests. *Servers* run network operating systems. Windows NT Server and *NetWare* are both network operating systems.

New Technology File System (NTFS)   A secure, transaction-oriented *file system* developed for Windows NT that incorporates the Windows NT *security* model for assigning *permissions* and *shares*. NTFS is optimized for hard drives larger than 500MB and requires too much overhead to be used on hard disk drives smaller than 50MB. Windows 95 cannot read or write to an NTFS *partition*.

non-browser   A computer on a network that will not maintain a list of other computers and services on the network. See also *browser, browsing*.

NTFS   See *New Technology File System*.

O

object   Almost anything in Windows 95. In Microsoft's object-oriented approach to the Windows 95 interface, files, *folders*, printers, *programs*, the *Desktop* itself, hard drives, the monitor, the keyboard, and so on are considered objects. The characteristics of an object are controlled by that object's *properties*.

Object Linking and Embedding (OLE)   A mechanism that allows Microsoft Windows applications to include each other's creations, such as a graphics image or a spreadsheet, in files. An OLE object incorporated in a document can be edited or modified by the *program* that created it; the user can double-click on that object to invoke its originating program.

ODI (Open Data-link Interface) real-mode drivers   Novell's older standard for *drivers* used to install network cards. For Windows 95, these drivers are loaded from the AUTOEXEC.BAT file. ODI drivers include LSL, NE2000, IPXODI, VLM, or NETX.

Open Graphics Language (OpenGL)   A standard interface for the presentation of two- and three-dimensional visual data.

Open Systems Interconnection model   See *OSI model.*

OpenGL   See *Open Graphics Language.*

operating system   A collection of services that form a foundation upon which applications run. Operating systems may be simple I/O (input/output) service providers with a command *shell*, such as MS-DOS, or they may be sophisticated, *preemptive multitasking, multiprocessing* applications platforms like Windows 95.

optimization   Any effort to reduce the workload on a hardware component by eliminating, obviating, or reducing the amount of work required of the hardware component through any means. For instance, file *caching* is an optimization that reduces the workload of a hard disk drive.

OSI (Open Systems Interconnection) model   A model for network component interoperability developed by the International Standards Organization (ISO) to promote cross-vendor compatibility of hardware and software network systems. The OSI model splits the process of networking into seven distinct services: *Physical layer, Data Link layer, Network layer, Transport layer, Session layer, Presentation layer,* and *Application layer.* Each layer uses the services of the layer below to provide its service to the layer above.

OSR2   A newer release of Windows 95, also called the B version. This version includes all the patches to the original version of Windows 95, plus additional features such as *FAT32.*

P

packet   A piece of information that is exchanged between computers. A packet usually contains the source and destination addresses, as well as the actual data being exchanged.

page fault   Occurs when there is a call for a data page that is not in physical memory (RAM). When the system has a page fault, it is reading information from hard disk rather than memory. Excessive page faulting can result in poor overall performance. See also *thrashing*.

page file   See *swapfile*.

paging   The process of transferring some data pages out to a *swapfile* when the physical RAM becomes full. Also called "demand paging."

partition   A section of a hard disk that can contain an independent *file system volume*. Partitions can be used to keep multiple *operating systems* and file systems on the same hard disk.

PCI (Peripheral Connection Interface)   A high-speed, 32/64-bit *bus* interface developed by Intel and widely accepted as the successor to the 16-bit *ISA* interface. PCI devices support I/O (input/output) *throughput* about 40 times faster than the ISA bus.

PDC   See *primary domain controller*.

peer   A networked computer that both shares *resources* with other computers and accesses the shared resources of other computers. A nondedicated *server*. See also *client*.

peer-to-peer   A networking or messaging system in which each computer can be both a *client* and a *server*. In Windows 95, this type of sharing can be configured and used by end users without special server configuration.

Peripheral Connection Interface   See *PCI*.

permissions   Assignments of levels of access to a *resource* made to *groups* or users. Administrators can assign permissions to allow any level of access, such as read only, read/write, or delete, by controlling the ability of users to initiate *object* services. Permissions are used to assign rights to users in a Microsoft or *NetWare* network when *User level security* is being used in Windows 95.

Personal Web Server (PWS)   A Web *server* component for Windows 95. PWS can enable Windows 95 to act as a full-service Web server. PWS comes with *OSR2*, and can be downloaded for earlier versions of Windows 95.

Physical layer   In the *OSI model*, the cables, connectors, and connection ports of a network. The passive physical components required to create a network.

PIF (Program Information File)   A file that allows MS-DOS-based *programs* to coexist with Windows programs. A PIF is a configuration header file for the MS-DOS *virtual machine*.

Plug and Play   The technology that allows installation of Plug-and-Play hardware into a Windows 95 system without needing to configure the hardware or the computer system. When a new Plug-and-Play device is added, Windows 95 will automatically detect and configure the device.

Point and Print   A Windows 95 method used to install *driver* files for a networked printer by dragging the Point-and-Print printer icon from the networked PC to the Printers *folder*. Documents can be printed to networking printers by simply dragging and dropping them onto the printer icon.

Point-to-Point Protocol   See *PPP*.

Point-to-Point Tunneling Protocol   See *PPTP*.

policy   See *system policy*.

Policy Editor   See *System Policy Editor*.

post office   A central location for storage of *e-mail* messages. This storage can be on a workstation's hard drive or on a network *server*. Windows 95 comes with an e-mail post office that is designed for *peer-to-peer* networks.

PPI   See *Print Provider Interface*.

PPP (Point-to-Point Protocol)   A *Data Link layer* transport that performs over point-to-point network connections such as serial or modem lines. PPP can negotiate any *transport protocol* used by both systems involved in the link and can automatically assign *IP*, *DNS*, and *gateway* addresses when used with *TCP/IP*.

PPTP (Point-to-Point Tunneling Protocol)   *Protocol* used to create secure connections between private networks through the public Internet or an *ISP*. PPTP is the protocol used to create *VPNs* (Virtual Private Networks).

preemptive multitasking   A *multitasking* implementation in which an interrupt routine in the *kernel* manages the *scheduling* of *processor* time among running *threads*. The threads themselves do not need to support multi-tasking in any way because the *microprocessor* will preempt the thread with an interrupt, save its state, update all thread priorities according to its scheduling algorithm, and pass control to the highest *priority* thread awaiting execution. Because of the preemptive nature, a thread that crashes will not affect the operation of other executing threads.

Preferences   Characteristics of user *accounts* on a *server*, such as password, profile location, *home directory*, and *logon script*.

Presentation layer   That layer of the *OSI model* that converts and, if necessary, translates information between the *Session* and *Application layers*.

primary domain controller (PDC)   The *domain server* in a Windows NT system that contains the master copy of the *security*, computer, and user *accounts databases* and that can authenticate workstations. The PDC can replicate its databases to one or more backup domain controllers. The PDC is usually also the *master browser* for the domain.

print driver   The software that understands a specific print device's command set. Each print device has an associated print *driver*.

Print Provider Interface (PPI)   A modular interface with interchangeable components that allows third-party vendors to seamlessly integrate network *print drivers* into Windows 95.

print queue   A *folder* where print jobs are held until they are printed.

print server   A computer on which the printers in a network are defined. When a user sends a job to a network printer, it is actually sent to the print server first.

print spooler   A directory or *folder* on the *print server* that actually stores the print jobs until they can be printed. The print server and print spooler should have enough hard disk space to hold all of the print jobs that could be pending at any given time.

priority   A level of execution importance assigned to a *thread*. In combination with other factors, the priority level determines how often that thread will get computer time according to a *scheduling* algorithm. See also *preemptive multitasking*.

process   A running *program* containing one or more *threads*. A process encapsulates the protected memory and environment for its threads.

processor   A circuit designed to automatically perform lists of logical and arithmetic operations. Unlike *microprocessors*, processors may be designed from discrete components rather than be a monolithic integrated circuit.

program   A list of *processor* instructions designed to perform a certain function. A running program is called a *process*. A package of one or more programs and attendant data designed to meet a certain application is called software.

Programming Information File   See *PIF*.

Programming Interfaces   *Interprocess communications* mechanisms that provide certain high-level services to running *processes*. Programming interfaces may provide network communication, graphical presentation, or any other type of software service.

property   A characteristic of a Windows 95 *object* Properties include a wide variety of attributes that can be examined and changed. For example, changing the wallpaper on the *Desktop* is done through the Desktop's properties; swapping the left and right mouse buttons is done through the mouse's properties.

protected mode   The Windows 95 32-bit mode of operation, which offers superior performance, protection, and *security* compared with *real mode*. Protected mode requires a 386-compatible CPU, and an *operating system* that supports it.

protocol   An established communication method that the parties involved understand. Protocols provide a context in which to interpret communicated information. Computer protocols are rules used by communicating devices and software services to format data in a way that all participants understand. See also *transport protocol*.

PSTN   See *Public-Switched Telephone Network.*

Public-Switched Telephone Network (PSTN)   A global network of inter-connected digital and analog communication links originally designed to support voice communication between any two points in the world, but quickly adapted to handle digital data traffic when the computer revolution occurred. In addition to its traditional voice support role, the PSTN now functions as the *Physical layer* of the Internet (in the *OS model* architecture) by providing dial-up and leased lines for the interconnections.

R

RAS   See *Remote Access Service.*

real mode   The older, Windows 16-bit mode of operation. Windows 3.*x* and MS-DOS 6.*x* are written to 16-bit standards. See also *protected mode.*

Recycle Bin   The Windows 95 utility that keeps track of deleted files and allows users to recover them.

redirector   A software service that redirects user file I/O (input/output) requests over the network. The redirector can go either to local *resources* or to a *NetWare*, Windows NT, or other network *server.*

Reduced Instruction Set Computer (RISC)   A *microprocessor* technology that implements fewer and more primitive instructions than typical microprocessors and can therefore be implemented quickly with the most modern semiconductor technology and speeds. *Programs* written for RISC microprocessors require more instructions (longer programs) to perform the same task as a normal microprocessor, but are capable of a greater degree of *optimization* and therefore usually run faster.

registry   A *database* of settings required and maintained by Windows 95 and its components. The registry contains all the configuration information used by the computer. It is stored as a hierarchical structure and is made up of keys, subkeys, and value entries. You can use the Registry Editor (REGEDIT) to change these settings.

Remote Access Service (RAS) A service that allows network connections to be established over telephone lines with modems or digital *adapters*. The computer initiating the connection is called the RAS client; the answering computer is called the RAS host. See also *Public-Switched Telephone Network*.

remote procedure calls (RPC) A network *interprocess communications* mechanism that allows an application to be distributed among many computers on the same network.

Remoteboot A service that starts diskless workstations over a network.

resource Any useful service, such as a shared network directory or a printer. See also *share*.

Ring 0; Ring 3 See *x86 ring architecture*.

RIP (Routing Information Protocol) A *protocol* within the *TCP/IP* protocol suite that allows *routers* to exchange routing information with other routers. A variant of RIP also exists for the *IPX/SPX* protocol suite.

RISC See *Reduced Instruction Set Computer*.

roaming user profile A *user profile* that is stored and configured to be downloaded from a *server*. Roaming user profiles allow users to access their profile from any location on the network.

router A *Network layer* device that moves *packets* between networks. Routers provide internetwork connectivity.

Routing Information Protocol See *RIP*.

RPC See *remote procedure calls*.

S

Safe mode A *boot* mode that bypasses loading the *registry*, CONFIG.SYS, and AUTOEXEC.BAT files. It does not load any network functionality or *protected-mode drivers*. Safe mode starts Windows 95 in standard VGA and loads HIMEM.SYS, IFSHLP.SYS, and the PATH statement from MSDOS.SYS.

SAP (Service Advertising Protocol)   A *NetWare packet*, broadcast from the *server* every 60 seconds, that contains the server name and the shared *resources* it has. Windows 95 can also generate a SAP so that NetWare *clients* will see the Windows 95 machine as a NetWare server.

ScanDisk   A *program* that looks for errors on the hard disk. ScanDisk can find and fix errors in *folders* or files.

scheduling   The process of determining which *threads* should be executed according to their *priority* and other factors. See also *preemptive multitasking*.

SCSI (Small Computer Systems Interface)   A high-speed, parallel-*bus* interface that connects hard disk drives, CD-ROM drives, tape drives, and many other peripherals to a computer. SCSI (pronounced "scuzzy") is the mass-storage connection standard among all computers except IBM compatibles, which may use SCSI or *IDE*.

search engine   A Web site dedicated to responding to requests for specific information, searching massive locally stored *databases* of *Web pages*, and responding with the *URLs* of pages that fit the search phrase.

security   Measures taken to secure a system against accidental or intentional loss, usually in the form of accountability procedures and use restriction.

Serial Line Internet Protocol   See *SLIP*.

server   A computer dedicated to servicing requests for *resources* from other computers on a network. Servers typically run *network operating systems* such as Windows NT Server or *NetWare*. See also *client/server*.

Server Message Block   See *SMB*.

Service Advertising Protocol   See *SAP*.

Session layer   The layer of the *OSI model* dedicated to maintaining a bi-directional communication connection between two computers. The Session layer uses the services of the *Transport layer* to provide this service.

share   A *resource*, such as a directory or printer, shared by a *server* or a *peer* on a network.

Share level security   The default level of *security* used in Windows 95 (and Windows for Workgroups). Share level security is based on passwords assigned to shared *resources*. See also *User level security*.

shell   The user interface of an *operating system*; the shell launches applications and manages *file systems*.

shortcut   A special instruction, or pointer, to launch an *object* (*program*, file, printer, and so on) with Windows 95. Shortcuts are usually stored on the *Desktop*, but they can be stored in *folders* as well. Deleting or editing a shortcut does not affect the original object. Shortcuts are identified with an .LNK extension.

Simple Network Management Protocol   See *SNMP*.

SLIP (Serial Line Internet Protocol)   An implementation of the *IP* (Internet Protocol) over serial lines. SLIP has been obviated by *PPP*.

slow link   Networking across telephone lines rather than over a standard network cable. Modem connections to a network are considered slow links because they generally run between 14,400 to 28,800 bps on an analog modem and up to 128,800 bps on a digital modem using *ISDN* (Integrated Services Digital Network) connections. A network cable can run between 4.2 million to 10 million bps, or 65 to 200 times faster than a modem connection.

Small Computer Systems Interface   See *SCSI*.

SMB (Server Message Block)   The language Microsoft *servers* use to communicate on a network.

SNMP (Simple Network Management Protocol)   An Internet *protocol* that manages network hardware such as *routers*, switches, *servers*, and *clients* from a single client on the network.

spooler   A service that buffers output to a low-speed device such as a printer so the software outputting to the device is not tied up waiting for it.

Startup disk   A bootable floppy disk with Windows 95 startup files that can be used to *boot* or troubleshoot a Windows 95 machine. Windows 95 can create a Startup disk during Windows 95 installation, or later, through the Add/Remove Programs applet in the *Control Panel*.

subnet mask   A number mathematically applied to *IP addresses* to determine which IP addresses are a part of the same subnetwork as the computer applying the subnet mask.

swapfile   The *virtual memory* file on a hard disk containing the memory pages that have been moved out to disk to increase available RAM.

System Monitor   A Windows 95 utility that monitors system parameters and statistics. For example, the System Monitor can be used to monitor *virtual machine* usage, *page faults*, and *threads*.

system policy   A method used to control what a user can do and the user's environment. System policies can be applied to a specific user, a *group*, a computer, or all users. System policies work by overwriting current settings in the Windows 95 *registry* with the system policy settings. For Windows 95, system policies are created through the *System Policy Editor*. In Windows NT, policies affect restrictions on password use and rights assignment and determine which events will be recorded in the Security log.

System Policy Editor   A Windows 95 utility used to create *system policies*. This program is not installed by default; it must be installed from the Windows 95 CD-ROM (found within the Administrative Tools group).

T

TAPI   See *Telephony Application Program Interface*.

Task Manager   A Windows 95 application that allows users to view and close running *processes*. The Task Manager can also be used to view CPU and memory statistics. Press Ctrl+Alt+Del to launch the Task Manager.

Taskbar   The gray bar at the bottom of the Windows 95 screen, which replaces the Task Manager of previous versions of Windows. The Taskbar holds buttons that represent running *programs* as well as the Start menu button. It is used to switch between running programs and to open the Start menu.

TCP (Transmission Control Protocol)   A *Transport layer protocol* that implements guaranteed *packet* delivery using the *Internet Protocol*. See also *TCP/IP*.

TCP/IP (Transmission Control Protocol/Internet Protocol) A suite of network *protocols* upon which the global Internet is based. TCP/IP is a general term that can refer either to the *TCP* and *IP* protocols used together or to the complete set of Internet protocols.

Telephony Application Program Interface (TAPI) A standard way for *programs* to interact with the telephony functionality in Windows 95.

templates ASCII files with an .ADM extension used to create Windows 95 *system policies*. Entries in a template correspond to subkeys and values in the *registry*.

thrashing Excessive *page faults*. This can occur when RAM runs low, and *programs* and data are paged out to the hard disk. Thrashing can often be eliminated by adding more memory or using fewer applications at one time.

thread A list of instructions running in a computer to perform a certain task. Each thread runs in the context of a *process*, which embodies the protected memory space and the environment of the threads. *Multithreaded* processes can perform more than one task at the same time. See also *multitasking*.

throughput The measure of information flow through a system in a specific time frame, usually one second. For instance, 28.8Kbps is the throughput of a modem: 28.8 kilobits per second can be transmitted.

Token Ring A *Data Link layer* standard for local-area networking. Token Ring implements the token-passing method of arbitrating multiple-computer access to the same network. Token Ring operates at either 4 or 16 megabits per second (Mbps). FDDI is similar to Token Ring and operates at 100Mbps.

Transmission Control Protocol See *TCP*.

Transmission Control Protocol/Internet Protocol See *TCP/IP*.

Transport layer The *OSI model* layer responsible for the guaranteed serial delivery of *packets* between two computers over an internetwork. *TCP* is the Transport layer *protocol* for the *TCP/IP transport protocol*.

transport protocol A service that delivers discrete *packets* of information between any two computers in a network. Transport protocols may operate at the *Data Link*, *Network*, *Transport*, or *Session layers* of the *OSI model*. Higher-level, connection-oriented services are built upon transport protocols.

U

UNC (Universal Naming Convention) A multivendor, multiplatform convention for identifying shared *resources* on a network.

Uniform Resource Locator See *URL*.

universal driver A *driver* written by Microsoft that contains the bulk of the code that makes up the entire driver. A universal driver, such as a *print driver* or the Unimodem driver, is used in conjunction with a *mini-driver*, supplied by the manufacturer.

Universal Naming Convention See *UNC*.

Unix A *multitasking, kernel*-based *operating system* developed at AT&T in the early 1970s and provided (originally) free to universities as a research operating system. Because of its availability and ability to scale down to *microprocessor*-based computers, Unix became the standard operating system of the Internet and is the closest approximation to a universal operating system that exists. Most computers can run some variant of the Unix operating system.

URL (Uniform Resource Locator) An Internet standard naming convention for identifying resources available via various *TCP/IP* application *protocols*. For example, http://www.microsoft.com is the URL for Microsoft's *World Wide Web server* site; ftp://gateway.dec.com is a popular *FTP* site. A URL allows easy hypertext references to a particular resource from within a document or mail message.

User level security A level of *security* that allows Windows 95 to share its *resources* by granting rights to existing users and *groups* from an existing Windows NT or *NetWare server*. See also *Share level security*.

user profile A method used to save each user's Desktop configuration. See also *local user profile, mandatory user profile, roaming user profile*.

username A user's *account* name in a *logon*-authenticated system. See also *security*.

V

Vcache   A *protected-mode* hard drive *caching program* that is integrated into Windows 95.

VCOMM   A Windows 95 *driver* that communicates with the serial ports and modems.

virtual machine (VM)   A method used by Windows 95 to fool *programs* into thinking that they have exclusive access to all system hardware. Virtual machines run in Ring 3 of the Windows 95 system architecture and use a message-passing technique to access memory and hardware. Two types of virtual machines exist in Windows 95: a System VM and multiple MS-DOS VMs. All Windows-based programs run in the System VM. Each MS-DOS-based program runs in its own MS-DOS VM. See also *x86 ring architecture*.

virtual memory   A *kernel* service that stores memory pages not currently in use on a mass-storage device to free up the memory occupied for other uses. Virtual memory hides the memory-swapping process from applications and higher-level services. See also *swapfile*.

Virtual Prinvate Nework   See *VPN*.

VM   See *virtual machine*.

volume   A collection of data indexed by directories containing files and referred to by a drive letter. Volumes are normally contained in a single *partition*, but volume sets and stripe sets extend a single volume across multiple partitions. Windows NT is required in order to build a volume or stripe set.

VPN (Virtual Private Network)   A secure connection to the Internet using PPTP.

W

Web browser   An application that makes *HTTP* requests and formats the resultant *HTML* documents for the users. Most Web browsers understand all standard Internet *protocols*.

Web page   Any *HTML* document on an *HTTP server*.

Win16   The set of application services provided by the 16-bit versions of Microsoft Windows: Windows 3.1 and *Windows for Workgroups 3.11.*

Win32   The set of application services provided by the 32-bit versions of Microsoft Windows: Windows 95 and Windows NT.

Windows 3.11 for Workgroups   The current 16-bit version of Windows for less-powerful, Intel-based personal computers. This system includes *peer*-networking services.

Windows 95   The current 32-bit version of Microsoft Windows for medium-range, Intel-based personal computers. This system includes *peer*-networking services, Internet support, and strong support for older DOS applications and peripherals.

Windows Explorer   The default *shell* for Windows 95 and Windows NT 4.0. Explorer implements the more flexible *Desktop object* paradigm rather than the Program Manager paradigm used in earlier versions of Windows.

Windows Internet Name Service (WINS)   A network service for Micro-soft networks that provides Windows computers with Internet numbers for specified *NETBIOS* names, facilitating *browsing* and intercommunication over *TCP/IP* networks.

Windows NT   The current 32-bit version of Microsoft Windows for pow-erful Intel, Alpha, PowerPC, or MIPS-based computers. This system includes *peer*-networking services, *server*-networking services, Internet *client* and server services, and a broad range of utilities.

WINS   See *Windows Internet Name Service.*

workgroup   In Microsoft networks, a collection of related computers, such as a department, that don't require the uniform *security* and coordination of a *domain*. Workgroups are characterized by decentralized management as opposed to the centralized management that domains use.

World Wide Web (WWW)   A collection of *Internet servers* providing hypertext-formatted documents for Internet *clients* running *Web browsers*. The World Wide Web provided the first easy-to-use graphical interface for the Internet and is largely responsible for the Internet's explosive growth. See also *HTML, HTTP.*

write-back caching   A *caching optimization* technique wherein data written by applications is cached until the cache is full or until a subsequent write operation overwrites the cached data. Write-back caching can significantly reduce the write operations because many write operations are subsequently obviated by new information. Data in the write-back cache is also available for subsequent reads. If something happens to prevent the cache from writing data to the application, the cache data will be lost. See also *write-through caching*.

write-through caching   A *caching optimization* technique wherein data written to applications is kept in a cache for subsequent rereading. Unlike *write-back caching*, write-through caching immediately writes the data to the application and is therefore less optimal but more secure.

WWW   See *World Wide Web*.

X

X.25   A standard that defines *packet*-switching networks.

x86 ring architecture   An architecture that supports multiple levels of *processor*-provided protection for running *programs*. These levels are called *rings*. Transitioning between rings uses a lot of time and system resources. In order to increase speed and reduce errors, Windows 95 uses only two rings in the *x*86 architecture: Ring 0 and Ring 3.

Index

NOTE: Page numbers in *italics* refer to figures; page numbers in **bold** refer to primary discussions of topic.

O

Object Linking and Embedding (OLE), 738
object-oriented approach, 102
object-sensitive menus, 107–108
objects, 737
   selecting, 106
ODI drivers, 738
   for NetWare clients, 387
Office 97, Web page creation in, 580–581
OLE (Object Linking and Embedding), 738
   Registry information about, 191, 193
Open command, for Network Neighborhood, 310
Open files, monitoring, 604
Open Graphics Language (OpenGL), 738
open programs
   moving among, **103–104**, 173
   and performance, 608
open protocol, 319
Open sockets, monitoring, 601
Open Systems Interconnection (OSI) model, 738
Open window. *See* Windows Explorer, Open window
open windows, Desktop with, *104*
operating system, 738
   components, **87–88**
   information from Microsoft Diagnostics, 593
   and Plug and Play, **699**
optimization, 738
Option Properties dialog box, 174
Options dialog box
   for Exchange client

General tab, *555*
   Services tab, *549*
Options menu for Help, *115*
orphaned files, in briefcase, 537
OS/2, 33
   compressed drives and, 257
   support for NetWare servers, 387
OSI (Open Systems Interconnection) model, **298–300**, *300*, 738
   Windows 95 and, **301–302**
OSR2, 738
Other memory, monitoring, 603
Out of Memory errors, in Windows 3.*x*, 223
Outlook Express, *575*, *576*
outside line, dialing pause to access, 511

P

.PAB file extension, 552
packet, 739
page fault, 80, 739
   monitoring, 603
   tracking with System Monitor, 81–82
Page-ins, monitoring, 603
Page-outs, monitoring, 603
page table, 80
PAGEFILE.SYS, 83
pages in memory, 80
paging, 739
paging file, 609
paper size for printing, 428
parallel cables, 530
parent folder, 155
parity, for modem connection, 506

MCSE ELECTIVE STUDY GUIDES FROM NETWORK PRESS®

ybex's Network Press expands the definitive study guide series for MCSE candidates.

ISBN: 0-7821-2224-8
688pp; 7¹/₂" x 9"; Hardcover
$49.99

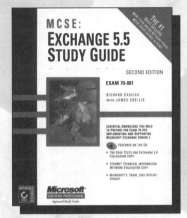

ISBN: 0-7821-2261-2
848pp; 7¹/₂" x 9"; Hardcover
$49.99

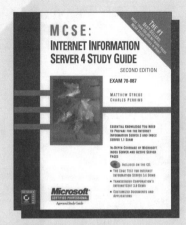

ISBN: 0-7821-2248-5
704pp; 7¹/₂" x 9"; Hardcover
$49.99

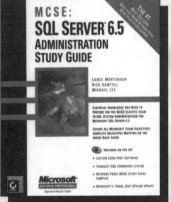

ISBN: 0-7821-2172-1
672pp; 7¹/₂" x 9"; Hardcover
$49.99

ISBN: 0-7821-2194-2
576pp; 7¹/₂" x 9"; Hardcover
$49.99

ISBN: 0-7821-1967-0
656pp; 7¹/₂" x 9"; Hardcover
$49.99

Microsoft® Certified
Professional
Approved Study Guide

NETWORK PRESS®
SYBEX

STUDY GUIDES FOR THE MICROSOFT CERTIFIED SYSTEMS ENGINEER EXAMS

NETWORK PRESS® PRESENTS
MCSE TEST SUCCESS
THE PERFECT COMPANION BOOKS TO THE MCSE STUDY GUIDES

MCSE Test Success:
NETWORKING ESSENTIALS
EXAM 70-058
TODD LAMMLE

GET READY FOR THE EXAM—
OBJECTIVE BY OBJECTIVE

MASTER ALL THE MATERIAL
YOU NEED TO KNOW

PRACTICE ON 500 REVIEW
QUESTIONS AND SAMPLE
TEST QUESTIONS

ISBN: 0-7821-2146-2
352pp; 7¹/₂" x 9"; Softcover
$24.99

MCSE Test Success:
NT SERVER 4
EXAM 70-067
LISA DONALD

GET READY FOR THE EXAM—
OBJECTIVE BY OBJECTIVE

MASTER ALL THE MATERIAL
YOU NEED TO KNOW

PRACTICE ON 500 REVIEW
QUESTIONS AND SAMPLE
TEST QUESTIONS

ISBN: 0-7821-2148-9
352pp; 7¹/₂" x 9"; Softcover
$24.99

Here's what you need to know to pass the MCSE tests.

- Review concise summaries of key information

- Boost your knowledge with 400 review questions

- Get ready for the test with 200 tough practice test questions

MCSE Test Success:
NT WORKSTATION 4
EXAM 70-073
TODD LAMMLE
LISA DONALD

GET READY FOR THE EXAM—
OBJECTIVE BY OBJECTIVE

MASTER ALL THE MATERIAL
YOU NEED TO KNOW

PRACTICE ON 550
REVIEW QUESTIONS AND
SAMPLE TEST QUESTIONS

ISBN: 0-7821-2149-7
400pp; 7¹/₂" x 9"; Softcover
$24.99

MCSE Test Success:
NT SERVER 4
IN THE ENTERPRISE
EXAM 70-068
LISA DONALD

GET READY FOR THE EXAM—
OBJECTIVE BY OBJECTIVE

MASTER ALL THE MATERIAL
YOU NEED TO KNOW

PRACTICE ON MORE THAN 500
REVIEW QUESTIONS AND SAMPLE
TEST QUESTIONS

ISBN: 0-7821-2147-0
442pp; 7¹/₂" x 9"; Softcover
$24.99

Other MCSE Test Success titles:

- **Core Requirements Box Set**
  (4 books, 1 CD)
  [ISBN: 0-7821-2296-5] April 1998

- **Windows® 95**
  [ISBN: 0-7821-2252-3] May 1998

- **Exchange Server 5.5**
  [ISBN: 0-7821-2250-7] May 1998

- **TCP/IP for NT® 4**
  [ISBN: 0-7821-2251-5] May 1998

Microsoft® Certified
Professional
Approved Study Guide

NETWORK PRESS® SYBEX®

MCSE CORE REQUIREMENT STUDY GUIDES FROM NETWORK PRESS

Sybex's Network Press presents updated and expanded second editions of the definitive study guides for MCSE candidates.

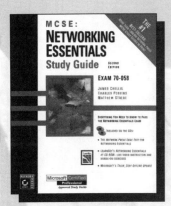

ISBN: 0-7821-2220-5
704pp; 7¹/₂" x 9"; Hardcover
$49.99

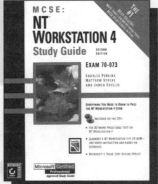

ISBN: 0-7821-2223-X
784pp; 7¹/₂" x 9"; Hardcover
$49.99

ISBN: 0-7821-2222-1
832pp; 7¹/₂" x 9"; Hardcover
$49.99

ISBN: 0-7821-2221-3
704pp; 7¹/₂" x 9"; Hardcover
$49.99

ISBN: 0-7821-2256-6
800pp; 7¹/₂" x 9"; Hardcover
$49.99

A $50.00 SAVINGS!

MCSE Core Requirements
Box Set
ISBN: 0-7821-2245-0
4 hardcover books;
3,024pp total; $149.96

STUDY GUIDES FOR THE MICROSOFT CERTIFIED SYSTEMS ENGINEER EXAMS

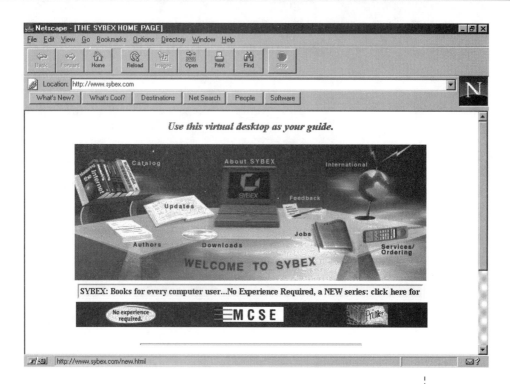

Official Microsoft Objectives for Exam 70-64 : Implementing and Supporting Microsoft® Windows® 95

 Exam objectives are subject to change at any time without prior notice and at Microsoft's sole discretion. Please visit Microsoft's Training & Certification Web site (www.microsoft.com/Train_Cert) for the most current exam objectives listing.